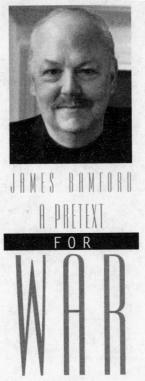

JAMES BAMFORD

A PRETEXT

FOR

WAR

James Bamford, the author of the bestsellers *Body of Secrets* and *The Puzzle Palace*, has written extensively on national security issues, including investigative cover stories for *The New York Times Magazine*, *The Washington Post Magazine*, and *The Los Angeles Times Magazine*. Formerly the Washington investigative producer for ABC's *World News Tonight with Peter Jennings*, and a distinguished visiting professor at the University of California, Berkeley, he lives in Washington, D.C.

A PRETEXT FOR WAR

9/11, IRAQ, AND THE ABUSE OF AMERICA'S INTELLIGENCE AGENCIES

JAMES BAMFORD

ANCHOR BOOKS
A Division of Random House, Inc.
New York

To Mary Ann

And to my father, Vincent

In memory of my mother, Katherine

And to Tom, Paula, and Christina

FIRST ANCHOR BOOKS EDITION, MAY 2005

Copyright © 2004, 2005 by James Bamford

The Library of Congress has cataloged the Doubleday edition as follows:
Bamford, James.
A pretext for war : 9/11, Iraq, and the abuse of America's intelligence agencies /
James Bamford.
p. cm.
Includes index.
1. Iraq War, 2003. 2. Intelligence service—United States. 3. United States—Politics and
government—2001– I. Title.
DS79.76.B36 2004
956.7044'3—dc22
2004050040

Anchor ISBN: 1-4000-3034-X

Author photograph © Tom Wolff

www.anchorbooks.com

Printed in the United States of America
10 9 8 7 6 5 4 3 2

Whoever fights monsters should see to it that
In the process he does not become a monster.
And when you look long into an abyss
The abyss also looks into you.

—Friedrich Nietzsche, *Beyond Good & Evil: Prelude to a Philosophy of the Future,* trs. W. Kaufmann, (New York: Vintage, 1989), Part 4, p. 89.

While nothing is easier than to denounce the evildoer,
nothing is more difficult than to understand him.

—Fyodor Mikhailovich Dostoevsky

Allow the President to invade a neighboring nation, whenever he
shall deem it necessary to repel an invasion, and you allow him to
do so, whenever he may choose to say he deems it necessary for
such a purpose—and you allow him to make war at pleasure. . . .
If, today, he should choose to say he thinks it necessary to invade
Canada, to prevent the British from invading us, how could you
stop him? You may say to him, "I see no probability of the British
invading us" but he will say to you, "Be silent; I see it, if you don't."

—Representative Abraham Lincoln, letter to William H. Herndon, February 15, 1848. (*The Collected Works of Abraham Lincoln,* ed. Roy P. Basler, vol. 1, 1953, pp. 451–52)

CONTENTS

PART I

DESTRUCTION

CHAPTER 1

ROME

Tech. Sgt. Jeremy Powell's heart started pounding and he quickly raised his hand and started waving it vigorously to get attention. He sat in a quiet pool of emerald light, staring at a matrix of slowly moving white dots, cryptic flashing letter-number combinations, lines going in all directions, and green circles that would form at the center and then expand outward, like a ripple from a stone tossed in a morning pond. Represented by every dot was a small cross-section of humanity, packed in an aluminum tube and traveling in the air near the speed of sound. Jeremy Powell was sitting in front of a glowing radar screen, scanning the skies over America's East Coast for any indication of attack, invasion, or airborne drug dealers.

This green room, like a leprechaun's lair, was the Operations Command Center of "Huntress Control"—the Air National Guard's Northeast Air Defense Sector. Located in the sleepy town of Rome in central New York, it was part of the North American Aerospace Defense Command—NORAD—a relic from the days of bomb shelters, air raid warnings, and fears of invading Russians. Besides being centrally located and free from major urban electromagnetic interference, Rome was an appropriate venue for America's twenty-first-century lookouts. It was the place where the American flag first flew in the face of battle, during the American Revolution at Fort Stanwix, located in what is now the center of the city of Rome. And it was the home, and final resting place, of Francis Bellamy, author of the Pledge of Allegiance.

Lt. Col. Dawne Deskins, her eyes now adjusted to the eerie light that greeted the start of her dozen-hour shift, saw Jeremy Powell's hand waving. As the airborne control and warning officer at the center, she was expecting more activity than usual this morning because of the drill. September 11, 2001, was the fourth day of a weeklong exercise code-named "Vigilant Guardian." It was designed to create a fictional crisis affecting the United States and test the network of radar watch stations around the country. Like a rerun of an old movie, the scenario involved Russian bombers flying over the North Pole in attack formation. The Rome command center was responsible for monitoring more than half a million square miles of airspace, from the Montana–North Dakota border to the coast of Maine down through South Carolina. Included were the skies over New York City and Washington, D.C. Should a crisis develop, the radar specialists could pick up the phone and alert fighter pilots at National Guard units at Burlington, Vermont; Atlantic City, New Jersey; Cape Cod, Massachusetts; and Duluth, Minnesota.

A moment earlier, Powell had taken a call from Boston Center. "Watch supervisor, I have a possible hijack of American 11 heavy," a Boston military liaison with the Federal Aviation Administration (FAA) told him. "Recommend notifying NORAD." Powell passed the information on to Deskins. *Part of the exercise*, Deskins thought to herself, until the direct phone line to the FAA began flashing. It was 8:40 A.M.

Forty-one minutes earlier, at 7:59 A.M., American Airlines Flight 11 had lifted off from Boston's Logan International Airport with eighty-one passengers and eleven crewmembers, and knifed into the crystal-blue sky. "Good morning," said the captain to the air traffic controllers disappearing quickly below. "American 11 heavy with you passing through, ah, two thousand for three thousand." As the flight climbed steeply from two to three thousand feet, window-seat passengers could clearly see the glint of sunlight reflecting off the gold dome of the State House high atop Beacon Hill. "Good morning," replied a controller at Boston departure radar. "Traffic ten o'clock, two miles, maneuvering."

Early September and a good time to be traveling. The weather had broken and it was clear and cool in the Northeast. The thunderstorms of summer were past, as was the hectic Labor Day holiday. And September 11 was a Tuesday, statistically one of the least busy travel days of the week. For the passengers aboard Flight 11, less than half full, it meant empty middle seats in which to stretch out for the long trip to Los Angeles. Normally capable of carrying up to 269 passengers, the twin-engine Boeing 767—a mechanized marvel made up of 3.1 million parts—was one of the long-haul workhorses for American Airlines. Sloshing around in the wings and other cavities was up to 10,000 gallons of highly explosive fuel.

"We have him in sight," replied the pilot. At fifty, John Ogonowski had been flying for half of his life, first in the Air Force at the end of the Vietnam War, and, beginning in 1979, with American. Earlier that morning, he had left the bucolic tranquility of his 150-acre farm in the northern Massachusetts town of Dracut. A sweeping expanse of fields and fruit trees, dotted with farm machinery and stonewalls, it was where the round-faced Ogonowski, a fourth-generation farmer, found peace. Down from the clouds, he spent his time laboriously plowing, cleaving, and harrowing the soil. "When his hands were dirty and his pants were filthy, he was always pretty happy," said his brother, James.

As the plane passed over the small Massachusetts town of Gardner, about forty-five miles west of Boston, the smell of coffee was starting to drift through the cabin. Flight attendants were just beginning to prepare the hot breakfasts of omelets, sausages, and fruit cups. Seated in business class, in seat 8D, was thirty-three-year-old Mohamed Atta, clean-shaven and in casual clothes. Instead of lowering his food tray, he pulled his small black shoulder bag from under the seat in from of him, withdrew a hardened plastic knife and a box cutter, and stepped into the aisle. At that same moment, as if choreographed, four other men assigned to Row 8 also rose and headed toward the front of the plane.

Sitting in front of a twenty-seven-inch, high-resolution Sony TV console, the controller could see Flight 11's key information—its altitude, direction, and identifying number. John Ogonowski heard again the crackle of a traffic controller in his earphones. "AAL11, your traffic is at, uh, two o'clock, twenty miles southwest-bound, MD-80," the controller said, alerting Ogonowski to a McDonnell Douglas MD-80 nearby.

"AAL11, roger," said the captain, adding, "twenty right, AAL11."

At that very moment, 8:13 A.M., the move was on. Atta and his men began their assault. First they used their knives to stab the two first-class flight attendants, Barbara Arestegui and Karen Martin. Then they slashed the throat of a business-class passenger who had apparently attempted to come to their rescue. As he lay on the floor of the plane, bleeding severely, the hijackers began spraying something in the first-class section to keep people away from the front of the plane. Then they made their way into the cockpit carrying a device with yellow wires hanging from it, which they said was a bomb. "Don't do anything foolish," one of the men yelled in English to the pilot and copilot. "You're not going to get hurt."

But likely within minutes, the door to the cockpit was locked, the two pilots were killed, and Atta took over the left seat. Suddenly one wing dipped severely while the other rose high, nearly tipping the plane on its side, before the aircraft stabilized. As the plane turned south toward New York, the flight attendants provided oxygen to the injured people and used the public address system to request the assistance of any doctor or nurse on board. In the coach section, passengers remained calm, thinking there was just some medical emergency.

Sixteen seconds later, unaware of the horror then taking place in the blood-splattered cockpit, the Boston controller again radioed Flight 11. "AAL11. Now climb maintain FL350," he said, giving the pilot permission to climb from 29,000 to 35,000 feet. Hearing nothing, he repeated the message ten seconds later, and again eleven seconds later, and once more fifteen seconds later at 8:14:23—but still no reply. By 8:15, the air traffic controller in Boston was becoming greatly concerned. Despite his numerous calls, there was only a deathly silence from American Flight 11. He switched to the emergency frequency, 121.5. "AAL11, if you hear Boston Center, ident please or acknowledge," repeated the controller, his voice rising.

At 8:24, frightening words poured from his earphones. "We have some planes," said a voice. "Just stay quiet, and you'll be okay. We are returning to the airport." It was a message, likely from Mohamed Atta, intended for his passengers. But it was relayed to the Boston Center possibly as a result of Captain Ogonowski secretly activating the "push to talk" button on the plane's wheel before being killed, or accidentally by Atta as he took his place. The depressed button allowed the controller to hear what was going on at that moment in the cockpit. "We have more planes. We have other planes," the hijackers said. "And, uh, who's trying to call me here?" asked the controller, wondering if it was his missing Boeing 767. "AAL11, are you trying to call?"

Then another troubling message. "Okay. If you try to make any moves, you'll endanger yourself and the airplane. Just stay quiet." And finally, at a second before 8:34, came one more. "Nobody move, please," said the voice. "We are going back to the airport. Don't try to make any stupid moves."

Six minutes later, at 8:40, the military liaison at Boston's FAA notified NORAD's Northeast Air Defense Sector Operations Center at Rome, New York. "We have a hijacked aircraft and I need you to get some sort of fighters out here to help us out," he told Dawne Deskins. The transponder on Flight 11 was no longer working, he said. Also, the Los Angeles–bound plane had suddenly made an unexpected left turn toward New York City. And then there were the frightening transmissions. Get "some F-16s or something" airborne, he pleaded. Deskins asked for Flight 11's latest position, but when the operator looked for it, it had disappeared. "American 11 heavy, Boston Center. Your transponder appears to be inoperative. Please recycle," said one of the controllers, repeating it several times. "American 11 heavy, how do you read Boston Center? Over."

As the plane was crossing from Massachusetts into New York, Atta turned off the plane's transponder, the device that transmits the plane's identification, speed, altitude, and location to the FAA's radar systems. Without the transponder information, Boston could still track it on its primary radar using faint "skin paint" returns, but for the technicians in Rome, like Jeremy Powell, finding the dot in the maze of moving and blinking images on his screen would be very difficult. At that moment, there were approximately 2,500 planes in the air over the Northeast alone. "We were going by the old-fashioned method of 'what was his last known speed, his last known heading, his altitude?'" said Powell. "And we were trying to kind of map it out on the scope."

"We'll direct the intercept," said the Boston liaison officer.

"Just get something up there." Deskins rushed up a short flight of stairs to the weapons desk in the "Battle Cab," a glassed-in balcony that overhung the Ops Room like a corporate suite at a football stadium. Her commanding officer, Air Force Colonel Robert Marr, was in the room working on the drill. "I have FAA on the phone, the shout line, Boston Center. They said they have a hijacked aircraft," she told him. "He says it's going to New York." Suddenly, she wondered why a large jet would be commandeered to go such a short distance.

As American Flight 11 continued tearing toward New York City, two courageous flight attendants, huddling out of sight, managed to telephone fellow colleagues with key details of what was taking place. "Listen, and listen to me very carefully. I'm on Flight 11. The airplane has been hijacked," said Amy Sweeney, a thirteen-year veteran of the airline. She was talking to American Airlines ground manager Michael Woodward at Boston's Logan Airport. Nearby, another flight attendant, Betty Ong, who had been with the airline a year longer than Sweeney, was also able to call an airline official on the ground. She reached Vanessa Minter, an agent at the airline's reservation center in Raleigh, North Carolina.

For twenty-five minutes, both flight attendants were able to communicate over crew telephones in the coach section of the plane. They relayed key details of the hijacking in real time, including the bloody way in which the men took over the cockpit. From the seat numbers Sweeney was able to pass on, airline officials were able to pull up such vital details as the hijackers' names, addresses, phone numbers, and credit-card information—including that of Mohamed Atta. She said they were all males and appeared to be of Middle Eastern descent. While calm, Sweeney and Ong were also very concerned. "Pray for us," Ong said repeatedly. "Pray for us."

Up in the Battle Cab, Colonel Marr called the man in charge

of NORAD for the continental United States, Maj. Gen. Larry Arnold at Tyndall Air Force Base in Florida. Thin, with short brown hair, Arnold was a command pilot with more than 4,000 hours flying nine different aircraft, including the F-16 and F-15. As he was walking out of a teleconference, someone came up and told him Rome was on the phone. "Boss, I need to scramble Otis," Marr said, referring to Otis Air National Guard Base on Cape Cod. Normally, the Secretary of Defense is the one who must give the approval to intercept a hijacked plane, but Arnold decided to make the decision on the spot. "Go ahead and scramble them, and we'll get the authorities later," he said.

As with most of the East Coast that Tuesday morning, the sky over Cape Cod was cloud-free and royal blue. Tucked away in the seaside resort community of Falmouth, Massachusetts, Otis Air National Guard Base was home of the 102nd Fighter Wing. Out on the tarmac, two F-15s sat "cocked and loaded" with weapons and extra gas on board. The two pilots on alert that morning, Maj. Daniel Nash and Lt. Col. Timothy Duffy, were in the control room scanning the charts and schedules that lined the walls, when the traffic control tower at Otis told them of a possible hijacking of an American Airlines flight out of Boston.

Although no scramble alarm had yet been received, the two quickly put on their flight suits and began walking to the waiting fighters. Duffy was a part-time Guardsman who just happened to be on duty that day. The thirty-five-year-old Nash, a beefy pilot with neatly trimmed brown hair, had joined the 102nd about a year and a half earlier. He had been on a number of alerts, but they usually turned out to be false alarms, such as an unknown aircraft approaching the coast that turned out to be a military plane. But he had a different feeling about this one.

On board Flight 11, it was obvious that the plane's movements were becoming more erratic; the aircraft was descending rapidly, almost in a dive, as it neared New York City. Nevertheless, the passengers, perhaps out of fear, remained relatively calm, with no hysteria or screaming. Over the crew phone, Woodward asked flight attendant Sweeney to see if she could spot anything familiar. "I see the water. I see the buildings. I see buildings," she said, adding that the plane was flying very low.

In Manhattan, forty-eight-year-old Steve McIntyre left his Upper West Side home a good half hour earlier than usual and was just arriving at the World Trade Center. The Director of Regulatory Affairs for the American Bureau of Shipping, his office was on the ninety-first floor of Tower One. For nearly a quarter of a century, since graduating from the University of Michigan's Naval Architecture School, he had worked for the company, which sets standards for maritime safety.

By 8:46 A.M. on September 11, between five and seven thousand other people were at work in each of the two towers. Few tourists had arrived, and the observation deck wasn't scheduled to open until 9:30.

From McIntyre's north-facing office, the entire city was laid out below him. Silver towers and glass walls radiated in the sun, and flat, tar-covered rooftops with stubby chimneys stretched to the arched horizon. The glare was so great that he had to close the blinds before sitting down at his computer to begin plowing through his e-mail. Suddenly, he heard what he thought was the roar of jet engines followed by a shadow crossing the blinds.

Another employee of the American Bureau of Shipping, George Sleigh, a British-born naval architect, was talking on the phone when he, too, heard the roar of jet engines. He glanced out his window and a thought instantly crossed his mind: *The wheels are up, the underbelly is white, and man, that guy is low.*

Nearby in the office, Claire McIntyre, no relation to Steve

McIntyre, was checking her e-mail when she heard the same sound—the blast of a jet engine. *Impossible,* she thought. Then, to her horror, she looked up to see the wing and tail of a colossal plane coming right at her at nearly the speed of sound. *Oh my God, all my people,* she thought. Screaming, she bolted from her office and raced into the hall to alert the rest of the staff. "Everyone, get out now," McIntyre yelled at the top of her voice. At the same moment, Steve McIntyre also realized it was a plane but had no idea of its size. *Oh, shit,* he thought to himself. *Someone's lost control of a private Learjet.*

Nearly one hundred floors below, French filmmakers Jules and Gedeon Naudet were shooting scenes for their documentary about a typical day in the life of a rookie New York fireman. As they were zooming in on men closing a sewer grate, they heard the sound of a low-flying plane. Curious, they pointed the camera almost straight up as American Flight 11 streaked across the lens headed directly for the building.

At Boston's Logan Airport, ground manager Michael Woodward was still holding the telephone to his ear, listening to flight attendant Amy Sweeney describe the approaching buildings before she took a very slow, deep breath. "Oh, my God!" she said quietly, calmly. And then there was just very, very loud static.

For a fraction of a second, the event seemed almost graceful. At 8:46:26, the building simply swallowed up the plane. But in the blink of an eye, when the jet's tanks containing 10,000 gallons of fuel suddenly compressed like crushed Coke cans, a massive fireball exploded with a force equal to 480,000 pounds of TNT. So powerful was the explosion that it registered a .09 on the Richter scale, used to measure earthquakes.

Flight 11 entered between floors 93 and 98, just two floors above the heads of Steve McIntyre, Claire McIntyre, and George Sleigh, shaking and oscillating the entire building as if an earthquake had struck. In the American Bureau of Shipping, an interior wall and ceiling crumbled. One employee, encased in debris, had to be extricated from his cubicle. People began grabbing fire extinguishers while another person had the presence of mind to soak a fat roll of paper towels. Sleigh crawled out from the rubble while Steve McIntyre left to check the fire exits.

The three had no idea how lucky they were. The concrete slab above their heads would become the dividing line between survival and tragedy—a ceiling of life for those below it, a floor of death for those on top of it. None of the 1,344 people then struggling on the floors above them would make it out alive.

Seconds after the blast, the cockpit crew aboard U.S. Airways Flight 583 heard Flight 11's eerie final gasp. "I just picked up an ELT on 121.5," the pilot told New York air traffic control, referring to an emergency locator transmitter and its frequency. "It was brief, but it went off." The sound probably came from the black box aboard the doomed American flight in the second before it vaporized. "We picked up that ELT, too," reported a pilot on Delta Airlines Flight 2433. "But it's very faint."

Slowly, it was beginning to dawn on New York Control just what had taken place. "Anybody know what that smoke is in lower Manhattan?" asked another pilot flying over the area. "A lot of smoke in lower Manhattan coming out of the top of the World Trade Center—a major fire."

At the Rome Ops Center, somebody ran into the room and said they had just heard about a plane hitting the World Trade Center. A few minutes later, Boston Center was called with the news that the plane was American Flight 11. Dawne Deskins picked up the telephone and called Maj. Don Arias, the public affairs officer for NORAD. "We think the aircraft that just hit the World Trade Center was American Airlines Flight 11," she said. In response, Arias gasped. "Oh, God. My brother works in the World Trade Center," he said.

Arias, a former New York City firefighter, called his brother immediately. What his brother related was bedlam in hell. "He says, 'You're not gonna believe what I'm looking at here.' I said, 'What?' He says, 'People are at the windows.' He says, 'There's a guy falling out of the building next door.' He says, 'There are people jumping.' And I said, 'You know, I—I think, I just got a call from the Northeast Air Defense Sector. There's a hijacked plane. I think that's the plane.'"

At about the same moment that Flight 11 slammed into Tower One, a Klaxon at Otis Air National Guard Base let out a series of deafening blasts and red lights began flashing in the corner of the alert barns, sending a flock of seagulls flapping into the air. "This is an official military scramble," said the public address system. "Alert pilots report to your battle stations." Already halfway to their jets, Nash and Duffy began racing as crew chiefs quickly pulled protective covers from the two vintage F-15 Eagles, built in 1977. Chocks were yanked from beneath the wheels and the heat-seeking and radar-guided missiles were armed. At 8:52 A.M., a red light turned green and the F-15s screamed down the tarmac.

Ten minutes earlier, at 8:42 A.M., concern had deepened when a flight controller at Boston Center suddenly became concerned about another plane, United Airlines Flight 175. Like American Flight 11, it was a Boeing 767 destined for Los Angeles. "Looks like he's heading southbound, but there's no transponder, no nothing, and no one's talking to him," he told his supervisor. A minute later, Deskins at the Rome command center received the new alert on the "shout line" from Boston Center.

Sitting in the pilot's seat was Victor Saracini, a fifty-one-year-old Navy veteran from Pennsylvania who often took his guitar along with him on flights. Saracini had also heard the troubling

messages from Flight 11 and notified New York Air Route Traffic
Control Center in Ronkonkoma, New York. "We heard a suspicious
transmission on our departure from Boston," said Saracini.
"Sounds like someone keyed the mike and said everyone stay in
your seats." What Saracini did not know was that he had his own
set of hijackers on board.

By the time Duffy and Nash were airborne, they were
already too late for Flight 11. Nevertheless, the fighter pilots still
had a chance of catching up to United Flight 175. But distance and
time were critical factors. Cape Cod was nearly two hundred miles
from downtown Manhattan. Duffy pushed his throttle to Mach
1.2, nearly 900 miles per hour. Going at such a supersonic speed
was normally something for which they needed permission. Nash
called Duffy on the radio. "Duff, you're super," he said. "Yeah, I
know," said Duffy. "You know, don't worry about it." Duffy then
called for a location of the target. "Your contact's over Kennedy,"
came the response. "Okay, I know where that is," said Duffy and
they turned toward New York's Long Island. At that moment, they
were 153 miles from the World Trade Center.

Another Air National Guard base with F-16s was located at
Atlantic City, New Jersey—and Flight 175 would pass within just
four minutes of the base before turning north to New York City. At
the time, two Air Force F-16 jet fighters were simply practicing
bombing runs above a scruffy patch of Pine Barrens near Atlantic
City, just eight minutes away from Manhattan. But they were not
armed for air-to-air combat, and to land, rearm, and get airborne
again would take too long.

The two aircraft were based at the Air National Guard's
177th Fighter Wing at Atlantic City International Airport in
Pomona, New Jersey. Throughout the Cold War, two scramble-
ready jets had always been on alert in Atlantic City. But because of
budget cutbacks beginning in 1998, the wing's mission had been

changed. Instead of the jets being ready to take off on a moment's notice, they were both assigned to unarmed bomb practice. On September 11, 2001, the entire United States mainland was protected by just fourteen planes spread out over seven bases.

By 8:48, there was no question that a major crisis was unfolding, possibly that the United States was under attack by terrorists. It was known that at least two commercial airliners had been hijacked. Worse, nearly half an hour earlier, at 8:24, a Boston controller had heard one of the hijackers threatening the pilots and saying, "We have more planes. We have other planes." It was then that NORAD and the command's top general in charge of the continental United States had been notified. He authorized a "battle stations" alert and scrambled heavily armed F-15 jet fighters into the air. Should the fighters catch up with the passenger planes, the only defense would be to shoot them down, though only the President of the United States could give such an order. Then a large plane crashed into Tower One of the World Trade Center.

At 8:47, the CNN program *Live at Daybreak* was carrying a fluffy report on a maternity-wear fashion show in New York. Then, at 8:48, anchor Carol Lin broke into a commercial about debt relief. "This just in," she said. "You are looking at . . . obviously a very disturbing live shot there—that is the World Trade Center, and we have unconfirmed reports this morning that a plane has crashed into one of the towers of the World Trade Center." CNN then switched to Sean Murtagh, the network's vice president of finance, who had observed the crash from the twenty-first floor of 5 Penn Plaza. "I just witnessed a plane that appeared to be cruising at a slightly lower than normal altitude over New York City. And it appears to have crashed into—I don't know which tower it is—but it hit directly in the middle of one of the World Trade Center towers," he said during the live telephone interview. "It was a jet, maybe a two-engine jet, maybe a 737 . . . a large passenger commercial jet. . . . It was teetering back and forth, wing-tip to wing-tip, and it looks like it has crashed into— probably, twenty stories from the top of the World Trade Center— maybe the eightieth to eighty-fifth floor. There is smoke billowing out of the World Trade Center."

At that moment, George W. Bush was sitting in the back of his limousine in Sarasota, Florida. His motorcade was about six blocks from the Emma E. Booker Elementary School, where the President was to meet a class of second-graders, when presidential press secretary Ari Fleischer, traveling in a separate car, received a phone call. "Oh, my God, I don't believe it," he said to the caller. "A plane just hit the World Trade Center," he announced to others in the car.

When Bush arrived at the elementary school, Fleischer, along with aides Karl Rove and Dan Bartlett, were standing on the sidewalk waiting to brief the President on the crash. "The President was surprised," said Fleischer. "He thought it had to be an accident." Yet despite having a secure STU-III phone next to him in the presidential limousine and an entire national security staff at the White House, it appears that the President of the United States knew less than tens of millions of other people in every part of the country who were watching the attack as it unfolded. Once in the school, the President ducked into an empty classroom and spoke on the phone with his national security advisor, Condoleezza Rice, and asked her to keep him informed. Yet even then, at almost 9:00, neither Rice nor Bush was aware that the United States had gone to "battle stations" alert and had scrambled fighter jets into the air to intercept and possibly take hostile action against multiple hijacked airliners, something that was then known by hundreds of others within NORAD, the Federal Aviation Administration, and the Pentagon.

With the President in Florida and no White House briefing that morning, George Tenet, the Director of Central Intelligence, was taking it easy. Instead of going in to work, he was having a leisurely breakfast with an old friend, David Boren, in the royal splendor of Washington's St. Regis, a hotel built in the style of an Italian Renaissance palace. Surrounded by European antiques, Palladian windows, a Louis XVI chandelier, and rich damask draperies, the two chatted about families over omelets and triangles of buttered toast. Boren, the former chairman of the Senate Intelligence Committee, and now president of the University of Oklahoma, had been Tenet's "godfather" as the former Intelligence Committee staff director rose to the top of the spy world.

At their table next to a window overlooking K Street, Tenet was completely unaware of the first plane hitting the World Trade Center, or of the hijackings, or of the "battle stations" alerts. It was not until sometime after the second plane hit Tower Two, after much of the country knew of the terrorism, that the Director of Central Intelligence received a phone call. "Mr. Director, there's a serious problem," an aide told him. Officials in the blue-carpeted CIA Operations Center on the seventh floor of the agency had learned of the attack from CNN. It would be after 9:30 when the Director was back in his office at CIA headquarters.

Air Force Lt. Gen. Michael Hayden, the director of the ultra-secret National Security Agency, was in his office at the time of the attack. He was standing a few feet from his desk, behind a tall wooden speaker's table, when he first heard the news. In the middle of a meeting with a small number of senior officials, his executive assistant, Cindy Farkus, walked in and told him about a plane hitting the World Trade Center. "The immediate image I had was a light plane, off course, bad flying," he recalled in a January 2004 interview in his office.

High up on the eighth floor of NSA's Ops Building 2B, in the brilliant sunshine of September 11, 2001, Hayden could clearly see the "company town," Laurel, Maryland, from the square eaves-dropping-proof window directly behind his desk. Ironically, only a few miles away in the Valencia Hotel, Khalid Almihdhar and Nawaf Alhazmi had planned and plotted with Mohamed Atta the morning's attacks. Now they were on American Airlines Flight 77, forcing their way into the cockpit at that very moment, and changing the plane's destination from Los Angeles to the Pentagon.

Hayden's office, and those of his deputy and executive director, occupies the southwest corner of the top floor of a massive, dark-glass cube-shaped building that towers above a secret town. Nicknamed Crypto City, the expansive complex includes such things as a plant that produces disposable codebooks known as "one-time pads" for covert spies and another that fabricates silicon chips for cryptographic machines.

Hayden's office reflects deep loyalty to his native Pittsburgh. Against a beige wall is a large bookcase containing mementos from his hometown football and baseball teams, the Pittsburgh Steelers and Pirates. On another wall is a framed, yellowing newspaper article from October 1941 announcing that his father, Harry V. Hayden, Jr., had been inducted into the service as a private and had arrived in Northern Ireland. In the center of the large office is a dark conference table surrounded by eight chairs; a maroon-colored couch sits off to the side.

On a table behind his high-backed, padded leather chair are two computers, one for classified and the other for unclassified work. There are also a series of telephones on the table. One is for internal calls, another is a secure STU-III for secret external calls, a black "executive phone" connects him to other senior officials, and a white phone has buttons that can put him through instantly to the Secretary of Defense and Chairman of the Joint Chiefs of Staff.

Earlier, at 8:00 A.M., Hayden had gone down to the National Security Operations Center (NSOC, pronounced "n-sock") in the Ops 1 Building for his regular meeting with all of his senior staff. "It's something I started here because I wanted the seniors to get a sense of the ops tempo," he said. Among the more worrisome items that morning was the assassination two days earlier of Afghan opposition leader Ahmed Shah Massoud. Two suicide bombers posing as journalists detonated a bomb hidden in their TV camera during an interview with Massoud on Sunday, and it was suspected that Osama bin Laden and the Taliban were responsible. The assassins were believed to have been Arabs who had come from the Taliban-controlled capital, Kabul.

Following the ops briefing, Hayden went to the small attached conference room for a quick staff meeting. He returned to his office for a meeting with his senior staff just as American Airlines Flight 11, piloted by Mohamed Atta, plowed into Tower One of the World Trade Center.

Notified of the crash, Hayden walked over to his walnut desk, neatly arranged with a penholder from his days as the number-two commander in Korea, a notepad printed with the word "DIREC-TOR," and a Brookstone world clock. On the left side were two television sets, one connected to the outside world with CNN muted, and the other connected to the agency's own secret internal television network. Hayden glanced at CNN just as they began showing scenes from the first strike. "I thought that was a big fire for a small plane," he said, and then continued with his meeting.

In Tower One, fighting the blinding, choking, oily smoke, black as chimney soot, Steve McIntyre made his way out to the nearly impassable hallway and began looking for the emergency stairwells. The first one he tried was filled with water and debris. After locating the second emergency exit, he found it dark and worse than the first. "Where the hell is the third fire-stair?" he cursed. A few seconds later he found it, but in the rubble-filled darkness he slipped on a piece of gypsum board and fell, sliding down to the next landing and then bouncing down to another. Fellow worker George Sleigh also made it to the stairwell after going back for his briefcase. Minutes later, the entire office exploded in flames.

Throughout the building, terrorized people were dialing 911 on cell phones and pleading for help from fire rescue, which was sending every piece of emergency equipment in its inventory to the Trade Center. At 8:56, a man from the eighty-seventh floor called in, yelling that his office was on fire and there were four other people with him.

Picking himself up from his long tumble, Steve McIntyre knew that he had found the only way out and headed back up to get the other employees. He noticed that very few people were passing him coming down. Above McIntyre's office was the giant insurance, consulting, and financial firm Marsh & McLennan, occupying floors 93 to 100. And above them, from 101 to 105, was Cantor Fitzgerald, a large bond dealer. One of the World Trade Center's oldest tenants, it had gradually taken over five floors as it grew. Finally, there was Windows on the World, the famous restaurant with its breathtaking views, on the 106th and 107th floors.

Christopher Hanley, who worked for a division of Reuters on Sixth Avenue, was among 150 people attending a special breakfast conference at Windows on the World. At 8:57, he called fire rescue to tell them the room was filling with smoke and people could not get down the stairs.

A few minutes later, Christine Olender, the thirty-nine-year-old assistant general manager of Windows on the World restaurant, called the Port Authority requesting help for the approximately 170 guests and staff with her. "We're having a smoke condition," she said. "We have most people on the 106th floor—the 107th is way too smoky. We need direction as to where we need to direct our guests and our employees, as soon as possible." A Port Authority police officer responded, "Okay. We're doing our best—we've got the fire department, everybody, we're trying to get up to you, dear. All right, call back in about two or three minutes, and I'll find out what direction you should try to get down." Olender continued, "The stairways are full of smoke . . . and my electric . . . phones are out . . . The condition up on 106 is getting worse," she said. The officer asked her to call back in two minutes.

By then the situation had rapidly deteriorated. Olender called back, this time pleading for help. "The situation on 106 is rapidly getting worse," she yelled. "We . . . we have . . . the fresh air is going down fast! I'm not exaggerating." Port Authority police officer Ray Murray answered the call. "Uh, ma'am, I know you're not exaggerating," he said. "We're getting a lot of these calls." By now she was desperate. "What are we going to do for air?" "Ma'am," said Murray, "the fire department—" Olender cut in, "Can we break a window?" Murray responded, "You can do whatever you have to to get to, uh, the air."

Other people were trapped in elevators and calling the Port Authority Police for help. "Listen, this is Tony Savas," said a seventy-two-year-old Port Authority construction inspector. "If you can, I'm on the seventy-eighth floor, I'm trapped in the elevator. Water and debris is coming down. And I'm in car number 81-A. Please send somebody to open the doors."

Many feared more planes were on their way. A Port Authority police officer named Tommy telephoned his mother to tell her not to go out. "I'm at work," he said. "Just stay in. Don't do nothing. There's . . . this is bad. They got planes all over the radar, coming into the New York area. They think everything is going to start hitting." "Oh, Tommy," his mother pleaded, "please promise you'll call me again!" "Right, Ma," said Tommy, "it's going to be a while, all right? But just don't even go out. I mean, they got planes on the radar. They think they are going to start crashing all over Manhattan."

Over at Tower Two, about two-thirds of the occupants headed down the emergency stairwells soon after the crash. But after a few minutes, once it was determined that their tower was not affected, they were told that they could return to their offices, and some did. One was Sean Rooney, a fifty-year-old vice president for Aon, one of the numerous insurance and financial services firms that populated the twin towers. At the time of the attack on Tower One, his wife, Beverly Eckert, a vice president with GeneralCologne Re, was attending a conference in her Stamford, Connecticut, offices. Hearing of the explosion at the World Trade Center, she quickly went for her phone, where she found a message from Rooney. "It's the other building," he said. "I'm all right. But what I'm seeing is horrible." Relieved, Eckert went back to her meeting.

When Steve McIntyre returned to American Bureau of Shipping after finding an open emergency stairwell, the other employees were gathered in the reception area. Quickly, they began making their way down. Despite the confusion, Claire McIntyre had managed to grab her pocketbook and flashlight. "The first two flights were dark," she recalled, "with no emergency lights, and water was pouring down the stairs. We could barely see, and I put my flashlight on. Then the emergency lights came on, and water was still flowing down." But the slick, oil-covered debris was treacherous and colleague Emma "Georgia" Barnett slipped and fell down three flights of stairs. She got right back up, but this time she tripped over a hose, injuring her knee. Still, determined to survive, she continued down with the rest.

As the occupants of Tower One struggled to get out, air traffic personnel were becoming increasingly worried about the fate of United Flight 175 out of Boston. At 8:52, the same moment Duffy and Nash became airborne from Otis Air National Guard Base, a technician at New York Control once again tried to reach the missing aircraft. "UAL175," he said, "do you read New York?" But, just as with Flight 11, there was only icy silence. Growing more and more concerned, he checked that his equipment was working correctly and asked whether other locations may have picked him up. "Do me a favor, see if UAL175 went back to your frequency," he asked a southern traffic control center. "He's not here," came the response.

After another minute of agonizing quiet, the controller expressed his suspicion. "We may have a hijack," he told a colleague. "I can't get ahold of UAL175 at all right now, and I don't know where he went to. UAL 175, New York," he called again. But by then the hijackers were in full control of United Flight 175. Near Albany, they made a U-turn back to the east and were at that moment screaming south toward Manhattan over the Hudson Valley at about 500 miles per hour—more than double the legal airspeed. The hijack pilot probably followed the Hudson River, like a thick line on a map, directly toward his target: Tower Two of the World Trade Center.

Among those watching the events unfold on television was John Carr, the president of the National Air Traffic Controllers Association. Shortly before nine, his cell phone beeped. "Hey, John, are you watching this on TV?" said one of his associates. "Yeah, I am," replied Carr. "That's American 11," said the friend. Carr nearly dropped his coffee. "My God, what are you talking about?" he said. "That's American 11 that made that hole in the World Trade Center." Carr still could not believe it. "You're kidding me," he said. "No," replied his friend. "And there is another one that just turned south toward New York." Then, referring to United Flight 175, he added ominously, "We lost him, too."

Over in Tower One, Steve McIntyre and his fellow employees were still attempting to make their way down the crowded and rubble-strewn stairwell. "We stopped at around the eighty-fifth floor to take stock and to calm each other," McIntyre recalled. "That was much better. We realized the fire was above us and that it was clear below. We just had to get down." His emotional state was "up and down like a yo-yo," he said. "We were completely encased in tunnels. And then we would open a door onto a floor and there would be guys fighting a fire, and then we would open another door and there would be people just milling around." As people or debris blocked their paths, they would zigzag across floors to other emergency stairwells. By the time they reached the sixties, Claire McIntyre was exhausted. "I was thinking: 'How much more to go?'" she said.

Sixty miles to the south, at Washington's Dulles International Airport, American Airlines Flight 77 bound for Los Angeles was getting ready to board. At 7:18, Khalid Almihdhar and Nawaf Alhazmi faced their final security hurdle. Having evaded the CIA, NSA, FBI, INS, State Department, and assorted other intelligence and security organizations with barely a drop of sweat, they now simply needed to get through airport security and they were home free to carry out their deadly suicide mission.

Their hand luggage likely contained such things as a shiny silver Leatherman utility pocket knife—a spring-action tool-style device that opens up at the center into miniature pliers and has an assortment of blades, wire cutters, screwdrivers, and other attachments fitted into it. Because it had a blade of less than four inches, it would have been permitted, whether in their bag or on their person. They also may have had razor-sharp box cutters, which would have been forbidden unless the blades were removed. Another item they likely carried were aerosol cans containing Mace or pepper spray—also prohibited. Finally, at least one of them probably had some sort of square- or rectangle-shaped object and a number of colored wires, which, when attached, would look like a bomb.

But the Mace may have been camouflaged as hair spray; the box cutter may have been empty, with the small, slim blade easily hidden elsewhere; and the phony bomb could have simply been an innocent-looking box with some wires packed separately. At the time, security was haphazard at best. There had not been an airline hijacking or bombing in the United States for more than a decade, and most of the people who operated the security checkpoints were low-paid contract workers with minimal experience.

Alhazmi placed his carry-on bag on the conveyor belt and walked through the arched magnetometer. Suddenly, there was a deep electronic buzz. A security official directed him to walk through another, secondary magnetometer. Again the alarm went off. Finally, a guard asked him to stretch out his arms and passed a metal-detecting wand around his body. Not discovering any guns or long knives, the security official allowed Alhazmi to pass. Then his hand luggage was swiped by an explosives trace detector and found to be harmless. Like the four other members of the team, he successfully evaded the final check.

At 8:16, the wide-body jet began to taxi away from the terminal. "American 77, Dulles tower," said the controller. "Runway three zero, taxi into position and hold. You'll be holding for landing traffic one left and for wake turbulence spacing behind the DC-10." Among the sixty-four people on board was Barbara Olson, a cable-TV talk-show regular who turned bashing the Clintons into a professional blood sport. Her husband was Theodore Olson, the Bush administration's solicitor general. Also on board were Khalid Almihdhar, Nawaf Alhazmi, Hani Hanjour, and two others from the Valencia Motel in Laurel, Maryland, near the headquarters for the National Security Agency.

As American Flight 77 nosed skyward, Danielle O'Brien, an air traffic controller in the Dulles tower, passed them on to another controller at a different frequency. "American 77, contact Washington center one two zero point six five," she said. Then she added, "Good luck." Later, she thought how odd that was. "I usually say 'Good day' as I ask an aircraft to switch to another frequency, or 'Have a nice flight.' But never 'Good luck.'"

At 8:56, just as the fighter pilots took off from Otis Air National Guard Base and controllers were becoming very worried about United Flight 175 from Boston, an air traffic controller in Indianapolis was getting the same kind of jitters. American Airlines Flight 77 was not answering his call. "American 77, Indy," he kept repeating. The controller then called American Airlines operations to see if they could raise the crew. They also had no luck, so the controller asked a different operator to try again. "We, uh, we lost track control of the guy," said the Indianapolis controller. "He's in coast track, but we haven't . . . we don't [know] where his target is and we can't get ahold of him. You guys tried him and no response. We have no radar contact and, uh, no communications with him, so if you guys could try again."

"We're doing it," said the American Airlines operator. But there would be only silence.

At 9:00 A.M. on September 11, 2001, there were 4,205 planes in the skies over the United States.

Just across the Hudson River from Manhattan, high up in Newark, New Jersey's air traffic control tower, forty-one-year-old controller Rick Tepper was looking out the facility's large windows when all of a sudden he saw a large explosion at Tower One of the

World Trade Center. "Wow! Look at that," he said, having no idea what had caused it. "How are they going to put that out?"

A few minutes later, Tepper received a call on the high-priority "shout line" from another controller at New York Center. "We've lost an aircraft over Manhattan," he was told. "Can you see anything out your window?" But Tepper still had not connected the two events. "No," he said. "I don't see anything. But one of the towers, one of the Trade Towers, is on fire."

About fifteen minutes later, the "shout line" rang again and this time the controller asked Tepper if he had any idea as to the location of United Flight 175. "Can you see him out the window?" he was asked. In the distance, high above the New Jersey ship-yards, Tepper caught sight of the plane as it was heading for Manhattan, traveling north over the Hudson River. It was moving too fast, Tepper felt, and rocking from side to side. Suddenly, its nose began pointing down as if in a dive. Then it began banking left and right, moving ever faster as it began to level off—something he had never seen before.

In her Manhattan apartment a few blocks from the World Trade Center, Mable Chan, a producer for the NBC program *Dateline*, was getting ready for work when she heard the first reports of the plane crash into Tower One. "I immediately rushed out of the bathroom with a toothbrush stuck in my mouth," she recalled. "My eyes were wide open and glued to the tube." Frustratingly, she kept getting a busy signal as she quickly began dialing her office to get her assignment to begin covering the story. "I decided to try sending a computer message to my boss," she said. "While I was dialing up for connection, I suddenly heard a thunderous engine sound roaring past the window on my right side."

At that moment, on the ABC News program *Good Morning America*, correspondent Don Dahler in New York was giving hosts

Diane Sawyer and Charles Gibson an update on the Trade Center explosion. "It appears that there is more and more fire and smoke enveloping the very top of the building," he said as the camera focused on the twin towers, "and as fire crews are descending on this area it does not appear that there is any kind of an effort up there yet. Now, remember— Oh, my God!"

In a flash, a large commercial jetliner, tilted to one side, zoomed across the television screen and smashed into floors 78 through 84 of Tower Two, pushing desks, people, and file cabinets out the windows. Paper began to slowly rain down, sparkling in the sun like confetti. Then, a fraction of a second later, United Flight 175 exploded with the force of a fuel-air bomb, sending superheated flames and dense, midnight-black smoke in all directions. It was 9:02:54.

"My God!" repeated Sawyer, almost in a whisper. "That looks like a second plane," said Gibson flatly and with no emotion, as if describing a passing city bus. "I just saw another plane coming in from the side. That was the second explosion—you could see the plane come in, just on the right-hand side of the screen. So this looks like it is some kind of concerted effort to attack the World Trade Center that is under way in downtown New York."

High in the sky, Officer Timothy Hayes, a helicopter pilot for the New York Police Department's aviation unit, noticed something out of the corner of his eye. He was the first to arrive at Tower One after it was hit by Flight 11 and was reporting on the fire back to his headquarters when he saw another jet coming right at him. "I realized how close it was coming to us," he said. "I thought it was going to impact our aircraft. So we climbed. He went underneath us." Then he realized what was happening. "Jesus Christ," he yelled to his partner, "there's a second plane crashing."

On the phone, sitting at his desk on the eighty-first floor, was Fuji Bank loan officer Stanley Praimnath. "What I saw was the biggest aircraft ever, bearing down towards me, eye level eye contact. It's coming towards me. I can still see the letters on the wing and the tail; big red letters. I screamed, dropped the phone, and dove under my desk."

In Newark's tower, Rick Tepper was still holding on to the telephone as he followed Flight 175 up the Hudson River into Manhattan. "Oh my God!" he shouted. "He just hit the building."

"It was the most excruciating sound you could ever hear," said Stanley Praimnath as the plane sliced into his office. "It was like steel ripping against steel. And the revving of the engine just before it hit—it's like the sound is still in my ears, it's ringing. The wing was stuck in the office door, twenty feet from where I was." Trapped, Praimnath began yelling. "Oh please, somebody help me," he cried. "Help me, help me, don't leave me to die, I don't want to die."

Three floors above, on the eighty-fourth floor, Brian Clark, executive vice president of Euro Brokers, dropped into a football stance when a wing of the Boeing 767 smashed into his floor. "Boom, boom," he recalled. "There were these distinct two noises right after one another and in an instant our room just fell apart." The tower shuttered, floors buckled, and walls collapsed. "For ten seconds," he said, "it felt like ten seconds, the building swayed toward the Hudson River, just one way, it kept going and I thought it was never going to stop. I thought the building was going over." But it suddenly snapped back.

At the time of the impact, NORAD's two fighters from Otis Air National Guard Base were still seventy-one miles away—seven minutes' flying time.

When United 175 rammed into Tower Two, NORAD's public affairs officer, Maj. Don Arias, was talking to his brother in the building. "Well, I better get out of here," his brother said quickly, then hung up. He never made it out.

Hearing of the second explosion, Beverly Eckert once more grabbed the phone to call her husband, Sean Rooney. Again, another message was waiting—but it had come in prior to the most recent event. "Just letting you know I'll be here for a while," Rooney said. "They've secured the building." After trying unsuccessfully to call him, she rushed home to Glenbrook, Connecticut.

By then, the two had been married for twenty-one years, and had known each other since meeting in their native Buffalo in 1967. For Rooney, it was a long commute to the World Trade Center every day, but he greatly enjoyed playing carpenter, plumber, electrician, and mason at his home in Connecticut. Since buying the house fourteen years earlier, he had added cement steps to the front door, built a fireplace mantel in the living room, and laid marble floors in the master bathroom. He even cultivated an herb garden. Eckert especially liked the way her husband laughed—and how it would make his shoulders shake. But now she was very worried.

In Tower Two, dense smoke had engulfed the upper floors and the stairwells. People tried to decide whether to fight their way down through the choking darkness or up to the roof and possible rescue by helicopter. On the eighty-fourth floor, Brian Clark pushed the fallen rubble off his back and began organizing a rescue.

"Come on, everyone. Let's go," he yelled to fellow workers. A fire warden for his company, Clark was carrying a whistle and a flashlight as he led five colleagues to Stairway A.

Three floors down, on the eighty-first floor, two people heading up warned them about going any farther. "You can't go down," said a woman. "The floors are in flames. We have to get above the smoke and fire." For a moment or so, the group pondered, then four decided to go up and Clark and coworker Ronald DiFrancesco continued down. Suddenly, there was a noise—bang, bang, bang—coming from the destroyed offices of Fuji Bank. "Help! I'm buried!" someone yelled. "Can anybody help?" The shouts were coming from loan officer Stanley Praimnath. Clark managed to free him from the debris, and he joined the two as they continued down the stairwell and into the heavy smoke.

By then the smoke was becoming thicker and breathing was difficult. DiFrancesco turned around and climbed to the ninety-first floor. Exhausted, he rested there for ten minutes and then, determined to get out, headed back down the stairwell and began pushing into the black, suffocating soot.

Soon after Beverly Eckert reached her house, only about a mile away, the phone rang. It was Rooney. "Sean," she yelled, elated, "where are you?" But the news was not good. Coughing and gasping for air, he said he was trapped on the 105th floor of the burning Tower Two. "Why are you there?" Eckert asked, confused and afraid, knowing he worked seven floors below. As with the employees of Euro Brokers, Rooney had first tried to climb down the emergency stairwell, making it to somewhere around the seventy-sixth floor. But the heat and smoke had become too intense, driving him back.

Then, like Brian Clark's colleagues, Rooney turned around and tried to escape to the observation deck on the 107th floor. But when he got there, he found the thick steel door firmly sealed. "The roof doors were locked," he told Eckert. "How could they be locked?" she said, frantic for Rooney to find a way out. "Please, just try it again. Try it again, maybe it was just jammed when the building got hit." But Rooney said there was no use, he was sure it was locked.

He told Eckert that he was now on the north side of the building, and Eckert said she would pass the information on to the rescue workers. Confused as to what was happening around him, Rooney asked his wife what she could see on the television. "Where's the fire?" he said. Eckert said there was fire on his side of the building, but it was many floors below. "The smoke is heavy," Rooney said. "I don't understand why the fire suppression isn't working."

"Maybe they can get a helicopter to you," said Eckert, desperately trying to get her husband to the roof and possible rescue. "Please try the door again. Pound on it. Maybe someone is on the other side and will hear you. Who is with you?" she asked. "I'm alone," said Rooney. "Some other people are in a conference room nearby." He then went back to the observation deck to try the door once again.

Shortly after nine at NSA, Cindy Farkus again broke into Lieutenant General Hayden's meeting, but this time she was almost running. Another plane had hit the second tower, she said. "One plane's an accident, two planes is an attack," said Hayden, who immediately adjourned his meeting and asked Farkus to quickly summon the agency's top security officials to his office.

That was not the way it was supposed to be. NSA was not supposed to find out about an airborne attack on America from CNN, after millions of other Americans had already witnessed it. It was supposed to find out first, from its own ultrasecret warning center, and then pass the information on to the White House and the strategic military forces.

Among the agency's most secret units is the Defense Special Missile and Astronautics Center (DEFSMAC), located within the

NSA center. At the entrance is its seal: an orbiting satellite and a patch of stars above the earth. Even within the intelligence community, DEFSMAC (pronounced "deaf-smack") remains little known. In fact, its purpose is to serve as the nation's chief warning bell for a planned attack on America. It serves as the focal point for "all-source" intelligence—listening posts, early-warning satellites, human agents, and seismic detectors.

Secretary of Defense Robert S. McNamara established the joint NSA-DIA activity at NSA on April 27, 1964, largely as a result of the Cuban missile crisis. "You didn't want NORAD fooling around in technologies that they didn't understand, or trying to evaluate a bunch of raw data, so DEFSMAC was put in," said Lt. Gen. Daniel O. Graham, the former director of the Defense Intelligence Agency. Since its beginning, the organization has been headed by an NSA civilian with a DIA colonel as deputy director.

As other warning organizations shrank with the end of the Cold War, DEFSMAC more than doubled its size to more than 230 people. This included a new, eighty-five-person operations center. Where once DEFSMAC had only Russia and China to monitor, its widely dispersed targets continued to grow to include India, North Korea, Iran, Iraq, and Pakistan.

DEFSMAC watches the earth as a physician listens to a heart, hoping to detect the first irregular beat indicating that an attack is about to take place. "It has all the inputs from all the assets, and is a warning activity," a former senior NSA official once explained. "They probably have a better feel for any worldwide threat to this country from missiles, aircraft, or overt military activities, better and more timely, at instant fingertip availability, than any group in the United States."

Upon receiving indicators that an attack was imminent, DEFSMAC officials would immediately send out near-real-time and in-depth, all-source intelligence alerts to almost two hundred "customers," including the White House Situation Room, the National Military Command Center at the Pentagon, the DIA Alert Center, and listening posts around the world. At the same time, elsewhere within DEFSMAC, analysts would be closely monitoring all intercepts flooding in; examining the latest over-head photography; and analyzing data from early-warning satellites 22,300 miles above the equator. DEFSMAC would then flash the intelligence to the U.S. Strategic Command at Offutt Air Force Base in Nebraska, NORAD at Cheyenne Mountain in Colorado, and other emergency command centers.

But on the morning of September 11, DEFSMAC learned of the massive airborne attacks after the fact—not from America's multibillion-dollar spy satellites or its worldwide network of advanced listening posts, or its army of human spies, but from a dusty, off-the-shelf TV set.

Shortly after 9:00, General Hayden's principal concern was not finding the next target but becoming the next target. He summoned his top internal and physical security people to his office. "My intention," he said, "was to plumb their minds, to determine what do we do now to protect ourselves."

From the ground, NSA is one of the most well-protected facilities on earth. Hidden from the outside world by tall earthen berms and thick forest trees, it is surrounded by a labyrinth of barbed-wire fences, massive boulders placed close together, motion detectors, hydraulic antitruck devices, thick cement barriers, and cameras that peer down from rooftops. As part of the agency's perimeter-security antiterrorism program, all vehicles and cargo passing through the inner fences must first be inspected for bombs and other threats in a $4 million screening center. There, an Explosive Detection Canine Unit, consisting of a team of handlers and eleven specially trained Dutch Shepherd and Belgian Malinois bomb-sniffing dogs, inspect the vehicles.

The agency also has its own police force, complete with a mobile Emergency Response Communications Command Post equipped with both STU-III secure cellular telephones and also encrypted closed-circuit television systems. Should a threat be detected, the director could call out the agency's Special Operations Unit/Emergency Reaction Team. Dressed in black paramilitary uniforms and wearing special headgear, they brandish an assortment of weapons, including Colt 9mm submachine guns. Attached to the team are two military medics assigned to NSA's Medical Center. During periods of heightened alert, and at other times as a deterrent, the team, known as the "Men in Black," are posted at the perimeter gates.

But all of that security was designed to prevent a ground attack. From the air, NSA was just as vulnerable as a large unprotected shopping mall.

Disturbingly, the story George W. Bush often tells of his learning of the attacks cannot possibly be true. "I was sitting outside the classroom waiting to go in," he told an audience in Florida on December 4, 2001, "and I saw an airplane hit the tower—the TV was obviously on, and I used to fly myself, and I said, 'There's one terrible pilot.' And I said, 'It must have been a horrible accident.'" He repeated the story a month later, on January 5, 2002, to another audience in California. It is the version that is on the White House Web page. "When we walked into the classroom, I had seen this plane fly into the first building. There was a TV set on. And you know, I thought it was pilot error and I was amazed that anybody could make such a terrible mistake."

The problem with the account is that there was no video of the first plane hitting the World Trade Center until later that day. The only video was of the second plane hitting the World Trade Center at 9:02:54. It's possible that he saw those images on live television when he ducked into an empty room set up so he could talk with Condoleezza Rice at the White House. He reportedly did not enter the class until 9:04, more than a minute after the United Flight 175 smashed into Tower Two. Thus, he may have learned of the second plane even before he went in to address the seven-year-olds. That would raise a serious question of judgment: How could a president ignore what to millions of people was an obvious terrorist attack and just go about a political photo op as if nothing had happened?

If he had not seen the second attack and could not have seen the first attack, then how could he make the later claims? Few people can ever forget the moment they first learned of the events of 9/11, especially if the person happens to be the President of the United States.

Whether or not Bush learned of the second attack before he went into Sandra Kay Daniels's second-grade class, he certainly knew about it after his chief of staff, Andrew Card, notified him of the event minutes later, at 9:06. "A second plane hit the second tower," said Card. "America is under attack." At that moment, a look of befuddlement passed over the President's face, the look of a man who couldn't—or wouldn't—believe what he was hearing.

Bush would later boast to reporters that at that moment he made his decision in favor of war. "They had declared war on us," he said, "and I made up my mind at that moment that we were going to war." For a commander-in-chief who had just decided to launch his country into a war, a rare and enormous event, George Bush seemed strangely uninterested in further information. He did not demand to speak to the Secretary of Defense. Nor did he ask for George Tenet, the Director of the CIA, to determine what kind of intelligence there was on what had taken place. There were no questions to Andy Card or Condoleezza Rice about whether there had been any additional threats, where the attacks were coming from, how to best protect the country from further devastation, or the current status of NORAD or the FAA or the Federal Emergency Management Agency. Nor did he ask that Air Force One prepare to return him to Washington at once.

Instead, he simply turned back to the photo op. "Hoo!" he cheered as the electronic flashes continued to blink and the video cameras rolled. "These are great readers. Very impressive!" Precious minutes and seconds were ticking by and many more lives were still at risk, but the President of the United States did not budge from his small, second-grade chair. The enormity of the reality waiting for him would have to wait.

By then, at one of the most critical moments in American history, the country had essentially become leaderless. Both towers of the World Trade Center had been blown up by large commercial airliners with thousands of people feared dead. One crash took place on live television. At least one other commercial jet— American Flight 77 from Washington's Dulles Airport, bound for Los Angeles—was missing. And unknown yet was the presence of hijackers on a fourth plane waiting to take off at Newark International Airport. NORAD had launched fighters to intercept and possibly shoot down one of the aircraft, but such a decision would require the President's order.

"Really good readers, whew! These must be sixth-graders!" the President effused. "Thank you all so very much for showing me your reading skills. I bet they practice, too. Don't you? Reading more than they watch TV? Anybody do that? Read more than you watch TV?"

The U.S. military command was equally out of touch as the horror continued to unfold on television. The Chairman of the Joint Chiefs of Staff, Army General Henry Shelton, was somewhere over the Atlantic en route to Europe. That left his deputy, Air Force General Richard Myers, the Vice Chairman, in charge of the country's armed forces. But incredibly, he would remain unaware of what was going on around him during the entire series of attacks.

Myers was on Capitol Hill waiting to meet with Georgia Senator Max Cleland about his upcoming confirmation hearings to become the new Joint Chiefs chairman. While in Cleland's outer office, he watched live television reports following the first crash into the World Trade Center and then went into Cleland's office for his routine meeting. There he would remain for the next forty-five minutes, self-promoting his talents to lead the military as the rest of the targets were attacked and the country succumbed to enormous death and destruction.

Through it all, the general in charge of the country's military was completely ignorant of the fact that the United States was under its worst attack in nearly two centuries. Nor did he know that about forty minutes earlier, the President had decided to declare war. "It was initially pretty confusing," Myers later said. "You hate to admit it, but we hadn't thought about this."

As President Bush continued reading with the second-graders, the situation within the burning towers of the World Trade Center was becoming ever more desperate. At 9:06, NYPD helicopter pilot Timothy Hayes radioed the message "Unable to land on roof. . . . Captain, this is impossible. This is undoable. I can't see the roof." He later added, "The smoke had covered 90 percent of the entire roof, so I couldn't even see the roof to make an evaluation of where we could go. We were looking at probably fifteen to twenty stories burning simultaneously. Probably well over a thousand degrees, you know, if not more. I never felt so helpless and guilty in my life. When you get there with these millions of dollars of equipment . . . and there was absolutely nothing we could do. There was nothing. We couldn't get on that roof, we couldn't get people out of that building."

Hayes could actually see people inside the buildings, leaving him with the heart-wrenching feeling that people were trapped and he couldn't reach them. As he pulled away, the hundreds or thousands still trapped on the upper floors of the towers saw their last hope disappear. Some flapped draperies to try to attract attention. Without someone to break open the locked doors to the roof or pluck them from it, all they could do was hang out of windows trying to find some smoke-free air to breath. The towers had now become sky-high chimneys.

Within minutes, people began jumping, preferring a quick death to burning alive or suffocating from the smoke. "People falling out of building," said the pilot of the chopper. "Jumper," he added. And they just kept coming. "Several jumpers from the Window [Windows on the World] at One World Trade Center." By 9:09, people were also beginning to throw themselves out of Tower Two. "People are jumping out the side of a large hole," said a caller to fire rescue. "Possibly no one catching them."

On the street, Port Authority police officers reported the horrible scene unfolding in front of them. "There's body parts all over the place," said one officer. "So much—bodies blew out of the building. . . . There's got to be hundreds of people killed in there. There's body parts like five blocks away." Another reported, "I've got dozens of bodies, people just jumping from the top of the building onto . . . in front of One World Trade . . . bodies are just coming from out of the sky."

"Christian! Christian! Christian!," Mable Chan began yelling on the sidewalk of Greenwich Street near Tower One. Minutes before, the NBC *Dateline* producer had heard the second plane thunder past the window of her apartment and then the giant BOOM as it smashed into Tower Two. Now she had just spotted her colleague Christian Martin, also an NBC producer, whom she was trying to locate in order to begin covering the story.

Unable to find their camera crew, Chan and Martin offered a tourist $500 for a one-day rental of his small video camera. Then they began realizing the horror taking place around them. "Christian, I just saw an elbow!" Chan said. "Over there on the roadside, it's charred." Christian Martin looked where Chan was pointing. "Shit!" he said in disgust. "This shit has to be a terrorist act." "And we're in the middle of it," added Chan.

Like people trapped on a sinking ship seeking the highest point above the water, those in the twin towers, blocked from going down, were climbing up as high as they could go. But it would be a climb to nowhere. "A hundred and twenty people trapped on the 106th floor," exclaimed a caller in Windows on the World. "A lot of smoke . . . Can't go down the stairs!" "Evacuation to the top floor of World Trade Center," said another caller a few seconds later. The problem was the same at Tower Two. "Hundred and fifth floor," a caller yelled. "People trapped! Open roof to gain access!" But, ironically, although some would make it to the roof through open doors, other doors were locked to keep potential jumpers, and simple spectators, off. Nevertheless, because of the dense smoke, even those who made it to the roof were doomed. "The roof of the South Tower," said NYPD helicopter pilot Timothy Hayes, "was totally obscured."

At 9:13, the photo op over, Bush rose to his feet to leave the classroom—seven minutes after being notified of the attacks by Card and deciding to go to war. And eleven minutes after possibly seeing the second attack himself.

For more than half an hour, air traffic controllers in both Washington and Indianapolis had been searching madly for American Flight 77, which took off from Washington's Dulles Airport for Los Angeles at 8:16 A.M. At 8:56, all contact was lost. "You guys never been able to raise him at all?" asked a radar operator at Indianapolis Control. "No," said the air traffic controller. "We called [the] company. They can't even get ahold of him, so there's no, no, uh, no radio communications and no radar."

At the heart of the FAA's massive nationwide network is its control center in Herndon, Virginia, a NASA-like Mission Control facility with walls covered with video screens and small blinking lights on expansive electronic maps. Hours earlier, Ben Sliney arrived for his first day at work as national operations manager, the person responsible for juggling all the flights in the air and making sure they land safely. A lawyer, he once brought the FAA to court on behalf of air traffic controllers.

By 9:15, with two planes crashed into the World Trade Center and another still missing, the FAA was in full crisis mode. At the front of the control room, flight numbers were quickly scribbled on a white dry-erase board. They belonged to planes suspected of being hijacked. Other staff workers manned telephones, calling airlines to determine the status of various questionable flights. As aircraft were checked out, their flight numbers were scratched off the list. By 9:20, there were still eleven flight numbers on the list, including American 77.

After taking a quick survey of the most experienced controllers in the room and talking with others across the country during a massive conference call, Sliney began seeing the pattern as a possible wave of terrorist attacks. His first move was to immediately halt all flights bound for New York and New England. Then Washington, D.C., was added to the list, followed by Los Angeles, where the two planes that crashed into the Trade Center were bound. Finally, at 9:25, with Flight 77 growing more worrisome, Sliney made a bold decision. He ordered a full groundstop—all commercial and private flight activity across the country was grounded; no flights were to take off for any reason. At that moment, there were 4,452 planes over America.

A moment earlier, at 9:24, the FAA had alerted officials at NORAD about the missing American Flight 77. Officials there immediately sent out a scramble order to their Air National Guard unit at Langley Air Force Base in Hampton, Virginia. At 129 miles away, it was the closest alert base to Washington.

As Langley's scramble horn blared and the battle stations light turned yellow, Maj. Dean Eckmann, a Northwest Airlines pilot serving his regular National Guard rotation, ran for his fighter. Joining him were Maj. Brad Derrig and Capt. Craig Borgstrom. Six minutes later, NORAD's three F-16s, each loaded with six missiles, were wheels up. The mission for Eckmann and his two fellow pilots was to somehow find Flight 77 before it found its target, and possibly shoot it down. But that would require the authorization of the President, still in an elementary school in Sarasota, Florida. "I don't think any fighter pilot in the United States would have ever thought they would be flying combat air patrols over American cities," Eckmann said. "That was huge, huge culture shock."

At 9:29, Dulles tower air traffic control operator Danielle O'Brien spotted an unidentified blip on her radar screen. Although she didn't know it at the time, it was the missing Flight 77. Seventy minutes earlier, she had bid farewell to the flight crew with her uncustomary "good luck." The alarmed controllers quickly called to warn their colleagues at Reagan National Airport, which was located close to downtown Washington. "Fast-moving primary target," they said, indicating that a plane without a transponder was heading their way.

At the time, the plane was about twelve to fourteen miles southwest of Dulles and moving at lightning speed. Tom Howell, the controller next to O'Brien, glanced over at her screen and his eyes grew wide. "Oh my God!" he yelled. "It looks like he's headed to the White House! We've got a target headed right for the White

House!" At full throttle, American Flight 77 was traveling at about 500 miles per hour directly toward P-56, the prohibited airspace surrounding the White House and the Capitol. Because of its speed and the way it maneuvered and turned, everyone in the radar room of Dulles Airport's tower assumed it was a military jet.

Among the passengers on Flight 77 were the hijackers from the Valencia Motel in Laurel, Maryland, and Barbara Olson, wife of U.S. Solicitor General Ted Olson. Originally, Barbara Olson had planned to fly to Los Angeles the day before, on Monday, September 10. But because her husband's birthday was on the eleventh, she decided to leave the next morning so she could spend a little time with him on that day. After saying good-bye early in the morning, she called him at the Justice Department about 7:40, just before boarding the plane, which was scheduled to depart at 8:10.

Shortly after nine, Olson heard about the hijackings and quickly turned on his office television, worried that one of the planes might be Barbara's. But after a brief mental calculation, he figured her plane could not have gotten to New York that quickly.

Suddenly, a secretary rushed in. "Barbara is on the phone," she said. Olson jumped for the receiver. "Our plane has been hijacked!" she said quickly, but after a few seconds the phone went dead. Olson immediately called the command center at Justice and alerted them to the fact that there was yet another hijacked plane—and that his wife was on it. He also said she was able to communicate, though her first call had been cut off.

Minutes later, Barbara called back. Speaking very quietly, she said the hijackers did not know she was making this call. All the passengers, she said, had been herded to the back by men who had used knives and box cutters to hijack the plane. The pilot, she said, had announced that the plane had been hijacked shortly after takeoff.

Ted Olson then told her about the two other planes that had been hijacked that morning and flown into the World Trade

Center. "I think she must have been partially in shock from the fact that she was on a hijacked plane," Olson recalled. "She absorbed the information."

"What shall I tell the pilot? What can I tell the pilot to do?" Barbara said, trying to remain calm. Ted asked if she could tell where the plane was at that moment. She said she could see houses and, after asking someone, said she thought the plane was heading northeast.

Then they reassured each other that the plane was still up in the air, still flying, and that it would come out all right. "It's going to come out okay," Olson told his wife, who agreed. But Ted Olson knew the situation was anything but all right. "I was pretty sure everything was not going to be okay," he recalled. "I, by this time, had made the calculation that these were suicide persons, bent on destroying as much of America as they could." "I love you," she said as they exchanged feelings for each other. Then the phone suddenly went dead again. While waiting for another call, Olson remained glued to the television. It was now about 9:30.

In Florida at that moment, far away from the madness in New York, President Bush had finished his photo op and had been given a quick update on the state of the crisis. Then he strolled into the school's library, where he had originally planned to give a speech promoting his education policies. Instead, he told the children and teachers that he would have to leave.

"I, unfortunately, will be going back to Washington," he said, because the country had suffered "an apparent terrorist attack." With one brief exception, that was the last anyone would see of either the President or Vice President until long after the crisis ended.

Within the tower at Dulles Airport, the tension rippling through the air was almost visible. The supervisor in the radar room began a countdown as the unknown plane got closer and closer to the White House. "He's twelve miles west," he said. "He's moving very fast eastbound— Okay, guys, where is he now? . . . Eleven miles west, ten miles west, nine miles west." About that point, John picked up the phone to the Secret Service office at the White House. "We have an unidentified, very fast-moving aircraft inbound toward your vicinity," he said, counting down the miles. "Eight miles west. Seven miles west."

At the White House the warning came into the tightly packed Situation Room, down a flight of stairs from the Oval Office, where three watch officers continuously monitor computers carrying reports from the various intelligence agencies. A rush of fear suddenly washed over Franklin C. Miller, the Director for Defense Policy. *The White House could be going down,* he thought. Then he had an aide send out an e-mail with the names of those present "so that when and if we died, someone would know who was in there," he said.

Secret Service officers quickly rushed into Vice President Dick Cheney's office. "We have to move," said one agent. "We're moving now, sir; we're moving." Once out, they hustled him down to the Presidential Emergency Operations Center, a special tubelike bunker under the East Wing of the building. The rest of the White House staff were told to get out and away from the building as quickly as possible. "Get out, get out, this is real," shouted members of the bomb squad running through the building. "All the way to H Street, please," one uniformed Secret Service officer yelled. "Women, drop your heels and run, drop your heels and run," yelled one Secret Service agent. "Suddenly, the gates that never open except for authorized vehicles just opened and the whole White House just flooded out," recalled Press Secretary Jennifer Millerwise.

"Six miles," said the superviser. "Five miles, four miles." He was just about to say three miles when the plane suddenly turned away. "In the room, it was almost a sense of relief," recalled air traffic controller Danielle O'Brien. "This must be a fighter. This must be one of our guys sent in, scrambled to patrol our capital and to protect our president, and we sat back in our chairs and breathed for just a second. In the meantime, all the rest of the planes are still flying and we're taking care of everything else."

But then the plane suddenly turned back, making a 180-degree half-loop. "He's turning back in!" O'Brien yelled. "He's turning back eastbound!" O'Brien's fellow traffic controller, Tom Howell, also saw the turn and began to yell to the supervisor. "Oh my God, John, he's coming back!"

"We lost radar contact with that aircraft," recalled O'Brien. "And we waited. And we waited. And your heart is just beating out of your chest waiting to hear what's happened."

Arlington, Virginia, police officer Richard Cox could hardly believe his eyes. He grabbed for his microphone and called dispatch. "It's an American Airlines plane, headed east down over the pike, possibly toward the Pentagon," he said excitedly.

At that same moment, Father Stephen McGraw was in traffic so heavy it was almost at a standstill. A Catholic priest, he was driving to a graveside service at Arlington National Cemetery but mistakenly took the Pentagon exit onto Washington Boulevard. Suddenly, McGraw felt the teeth-rattling roar of a large aircraft only about twenty feet above the roof of his car. He looked out just as the plane clipped an overhead sign and then toppled a light pole, injuring a taxi driver a few feet away. "It looked like a plane coming in for a landing," he said. "I mean, in the sense that it was controlled and sort of straight." A second later, American Flight 77 smashed into the gray concrete wall of the Pentagon. The jet hit with such force that it penetrated four of the five concentric rings of corridors and offices surrounding a gazebo in the center court, long nicknamed Ground Zero.

"I saw it crash into the building," said McGraw. "There was an explosion and a loud noise, and I felt the impact. I remember seeing a fireball come out of two windows [of the Pentagon]. I saw an explosion of fire billowing through those two windows. I remember hearing a gasp or scream from one of the other cars near me. Almost a collective gasp, it seemed."

It was 9:37 A.M.

Nearby in another car was Aydan Kizildrgli, a student from Turkey who was just learning English. "Did you see that?" he shouted to the next car. Traffic along the highway came immediately to a halt as people jumped out of their cars and began putting their cell phones to their ears. Stunned and dazed, Kizildrgli left his car on the road and began walking aimlessly for half an hour.

Minutes later, in the Dulles Airport tower, the words of an air traffic controller at Reagan National Airport came over the loudspeaker. "Dulles, hold all of our inbound traffic," said the voice. "The Pentagon's been hit."

"I remember some folks gasping," recalled O'Brien. "I think I remember a couple of expletives."

"It's just like a big pit in your stomach because you weren't able to do anything about it to stop it," said Tom Howell. "That's what I think hurt the most."

At the Justice Department, Ted Olson heard on the television that an explosion had taken place at the Pentagon. Although no one identified the aircraft involved, he knew it was Flight 77, carrying his wife. "I did and I didn't want to," he recalled. "But I knew." Late that night, when he finally got to bed around 1 A.M., Olson found a note under his pillow that Barbara had left for his birthday. "I love you," she wrote. "When you read this, I will be thinking of you and will be back on Friday."

CHAPTER 3

CLEVELAND

Minutes after the crash, Maj. Dean Eckmann and his two fellow
NORAD fighter pilots from Langley Air Force Base were approaching Washington and could see the smoke. At first Eckmann thought
it might be a plane crash near Reagan National Airport. Then,
about twenty miles away, he saw that it was coming from the
Pentagon. "My initial thought was that it was a truck bomb," he
said. "We didn't actually find out it was an airliner until the next
day." Then he heard an air traffic controller say, "The Secret Service
is now in the building," followed by another military message saying, "We need to protect the house." "What I drew from that is, we
need to protect the White House." He added, "It was the first time
in my career that I ever actually wanted to go out and use my airplane to kill someone."

Thousands of feet below and only minutes before, the Secret
Service had placed an emergency call to the Air National Guard
unit at nearby Andrews Air Force Base. Answering the phone was
Lt. Col. Marc H. Sasseville, director of operations for the 113th Air
National Guard Wing. Get whatever you have in the air immedi-
ately, he was told, to protect Washington and particularly the
White House.

Given that much of America had realized that the country

was under attack since a few minutes after nine, it would seem logical that those aircraft should have been sent aloft well before the Pentagon was attacked. In fact, protecting the Washington, D.C., area is part of its charter: ". . . as part of its dual mission, the 113th provides capable and ready response forces for the District of Columbia in the event of a natural disaster or civil emergency." Why there were no aircraft launched earlier has never been adequately explained.

Sasseville quickly grabbed three F-16 pilots. "I have no idea what's going on, but we're flying," he told them. "Here's our frequency. We'll split up the area as we have to. Just defend as required. We'll talk about the rest in the air." The four rushed to the prep area and zipped up their g-suits and checked their parachute harnesses.

As the pilots were grabbing for their helmets, another urgent call came in from the Secret Service. "Get in the air now!" someone screamed. At almost the same instant, another White House official telephoned on a different line and said the entire Washington area had been declared "a free-fire zone." Sasseville told his three fellow pilots, "That meant we were given authority to use force, if the situation required it, in defense of the nation's capital, its property and people."

But these aircraft were part of the 121st Fighter Squadron of the D.C. National Guard—not NORAD. Thus they were not on alert. As a result, they had little or no weapons. Sasseville raced to the flight line with his wingman and jumped into the waiting F-16s armed only with five seconds' worth of nonexplosive 20mm training rounds—metal slugs. AIM-9 missiles were being installed on two other fighters, but Sasseville felt he had no time to waste. "I was still turning things on after I got airborne. By that time, the [NORAD] F-16s from Langley were overhead—but I didn't know they were there," he recalled. "We all realized we were looking for an airliner—a big airplane . . . the track looked like it was headed toward D.C. at that time."

Another F-16 pilot, Maj. Billy Hutchison, just landed after being recalled from a training operation in North Carolina. He also had no active weapons but was told to get airborne immediately. Like Sasseville and his wingman, if it came to preventing another airborne terrorist attack, Hutchison knew he had few options. All, however, were prepared to likely sacrifice their lives by using their aircraft to ram the hijacked plane.

Sasseville at least had a five-second burst of dummy rounds. His first option was to shoot from behind the passenger jet and "try to saw off one wing. I needed to disable it as soon as possible—immediately interrupt its aerodynamics and bring it down." But if that didn't work, the only shot he had left was "to hit it— cut the wing off with my wing. If I played it right, I'd be able to bail out. One hand on the stick and one hand on the ejection handle, trying to ram my airplane into the aft side of the [airliner's] wing," he said. "And do it skillfully enough to save the pink body . . . but understanding that it might not go as planned. It was a tough nut; we had no other ordnance."

News of American Flight 77's crash into the Pentagon removed any doubt from Ben Sliney's mind. At the FAA's control center, about fifteen miles south of the Pentagon, he boomed, "Order everyone to land! Regardless of destination! Let's get them on the ground!" It was a breathtaking decision. For the first time in history, every commercial and private plane over the United States was immediately ordered out of the sky. At that moment, there were 3,949 planes over the country. A few minutes later, Secretary of Transportation Norman Mineta agreed. But when told that even with the order it could still be overridden by pilot discretion, Mineta snarled, "Fuck pilot discretion, bring down all the planes."

L. Kemp Ensor, the National Security Agency's associate director for security, walked into the director's office with his assistants just as Lieutenant General Hayden heard some early reports about the explosion at the Pentagon. "As they were walking through the door, I knew exactly what we needed to do and I said all nonessential personnel out of here. Out of the complex," said Hayden. "A couple of reasons for it—one was just pure safety. Second was . . . the strength of the agency is our intellectual capital. The agency goes down in the elevators at night. Computers are nice, but what makes it run is the people. And there was certainly no better way to protect the people than to send them home on the dispersal plan. Everyone knows where they're going, and everyone can protect in place in their own quarters. So all nonessential personnel were to leave the building."

NSA was an easy target to hit. Nicknamed Crypto City, it consists of more than fifty buildings containing more than seven million square feet of space. The parking lots alone cover more than 325 acres and have room for 17,000 cars.

A key problem was that much of NSA's most critical functions were consolidated in single buildings. Among the most important was the Tordella Supercomputer Building, which housed the agency's electromagnetic brain. A 183,000-square-foot facility with nearly windowless walls decorated with light-colored enamel metal panels, it contains probably the largest collection of supercomputers in the world. The thinking machines are so powerful, they require the same amount of electricity (29 megavolt-amperes) needed to power half the city of Annapolis, Maryland's capital. Among the machines whirring out code-breaking solutions and analyzing intercepted messages were the CRAY Y-MP EL, the Silicon Graphics Power Challenge, and the IBM RS/6000 SP, with a capability of crunching through two billion instructions per second.

Not only did the building contain NSA's electronic brain, it also housed much of its memory. To store the massive amounts of data flowing in from its worldwide listening posts, NSA linked together several computers the size of telephone booths. The system is capable of storing five trillion pages of text—a stack of paper 150 miles high.

But it was NSA's human brainpower that most concerned Hayden.

Throughout NSA, loudspeakers began sounding. "All non-essential personnel are to leave the building," came the announcement over and over. But many of the 16,000 employees in "Crypto City" and its surrounding facilities were unsure as to whether that meant for a brief time or for the day, so quite a few went to their cars and just waited. Eventually, a massive traffic jam formed as they all began heading for the Baltimore-Washington Parkway.

Following definite word that the Pentagon had been struck and that there was still one or more hijacked aircraft headed toward Washington, NSA Director Hayden ordered the three to four thousand remaining essential personnel to immediately leave the agency's three tall towers. They were to relocate to the three-story Ops 1 Building, the old low-rise A-shaped structure that was the agency's first home in Fort Meade. All four buildings were interconnected, so employees never had to go outside.

In Ops 1, Hayden and his top staff marched through the automatic glass doors of the third-floor National Security Operations Center (NSOC), which was the agency's "war room." Above the door was the seal of the Central Security Service, NSA's own military, and below, inlaid in the flooring, were the Center's initials.

Normally quiet and sedate, the NSOC suddenly became a beehive of activity, with watch officers and signals intelligence officials fielding messages to and from the worldwide listening posts searching for answers in the dim light. All were watching for

a CRITIC (Critical Intelligence) message—the highest prece-
dence—warning of where the next attack might come.

The one group Hayden could not move to Ops 1 was the
counterterrorism unit, eight floors up on the top of Ops 2B.
Hayden visited the unit and described the employees working
there as "emotionally shattered." "One of the more emotional
parts of the day, for me," said Hayden, "I went into our CT [coun-
terterrorism] shop and our logistics folks were tacking up blackout
curtains because we can't move the CT shop in the midst of this."
Maureen Baginski, the head of signals intelligence, visited the
group and tried to calm them down. Hayden called his wife,
Jeanine, at their home a few miles away in Fort Meade and asked
her to locate their children.

Shortly after the Pentagon attack, Hayden ordered the counterterrorism unit to focus their attention on Middle Eastern intercepts
and to translate and analyze them immediately as they were
received, rather than starting with the oldest in the stack first, as
was normally the case. At 9:53 A.M., less than fifteen minutes after
Flight 77 hit the Pentagon, analysts picked up a phone call from a
bin Laden operative in Afghanistan to a phone number in the former Soviet republic of Georgia. The person in Afghanistan said
that he had "heard good news," and indicated that a fourth target
was yet to be hit—a possible reference to United Flight 93 that
would crash in Pennsylvania before reaching its intended target in
Washington. "I got in touch with George Tenet," said Hayden. "He
said, 'What do you have?' and I passed on whatever information we
had." Hayden then called his wife back, said he was okay, and found
out that his children had been located and were safe.

As rescue workers began racing to the Pentagon, it was quickly
becoming clear to air traffic controllers in Cleveland that still
another passenger jet—the fourth—was in the process of being

hijacked. This time it was United Flight 93, which had taken off at 8:42 that morning from Newark International Airport en route to San Francisco. At the controls was Capt. Jason Dahl, a NASCAR fan from Littleton, Colorado. Shortly after nine, following the attacks on the World Trade Center, he had heard a brief *ping* on his company computer. It was an electronic alert notifying him of a message from United's operations center near Chicago. In green letters on a black background came a warning to be careful of someone trying to break into the flight deck. "Beware, cockpit intrusion," it said. "Confirmed," typed one of the pilots, acknowledging the message.

At about 9:28, as the plane was flying near downtown Cleveland, Captain Dahl radioed Cleveland Control a cheerful greeting. "Good morning, Cleveland," he said. "United 93 with you at 3-5-0 [35,000 feet]. Intermittent flight chop."

But back in the main cabin there was pandemonium. Three men who had tied red bandannas around their heads were taking over and herding the passengers to the back of the plane, near the galley. Seconds later, the Cleveland controller heard the frightening sound of screaming in the cockpit. "Somebody call Cleveland?" he asked. There was no answer, just the muffled sounds of a struggle, followed by silence for about forty seconds. Then the Cleveland controller heard more struggling, followed by someone frantically shouting, "Get out of here! Get out of here!" Finally, the microphone once again went dead.

Unsure of what he actually heard, the controller called another nearby United flight to see if they might have picked up the broadcast. "United 1523," he said, "did you hear your company, did you hear some interference on the frequency here a couple of minutes ago, screaming?" "Yes I did," said a crewmember of the United flight. "And we couldn't tell what it was either." The pilot of a small executive jet also heard the commotion. "We did hear that yelling, too," he told the Cleveland controller.

"Any airline pilot with any experience, and I've had quite a bit," said veteran commercial pilot John Nance, "who sits up there strapped into a seat knows what happened here: two of my brethren being slashed to death. In the cockpit, I think what happened is the pilots had been subdued. I think their necks had been slashed. And they're strapped in, they've got no way of defending themselves. You can't turn around and fight. They're just sitting ducks."

Suddenly, the microphone aboard United Flight 93 came to life again, but this time with a foreign-sounding voice. "Ladies and gentlemen, here it's the captain, please sit down. Keep remaining sitting. We have a bomb aboard." Startled, the Cleveland controller called back. "Say again slowly," he said. But silence returned to Flight 93.

Despite having just seen the twin attacks on the Trade Center on television, Senate Majority Leader Tom Daschle decided to go ahead with his weekly leadership team meeting in Room 219 of the Capitol Building. But at about 9:45, Senator Patty Murray glanced out the conference room's windows and let out a yell. "Look," she hollered. "There's smoke!"

"With that we all rushed to the window," recalled Daschle. "None of us could believe what we were seeing. There, beyond the Washington Monument, just across the Potomac, thick plumes of black smoke were billowing up from the spot where the Pentagon stands. I know it's a cliché, but I really could not believe my eyes." Daschle and the other senators raced back to their offices in utter confusion. "It's hard to fathom," Daschle later candidly admitted, "that our leaders in the upper levels of government in Washington, the people we turn to for confidence and security in times of crises, might, at just such a time, be as utterly clueless as everyone else."

Within Washington, evacuation of federal and congressional officials—something that should have been well planned after nearly half a century of Cold War tensions—instead became more like an episode of *Monty Python's Flying Circus*. Congress, like the rest of government, knew far less about what was going on than someone watching CNN from their bed.

"A plane is heading for the Capitol!" said a reporter excitedly. Suddenly senators, members of Congress, staff, and visitors all began charging down hallways, pushing through doors, crowding onto elevators, and running down stairwells in a mad effort to escape the building. "Get off the sidewalks," yelled a Capitol police officer. "Moving everybody back. Moving everybody back."

"The scene was total chaos," said Daschle. At the same time, because no alarm system was ever activated, other people remained in their offices oblivious to what was going on around them. It was the first time in history that the entire United States Capitol had been evacuated. "There was starting to be a sense of panic," said one congressional official with detailed knowledge of the security measures.

After wandering around aimlessly outside of the Capitol Building for about half an hour, many senators and members of Congress were directed to the Capitol Police offices, located about a block and a half away on the top of a decrepit brick building. The worried officials feared that they were the next targets and, lacking any better ideas, quickly yanked down the shades. "People were just as fearful as I've seen," said Daschle. "I saw looks in senators' faces, looks in staff faces that I've never seen before."

In New York, the situation in Tower Two had grown even more critical and the calls to fire rescue more desperate. At 9:36, a woman called from an elevator saying she and others were trapped inside. "They are dying," said the report. Eighty-three elevator mechanics from ACE Elevator had left the two buildings following the crash into Tower Two. Dozens of people were left trapped inside the elevators—ninety-nine in each tower—at the time. One elevator mechanic from another company charged into the burning buildings from the street but died trying to rescue people.

Another call was from a woman named Melissa. The floor was very hot, she said. There were no available doors. She was going to die, she said, but first wanted to call her mother. Still another call had no voice, only the sound of people crying.

Back on the 105th floor, Sean Rooney again called his wife, Beverly Eckert. She could hear her husband was having tremendous difficulty breathing. "I can't get the door open," he said. "I pounded and the smoke is very thick. I passed out." Eckert asked him how bad the smoke was now. "It's getting bad," said Rooney. "The windows are getting hot." Eckert asked him if anyone else was there. Rooney said there were other people nearby but he was alone. Gathered in a conference room on the same floor were at least two hundred other people who had also hoped to escape to the roof and be rescued. Instead, like Rooney, they were all trapped.

By now Eckert knew there was little hope left. "Sean," she said with great sadness, "it doesn't seem to me that they are going to be able to get to you in time. I think we need to say good-bye." For the next few minutes, the two talked about their love and the happy years they had spent together. Eckert said she wished she were there with him. Rooney asked her to give his love to everyone. "I love you," he said.

The time was getting very short in Tower Two. At 9:47, in an office near Rooney on the 105th floor, a woman called fire rescue with an ominous message. The floor underneath her, she said, was beginning to collapse.

About the same moment, Ronald DiFrancesco, who had changed his mind after climbing to the ninety-first floor and turned around and headed back down through the smoke, finally emerged from Tower Two. A short while before, fellow worker

Brian Clark and Fuji Bank's Stanley Praimnath had also made it out successfully. But just then, a short distance from the entrance, DiFrancesco saw a fireball racing toward him and he tried to block it with his arms in front of his face.

Over the phone, Eckert suddenly heard an enormous explosion followed by a crack and then a roaring sound. "The floor fell out from underneath him," she said. "It sounded like Niagara Falls. I knew without seeing that he was gone." With the phone cradled next to her heart, she walked into another room and on the television she could see Tower Two collapsing—the first tower to go down.

"I will always be grateful that I was able to be with him at the end and that we had a chance to say good-bye," Eckert said. "He was so calm. It helped me in those final moments. So many people missed the last phone call. So many are saying, 'If only I had a final chance to say good-bye.'"

DiFrancesco was thrown to the ground, bones were broken, his arms were burned, and his lungs were singed, but he was alive. Rescue workers quickly gathered him up and took him to St. Vincent's Hospital, where he later recovered. He would be the last person out of Tower Two.

Mable Chan, the NBC *Dateline* producer, had just spotted a police helicopter near the top of Tower Two. "I thought to myself that it must have been the rescue chopper trying to save people trapped inside. I wanted that shot, I needed that shot." Then she suddenly let out a chilling scream. "Ahhhhh—Oh my God! Oh my God!" She recalled, "Everyone around me started screaming and squealing."

"It's down!" shouted a reporter in a helicopter. "The whole tower, it's gone! Holy crap!" The time was 9:59:04.

A stampede began on the streets as everyone began pushing and rushing to escape the collapsing skyscraper. Producer Mable Chan, wafer-thin with black flowing hair, was immediately swept up as if caught helplessly in a raging rapid. "Soot and fragments were gushing out and the crowd was about to run me over," she recalled. "I finally turned around and started fleeing for my life, but thick layers of charcoal gray dirt came over me."

She was knocked facedown on the hard cement, and a shoe kicked her in the side, another crushed her left knee, and still another struck her neck. Bleeding, her jeans ripped, she looked up. "I only saw feet running in front of my eyes and heard screaming men and women swirling around me. I asked myself, 'Is this it?'" But she struggled to her feet and found temporary safety in a satellite truck owned by the local cable televison channel, New York One.

At that moment, F-15 pilots Daniel Nash and Timothy Duffy, who had scrambled into the air from Otis Air National Guard Base on Cape Cod an hour earlier in a futile attempt to catch up with Flight 11, were patrolling the skies over New York City. Although they had been unable to reach the aircraft before it crashed into Tower One, there was probably nothing they could have done anyway. "If we had intercepted American 11, we probably would have watched it crash," said Nash. "We didn't have the authority to [shoot it down]. We didn't suspect they would use kamikaze tactics that morning. We weren't ready for that type of an attack, to quickly shoot down one of our own airplanes."

As they were steering aircraft away from Manhattan, facing away from the city, they turned to see Tower Two vanish in a gray cloud. "When we turned around, all we saw was lower Manhattan covered in dust and debris," said Nash, who thought he was witnessing another attack. "Then Duff said over the radio, 'It looks like the building collapsed.' I thought to myself, 'There were just tens of thousands of people killed.' I thought it was the start of World War III."

Back at NORAD's Battle Cab in Rome, New York, Col. Robert Marr saw the building collapse on television and felt a profound sense of helplessness. "I have determined, of course, that with only four aircraft, we cannot defend the whole northeastern United States," he said. "That was the sensation of frustration, of 'I don't have the forces available to do anything about this.'"

It was nearly ten o'clock when the eleven exhausted, blackened, but alive employees of the American Bureau of Shipping at last reached the bottom of Tower One, having started down from the ninety-first floor nearly an hour before. "I was thinking, 'Okay, great, we're safe,'" recalled Steve McIntyre. "But outside I could see all this falling debris flying around. I thought, 'We've being coming down for an hour, what the hell is this?'" Fellow worker George Sleigh, bruised and bloodied, had separated from his colleagues and made it to an ambulance just as a police officer began shouting. "Get out!" he yelled. "Get out! The building is coming down!"

McIntyre was helping a fellow employee named Ruth, who had sprained her ankle. Having made it to the lobby floor, the two managed to get across the plaza to an exit on the eastern side of the center where there was an escalator up to Church Street. "We're okay," McIntyre said to Ruth. "We get up this escalator and we're okay." Just at that moment, Tower Two collapsed.

"And then there was a big rumble and a huge roar," recalled McIntyre. "Everybody shouted 'Run,' and then a huge wind came through there. I remember distinctly being lifted off my feet and blown down the hall, I don't know how far. Ruth was holding on to me, but we were ripped apart. I had no conception of what was happening. It went through my mind that a bomb had gone off in the subway. Then the plume came through and there was an opaque blackness. It was not an absence of light. It was opaque. My glasses were gone. I put my hand in front of my face and I couldn't see it. I thought, 'A bomb has gone off and I'm going to die right here of smoke inhalation.'

"Then I realized that it wasn't smoke, that it was just very heavy air. There was all this stuff on the floor, but it was light stuff. I was coated in it, as if I'd been immersed in a vat of butter. And the exposed skin on my arm was all pocked from tiny glass shards, maybe a hundred of them. We must have been on the very edge of the blast field when number two came down." In the darkness, McIntyre ran into a glass storefront, but eventually he saw a flashlight and heard someone yelling, "Come to me." A short time later, McIntyre again saw daylight and freedom. Half an hour later, at 10:28:31, Tower One also collapsed.

As Tower Two began to crumble, the presidential motorcade was crossing DeSoto Road as it came onto the tarmac of Sarasota's Bradenton International Airport. Off to the side was Jones Aviation, where less than a year earlier Mohamed Atta and Marwan Al-Shehhi had taken flying lessons. Moments later, the presidential limousine came to a stop at the foot of the portable stairway and Bush quickly rushed for the doorway of the giant jet. "The President, famous for his courtesy, hurried past the local officials who had gathered to see him off," said surprised Florida Republican Congressman Dan Miller, who had earlier been invited to fly back to Washington with Bush.

Once inside, Bush turned left and then right and walked into his airborne office on the right side of the forward portion of the plane. For security, whenever the jet lands, the pilot keeps the right side away from a terminal. The presidential suite was the ultimate in luxury. Decorated in muted brown and beige tones, the office featured a sleek wraparound wooden desk against the right bulkhead facing aft. Behind his tall, executive-style chair was a matching wooden credenza. The next room forward, taking up the nose of the plane, was his stateroom with two long tan leather couches that converted into beds with dark blue blankets decorated with

the gold presidential seal. The forward bulkhead featured a wall
mural that resembled a desert sunset. Between the stateroom and
the office was a bathroom with full shower.

To many in the presidential party, the sight of the massive
blue and white jet brought a sense of safety and relief. Miller and
a fellow Florida Republican, Congressman Adam Putnam, were
led up the rear stairs and into the aft section of the plane. Within
five minutes, just about the time Tower Two was about to collapse,
Air Force One was moving down the runway. Hanging from the
wings like giant silver locomotives, the four General Electric tur-
bofan engines let out a Niagara-like thunder as 56,750 pounds of
thrust shot from them.

"As the President sat down in his chair, [he] motioned to the
chair across from his desk for me to sit down," said Karl Rove,
Bush's chief political advisor. "Before we could, both of us, sit
down and put on our seat belts, they were rolling the plane. And
they stood that 747 on its tail and got it about 45,000 feet as quick
as I think you can get a big thing like that up in the air."

The first call Bush made was to Vice President Cheney in the
White House presidential bunker, where officials were viewing
the rogue odyssey of United Airlines Flight 93 with growing fear.
By now they were certain that it had been hijacked somewhere
over the Midwest and was heading back toward Washington.
Along with the Capitol Building, the White House was the most
logical next target. Deep underground, a staffer would enter the
bunker every few minutes and update Cheney, as well as Secretary
of Transportation Norman Mineta and National Security Advisor
Condoleezza Rice, with the plane's latest position and trajectory.

By then, most workers had fled from the White House and the
Capitol Building. From the beginning, the Secret Service had been
constantly urging Cheney to leave by helicopter for the secret presidential relocation headquarters on the Maryland–Pennsylvania

border known as Site R. That was the appropriate procedure when time permitted, as in this case. But Cheney refused to budge from the bunker.

The thought that the White House might be destroyed while the president or vice president was in the presidential bunker had worried doomsday planners in the 1950s. The small shelter was originally built in 1934, at the same time that the East Wing was constructed. In 1942, when Franklin D. Roosevelt had the wing rebuilt, it was updated but it was still considered just an "air raid shelter" and designed to survive little more than a few conventional bombs. There were also rumors at the time that the shelter was connected to an escape tunnel that led to the Treasury Building, with its thick vaults, across the street.

Because of the bunker's vulnerability, an enormously secret plan was developed to attempt a rescue of the president and vice president from it. Code-named Outpost Mission, the operation involved the creation of a secret unit known as the 2857th Test Squadron, stationed outside the Washington blast zone at Dover Air Force Base in Delaware. Masquerading as a rescue force for civil and military emergencies, its sole job was to extract the president and vice president from the rubble of the White House after a nuclear attack.

Following a blast over Washington, the team was to board helicopters packed with decontamination kits, acetylene torches, crowbars, and other rescue equipment and land on the White House lawn. Extra radiation suits in canvas bags were carried for the presidential family. If the rubble covering the bunker was too heavy for their equipment, another secret presidential rescue unit stood by with large cranes and other heavy equipment. But the units were disbanded in 1970 and never replaced.

As United 93 got closer and closer to the White House, covering a mile every seven seconds, Cheney conferred with Secretary of Defense Donald Rumsfeld and then asked Bush to order the United jetliner shot down.

At the time, however, there was still a chance that the plane might be saved. Unlike the earlier flights, passengers using cell phones were able to talk to loved ones who told them about the other hijackings and their tragic outcomes. Believing they had no other choice, they grabbed everything they could muster as improvised weapons. Armed with little more than plastic knives, broken dishes, and boiling hot water, a number of passengers began rushing the cockpit, where the hijackers had barricaded themselves in. With the angry mob on the other side of the door, the hijackers may have realized that they had waited too long to take over the plane. As Flight 93 began slowly making its way back toward the East Coast from Cleveland, the passengers had time to organize.

"The significance of saying to a pilot that you are authorized to shoot down that plane full of Americans is a, you know, it's an order that had never been given before," said Cheney. On Air Force One, Bush issued the order. "The President did give the order to shoot down a civilian plane if it was not responding properly," Condoleezza Rice said. Bush, however, immediately passed the buck back to Cheney, leaving the decision to him as to whether to give the final okay to shoot down the plane. "The President gave the VP authority to make that call. It was a chilling moment, chilling moment," recalled White House photographer David Bohrer, who was present at the time.

A few minutes later, Cheney passed the order to Army Brig. Gen. W. Montague Winfield in the Pentagon's War Room. "The President had given us permission to shoot down innocent civilian aircraft that threatened Washington, D.C.," Winfield said. "In the National Military Command Center, everything stopped for a short second as the impact of those words sunk in."

"DOD, DOD." Richard Clarke was sitting at a conference

table facing a bank of blinking television monitors in the White House Secure Video Conferencing Center. Located on the ground floor of the building, the center was used during emergencies to bring senior government officials together to try to work out the problem. Finally reaching the Pentagon, Clarke passed on Bush's message:

"Three decisions. One, the President has ordered the use of force against aircraft deemed to be hostile. Two, the White House is also requesting fighter escort of Air Force One. Three, and this applies to all agencies, we are initiating COG. Please activate your alternate command center and move staff to them immediately." COG was Continuity of Government, a supersecret doomsday plan to keep the Federal government running no matter how badly it was attacked.

Sitting in the glassed-in Battle Cab of NORAD'S Northeast Air Defense Sector Operations Center at Rome, New York, Air Force Colonel Robert Marr received the call. Then he sent out word to air traffic controllers to instruct fighter pilots to destroy the United jet-liner and any other threatening passenger plane. "United Airlines Flight 93 will not be allowed to reach Washington, D.C.," said Marr.

Maj. Daniel Nash, the F-15 pilot from Cape Cod, heard the message while patrolling over Manhattan. "The New York controller did come over the radio and say if we have another hijacked aircraft we're going to have to shoot it down," he said. "From where we were sitting, you could see there were people dying and it had to stop. So if that's what it's going to take, that was our job. We would have done it."

At the time, the closest fighters to United Flight 93, now over Pennsylvania, were two F-16 pilots engaged in a training exercise in the vicinity of Selfridge Air National Guard Base near Detroit. They were instructed to immediately turn south and attempt to intercept Flight 93. But since they were being diverted from a training mission, the fighters were unarmed. "Sir, what are they gonna do?" asked Colonel Marr's mission crew commander. "We're gonna put them as close to that airplane as they can get," Marr said, "in view of the cockpit, and convince that guy in that airplane that he needs to land."

But Marr knew they were dealing with more than hijackers; they were faced with suicide terrorists with whom there could be no gentle persuasion or threats of force. Thus, admitted Marr, the only solution would be for one of the fighter pilots to give up his own life by crashing into the United Airlines jet. "As military men," he said solemnly, "there are times you have to make sacrifices."

Knowing they were fighting for their lives, the passengers on Flight 93 began storming the locked cockpit. On the other side of the door, there were frantic discussions about fighting back. One of the hijackers suggested turning off the oxygen—they themselves could breathe through their face masks. As the confusion increased, the plane began to wobble and then lose altitude.

Soon after, people for miles around could see a cloud of gray smoke billowing above the trees and low-rise buildings of Shanksville, Pennsylvania, about 175 miles north and west of Washington. The cloud, coming from a fifty-foot crater, was all that remained of United Airlines Flight 93. At 10:03, one hundred and ten minutes after the takeoff of American Flight 11, the terrorist attacks of September 11 at last came to an end, amid the red barns, white churches, and copper pastures of rural Somerset County.

CHAPTER 4

SITE R

Even the reporters in the rear of Air Force One were surprised at the quick getaway. "It seemed we were 'wheels up' in nanoseconds," said Ellen Eckert, a White House stenographer. "The chatter in the press section of the plane where I was sitting was 'Where are we going? Where are we going?' And we were looking out the windows, trying to see if we could figure out geographically where we were going."

Within minutes, it became clear to everyone that Air Force One was not going back to Washington. For the first time in history, it became not a symbol of power but of escape as the nation's commander-in-chief searched for a safe haven. The flight of George W. Bush from Sarasota was in stark contrast to the flight of Lyndon B. Johnson from Dallas, Texas, following the assassination of John F. Kennedy.

As on September 11, there were great worries on November 22, 1963, that the assassination was part of a larger plot to destroy or take over the government. It was during the fearsome days of the Cold War when missiles armed with nuclear warheads were pointed at cities across the United States. Yet Johnson flew straight back to Washington immediately after being sworn in on the plane in Dallas and gave a short talk on the tarmac at Andrews Air

Force Base several hours later, an act that brought confidence and stability to a shattered nation.

Bush could have easily ordered Vice President Cheney to a secure location outside Washington to preserve the continuity of government and then flown back to Andrews Air Force Base and given a defiant, Johnson-like speech. Then, with the public—and the rest of the world—feeling confident that despite the terrorist actions the U.S. government remained stable and firm, he could have gone back either to the White House or to one of the other highly protected, secure locations. That would have been the courageous thing to do.

Instead, the decision was made to leave Vice President Cheney in the White House while President Bush hopscotched around the country. Though reporters were told of a supposed call to the White House threatening Air Force One—the reason for President Bush's odyssey—later it was concluded that no such call or threat ever took place. "They've been unsuccessful in trying to track down whether there was such a call," one administration official told the Associated Press. CBS News reported the call "simply never happened," and *The Washington Post* headlined its article on the subject: "White House Drops Claim of Threat to Bush."

The post-apocalyptic plan for what became known as COG was originally drafted during the Eisenhower administration in the 1950s. It was a Top Secret blueprint for preserving the federal government following a devastating nuclear attack. "We would have to run this country as one big camp—severely regimented," Eisenhower instructed his advisors. This would be done by the imposition of martial law and the suspension of many civil liberties.

At the same time, Eisenhower initiated a major, but highly secret, series of construction projects designed to be emergency command centers for senior administration, military, and congressional officials. Other presidential command posts were created in aircraft, ships at sea, and even in tractor-trailers.

Most amazing was Eisenhower's creation of an entirely secret government made up of private citizens and several cabinet officers. They would run the country in the event that the top leadership in Washington was not able to escape to one of the emergency command posts. This outside government-in-waiting—which changed form over the years—lasted at least until the early 1990s and may still be in effect. But because of the enormous secrecy surrounding the program over the decades, few details about it have ever come to light.

In 1958, Eisenhower designated eight private citizens around the country to somehow find their way to the center of power after a nuclear attack and take over one of the emergency functions of government. One of those was Aksel Nielsen, fifty-seven, the Danish-born head of the Title Guaranty Company of Denver and an old fishing friend of Eisenhower. Shortly after March 6, 1958, he was handed a letter signed by Eisenhower on White House stationery and stamped "Secret."

"It is always possible that the United States might need suddenly to mobilize resources for a maximum national effort," read the letter. "Although it is my devout hope that this will never happen, the national interest requires that against that possibility we achieve and maintain a high state of readiness. I am delighted to know of your willingness to serve as Administrator of the Emergency Housing Agency in the event that a national emergency would compel its formation, and, accordingly, I hereby appoint you such Administrator effective upon activation of the agency. . . . In the event of an emergency, as soon as you have assured yourself, by any means at your disposal, that an Emergency Housing Agency has been activated, you shall immediately assume active direction of that agency and its function. This letter will constitute your authority."

Others who received similar letters were Dr. George Pierce Baker, a professor at Harvard Business School; Harold Boeschenstein, the president of Owens-Corning Fiberglas Corporation; John Ed. Warren, senior vice president of the First National City Bank of New York; and Frank Pace, Jr., president of General Dynamics Corporation. Two cabinet officers, James T. Mitchell, Secretary of Labor, and Ezra Taft Benson, Secretary of Agriculture, also received appointment letters. Ironically, Theodore Koop, the vice president of CBS at the time, was secretly designated the administrator of the Emergency Censorship Agency. His letter still remained classified in 2004.

In an enormous oversight, the Eisenhower White House failed to pass on details of their secret government to the incoming Kennedy administration, which discovered it by accident. What Kennedy did after that is still a mystery.

But during the presidency of Ronald Reagan, following the attempt on his life soon after he took office, the issue of how to run the country if the senior leadership was "decapitated" was again revived. To help resolve this problem, a plan known as the Presidential Successor Support System was developed—again in absolute secrecy. Once more, unelected private citizens from around the country and several cabinet officers were called upon to take command. But now, one of them would even assume the role of president.

Given overall responsibility for the secret government was Vice President George H. W. Bush, with Lt. Col. Oliver North, a key player in the Iran-contra scandal, as the National Security Council action officer. The operation was hidden under the cover name "National Program Office" and was run by a two-star general from a nondescript Washington office building. Among the key players in the shadow government were Dick Cheney, Donald Rumsfeld, and James Woolsey.

At the time, Cheney was a congressman from Wyoming; Rumsfeld was CEO of G. D. Searle & Co., which produced such products as Metamucil and Nutra-Sweet; and Woolsey was a lawyer in private practice. Except for Rumsfeld's brief stint as a Middle East envoy, none held a full-time position within the Reagan administration. Nevertheless, they all had high-level national security experience—Cheney served as White House Chief of Staff under President Gerald Ford, Rumsfeld was a former congressman and also served as Ford's Chief of Staff and later as Secretary of Defense, and Woolsey was Undersecretary of the Navy in the late 1970s.

Unlike Eisenhower, who had one team of private citizens and several cabinet officers, Reagan's shadow government was made up of three teams, each with a cabinet officer who would become president. In the lead-up to war or national emergency, or as soon after an attack as possible, each team would fly to a secure location somewhere within the United States. Each would be named after a color—such as the Red, Blue, or Green Team—and one would be predesignated as the lead group with the others as backups.

A key objective of the lead team was to get to the "doomsday plane," the National Emergency Airborne Command Post, which at the time was a modified Boeing 707. Code-named "Night Watch," the heavily protected aircraft could be refueled while airborne and stay aloft for days, where it would function as a flying war room, directing the battle as well as the country from 40,000 feet.

Team members included representatives from the CIA and other government departments. They would lead various national emergency functions, such as intelligence, defense, transportation, or medical services. Among those designated as emergency presidents during Reagan's years were Secretary of Agriculture John Block and Secretary of Commerce Malcolm Baldrige.

The existence of the secret government was so closely held that Congress was completely bypassed. Rather than through legislation, it was created by Top Secret presidential fiat. In fact, Congress would have no role in the new wartime administration. "One of the awkward questions we faced," said one of the participants, "was whether to reconstitute Congress after a nuclear attack. It was decided that no, it would be easier to operate without them." When George H. W. Bush was elected president, he continued the program, but with the Cold War over, President Bill Clinton decided to end it.

Shortly after taking off in Air Force One, however, Bush made his decision to reinitiate part of the plan. So secret was the decision that no one in Congress—and only Vice President Cheney and a very few within the executive branch—were notified of the establishment of an invisible shadow government. Not even Majority Leader Dennis Hastert or Senator Robert C. Byrd (D–W. Va.), the president pro tempore of the Senate, the officials who were by law the first and second in line of succession after the vice president, were informed.

Within a few hours of the decision, the first steps were taken. According to intelligence officers, nearly one hundred officials, some very senior, quietly began disappearing from Washington and turning up at the two key "doomsday" sites in Virginia and Pennsylvania. They were forbidden from telling even their spouses where they were going.

The Virginia site was located eight miles from the sleepy hamlet of Berryville, on a snaking stretch of County Route 601 deep in the Blue Ridge Mountains. Although originally code-named "High Point," President Dwight D. Eisenhower, the first chief executive to visit the facility, referred to it simply as "the hideout." It was there, during a "doomsday" rehearsal in May 1960, that Eisenhower first read Soviet Premier Nikita Khrushchev's speech denouncing his administration for sending a U-2 spy plane over the Soviet Union. The lying and cover-up by Eisenhower that followed, in an attempt to conceal his role in the intelligence disaster, became the biggest scandal of his presidency.

Today this bunker is known as the Mount Weather Emergency Operations Center and is operated by the Federal Emergency Management Agency. It is about forty-eight miles—twenty minutes by helicopter—from downtown Washington. Completed in 1958, the year following the Soviet Union's successful launch of its Sputnik satellite, it cost more than a billion dollars. To protect the 600,000-square-foot command post from powerful blasts, the entire complex rests on a series of giant, nuclear-shock-absorbing steel springs; roof areas are reinforced with 21,000 iron bolts pounded eight to ten feet into the rock.

The high plateau that became Mount Weather gained initial fame as the place where wireless telegraphy was born. In 1868, a Massachusetts dentist, Mahlon Loomus, attached a kite and wire to a telegraph key and flew it into a building cloud at the same time a colleague, nine miles away on another high ground, did the same thing. With both kites in the cloud, an electrostatic charge formed between them, linking the two telegraph keys. At the turn of the century, the U.S. Weather Bureau set up a small meteorological research observatory there, thus giving the mound its name. Later, following presidential approval, the hunk of granite was turned into a presidential command center.

On September 11, 2001, entrance to the secret seat of government was made through a guillotine gate and five-foot-thick, ten-foot-tall, twenty-foot-wide blast doors that weighed thirty-four tons. Like a small city, the underground world is made up of an emergency power plant, dormitory space for several thousand people, a hospital, radio and television studios, storage tanks capable of holding 500,000 gallons of water, and even a reservoir for fresh water. A

series of side tunnels accommodates a total of twenty office buildings, some of which are three stories tall. Other tunnels accommodate computer complexes that maintain redundant electronic
databases for the continuity of government. For those who die in the
strange cement bunker, the facility is equipped with its own crema-
torium, known as a "pathological waste incinerator."

During the Cold War, Mount Weather also contained a
"Bomb Alarm System," a huge electronic map of the United
States in a special room that would display glowing red lights
wherever nuclear explosions had taken place. The map was part of
an elaborate system, consisting of a network of sensors mounted
on telephone poles near ninety-nine cities and military bases
around the country. The devices would detect the pressure, heat,
and intense thermal flash of a nuclear blast and send a signal to
the Bomb Alarm. By 2001, the system had been upgraded and
modified through the use of early-warning satellites.

An especially appealing factor to the Bush officials was that
Mount Weather was not only secure from nuclear explosions, it
was also invulnerable to crashing passenger jets. In a bizarre accident on December 1, 1974, a TWA Boeing 727 jet plowed into the
fog-wrapped hill, killing all ninety-two persons on board but leaving the command center untouched.

Not far from Mount Weather is Mount Pony, which until the
late 1990s was the underground bunker for the Federal Reserve
Board. Located just east of Culpeper, Virginia, it was where the
nation's money supply would be managed in case of national
emergency. Built of one-foot-thick, steel-reinforced concrete, with
lead-lined shutters in the windows, the facility is covered by up to
four feet of dirt and surrounded by barbed-wire fences and a guard
post. Inside the building is a giant 23,500-square-foot vault, which
until 1988 held several billion dollars, shrink-wrapped on pallets
nine feet high, that were to be used to jump-start a ruined econ-

omy. The building also contained a cold-storage area for maintaining highly radioactive bodies and seven computers that would control the transfer of all American electronic funds. But by September 11, 2001, Mount Pony had been converted to a video and audio storage facility for the Library of Congress.

The other key location for the shadow government, and what, say intelligence officials, would become a principal hiding place for Vice President Dick Cheney, is "Site R"—a highly secret and well-protected military command post at Raven Rock Mountain on the Maryland–Pennsylvania border. Located ten miles west of Waynesboro, Pennsylvania, a speck on the map with a Main Street lined with dusty antique shops, pizzerias, and vacant storefronts, the mysterious facility is hidden behind a forest of trees from those passing by on State Route 16.

First opened in 1951 and nicknamed the "Underground Pentagon," the official name for Site R is the Alternate Joint Communications Center. Only about seven miles from Camp David, the facility also doubles, like Mount Weather, as a heavily fortified emergency presidential bunker. Aboveground is a sprawling, porcupine-like antenna farm, satellite dishes, and a helipad. But deep inside the hard greenstone granite mountain is a secret world of five buildings each three stories tall, computer-filled caverns, and a subterranean water reservoir.

Within hours of the attacks on September 11, local residents saw a sudden increase in activity around the Raven Rock facility. Commandos quickly joined the military guards surrounding the facility. Five helicopters landed on the helipad, a convoy of SUVs with black-tinted windows sped up Harbaugh Valley Road to the main gate, and tan buses began laboring up the steep, two-lane road to the heavily guarded, unmarked service entrance. Among those early to arrive was Deputy Secretary of Defense Paul Wolfowitz, the Pentagon's second in command.

"We don't even have to turn on the news. We hear planes and we know right away what is going on," said local resident Jerre Snider. "When they hid the Vice President, well, we knew where he was."

Two thousand miles to the west, another mammoth underground command center was going to war conditions for the first time in its history. Buried deep inside the bored-out heart of Colorado's Cheyenne Mountain, and protected by 1,750 feet of granite, is NORAD's citylike Operations Center, the principal node for America's air, missile, and space early-warning system. Spread out over four and a half acres, it contains fifteen two- and three-story buildings, each with its own tunnel; a convenience store; a chapel; and even a restaurant, the Granite Inn.

To prevent a cave-in, the 115,000 bolts shoring up the walls are constantly checked and tightened. And to cushion the shock of a nuclear blast, the entire facility rests on more than 1,300 half-ton springs that allow the entire city and its 1,100 residents to sway up to a foot horizontally in any direction in the event of a nuclear explosion or an earthquake.

Since the enormous construction project was completed in 1965, the prime task of the center was to look outward across the seas and over the pole for threatening missiles and bombers. Its data comes from early-warning satellites in geostationary orbit and giant radar complexes around the country. Every day, technicians track more than 8,000 objects in near-Earth orbit, most of which is "space junk." But since its start, the early-warning system has always been focused on what was coming in, not on what was already present in the country.

On the morning of September 11, Lt. Col. John Donovan, a forty-two-year-old missile officer, had not a hint of what was about to happen fifteen minutes after he went off duty. "We told the [next] crew it was pretty quiet," he said. His boss, Command

Director Jerry Hatley, an Army colonel, was partway down the mountain when he heard about the first attacks on the radio.

Also within the mountain was NORAD's Air Warning Center. Caught by complete surprise as well, the group was in the middle of a twice-yearly exercise when the attacks began. "We were correlating our reports with what we were seeing up there, and it's just disbelief," said Air Force Lt. Col. William Glover, in charge of the Center at the time. As the devastation began, they closed the massive three-foot-thick, twenty-five-ton baffled steel doors, built a third of a mile into the mountain. Using hydraulic pressure, it took less than a minute to slam them shut.

Once sealed inside and surrounded by billions of dollars' worth of the most sophisticated intelligence and early-warning equipment, tied into advanced spy satellites and building-size surveillance antennas, the nation's guardians were left to watch the country undergo its worst attack in nearly two centuries on $300 television sets tuned in to CNN. To many, it was impossible to escape thoughts of Pearl Harbor.

"The blast doors were closed that morning for the first time in anger since this place was opened for operations in 1966," said Canadian Air Force Brig. Gen. Jim Hunter, vice commander for the Cheyenne Mountain Operations Center. "We did what we call buttoning up the mountain. We closed the blast doors and everybody that was in the mountain was going to stay for a while. I've never been in combat, and that morning was the first morning that I had ever really faced a real threat. . . . Once I realized we had those blast doors closed, I think they could have launched airliners at this mountain all day and we never would have felt the effects of it, because we have twenty-six hundred feet of granite above us."

As the Bush administration's shadow government began setting up at Mount Weather and Site R, senior congressional leaders were also looking for a place to hide, and the decision, say intelligence officials, was to fly them to Mount Weather.

For decades, Congress had their hideout, code-named Casper and later Greek Island, secretly attached to the five-star Greenbrier Resort in White Sulphur Springs, West Virginia. Completed in 1962, the 112,000-square-foot bunker, in the remote Allegheny Mountains five hours' drive southwest of Washington, sits more than six stories beneath the hotel's luxury-suite West Virginia wing. In addition to a complete medical clinic, television studio, and decontamination showers to wash off radiation, the buried facility included separate chambers for the House of Representatives and the Senate, as well as a larger room for joint sessions.

The covert construction project took two and a half years to complete and used 50,000 tons of concrete. The steel-reinforced concrete walls are two feet thick, and the blast doors weigh more than twenty-eight tons and are twelve feet tall. The hinges alone weigh one and a half tons. It was constructed so that its large wheel-locking mechanism could operate only from within.

Inside there was enough space to accommodate about 1,000 people for two months. Should the crisis go on longer, however, the plans were to commandeer the entire resort, which can house 6,500 people. But with the Cold War over, the decision was made in 1995 to deactivate the facility, and by September 11, 2001, it had become a sightseeing attraction. Thus the need to send the senior congressional leaders to Mount Weather. With the Greenbrier bunker crawling with tourists, the rest of Congress was left to fend for itself.

Shortly after the Pentagon was attacked, House Majority Leader Dennis Hastert (R–Ill.), next in line of succession behind Vice President Dick Cheney, was whisked out of his office. "Two of my security people grabbed me—one on each side—and said we think a plane's coming for the Capitol," he said. "And so I was exited out, down through the tunnels, into our car and shuttled off at high speed to Andrews Air Force Base.

"I'm thinking to myself," Hastert recalled, "here I am Speaker of the House, something I never dreamed would ever happen to me, and we're evacuating the Capitol. It just can't be happening to us. I was put in a . . . one of our secure automobiles, and the next thing I knew I was hurtling through the back streets of Washington." From there he was put on a helicopter and flown to the secret facility. About a half hour later, Daschle and the rest of the Senate and House leadership followed.

"Immediately upon landing," recalled Daschle, "we were met by armed guards who escorted us through two massive steel doors and down into the underground 'secure location.' The room we were first taken into was more bare bones than I had imagined. It had nothing in it but a couple of tables, a few folding chairs, and bright fluorescent lights. It could almost have passed for a police interrogation room. We waited there a short while before we were led down a cavelike tunnel into a more spacious room, furnished with desks and cubicles and a console of television monitors arrayed much like a NASA command center." Sitting at some of those consoles were representatives of the alphabet soup of intelligence agencies, from the NSA to the CIA.

Like NSA, the CIA also evacuated many of its employees from its headquarters in Langley, Virginia. Director of Operations James Pavitt sent a message to all of the agency's stations. "I expect each station and each officer to redouble efforts of collecting intelligence on this tragedy," he said. But it was the officials assigned to the agency's secret New York City station who were facing the most serious jeopardy. The station was located at 7 World Trade Center, a sleek forty-seven-story office building in the shadow of the twin towers. Masquerading as an office of the U.S. Army Logistics Command, the station was part of the Directorate of Operations' National Resources (NR) Division.

NR case officers attached to the station were responsible for attempting to recruit foreign officials, mostly those assigned to the United Nations from high-priority countries. Others specialized in debriefing U.S. citizens who had traveled to countries of high interest to the CIA. The office also played a major role in providing intelligence to the FBI for their cases against defendants charged in the August 1998 embassy bombings in East Africa and the October 2000 attack on the USS *Cole*.

Soon after the two towers were attacked, all of the occupants of 7 World Trade Center, across Vesey Street from the towers, were safely evacuated. Later, blown debris would set the sixteen-year-old steel building on fire, and with the fireproofing systems completely inoperable, it would burn for hours. Eventually, the heat and flames likely reached tanks, stored just above and at ground level, containing some 36,000 gallons of diesel fuel used to run backup generators for the city's emergency command post, also located in the building. About seven seconds after the lower levels of the building began giving way, all two million square feet of it completely collapsed into its own footprint.

Because the attack caught the entire intelligence community by complete surprise, the information reaching the President on Air Force One was a jumble of disparate facts, rumors, and hypotheticals. There were only questions and no answers. The most reliable information was coming not from the CIA, NSA, FBI, or DIA, but from ABC, NBC, CBS, and CNN. Where the intelligence community was emptying its buildings and running for cover, the news organizations in New York and Washington were pulling everyone in and jumping on the story.

But the television signal aboard the presidential jet was haphazard. As a result, the President and those around him on the plane continually knew less than millions on the ground below them. "Everyone is watching the monitors, trying to get snippets of visual information, and the reception keeps going in and out," recalled Eric Draper, President Bush's personal photographer. "It was like a bad dream," he said.

Seated in one of the eight chairs around the plane's conference table, Florida Congressman Dan Miller also had difficulty getting much news from the flickering words and images on the television set. As a result, information—and rumors—were passed throughout the plane the old way, from mouth to mouth. Then, about twenty-five minutes into the flight, while flying over northern Florida, Miller and many of the others noticed the plane suddenly bank to the west. Through the window, he could see the unmistakable coastline of the Florida Panhandle, followed by Alabama and then Mississippi. "This is like a Tom Clancy novel," Miller kept thinking. "It can't be happening."

At that point, Bush had made a dramatic decision. Instead of going back to Washington, he would fly inland and seek a secure shelter. "We seemed to be flying forever," said ABC News White House correspondent Ann Compton. "And one of the Secret Service agents leaned over to me and said, 'Look down there, we're at 44,000 feet, and we're not going back to Washington.'" At the White House, presidential advisor Karen Hughes attempted to place a call to Bush. "The military operator came back to me and in—in a voice that, to me, sounded very shaken, said, 'Ma'am, I'm sorry. We can't reach Air Force One,'" said Hughes.

The plan was to fly to Barksdale Air Force Base near Shreveport, Louisiana. According to intelligence sources, a key reason for deciding to land there was that Barksdale was home to the U.S. Strategic Command's alternate underground command post, a bunker from which Bush could run a war if necessary.

It was also a place where the President could rendezvous with "Night Watch," the "doomsday plane." Once a specially outfitted Boeing 707 known as the National Emergency Airborne Command Post, by 2001 it had become a heavily modified military version of the Boeing 747-200, similar to Air Force One. Renamed the National Airborne Operations Center (NAOC), the aircraft was designed to be used by the President to direct a war in case of nuclear attack. During the Cold War, one of the four Night Watch aircraft was always in the air, twenty-four hours a day. But in the 1990s, the decision was made to keep the alert aircraft on the ground with the ability to take off on fifteen minutes' notice.

Whenever the President travels, one of the heavily shielded Night Watch alert aircraft, complete with battle staff, is moved to a base in his general vicinity. In a bit of black humor, crewmembers occasionally wear ball caps with the image of the grim reaper holding a sickle in one hand and a button in the other, with a mushroom cloud in the background. The caption reads: "Doomsday Aircrew Member—Don't Push Me."

In a matter of minutes, Air Force One had gone from a flying limousine to an airborne command post. With an onboard refueling capability through a small hump in the nose, airborne tankers could keep the plane aloft indefinitely, though after about five or six days the engine oil would begin to break down and it would have to land.

To protect against heat-seeking missiles, the plane has a sophisticated infrared jammer, code-named "Have Charcoal," flares designed to confuse the missiles, and other electronic countermeasures hidden inside its tail section. Its 238 miles of wire—more than twice the wiring found on a typical 747—is shielded to protect it from electromagnetic pulse generated by a thermonuclear blast.

In the cockpit of Air Force One, Col. Mark Tillman, the pilot, worried about security even on the presidential aircraft and ordered an armed guard posted outside his door. Then the Secret Service rechecked the identity of everyone on board and went over the emergency evacuation procedures. Another concern was that communications with air control on the ground would be overheard. "We actually have to consider everything we say," he told his crew. "Everything we do could be intercepted, and we have to make sure that no one knows what our position is."

On the upper deck, behind the cockpit, was the plane's near-windowless communications suite. There three radio operators controlled the plane's eighty-five air-to-ground telephones and its sophisticated encryption and communications systems—running the gamut from extremely low to ultrahigh to satellite frequencies. But during the flight, secret, encrypted calls were slow and they would occasionally cut out. At one point as Bush was talking to Cheney, the connection broke off in midsentence. "This is inexcusable," Bush shouted. "Get me the Vice President."

"Secure calls just take a while to establish sometimes," said one senior Bush advisor. "It's just the nature of encryption—encryption moving at 35,000 feet, at 500 to 600 miles an hour."

Secret Service agents passed messages to the communicators using their special code words. Bush was "Trailblazer," Laura Bush was "Tempo," Cheney was "Angler," Air Force One was "Angel," the White House became "Crown," and the Capitol "Punchbowl." "Angel to Crown, Angel to Crown" was often heard. Other code words were used for the hidden doomsday bunkers; Site R became WAR-46 and the alert doomsday plane was GORDO.

Rather than use his radio, Tillman called air traffic control over the onboard telephone and refused to tell them their destination or even what direction they were headed. "We have no clearance at this time; we are just going to fly across the United States,"

he said to one controller he spoke to. On the ground, there was confusion. "Okay, where's he going?" asked one air traffic controller.
"Just watch him," said another. "Don't question him where he's
going. Just work him and watch him. There's no flight plan in, and
right now we're not going to put anything in. Okay, sir?" "Copy
that," the other controller replied.

In a further security measure, passengers were ordered to
turn off their cell phones and Secret Service agents yanked their
batteries to prevent signals from revealing the plane's location.
They were also instructed that when they landed they could say
only that the President was at "an unidentified location in the
United States," and nothing more. "The strange part about it was,
here we are turning off cell phones and taking precautions, and
we see ourselves landing at Barksdale Air Force Base in Louisiana
on the TV," said Draper. "So much for not being found."

Air Force One landed at Barksdale at 11:45. Congressman
Miller looked out the window and was amazed at the array of sol-
diers in helmets and flak jackets packing automatic weapons, as
well as the assortment of armored vehicles that had surrounded
the plane. Bush was immediately taken to Building 245, the
Headquarters of the Eighth Air Force, in a blue Dodge Caravan.
Leading the motorcade was a green Humvee with an airman vis-
ible in the gun turret. By then signs on the base were displaying
"DEFCON DELTA" in large black type, the highest state of alert.
From the headquarters, Bush went to the commanding general's
quarters, where he spoke over a secure line with Cheney, Rice, and
Rumsfeld.

Then he videotaped a two-minute address—just 219 words—
to the nation that was to be shown later. "He looked nervous," said
The New York Times reporters David E. Sanger and Don Van Natta,
Jr. *The Washington Post* reporters Dan Balz and Bob Woodward
agreed. "When Bush finally appeared on television from the base

conference room," they wrote, "it was not a reassuring picture. He spoke haltingly, mispronouncing several words as he looked down at his notes." Judy Keen of *USA Today* noted that Bush "looked grim. His eyes were red-rimmed." An administration official later admitted, "It was not our best moment."

By then many in the press were beginning to question why the President hadn't returned to Washington during the grave crisis. The question was put to presidential counselor Karen Hughes, then at FBI headquarters. "Where's the President?" asked one reporter. "Is he coming back to D.C.?" asked another. Instead of answering, she simply turned on her heels and walked out of the room. NBC's Tim Russert, host of *Meet the Press* and the Washington bureau chief, also remarked about the nation needing the leadership of its president. Yet, rather than return to Washington, the decision was made to keep moving as quickly as possible in the opposite direction. It was a risky choice. "If he stayed away," reported London's *Daily Telegraph*, "he could be accused of cowardice."

In another secret wartime move, NORAD and the Secret Service decided to divert an AWACS airborne early-warning aircraft, with the capability to watch the skies for hundreds of surrounding miles, from a training mission off the coast of Florida to follow Air Force One. Fighters were also ordered aloft to protect the plane. "Air Force One, got two F-16s at about your—say, your ten-o'clock position," said one ground controller. "We were not told where Air Force One was going," recalled NORAD Maj. Gen. Larry Arnold. "We were told just to follow the President. We scrambled available airplanes from Tyndall [Air Force Base, Florida] and then from Ellington in Houston, Texas."

After the removal of most of the aides and press from Air Force One, it was again airborne. "Ari Fleischer told us, 'I can't tell you where we're going,'" recalled ABC News correspondent Ann

Compton. "And you got the distinct feeling it was because he didn't know. Because they didn't know." White House stenographer Ellen Eckert said, "I remember thinking it was like being on the *Twilight Zone* plane because there was nobody around anymore."

At five minutes past noon, CIA Director George Tenet passed to Secretary of Defense Rumsfeld the key information NSA had intercepted at 9:53, about fifteen minutes after the Pentagon had been hit. A bin Laden operative in Afghanistan had telephoned a number in the former Soviet republic of Georgia and asked if he had "heard good news?" At the same time, he had indicated that at least one more target was yet to be hit. Ten minutes later, United Flight 93 crashed in Pennsylvania on its way to a fourth target in Washington.

Air Force One's mysterious destination was Offutt Air Force Base, near Omaha, Nebraska, home of the United States Strategic Command—STRATCOM—the successor to the Cold War Strategic Air Command, SAC. Its deep bunker is the principal location from which the United States would direct World War III.

For several hours forklifts had been setting up a serpentine network of concrete barricades on the entrance roads to the base. Guards in camouflaged helmets and protective vests were posted around the perimeter, large trash containers were being hauled away from buildings, and bomb-sniffing dogs were checking all vehicles, resulting in the backup of hundreds of cars waiting to enter the gates.

Earlier that morning, of the five levels of security—Normal, Alpha, Bravo, Charlie, and Delta—Offutt was as usual at Normal. Following the attacks on New York and Washington, it was moved up to Bravo. Now it was at Delta. "Delta means an area," read a sign posted at Offutt's Kenney Gate, "where a terrorist attack has occurred or where intelligence has been received that terrorist action against a specific location or person is likely."

At 2:50 eastern time, Air Force One, accompanied by two F-16 jet fighters, landed at Offutt. A motorcade of eight vehicles drove out to meet it, and about fifteen minutes later Bush went "down the bunny hole," said ABC's Ann Compton. The tiny, cinder-block structure was the emergency escape exit for the underground command center.

"You go downstairs and go downstairs and go downstairs and you go downstairs," recalled Karl Rove. "I mean, it's a long way down, and then you emerge and go through a series of hallways and special doors, blast doors and so forth, and then you enter into a conference center, which is, you know, several stories underground."

Three stories down was the command center, a cavernous two-story war room with banks of dark wooden desks curved away from a giant projection screen on which was displayed the status of military forces around the world. To defend against biological warfare or lethal gas, the air pressure in the center is kept somewhat higher than the surrounding area and a sophisticated filtering system is used. The President took his seat surrounded by a multiservice battle staff.

It was like a scene from *Dr. Strangelove,* or *Seven Days in May.* Never before had all the pieces been in place for the instant launch of World War III. The military alert level was at its highest level in thirty years. The Vice President was in the White House bunker, senior administration officials were at Site R, congressional officials had been flown to Mount Weather, the Secretary of Defense and Vice Chairman of the Joint Chiefs of Staff were in the Pentagon War Room, and the President of the United States was in the nuclear command bunker at STRATCOM.

Only a few feet away from Bush was the fire-engine-red

double-locked "clanker box" containing the authentication codes required to send America's nuclear arsenal skyward. Another set of the codes was nearby in a black briefcase known as the "football," which is always carried by a military officer never more than a few yards from the President's side. A third authentication code, abbreviated in case of an emergency, was on a card in the President's wallet.

Once the codes are sent to American missile bases and ballistic submarines around the world, two people would open separate locks on their "clanker boxes"—so called because of the clanking sound made by the alarm when the safe is opened. Inside are thick envelopes stamped "Top Secret—SIOP ESI" containing documents and computer disks. SIOP ESI stands for "Single Integrated Operational Plan—Extra Sensitive Information." They are the nuclear war plan options—where, and how hard, to hit such targets as North Korea, Iraq, Iran, China, Russia, or Afghanistan.

Not far away, at Malmstrom Air Base in Montana, nuclear weapons watch officers were at their highest state of alert. They sat with "launch keys" dangling from their necks in control facilities buried sixty feet underground and protected by concrete and rebar walls four-and-a-half feet thick with eight-ton blast doors. Surrounding them were two hundred silos, each armed with an intercontinental ballistic Minuteman III missile, tipped with up to three deadly warheads inside a silver titanium shield.

It was "nerve-racking," said Air Force Capt. Rob Riegel, who was on duty on September 11. "If we get the authorized presidential directive," he later explained, "we go through several procedures, the final one of which is to insert the launch key . . . and put our hand on the cooperative launch switches. I have one. My deputy has two. And at the appropriate time, we'll turn those switches, look for indications, and hope that it works." He added, "It has to stay in the forefront of our mind how important it is what we do here, and it has to stay in the forefront of our mind how absolutely frightening it can be."

From the safety of his rabbit hole in Nebraska, George W. Bush conducted a National Security Council meeting via teleconference screens with his top aides back in Washington. "Who do you think did this to us?" he asked CIA Director George Tenet. "Sir, I believe it's Al Qaeda. We're doing the assessment, but it looks like, it feels like, it smells like Al Qaeda," he said. "Get your ears up," snapped Bush.

By the time it was over it was close to 4:30 on the East Coast, and except for the brief, two-minute taped comments made at Barksdale, no one had seen or heard from the President or even knew where he was. Republicans back in Washington were becoming worried. "I am stunned that he has not come home," said one Bush fund-raiser. "It looks like he is running. This looks bad." William J. Bennett, a former education secretary under President Ronald Reagan and a drug czar under former President George Bush, said that it was important for Bush to return to the White House as soon as possible. "This is not 1812," he said. "It cannot look as if the President has been run off, or it will look like we can't defend our most important institutions."

As the President sat in his hideout, officials were following the track of a commercial jetliner traveling from Spain to the United States that was giving off an emergency signal. "Do we have permission to shoot down this aircraft?" said a voice over a loudspeaker. "Make sure you've got the ID," said Bush. "You follow this guy closely to make sure." The alert eventually turned out to be a simple mistake. Many later considered it something of a miracle that no innocent passenger jets were accidentally shot down that day.

"We were able to determine that aircraft was not being hijacked by calling the company," said NORAD commander Maj.

Gen. Larry Arnold in Florida. "And so I just picked up the conference call and said, 'Mr. President, we have confirmation—that aircraft has turned around, is on the ground, and we have no other aircraft in the system.' And with that he got in his aircraft and flew back to Washington."

With the last plane out of the sky in virtually the entire Northern Hemisphere, Bush finally decided to return. It was after 7:00 when he finally arrived back at the White House, and he gave a brief report to the nation on live television at 8:30. But again, the speech was a disappointment. "Republican advisers to the administration said the speech fell flat, that it failed to meet either the magnitude of the day's events or the nature of the task ahead," noted *The New York Times*.

That night before bed, Bush jotted a note in his diary. "The Pearl Harbor of the 21st century took place today," he wrote. "We think it's Osama bin Laden."

PART II

DETECTION

CHAPTER 5

FLORENCE

One hundred and five miles south of Denver, in the arid, remote high desert along the Arkansas River, a sign says "Welcome to Florence, A Great Little Town!" Cradled on three sides by the Rocky Mountains, like cupped hands, the old boomtown is largely protected from the often severe Colorado winters and blustery summer storms. Life for the 3,600 townsfolk centers on Main Street, where one can shop for an old silver horse bit or Victorian glassware at the Blue Spruce Art & Antiques Shop, or get an iced café latte at Coffee Creations. When the alarm sounds at the fire station a few doors down, volunteers from throughout the town hurry to man the trucks. Given the sleepy, bucolic nature of Florence, deep in coal and cattle country, it hardly seems the place one would find America's most dangerous terrorist.

Living just south of town on State Highway 67, Ramzi Yousef was one of Florence's involuntary residents. His address was, and will be for some time, Box 6000, United States Penitentiary Administrative Maximum Facility (ADX), Florence, Colorado 81226. Otherwise known as the Alcatraz of the Rockies, the two-story, rectangular ADX is America's toughest prison—a "supermax."

By September 11, 2001, Yousef's world had shrunk to exactly eight feet by ten feet by twelve feet. That Tuesday was a day virtually identical to all others. Twenty-three hours of it was spent double-locked in a cement box behind a steel door and barred grate in the most secure wing of the most secure prison in America. Like the walls and the floor, the bed, desk, and stool were also made of poured concrete. His window, four inches wide, looked out on his small concrete recreation yard, which he could use one hour a day—but without any other human contact except for the watching guards. His sink had buttons instead of taps so the parts could not be disassembled and used as weapons or for suicide, and his toilet had an automatic shut-off valve to prevent him from stopping it up and flooding the cell. Among his four hundred neighbors were Unabomber Ted Kaczynski, Oklahoma bomber Terry Nichols, and, until he was executed, Nichols's coconspirator, Timothy McVeigh. Reed thin, with a bony physique, wavy raven-dark hair, and determined brown eyes, Yousef was in the sixth year of a 240-year sentence.

Nearly a decade earlier, Yousef, who speaks perfect English with a British accent, boarded a plane from Pakistan to New York's JFK Airport. The purpose of his visit was to exact revenge for America's financial and military backing of Israel's treatment of the Palestinians. Left behind in Pakistan was the mastermind of the plot, Yousef's uncle, Khalid Shaikh Mohammed. A cunning engineer, Khalid Shaikh had studied higher mathematics and jet propulsion amid long-leaf pines and antebellum mansions in Greensboro, North Carolina.

Khalid Shaikh had arrived in the United States in 1984 and first spent a semester at nearby Chowan College, a 155-year-old Baptist school in Murfreesboro with clinker-built, white-painted homes on the Meherrin River. "Khalid, he was so, so smart," recalled a fellow classmate who later became an advertising executive in Kuwait. "He came to college with virtually no English. But he entered directly in advanced classes. He was a funny guy, telling jokes twenty-four hours straight. He was focused. He wanted to get his degree and go home. He was so quiet, there was no indication that he was involved in [religious extremism]."

Following his semester at Chowan, which he used mostly to improve his English, Khalid transferred to North Carolina A&T in Greensboro, where he studied engineering, taking courses in the basics of power plants, combustion reactions, and jet engines.

Khalid Shaikh graduated from North Carolina A&T on December 18, 1986, having completed the requirements for his bachelor's degree in mechanical engineering in just two and a half years. Of the twenty-eight others receiving similar ME degrees, almost one-third came from the Middle East. Rather than return to Kuwait, Khalid chose to join his older brother, Zahed, in Peshawar, Pakistan.

At the time, Peshawar was the front door to the Soviet-Afghan war, and thousands of Arabs from around the Middle East were flooding into the city before heading across the Khyber Pass into Afghanistan to help expel the Russians. Like many places that become crossroads for a war, Peshawar bubbled with intrigue and danger. As cash and weapons flowed in and out, smuggling became a booming business, and covert-action specialists competed with revolutionaries for recruits. It was into such an atmosphere that Khalid Shaikh Mohammed emerged as he stepped off his flight from Greensboro and took a whiff of war.

Soon after arriving, he obtained a job as an assistant to Abdul Rasool Sayyaf, one of the leading Afghan warlords and a former Kabul University professor. His brother, Zahed, had several years earlier begun making a name for himself running large charities—organizations raising money for a variety of causes, from combat arms to child welfare—in Peshawar. Coordinating many of these charities was Sheik Abdullah Azzam.

Born near Jenin, in Palestine, Azzam had been among the

tens of thousands of Palestinians forced out of the West Bank during the Israeli occupation of 1967. In 1966, he received a bachelor's degree in Islamic law from Damascus University. But a year
later, the Israeli capture of the West Bank turned his village into
little more than a military camp. Bitter with hatred at the occupiers with their tanks and troops, Azzam joined Yasser Arafat's
PLO movement in southern Jordan. In 1973, he earned his doctorate in Islamic jurisprudence from Al-Azhar University in Cairo.

More determined than ever to bring a violent end to the
Israeli occupation of his lost Palestine, he also believed that the
fight should be based on Islamic principles and laws. Thus, rather
than return to Jordan, he instead accepted a teaching position in
Jedda, Saudi Arabia, at the King Abdul Aziz University. Among the
students who heard Azzam's emotional plea for an Islamic war
against Israel and its American benefactors was the wealthy son of
a Saudi construction magnate, Osama bin Laden.

With the outbreak of the Afghan revolt against the Soviet
invasion, Azzam saw his opportunity to rejoin the fight, and in
1979 he quickly exchanged the classroom for the battlefield.
Moving to Peshawar, a frontier town in northwest Pakistan, he set
up his Office of Services in a small shop among the city's winding
alleyways. The Office of Services was a sort of recruitment center
and central clearinghouse for Arab volunteers—mujahideen—
seeking to join the battle. Osama bin Laden, then twenty-two, followed his mentor to Peshawar and bankrolled the organization
with his millions in family inheritance.

It was through these connections that Khalid Shaikh and his
brother Zahed got to know Azzam, bin Laden, and Ayman
al-Zawahiri, a top associate of bin Laden. Later, he would also be
joined by another close relative, his nephew Ramzi Yousef, who
had left Kuwait to study electrical engineering in Wales. Yousef
made his first trip to Peshawar in 1988 during a summer break

from Swansea Institute of Higher Education, where he was studying computer-aided electrical engineering. Then he returned the
summer following graduation to train and offer instruction in
explosives at the Sadda training camp for mujahideen. Controlled
by Abdul Rasool Sayyaf, it was located in the wild Khumram
Agency (agency was the bureaucratic term for the buffer zone
between Pakistan and Afghanistan, which was managed by local
Pashtun tribesmen) near the border town of Parachinar.

On September 1, 1992, Khalid Shaikh Mohammed's nephew,
Ramzi Yousef, stepped off a Pakistan International Airlines jet
from Peshawar, Pakistan, at New York's JFK Airport. Yousef,
whose mother was Palestinian, would call himself "Pakistani by
nationality" but "Palestinian by choice." His goal was to punish
the United States for its support of Israel. "Since the U.S. government every year sends military and financial aid worth hundreds
of millions of dollars to Israel," he said, "all Muslims have the
right to regard themselves in a state of war with the U.S. government."

Arriving in New York without a visa, Yousef told immigration inspectors that he was requesting asylum. After being finger-
printed, he was released but ordered to show up for a later hearing.
From the airport he apparently took a taxi to the East Village of
Manhattan, where he met with Mahmoud Abouhalima. A graduate of one of Osama bin Laden's training camps, Abouhalima was
also a former associate of El Sayyid Nosair, who was acquitted of
charges he killed Rabbi Meir Kahane, the head of the Jewish
Defense League, an anti-Arab terrorist group. (Nosair was con-
victed on lesser charges in the Kahane case.) Abouhalima introduced Yousef to other former associates of Nosair, and then Yousef
moved in with Nosair's top supporter, Mohammed Salameh.

Shortly after his arrival in New York, Yousef was told of the group's plot to set off bombs at a dozen locations in New York associated with Israel. Yousef, however, instead suggested a much more ambitious target, one he and his uncle, Khalid Shaikh, had likely been planning for a long time: to bring down the soaring towers of the World Trade Center, the ultimate symbol of America's worldwide financial muscle.

Six months later, a yellow Ford Econoline Ryder rental van was driven down the sloping ramp into the World Trade Center garage and parked in a space next to a concrete wall on the B-2 level. Packed inside the 295 cubic feet of space behind the driver's seat was twelve hundred pounds of high explosive—a witch's brew of nitroglycerine, urea pellets, sulfuric acid, aluminum azide, magnesium azide, and bottled hydrogen. Attached to the bomb were four fuses, each twenty feet long and covered with surgical tubing to help prevent escaping smoke. Once lit, the fuses burned at the rate of one inch per two-and-a-half seconds. At 12:17 P.M. on February 26, 1993, the fuses reached the explosives, generating a massive blast consisting of more than 154,000 pounds of pressure per square inch. In that instant, the violent conflict between Israel and the Palestinians finally arrived in downtown Manhattan.

Hours later, the thick spiraling clouds of black and gray smoke pouring out of the World Trade Center were still visible as Ramzi Yousef rode to Kennedy Airport. In his pocket was a ticket on a Pakistan International Airlines flight to Karachi, and from there to Quetta, Pakistan, on the Afghanistan border. The fact that both towers remained standing, however, was a disappointment, one he planned to correct sometime in the future.

The next day, one of the members of the cell called the New York *Daily News* "tips line" and claimed responsibility for the bombing on behalf of the "Liberation Army," which was the name Yousef gave to his terrorist group. "We conducted the explosion at the World Trade Center. You will get our demands by mail.

This is the Liberation Army." The letter containing the demands was sent to *The New York Times*. It said that the World Trade Center was bombed in retaliation for American support for Israel and demanded changes in American foreign policy in the Middle East. If the demands were not met, the letter warned, more terrorist "missions" would be carried out against military and civilian targets in America and abroad. It also warned that future attacks could be carried out by "suicidal soldiers," a clear escalation in tactics.

Specifically, the letter declared:

OUR DEMANDS ARE:

1—Stop all military, economical, and political aid to Israel.

2—All diplomatic relations with Israel must stop.

3—Not to interfere with any of the Middle East countries interior affairs.

If our demands are not met, all of our functional groups in the army will continue to execute our missions against the military and civilian targets in and out the United States. For your own information, our army has more than hundred and fifty suicidal soldiers ready to go ahead. The terrorism that Israel practices (which is supported by America) must be faced with a similar one. The dictatorship and terrorism (also supported by America) that some countries are practicing against their own people must also be faced with terrorism.

The American people must know, that their civilians who got killed are not better than those who are getting killed by the American weapons and support.

The American people are responsible for the actions of their government and they must question all of the crimes that their government is committing against other people. Or they—Americans—will be the targets of our operations that could diminish them.

> LIBERATION ARMY
> FIFTH
> BATTALION

The CIA and FBI had no doubts about the authenticity of the message. This was because they found a second "Liberation Army" letter, never sent, on a computer disk seized from the office of one of the cell members in New Jersey. Although the letter had been deleted, computer experts were able to recover it. This second letter made it very clear that they were planning to return to finish what they had started at the World Trade Center.

> Unfortunately, our calculations were not very accurate this time. . . . However, we promise you that next time it will be very precise, and the World Trade Center will continue to be one of our targets in the U.S., unless our demands are met.

On September 11, 2001, shortly before seven, a late-model Volvo pulled up to a sidewalk in front of the headquarters for the National Security Agency at Fort Meade, Maryland, and a husky Air Force officer stepped out. Walking up a few cement stairs at Ops 2 Building, he pulled open a glass door, slipped his blue security badge into a reader, and pushed through the steel turnstile. Lt. Gen. Michael V. Hayden, the unpretentious director of the largest intelligence agency on earth, had arrived for work. "I drive myself or my son or wife will drop me off if they need the car," he says, "and more often than not they will drop me off." Bypassing his small private elevator, Hayden smiled, said "good morning," and crowded in with the other early-morning arrivals in one of the large employee elevators.

Up on the eighth floor, he walked to the end of the hallway and entered the executive suite containing the offices of the director, deputy director, and executive director. Once referred to as "Mahogany Row," the shiny wood was long gone. Instead, past the receptionist, the walls are covered with framed pictures of NSA's largest listening posts. Among them is Menwith Hill Station in central England, with its dozens of eavesdropping antennas hidden under radomes that look like giant Ping-Pong balls. Hayden took a left through an unmarked wooden door and entered his corner office.

By early September 2001, the National Security Agency had become not only the world's biggest spy organization but also the most sophisticated, pervasive, and secret. Since its birth on November 4, 1952, the singular objective of the NSA, responsible for worldwide electronic surveillance and code breaking, was to prevent a surprise attack. To that end, the agency had spent most of its existence—and its budget—focused on one target: the Soviet Union and its satellite states. For nearly half a century, the agency fought a secret war to break the defiant Russian cipher system and to eavesdrop on that nation's most secret communications. But by the early 1990s, the Evil Empire had died, a friendly Russia had taken its place, and the earth suddenly shifted underneath it. Decades of training and billions of dollars' worth of equipment were now out of date. No one knew where the next crisis would take place, or who the new enemies were. All Air Force Lt. Gen. Hayden, now Director of NSA, really knew for sure was that his agency was quickly becoming obsolete and he was running out of time to fix the problems.

Standing at his eavesdropping-proof windows, Director Hayden could survey his burgeoning empire—a top-secret town of more than sixty office buildings, warehouses, factories, laboratories, and living quarters—stretching far into the distance. At the heart of the invisible city was NSA's massive Headquarters/ Operations Building, a complex so large that the U.S. Capitol Building could easily fit inside it—four times over. A modern, boxy structure with floor after floor of dark, one-way glass, the complex looked from the outside like it could be a large insurance company or a stylish office building.

Born on March 17, 1945, Hayden grew up amid the steel mills and towering smokestacks of Pittsburgh's North Side, daydreaming about a career as a professional football player with the Pittsburgh Steelers. Harry Hayden, Sr., his father, worked the 3:30-to-midnight shift as a welder at the Allis-Chalmers plant, which built mammoth electrical transformers.

In college and graduate school at Duquesne University, he avoided hard math and science courses and instead studied history while earning money behind the wheel of a taxi and as a night bellman at the Duquesne Club. During the height of the anti–Vietnam War era of the late 1960s, when students were burning their draft cards, Hayden went in the opposite direction, excelling in ROTC and becoming a distinguished graduate of the program. He entered the Air Force in 1969, shortly after finishing graduate school, and spent most of his career in staff intelligence assignments, including a stint as an air attaché in Sophia, Bulgaria. Hayden was in Korea serving as deputy chief of staff for the United Nations Command when he secretly received word of his new assignment to NSA.

Arriving at NSA in April 1999, he found an agency holding on to its technology tail for all its life. The same organization that once blazed the path in computer science, going where the private sector feared or could not afford to go, was now buying off-the-shelf technology. "Most of what they [NSA] were expert in is no longer relevant," said a former director. "Getting them to embrace the new world has been traumatic. . . . All they're trying to do is hang on and survive."

The congressional intelligence committees also saw NSA's ship heading for the shoals and, like worried first mates, began sounding the alarm, pressuring NSA to quickly begin turning away from the rocky coast. For years, they believed, NSA's leadership had simply ignored the agency's many problems. "Congressional leaders told me at our first meeting," said Hayden, "that the agency had fallen behind and was in danger of irrelevance. The challenge was above all technological. As one congressional leader put it, 'You need to hit a home run your first time at bat.'"

In a candid talk, Hayden told his staff that what was at stake was nothing less than the very survival of NSA. "As an agency," he said, "we now face our greatest technological and analytic challenges—diverse and dynamic targets; nontraditional enemies and allies; a global information technology explosion; digital encryption; and others. Make no mistake, we are in a worldwide competition for our future."

One of the major problems confronting NSA was a growing switch in technologies throughout the world. Some of NSA's targets continued to use traditional methods of communications—unencrypted faxes and phone calls transmitted over microwaves and satellites—which NSA was still very capable of intercepting. But other targets had switched to far more complex communications systems—circuit encryption, fiber-optics, digital cellular phones, and the Internet. The problem was spending vast amounts of money, time, and expertise to develop ways to penetrate the new systems while not overlooking the old systems.

For NSA, day had become night in attempting to switch gears from fighting the Cold War to fighting terrorism—especially terrorists operating independently of foreign governments. "Our world kind of turned upside down," said one senior NSA official. "The target changed overnight on 9 November 1989, and we began to search for what our next target would be. That happened to everyone in the intelligence community. But at NSA it was far more revolutionary. Cyberspace has no geographic boundaries. The computer that decides what is happening in one place may be geographically in another part of the world. Traffic lights in a place like Nashville, Tennessee, are controlled by a computer in Chicago."

In the old days, said the official, you could tell what kinds of communications were being transmitted simply by the sound—the sounds of Sigint (signals intelligence). "You could tell a fax from a teleprinter just by the sound. The ear could tell you the mode of transmission. But now in the digital world, every single one of those sounds of Sigint became one sound—what we call a beat and a rush. There was no other identification. That began the change from the analog world to the digital world. Everything we had learned in the analog world in the way to approach a problem didn't work in the digital world."

Another advantage of the Cold War was that the Soviet Union, with its fixed military bases, naval ports, and airfields, was largely stationary and the military components were always chatting back and forth. Much of the communication among these units was transmitted over low-cost unencrypted high-frequency channels. Thus, by ringing the Soviet Union with massive high-frequency listening posts targeted at the various key communications nodes, they would be able to eavesdrop constantly.

Also, a large percentage of the world's communications were transmitted and received via satellite during the 1970s and 1980s. Thus, NSA needed to do little more than plant a giant dish-shaped antenna in an open field and collect the millions of phone calls, faxes, and other forms of communications falling into it like rain. Through a highly secret pact known as the UKUSA agreement,

NSA and its close partners in the United Kingdom, Canada, Australia, and New Zealand collected and then shared this world-wide satellite intelligence—a system known as Echelon.

Yet more and more communications companies had begun to switch their networks from satellites, with their half-second time delay and occasional atmospheric interference, to buried fiber-optic cables. Made up of bundles of tiny, hair-thin glass strands, fiber-optics offers greater volume, more security, and higher relia-bility. Where satellite communications are as easy to collect as sun-shine, fiber-optic signals require the skills of a mole. As telephone calls began going from deep space to deep underground, it began to spell eventual doom for Echelon.

"The powers that be are trying to kill it so fast because it's a legacy [outmoded system]," said one NSA official at the end of August 2001. "We probably won't even use it in two or three years. It's an outdated mode of Sigint. Just one percent of the world's communications travel by satellite now—and much of that is U.S. communications. The amount of intelligence gained from Echelon is still relatively high, because we've been so slow in going to those other modes of communications. There's talk about a 300-percent growth in fiber-optic communications, and the [digital] packet switching is now up through the roof." Instead of telecommunica-tions, many of the satellite companies were switching to serving the burgeoning growth in cable television channels.

Another NSA official agrees that Echelon has become largely obsolete but says it still provides useful, but limited, intelligence. "There are still things that you can pick up," the official said. "You can get some limited cell phone stuff where you have access to people using cell phones on the ground. You can get a little bit of cell phone stuff from space, but not as good as we'd like it. It's get-ting better, but it's hard. The bad guys are pretty disciplined about how they use it."

Even though the agency had developed a way to tap into fiber-optics, getting access to the cables buried in foreign countries was still a major problem. In 1990, the agency was so worried about the issue that it fought against export of the technology to Russia. The United States denied, for example, an export license to US West Inc. for a proposed trans-Siberian cable project. By 2000, NSA was facing a second, far more sophisticated generation of fiber-optic technology.

Also up was voice traffic, which had been increasing in volume at 20 percent a year. This was largely as a result of new digital cellular communications that were far more difficult for NSA to analyze than the old analog signals. Rather than consisting of voices, the digital signals were made up of data packets that may be broken up and sent a myriad of different ways. "Today you have no idea where that information is being routed," said one intelligence official. "You may have somebody talking on a telephone over a landline and the other person talking to them on a cell phone over a satellite. You don't know how it's being routed, it's going through all kinds of switches, the information is not where you think it is, and that's what has created the complexity and that's what we have to figure out how to deal with."

In the same way that NSA was facing enormous new difficulties switching from the Cold War to terrorism in its eavesdropping operations, it was having similar problems in code breaking.

"There was nothing more important than the Soviet cryptanalysis problem, and so we had literally thousands of people working on the problem," said one former senior NSA cryptanalyst whose career stretched into the late 1990s. "The successes were few and far between, and so the life of the cryptanalyst was not a lot of fun. You were working on data that was probably older than Korea sometimes. Many times if you made progress against it, it wasn't because you took on the mathematics. It was because of a

bust [a mistake on the part of the foreign cryptographer or an electrical or mechanical anomaly]. So cryptanalysts didn't really
develop very well in that environment because of their modest
expectations and virtually no success." Most of the progress, the
former official said, came from successful attacks on less difficult
Third World countries that were friendly to the Soviet Union.

During the Cold War, the cryptanalysts—code breakers—and
signals analysts were divided up among the three major area
groups: the Soviet Union and its satellite countries (A-5), China and
Communist Asia (B-6), and the rest of the world (G-4). Then, in
1992, in response to the end of the Cold War, they were all consolidated in a single new group: Z. "There were two issues," said the
official, "who was the enemy and what methodology do you use to
fight the new enemy?" The problem was that because so many
cryptanalysts knew only the old techniques and methods for attacking Russian codes and ciphers, they were applying the same methods to the new targets, such as China, and the countries suspected
of terrorism, such as Iran and Iraq. And they weren't working.
"The Soviet cryptanalysts wanted to take their methodology and
apply it to the PRC," the former official said. "It was an impossible
job. And that methodology was useless against terrorists."

In charge of all of NSA's eavesdropping and code breaking
was Maureen A. Baginski, the agency's director of Sigint, one of
the most powerful positions in the U.S. intelligence community.
Thin, petite, with thick dark eyebrows, wavy brown hair, and a gift
for speaking bureaucratese, she had a wood-paneled office that was
the NSA director's office during the first decade of the agency. It
was where the agency directed its worldwide electronic spies during the Cuban missile crisis of 1962—a time when Baginski was
still in high school. But by September of 2001, Baginski had been
with NSA for twenty-one years.

"The career path from college was studying to be a Russian

linguist, spending a year in the USSR—1976–1977—at a foreign-language institute—Moriz Torez, named after a good French Communist," she said. "My experience in the Soviet Union caused me to make a very deliberate decision to come and work in defense. I knew I wasn't willing to carry a weapon like my dad did, so I decided to look for a different kind of weapon and made a decision to come to NSA." After receiving a bachelor's degree in Russian and Spanish and a master's in Slavic languages from SUNY, Albany, she began her career at NSA teaching Russian and went on to become a signals operations officer, moving into NSA's epicenter, the National Security Operations Center (NSOC), which keeps watch over the agency's worldwide eavesdropping, code-breaking, and code-making operations. Eventually, she became the agency's top Russian expert and the senior official in charge of NSOC before General Hayden put her on the fast track to become the country's top international eavesdropper.

By 2001, Baginski was well aware that NSA had fallen dangerously behind and was now simply on a par with its enemies, including the terrorists.

"We were always out ahead in the technology arena," she said. "Over the past decade, we have lost that edge to industry. What has happened as a result is our adversaries and us have available the exact same technology, and it allows your adversary to have any kind of telecommunications technology anywhere in any mode all the time. Wireless, encryption, all of that has moved out of what was a sphere really for large government organizations into being readily available to anyone. So what you have is an adversary who because of the technology can operate at a speed of business that makes his decision cycle awfully short. And what we have to do is be able to operate at the same or faster speed and match his speed of business. So that's our challenge—it's to be able to operate in our adversary's information space, just the same way our adversary operates."

A major problem facing NSA is the needle-in-the-haystack conundrum. "Are we going deaf or are we drowning? The answer's yes," Baginski frankly admitted. "And it's not that we're not hearing or sensing things. It's that there's too much of it and it's too hard to understand, so the effect of the volume, velocity, and variety is deafening. There's so much out there."

With tens of millions of communications continuing to be vacuumed up by NSA every hour, by 2001 the system had become overwhelmed as a result of too few analysts. "U.S. intelligence operates what is probably the largest information-processing environment in the world," said former NSA Director William O. Studeman. "Consider this: Just one intelligence collection system alone can generate a million inputs per half hour." In other words, dozens of listening posts around the world each sweep in as many as two million phone calls, faxes, e-mail messages, and other types of electronic communications an hour. That enormous volume was one of the key issues that most worried former House Intelligence Committee Staff Director John Millis. "We don't come near to processing, analyzing, and disseminating the intelligence we collect right now," he warned. "We're totally out of balance."

According to General Hayden, the problem was in the numbers. "We are digging out of a deep hole," he said. To help correct the budget problems that caused so much grief for his predecessor, Hayden hired a chief financial manager, a first for NSA. Going outside the agency, Hayden chose Beverly Wright, a Harvard MBA with a background in investment banking. At the time of her selection, she was chief financial officer at Legg Mason Wood Walker in Baltimore, Maryland. Her job, according to Hayden, was to develop a management strategy for the agency and to "ensure that our mission drives our budget decisions" and not the other way around.

The hiring of Wright was no mere window dressing. When Hayden arrived at NSA, he found an ax waiting for him. Congress and the Clinton administration had directed that he slice away at the agency's personnel levels more than at any other time in history. In order to reduce the personnel rolls, NSA for the first time began turning over to outside contractors highly sensitive work previously performed exclusively by NSA employees, and scaled back its hiring to only about a hundred new employees a year. Ominously, a commission established to look into the intelligence community saw problems down the road in such a drastic cutback in hiring. "This is simply insufficient to maintain the health and continuity of the workforce," the report said. It went on to warn that if the pattern continued, NSA would face a future where large segments of its workforce will leave "at roughly the same time without a sufficient cadre of skilled personnel to carry on the work."

According to Hayden, "NSA downsized about one-third of its manpower and about the same proportion of its budget in the decade of the 1990s. That is the same decade when packetized communications (the e-communications we have all become familiar with) surpassed traditional communications. That is the same decade when mobile cell phones increased from 16 million to 741 million—an increase of nearly 50 times. That is the same decade when Internet users went from about 4 million to 361 million—an increase of over 90 times. Half as many landlines were laid in the last six years of the 1990s as in the whole previous history of the world. In that same decade of the 1990s, international telephone traffic went from 38 billion minutes to over 100 billion. [By 2002] the world's population will spend over 180 billion minutes on the phone in international calls alone."

Looking back, said Hayden, no one would have predicted such enormous growth. "Forty years ago, there were 5,000 standalone computers, no fax machines, and not one cellular phone. Today, there are over 180 million computers—most of them networked. There are roughly 14 million fax machines . . . and those numbers continue to grow. The telecommunications industry is making a $1 trillion investment to encircle the world in millions of miles of high-bandwidth fiber-optic cable. They are aggressively investing in the future."

Simply sending an internal e-mail, Hayden discovered, was a major problem. It takes "an act of God," he said, to send an e-mail message to all of the agency's 38,000 employees because of NSA's sixty-eight separate e-mail systems. Nor could the three computers on his desk communicate with one another.

Even if the system could eavesdrop on and process all the critical communications, most of it would go unread for days or weeks, if at all. This is a result of NSA's enormous lack of specialists in many key languages. By the summer of 2001, the number of NSA language specialists expert in the Afghan languages—Pashto and Dari—was almost nil. According to one senior intelligence official, they could be counted on one hand with fingers left over.

Aware of its myriad—and dangerous—shortcomings, the agency was attempting to self-diagnose its various disorders, some of which had become very obvious to Congressman Porter Goss, the chairman of the House Intelligence Committee. "What we said basically was we see a lot of management and very little leadership. And there is a major difference," said Tim Sample, Goss's staff director. "And we said that we saw a lot of people trying to do a lot of good work, but that Sigint in the future was in peril. And they were fairly harsh words, and they got a lot of people upset, though my sense is for those in the workforce there was a lot of head shaking up and down, going yeah, how do we fix this. And I will say this now, and I will say it again and again, the issue here was facing change."

Part of the problem, said Sample, was an attitude of self-reliance. "There was an attitude of 'we'll do it ourselves, thank you very much.' We understand that there are some changes, but we've been doing pretty well with what we've been doing, thank you. . . . There was an issue of financial accountability, and that was at best elusive. There was a sense of protecting fiefdoms. . . . From a management standpoint, we saw a major protection of bureaucracy. Many managers, especially at the more senior levels, didn't accept the writing on the wall. Not just the congressional writing on the wall, but the intelligence, the target writing on the wall. That somehow in our view, some of the management lost touch with the workforce."

Realizing that NSA's very existence depended on reform, Hayden issued an edict: "Our agency must undergo change if we are to remain viable in the future." Like someone who had just inherited an old car, Hayden decided to call in the repairmen to give him an estimate on what was wrong and suggestions on how to fix it. He put together two groups, one made up of middle-ranking insiders and the other composed of outside experts, to take a close look at what makes NSA tick, and directed them to write up report cards on what they found.

At the time, among the greatest obstacles to change were a number of hard-line traditionalists, among them the agency's deputy director, Barbara McNamara. They were constantly resisting the growing pressures to break away from NSA's insular, secrecy-obsessed culture and reach out to industry for help.

Yet members of the inside panel—whom Hayden referred to as "responsible anarchists"—had no hesitation in outlining a decade of mismanagement, bureaucratic squabbling, and poor leadership. Among the key findings was a need for "profound change [or] the nation will lose a powerful weapon in its arsenal." It pointed to the following specifics:

- NSA has failed to begin the organizational transformation necessary for success in the Information Age.

- NSA has been in a leadership crisis for the better part of a decade.

- Systems development is out of control.

- Duplicative efforts flourish because we have no single point of control for reviewing development across organizations.

- Critical data required by decision-makers . . . are often unavailable or difficult to retrieve.

- Decisions on financial resources, human resources, and customer engagement are often late or fatally flawed.

"In a broad sense," Hayden said, the panels painted a picture of "an agency that did not communicate with itself, or with others, well. Which—my view now, not theirs—is the by-product of a great deal of compartmentalization and insularity built up over almost half a century. A management culture that found it difficult to make the tough decisions, largely because the decisions were so tough." Also, he said, "They found that accountability was too diffused throughout the agency. I've used the phrase 'You damn near have to rent Camden Yards [home baseball field of the Baltimore Orioles] to get everybody that thinks he has a piece of the action in on a meeting.'"

On November 15, 1999, General Hayden instituted his "100 Days of Change." It was an ambitious plan to put many of the reforms into place in a little more than three months. At the same time, he sought to consolidate his power in order to blunt any opposition from the conservatives. "Even the best game plan," he warned, quoting legendary University of Alabama football coach Paul "Bear" Bryant, "ain't got no chance if the players don't execute it."

To deal with the growing language problems, Hayden turned to agency veteran Renee Meyer and appointed her the agency's first Senior Language Authority.

According to Meyer, even though nearly half the world (47 percent) speaks English, there is a growing tendency for people to return to local languages. "Cultural pride has reemerged," said Meyer. "People use their 'own' languages, and there are all kinds of speakers." The number of languages being used around the world, she said, is enormous—more than 6,500—many of which are growing. Also, it takes a tremendous amount of time to train language analysts in many of these "low-density" languages, such as those used in Afghanistan. Simply to reach the minimum professional capability—level 3—takes from three to eight years of study.

In the summer of 2001, the agency had at last completed a language database showing who in the agency spoke what languages and where in the world they were located. By the fall of that year, Meyer said, she hoped to complete Daily Language Readiness Indices—daily printouts of the constantly changing database that would be placed on the director's desk every morning. Thus, in the event of a crisis, the agency could identify and immediately locate everyone who spoke the critical languages of the area. When she was appointed to the new position, Director Hayden told her she had until October 15, 2001, to fix the system. A few months earlier, a congressional report issued a warning: "NSA is . . . not well-positioned to analyze developments among the assortment of terrorist groups."

For the residents of Bells Mill, a small neighborhood of drowsy homes in the well-heeled Maryland town of Potomac, the sight of the two black bulletproof SUVs, with Uzi-toting agents peering out the open rear windows, had become a daily routine. Early in the morning and early in the evening they would quietly arrive, one blocking traffic and the other pulling into the driveway of a tree-shrouded house in the middle of the block. Shortly after 7:00 A.M. on September 10, 2001, George John Tenet, the bulldog-chested CIA Director, stepped into the back seat. Waiting for him was the agency's presidential briefer along with a black, leather-bound folder with the presidential seal and gold letters—PRESI-DENT'S DAILY BRIEF.

Better known simply as the PDB, the document inside the folder summarizes the most important world events over the past twenty-four hours based on analysis of all U.S. intelligence capabilities, from spinning satellites to clandestine agents. It is perhaps the single most important report produced by the agency. "We truly are speaking truth to power," boasted the CIA's top analyst, Jami Miscik.

A right turn on Democracy Lane, a left on Democracy Boulevard, eighteen more miles, and the heavily armored Ford

Explorer would pull into the White House for the 8:00 A.M. briefing of President Bush. The twenty-five-minute ride would give Tenet a chance to make notes and read over the backup documents, such as communications intercepts and satellite photos, the aide had brought along. Prior to going to bed the night before, Tenet had already looked it over and made changes. Later, CIA analysts on the midnight shift updated the intelligence and printed up a final version.

During the previous administration, Tenet had a cool and distant relationship with President Clinton, who would occasionally keep his intelligence chiefs at arm's length. One former CIA director, R. James Woolsey, had only two semiprivate meetings with the President in two years and referred to his relationship with Clinton as "nonexistent." But although he had little use for the oral briefings, at least in the beginning of his presidency, he was an avid reader of the PDB, which normally ran around a dozen pages and often contained detailed analysis. Despite the secrecy and exclusivity of the PDB, Clinton would often complain that most days the document contained much that he had already read elsewhere. As a result, he allowed the PDB to be sent around to a wider circle of officials than previous presidents had permitted.

Bush, however, decided to limit the distribution of the PDB to only his top cabinet members and White House aides. At the same time, he reduced the size of the report to just seven to ten pages. With less analysis than before, most items were brief—less than a page in length. It was prepared, said one former senior intelligence official, with the understanding that Bush was a "multimodality learner who processes information better through questions and answers while reading along." In other words, he wasn't much of a reader.

Bush may have inherited a fondness for the PBD from his father. Charles A. Peters, who served for fourteen years as the CIA's

chief presidential briefer, said he briefed President Ronald
Reagan only three times during his eight years in the White
House. Vice President Bush, however, would get a briefing from
Peters every morning around eight in his office in the Old
Executive Office Building.

When he moved from the vice president's office into the
White House, Bush continued his morning briefings. "The
Presidential Daily Brief was the first order of business on my cal-
endar," he said. "I made it a point from day one to read the PDB
in the presence of a CIA officer and either [National Security
Advisor] Brent [Scowcroft] or his deputy." Peters said Bush was
very careful to keep the PDB free of political influence. Once, he
recalled, Bush became very angry when he learned that cabinet
members were trying to influence him by making suggestions on
what the CIA should put into the Daily Brief. John L. Helgerson,
the CIA's deputy director for intelligence while Bush was president, agreed. "He did not want us talking to anybody else," said
Helgerson, who was responsible for assembling and editing the
PDB. "It was his book, and he wanted to decide what went in it."

CIA Director Robert M. Gates would also brief the senior
Bush several times a week. "The relationship between the
President and the CIA Director, if close, can assist enormously in
the creation of foreign policy," he said. "But to be effective, the
Director has to be in the innermost circle. . . . The best part about
meeting face-to-face with the President was to get instantaneous
feedback on what his agenda was. He asked questions and we
would get answers to him, and thus had a direct dialogue with the
President that is most often missing in the normal daily mix of
things."

When George W. Bush was elected president, his father
unequivocally instructed his son to develop a close relationship
with his CIA chief. "The former president reinforced how impor-

tant it was that a president have face-to-face meetings with the CIA Director, rather than just receive his intelligence reports on paper," said White House Chief of Staff Andrew H. Card, Jr. "And so the President-elect told me, when I was the chief of staff-designate: 'Make sure that happens. I want to see the CIA Director and be able to talk with him.'"

Over the past eight months, Tenet and George W. Bush had "really hit it off," said one former senior agency official. Bush liked Tenet's streetwise, casual, and unpretentious style. It was get-to-the-point Texas-like, without a lot of jargon-cluttered bureau-cratese. "They're pragmatists, they talk sort of 'male talk,'" said Senator Bob Graham, who was chairman of the Senate Intelligence Committee. "George is a very smart person, but his rhetoric isn't theoretical. It's blunt. It's straightforward."

Arriving at the White House, an unlit cigar extending from the left corner of his mouth, the CIA Director power-strutted down the center of the short cement walkway toward the West Wing. George Tenet liked to keep to the center. It was the way he managed to survive as one of the longest-serving spy chiefs in the CIA's history, and the only Clinton holdover in Bush's inner circle. Through war and peace, Democratic and Republican administrations, quiet successes and noisy disasters, he defied the odds in a place lined with bureaucratic land mines and encircled by media snipers.

A Marine in dress uniform snapped to attention and in a single fluid motion pulled open the door to the West Wing Reception Room. It resembled an early-nineteenth-century drawing room, its many doors sparkled with ancient, highly polished brass handles, latches, and lockboxes. A multi-armed brass chandelier hung from the ceiling. And next to a two-hundred-year-old English library bookcase was Worthington Whittredge's stunning 1868 painting "Crossing of the River Platte." Looking around at the historic surrounding, waiting to give his daily Top Secret briefing to the President of the United States, George Tenet, a loudmouth kid from Queens, New York, who could never keep a secret, might have wondered how he got there.

Once described by a family friend as a child who was always talking and could never keep a secret, Tenet would later agree. "Nobody who knew me when I was younger believed that I would ever be the director of CIA," he said. "I had the biggest mouth in town. No one would ever believe I could keep a secret." But it was a trait he would teach himself. "I want to tell you that I have learned my lessons. I'm very discreet now; I don't say anything to anybody."

George Tenet's parents, both Greeks born in the Albanian-controlled province of New Epirus, settled into a two-story row house on Marathon Parkway in the Little Neck section of New York's Queens Borough. His father opened a Greek restaurant called the Twentieth Century Diner. Both Tenet and his twin brother, William, would later earn spending money there as busboys while attending P.S. 94, Junior High School 67, and Benjamin N. Cardozo High School. "Starting out with nothing, he made a success of the Twentieth Century Diner in Queens," recalled Tenet about his father. "He taught me to value hard work, to honor this great country, and to take nothing for granted, least of all family. He is gone now, but the strength of his influence on my life is undiminished."

In some respects, Tenet's upbringing was straight out of a Norman Rockwell painting. When not playing soccer or basketball in the church league, Tenet was an altar boy at St. Nicholas Greek Orthodox Church. It was a formative period in his life. "When I went to high school, I learned about discipline and hard work," he said. "I learned about being loyal to your family. I learned about taking care of people. I learned about standing up for what you believed in. I learned about never compromising what your core values are. And when you are sitting in a room with the President of the United States, and you have to gulp hard, because you have to tell him some very bad news, you have to have that inner being come from somewhere."

Tenet graduated from Cardozo High in 1971. He avoided Vietnam, apparently with a student deferment, and enrolled at Georgetown University's School of Foreign Service. With both Tenet and his brother—who would go on to become a cardiologist in Queens—attending college at the same time, tuition was a hardship for their parents. To help out, both brothers spent the summers serving moussaka and spanakopita at the Twentieth Century Diner and beer and pretzels at Patrick's Pub in Queens.

Then as today, Georgetown's School of Foreign Service was a prep school for both the State Department and the spy world. Currently, some four hundred graduates work at the CIA. Although his mother desperately wanted him to become a lawyer, Tenet decided instead to remain focused on world affairs and went to Columbia for a master's degree in international affairs. "I didn't go to law school and broke my mother's heart," he recalled.

He quickly got a job as Director of Research for the American Hellenic Institute, where he focused largely on Greek-Cypriot issues. "Read 'lobbying,'" Rick Horowitz said of the Greek-American public affairs group that would pepper members of Congress with requests for pro-Greek and anti-Turkish legislation. "I was a staffer myself," he recalled, "for a congressman who was a major player on some of those very same issues. We had meetings, George and I and our respective bosses did. We compared notes. We talked strategies."

From lobbying for Greek-Americans, Tenet moved on to pushing the worldwide virtues of photovoltaic cells as director of international programs at the Solar Energy Industries Association.

But it was world power, not sun power, that pulled at Tenet in the early 1980s. Seeking to get into the action, Tenet signed on as a staffer with John Heinz, the late Republican senator from Pennsylvania and wealthy heir to the "57 varieties" fortune. Viewed by many as a Republican John F. Kennedy, he was young, physically attractive, and a Renaissance man who had a taste for early American and European art. He was also a respected environmentalist who was interested in energy solutions. Tenet's background, which combined international affairs with three years in the energy field, appealed to Heinz, and he made him his national security and energy aide, and legislative director.

Three years later, in August 1985, Tenet transferred to the Senate Select Committee on Intelligence as designee to the vice chairman, Patrick Leahy, a liberal Democratic senator from Vermont. It was an exciting time to be on the inside; the "Year of the Spy" was unfolding and the East-West espionage wars were at their peak. Tenet's job was to direct the committee's oversight of all arms-control negotiations between the Soviet Union and the United States. Of particular concern was the ability of the various spy agencies to monitor the Intermediate Nuclear Force Treaty.

He worked in Room SH-219 in the Senate Hart Building— "the vault"—a windowless, steel-lined, heavily guarded warren of cubbyhole offices, with brown paper "burn-bags" next to each desk and paper shredders on thick file cabinets with large black combination dials. Known as a "SCIF" (pronounced "skiff" and standing for Secure Compartmented Information Facility), it also contained a hearing room with pink chairs arranged around a horseshoe-shaped table that was frequently scrubbed for bugs. The olive-green walls were decorated with the seals of the various spy agencies, and three secure video monitors faced the committee's seventeen senators seated around the table.

But Tenet's luckiest move came in 1987 when the Democrats

regained control of the Senate and David Boren, a senator from Oklahoma, was named chairman. Seeing Tenet as a moderate like himself, and with the personality of a football coach, he picked him ahead of more senior employees to be director of the committee's forty-member staff. It was a large step on a slippery ladder for a thirty-four-year-old with only five years of government service. But Boren liked Tenet's blunt, confident manner and became his "godfather," shepherding his career higher and higher up the ladder.

While working largely with the analysts and the technical spooks when assigned to arms control, Tenet now began focusing more heavily on human intelligence—"humint." Among his first assignments from Boren was to audit the shadowy, loosely controlled agent programs run by the CIA's Clandestine Service. By the time he was finished, he had forced the agency to pull the plug on two of its most secret covert operations. His staff discovered that CIA case officers worked against U.S. policy objectives in several foreign countries and may have allowed informants to steal funds. To correct the problem, Tenet helped strengthen the covert-action reporting requirements and facilitated the creation of a statutory inspector general at the CIA. He also drafted legislation to reorganize the entire U.S. intelligence community.

As chief of the intelligence committee staff during the end of the Cold War, Tenet was also in a very good position to see just how inadequate the CIA's human intelligence was—more Hollywood myth than reality. At the time, Milt Bearden, a highly regarded agency veteran who had previously served as chief in Pakistan during the Soviet war in Afghanistan, ran the agency's Soviet–East European Division. He and Tenet would occasionally get together in Bearden's second-floor office in the CIA's New Headquarters Building, the "NHB."

Recently completed, the NHB was designed to be state-of-the-art, with elaborate shielding to prevent electromagnetic eaves-dropping. In a massive atrium hung models of the agency's legendary spy planes, the U-2 and SR-71, and in a nearby courtyard was James Sanborn's sculpture "Kryptos," a maddeningly complex cipher built into an S-shaped copper screen near a bubbling pool of water. The new facility was connected to the Old Headquarters Building by a slightly curving tunnel called a "wave guide," which was designed to prevent electromagnetic emanations from passing from one building to the next. But despite the high-tech wizardry, Bearden's new office seemed patched together—with a wall not quite connecting with the door. "A pretty appropriate description of the agency," he joked.

Returning to headquarters after his extended assignment in Pakistan, Bearden was shocked to discover how bumbling and ineffective the agency's human intelligence efforts were against its longtime principal targets, the Soviet Union and its East European satellites. When a coup took place against Soviet Premier Mikhail Gorbachev in 1991, for example, the CIA station chief, David Rolph, didn't have a clue. "When David Rolph walked into the embassy Monday morning," said Bearden, "he did not realize that the coup had actually been under way since the day before, did not know that Mikhail Gorbachev and his family had been surrounded and cut off from all communications." Rolph actually learned of it from an embassy colleague who just happened to hear of it on the radio. "That's how the CIA's Moscow station chief found out about the coup that changed the twentieth century," said Bearden. "The CIA simply did not have any assets inside the Kremlin who were in a position to give the Americans detailed and timely information about when or where a coup might take place."

Although Bearden didn't know it at the time, the situation was even far worse. The few agents the CIA did manage to develop had years earlier been compromised, revealed to the Russians by agency turncoat Aldrich Ames. Thus, worse than no information, the Soviet agents may have unwittingly been passing on disinformation.

According to Bearden, the situation was no better in East Germany. "The CIA did not have any high-level agents in the East German government," he said in his book, *The Main Enemy*, coauthored with James Risen. "The CIA had no agents inside the internal security apparatus of the [East German] MfS, or in the HVA, the Hauptverwaltung Aufklarung, its foreign intelligence arm . . . the CIA had had no luck in recruiting even the dullest functionaries." The lack of human intelligence sources was driven home dramatically as the Berlin Wall collapsed in 1989. "The CIA had no human intelligence on the events as they were unfolding," said Bearden. "None of our human assets in the capitals of Eastern Europe and the Soviet Union were in a position to tell us what was going on; most were asking us what was happening."

With the end of the Cold War, CNN replaced the KGB as the agency's biggest competitor. "In truth," said Bearden, "the CIA didn't have spies with high-placed political access who could provide important political insights. How then should CIA officers try to satisfy policy makers hungry for a continuous flow of information? Tell them to turn on CNN and hope for the best? That was the awkward situation facing the CIA in East Berlin in November 1989. . . . It would be CNN rather than the CIA that would keep Washington informed of the fast-moving events in Berlin."

Before Boren left the committee chairmanship in 1993, he made sure to take care of his young charge. He first helped Tenet become the head of the intelligence team for President-elect Bill Clinton's transition, a position of high visibility. Then he pushed him for a key position in the Clinton White House as senior director for intelligence programs within the National Security Council. There he coordinated a number of Clinton's Presidential

Decision Directives—White House orders—dealing with issues ranging from intelligence priorities, to the effectiveness of U.S. counterintelligence activities, to policies on spy satellites.

By now Tenet's ladder was more closely resembling a swiftly moving escalator. In 1995, Boren helped him move into the number-two job at CIA, deputy director. Two years later, upon the resignation of agency director John Deutch, and the withdrawal of his designated successor, National Security Advisor Anthony Lake, Tenet reached the top. Clinton nominated him to become the next director.

Weary of their successful battle against Lake's nomination, which was largely a result of his liberal reputation, Republican senators were overjoyed with the possible choice of Tenet, whom most considered bipartisan and a centrist on most issues. At one point, during testimony in a closed hearing on the intelligence budget, a number of Republican senators began fawning over Tenet. Surprisingly to many, among those enthusiastically in Tenet's camp was Republican Senator Richard Shelby, the chairman of the intelligence committee. Hearing these stories, Clinton pushed up the timetable and that same March afternoon went on television and announced the nomination. Four months later, on July 11, 1997, Tenet was sworn in as the eighteenth director of Central Intelligence, at forty-four the second youngest in the agency's history.

"Washington is full of people who know how to scramble up the ladder of power. But George Tenet," wrote Eric Pooley of *Time*, "has set new records for both speed and elegance of ascent." Part of Tenet's success was due to his ability to keep a poker face when it came to partisan politics. Even today, Boren claims he does not know whether Tenet is a Democrat or a Republican. "I'm registered in one party," said Tenet, "but for the purposes of doing my job, no one should ever know because you have to serve everyone."

When Tenet moved from the deputy's office to the director's suite next door, he brought with him more than boxes of papers and desktop trinkets. He brought a new style. Where John Deutch had been the ultimate technocrat—distant, aloof, and somewhat scornful of the workforce—Tenet would become their coach and cheerleader rolled into one. Part of it, he said, came from his old days back at Cardozo High in Queens. "My high school soccer coach [Ed Tatarian] taught me more about how to run a big organization and take care of people, as I look back at it, than anybody ever taught me for the rest of my life."

Where Deutch was the geeky professor, absentmindedly walking home with top-secret disks in his pockets, Tenet became the tough but lovable mob boss—"Nobody bedda mess wit my crew." Although he had never been anything but a deskbound staffer, figuring budgets and collating data in windowless offices, his dark, ruddy complexion combined with his blunt Queens speech and father confessor demeanor allowed him to pull it off. Employees, fatigued from post–Cold War neglect, the Aldrich Ames spy scandal, and confusion at the top—five directors in six years—quickly took to Tenet, adopting him as one of their own. Behind his back, some even began calling him "Puff Daddy" because of the unlit cigar that became a trademark and the paternal feeling he exuded. "George is arguably the most popular CIA Director we've ever had," said former Deputy Director for Operations Jack Downing.

They also took to his casual, quirky style. "I'll come in and his door will be shut, and he'll be blasting opera music," said one employee, who noted that Andrea Bocelli, the blind tenor, was his latest favorite. "He'll be in sweatpants, unshaven—which is fine, you know, at seven A.M. So we'll start talking about what's in the papers, and what's in the President's Daily Brief. Then all of a sudden it's time for the eight o'clock meeting, when we go over the previous night's cable traffic. And he'll still be in sweats, unshaven—and that's fine. And then at eight-thirty there's a much bigger meeting of all the senior staff, and he's still in sweats. And you kinda begin to wonder . . . when's he gonna change?"

Also unlike some of his predecessors, Tenet had a well-developed sense of humor. "I know most of you probably thought Tom Cruise or Harrison Ford was going to show up," he once told a crowd at his old high school. "Instead, you got the short fat guy from Little Neck." One of his lifelong "tenets," he says, is "Laugh as much as you can. Never take yourself too seriously."

By the time Tenet arrived, the agency's Clandestine Service had reached a state of atrophy, largely as a result of post–Cold War budget cuts; the collapse of its longtime target, the Soviet Union; and a shift to massive technical collection by imagery and eavesdropping satellites. Throughout the 1990s, the CIA's overall personnel numbers were slashed by 23 percent and its slice of the budget pie became a narrow wedge. When handing out about $27 billion to the intelligence community as part of the 1999 federal budget, Congress gave the high-tech eavesdroppers at the National Security Agency a "huge increase," said one staffer, while leaving CIA's funding about level. A few weeks later, Congress awarded an additional $1.5 billion in emergency supplemental funds. The technical spies received what one observer called "a windfall"—nearly a billion dollars—while leaving less than 20 percent for human agents.

Not only had the Clandestine Service withered in size, for many years its performance had also been rapidly spiraling downward. Just as it had no useful spies in East Germany or Moscow during much of the Cold War, it also had no useful spies in Iraq prior to or during the first Gulf War, or in India at the time of its 1998 nuclear test. "I called Tenet," said Senator Richard C. Shelby, Chairman of the Senate Intelligence Committee, about the India test, "and he told me, 'We didn't have a clue.' I said, 'That's a strategic failure of intelligence,' and I got to thinking, 'I wonder what else they're missing big time.'" With regard to the 1998 bombing of the U.S. embassies in East Africa and the 2000 attack on the American destroyer *Cole*, Shelby added, "They didn't have a clue about these either."

Some began wondering if the agency ever had any serious spies anywhere. "The CIA is good at stealing a memo off a prime minister's desk," sneered former National Security Agency Director William Odom, a retired Army lieutenant general, "but they're not much good at anything else."

"We never recruited a spy who gave us unique political information from inside the Kremlin," admitted Robert Gates, the former Chief of Intelligence and later Director of CIA. Gates said that the first Gulf War might have proved a Waterloo of sorts for the Clandestine Service. "Perhaps the most compelling recent example of the gap between our technical and human capabilities was the Persian Gulf war," he said. "U.S. military commanders had superb imagery and signals intelligence, but we had only sketchy human intelligence on Iraq's intentions prior to invading Kuwait, Iraq's ability to withstand sanctions, and the status of Iraq's weapons program." Former Secretary of State James Baker was even more blunt. "U.S. intelligence assets on the ground were virtually nonexistent," he said.

Richard L. Russell, a seventeen-year veteran analyst at the CIA and now a member of the faculty of the National Defense University, agreed. "The greatest weakness of CIA's performance [during the first Gulf War]," he said, "was its lack of human assets inside the Iraqi regime able to report on Saddam's plans and intentions." Concluded Russell: "The poor human intelligence performance is not a lone incident in CIA's history. CIA has traditionally performed poorly in human operations against the United States's most ardent adversaries."

With regard to India, according to the report of the commission set up to examine the Indian intelligence failure, "The CIA had no spies worthy of the name in India." The report went on to say, "Its ability to pry information out of people is weak worldwide."

"The CIA's spy service has become an anachronism," argues Melvin A. Goodman, a twenty-four-year veteran Soviet analyst of both the CIA and the State Department. Now a professor at the National War College, he gave a number of examples of why the cloak-and-dagger spies have become endangered species. "CIA sources failed to decipher Leonid Brezhnev's intentions toward Czechoslovakia in 1968, Anwar Sadat's toward Israel in 1973, and Saddam Hussein's toward Kuwait in 1990. . . . It's time," he concluded, "to jettison the myth that only clandestine collection of information can ascertain the intentions of foreign leaders."

So far had the CIA's human capabilities dwindled by 1998 that it led House Intelligence Committee Chairman Porter J. Goss—himself a former CIA case officer—to declare, "It is fair to say that the cupboard is nearly bare in the area of human intelligence."

Nowhere was the decline of the Clandestine Service more visible than at Camp Peary, the CIA's 10,000-acre Special Training Center near Williamsburg, Virginia. Hidden under the cover name Armed Forces Experimental Training Activity, it was more commonly known by its nickname: The Farm.

Code-named ISOLATION, the base was originally built during World War II as a training facility for Navy Seabees. In 1951, the CIA acquired it, and since then it has been the agency's principal school for spies. At its height during the Cold War, the Spartan dormitories, worn classrooms, sweaty gym, and swimming pool were a beehive of activity as green recruits went through the Basic Operations Course. Veteran clandestine officers taught classes in field surveillance, infiltration and exfiltration, how to load and unload dead drops, and the best ways to make a "brush pass." Students on bicycles pedaled from the Magnolia Conference Center to the Laurel Classroom to the Team Development Areas, and on weekends the staff would hunt turkey and deer.

Advanced weapons and explosives training were held down the road at the agency's highly secret Harvey Point Defense Testing Activity. Located along Albemarle Sound near Hertford, North Carolina, the twelve-hundred-acre site was code-named ISOLATION-TROPIC and nicknamed "The Point." Like The Farm, it was completely hidden from view—tucked away on a small marshy peninsula of graying barns with faded tobacco advertisements, dirt roads, and endless expanses of snowy cotton and spindly stalks of corn. The CIA originally acquired the property in 1961 as a secret weapons-supply base for its failed Bay of Pigs operation in Cuba, and since then it has been used as the agency's bomb school. Veterans of The Point have taken part in every secret war from Congo to Iraq, and it is a key training base for the agency's paramilitary grenade-tossers assigned to the Special Activities Division.

Oddly, among the things they trained to do at Harvey Point was practice blowing up buses—Palestinian-terrorist style. "We made a school bus disappear with about twenty pounds of U.S. C-4," said former CIA officer Robert Baer. "For comparison's sake, we tried Czech Semtex and a few other foreign plastic explosives. Not that you really need anything fancy. We blew up one bus using three stacks of fertilizer and fuel oil, a mixture called ANFO [ammonium nitrate fuel oil] that did more damage than the C-4 had. The biggest piece left was a part of the chassis, which flew in an arc, hundreds of yards away. . . . We were also taught some of the really esoteric stuff like E-cell timers, improvising pressurized airplane bombs using a condom and aluminum foil, and smuggling a pistol on an airplane concealed in a mixture of epoxy and graphite. By the end of the training, we could have taught an advanced terrorism course."

Another CIA veteran of The Point during the 1970s was so repulsed by the terrorist bus-bomb training that he quit the agency. One of the exercises involved making a "mini-canon" from a #10 can packed with plastic explosives and then fastening it to the gasoline tank of the bus. "The incendiary projectile would rupture the tank and fling flaming gasoline the length of the bus interior," he said, "incinerating anyone inside. It was my lot to show the rest of the class how easily it could be done. It worked—my God, how it worked. I stood there watching the flames consume the bus. It was, I guess, the moment of truth. What did a busload of burning people have to do with freedom? What right did I have, in the name of democracy and the CIA, to decide that random victims should die? The intellectual game was over. I had to leave."

By the 1990s, Carolina's coastal breezes were carrying fewer and fewer muffled booms and bangs to the 2,000 townspeople of Hertford. And no longer did strangers turn up at the annual "Pig Out on the Green" celebration, where locals covered paper plates with steaming mounds of barbecue pork and runny coleslaw, and listened to southern rock in front of the Perquimans County Courthouse. And The Farm began to more closely resemble a dying religious retreat as the number of new operations officers sent there dropped to a dozen by mid-1995. By then, only eight hundred case officers were left in the field.

In 1994, following their bombing of the World Trade Center, Khalid Shaikh and Ramzi Yousef flew to the Philippines to aid a local terrorist organization, Abu Sayyaf. Organized by several dozen veterans from the Afghan war, the group was hoping to establish an independent Muslim nation in the southern part of the country. A Christian island in a Muslim sea, the Philippines is 95 percent Christian in a region where 25 percent of the world's Muslims live.

As part of their work for Abu Sayyaf, Yousef spent a short period of time in the Mindanao city of Basilan, where he trained around twenty members of the group in bomb-making. Khalid Shaikh and Yousef then moved to Manila, where they came up with a plan to assassinate the religious leader of the Christian world, the Pope, during a planned visit to the Philippines in January 1995. The assassination would also serve as a diversion for a much more ambitious terrorist operation, one that would be carried out at almost the same time against the United States.

Living in Manila, the two took full advantage of the lively nightlife in the neon-lit Malate nightclub district and the karaoke bars in Pasay City. "Hardly an Islamic fundamentalist," said BBC reporter Ben Anderson in Manila, "Khalid Shaikh Mohammed spent his time here dating local strippers. With over forty-three aliases between them, they went scuba diving at beach resorts and got drunk in strip clubs. One thing they didn't do was visit a mosque."

While Khalid Shaikh was entertaining the ladies in his white tuxedo at the Shangri-La Hotel in Makati, and advising Abu Sayyaf on guerrilla tactics, Yousef was building his bomb factory in Room 603 of the Dona Josefa Apartments. A neat but plain building with an open lobby, it catered mostly to short-term rentals by Middle Eastern tourists. From his top-floor window, Yousef had a view of the busy General Quirino Avenue that leads down to the shimmering waves of the South China Sea, and Manila Bay with its bobbing cargo ships waiting to unload.

A few blocks away was a nightspot, the Unplugged Acoustics bar, which had an eye-catching feature—an airplane mounted on the roof in such a way that it was made to look as if it had crashed. More important, the apartment was only a block away from the papal nunciature, which was to play host to Pope John Paul II during his visit, and plans were for the pontiff's motorcade to travel down General Quirino Avenue, right under their window.

In early January 1995, only a few weeks before the Pope was to arrive, Yousef's one-bedroom flat resembled a chemical lab in a B-grade Frankenstein flick. Sitting on unpacked crates of hot plates were odd-shaped vessels, open and sealed, bearing stamps from Pakistani and German chemical companies. Containing unpronounceable liquids—sodium trichlorate, nitrobenzoyl, methanamine—they gave off a variety of pungent odors and fumes. Also nearby were bundles of cotton and loops of red, yellow, green, and blue electrical wire. Several remote-control brass pipe bombs lay around like discarded toys.

Tucked into the corner of a bedside mirror, above a new crucifix, rosary, and a Bible, was a picture of the pope. Below was a box of Rough Rider lubricated condoms. There were beakers and thermometers, funnels and circuit breakers. Maps of Manila were scattered about, some with lines in red ink tracing the papal motorcade's route. A Pakistani passport, No. C665334, issued in Kuwait, sat on a table near a piece of paper with a phone message from a tailor: The priest's cassock that had been ordered was ready for a final fitting. In the kitchen were recipes from Hell: "Put 0.5 g of sodium hydroxide with 30 ml of warm water. Add to them 3 g of picric acid . . . very slowly add sulfuric acid to the liquid until its color is changed to orange, then to brown."

The passport belonged to Abdul Hakim Murad, a boyhood friend of Yousef's from Kuwait. Yousef had taught Murad the art of bomb-making in Lahore, Pakistan, and now his understudy was his terrorist helper in Manila. Only a small portion of the bomb-making ingredients, however, was intended for the pope. Just enough to outfit a suicide bomber dressed up as a priest, who would make his way to the vicinity of the pontiff and detonate the charge. But the papal assassination was intended as little more than an opening act, and diversionary tactic, for the main show, which was the reason for most of the explosives.

While Yousef was studying electrical engineering in Wales, Murad was in the United States attending flying schools in Texas, upstate New York, and North Carolina. On June 8, 1992, he received his commercial pilot's license from North Carolina's Coastal Aviation Inc. after completing 275 hours of flight time. Now he, Yousef, and Khalid Shaikh were planning a complex, highly coordinated series of bombings on nearly a dozen American airliners flying across the Pacific to U.S. airports. Its code name was Bojinka, "loud bang" in Serbo-Croatian. It was to take place about a week after the planned assassination of the pope during his visit to Manila from January 12 to 16, 1995.

On December 11, 1994, Yousef went to Ninoy Aquino International Airport near Manila to try out his newly developed air bomb. That evening, he boarded Philippine Airlines Flight 434 bound for Tokyo, with a stopover at the Philippine resort town of Cebu. A Boeing 747-200 jumbo jet, the plane carried 273 passengers and a crew of 20. To get past security, he had removed the liquid from a small bottle of contact lens solution and replaced it with cotton balls soaked in extremely explosive nitroglycerine. He had also modified the Casio digital watch he was wearing to work as a timing device. He did this by attaching electronic components to the alarm in the small space underneath the watch's calculator. All that was visible was a tiny plug. Tiny nine-volt batteries he had taken out of children's toys were hidden in the heels of his shoes.

After takeoff, Yousef went to the rest room and snapped a

small fusing system, made of lightbulb filaments and the two nine-volt batteries, into the plug on the back of his watch. Then he wrapped the watch around the device and set the timer for four hours. Returning to his seat, 26K—a window seat off the right wing near the center fuel tank—he hid the bomb in the life jacket pouch underneath his seat cushion. When the plane landed at Mactan-Cebu International Airport, Yousef was one of the forty-six passengers who deplaned.

A short while later, when the plane took off for Tokyo, Yousef was not aboard. Instead, seat 26K was now occupied by a Japanese industrial sewing machine maker, Haruki Ikegami, twenty-four, who was returning home from a business meeting in Cebu. At 11:43 P.M., about two hours into the flight, the alarm on the watch triggered the lightbulb filaments, which ignited the nitroglycer-ine-soaked cotton. The resulting blast nearly tore Haruki Ikegami in two, killing him instantly. At the time, the plane was over Minami Daito Island, 960 miles southwest of Tokyo. Ten others were wounded, and a hole ripped in the floorboard severed the aileron control cables that run the length of the aircraft and control the wing flaps. Despite severely crippled steering systems, the pilot was able to turn the plane around and land safely in Okinawa.

Although Flight 434 was not blown out of the sky, the bomb worked perfectly and encouraged Yousef and Murad, who began filling fourteen more contact lens solution bottles with nitroglyc-erine. The same technique would be used on the eleven American aircraft targeted over a two-day period, January 21–22. The bombers would come from the twenty or so people who made up Yousef's highly compartmentalized Manila cell.

But on January 7, 1995, as Yousef and Murad were cooking their deadly brew, a fire broke out in their apartment and Murad was captured and subjected to a lengthy, and torturous, interroga-tion. In addition to details on Bojinka, the techniques Murad described included an astonishing preview of what would take place in September 2001, just six years later.

According to a Filipino police report dating from 1995, "Murad's idea is that he will board any American commercial aircraft pretending to be an ordinary passenger, then he will hijack said aircraft, control its cockpit and dive it at the CIA headquarters. There will be no bomb or any explosive that he will use in its execution. It is a suicidal mission that he is very much willing to execute." Filipino authorities later told the Associated Press that they had shared the information immediately with FBI agents in Manila in 1995. "We shared that with the FBI," said Robert Delfin, Chief of Intelligence command for the Philippine National Police. "They may have mislooked [sic] and didn't appreciate the info coming from the Philippine police."

As with the World Trade Center bombing, Murad admitted that the airborne terrorism directed at America was a result of its support for Israel. "What do you mean by Liberation Army?" asked the interrogator. It was the same name Yousef had given the cell that had bombed the World Trade Center in New York one year earlier. Said Murad, "We shall liberate all the Muslims from the United States, from Israel." When asked whether he would die for his cause, Murad unhesitatingly said he would. "Yes," he said, "yes." He later added, "All my thinking was . . . that I should fight the Americans. I should do something to show them that we are . . . we could stay in their face."

Investigators in the Philippines also recovered Yousef's laptop computer and were able to read many of his messages. Among them was one outlining the purpose of the terrorism:

> If the U.S. government keeps supporting Israel . . . then
> we will continue to carry out operations inside and out-
> side the United States. . . . All people who support the

U.S. government are our targets in our future plans, and that is because all those people are responsible for their government's actions and they support the U.S. foreign policy and are satisfied with it.

Thus, by early 1995, terrorists had attempted to bring down the World Trade Center, were planning to blow up airliners, and were exploring the possibility of turning passenger planes into weapons of mass destruction and crashing them into American buildings. It was clear that the United States had become a target and would be at great risk in the future. It was equally clear that the reason for the attacks was the country's support for Israel and its occupation and treatment of the Palestinians.

In the late 1970s, Osama bin Laden had been a student and disciple of Abdullah Azzam, a Palestinian who, along with his family, had been forced out of his country by Israel in 1967, and who went on to become a professor at King Abdul Aziz University in Jedda, Saudi Arabia. Azzam not only taught Islamic law but also preached Islamic jihad against Israel for its actions against the Palestinians, a topic that resonated with bin Laden. When Azzam went to Peshawar, Pakistan, to help in the Afghan war against the Russians, bin Laden followed. "When the invasion of Afghanistan started," said bin Laden, "I was enraged and went there at once—I arrived within days, before the end of 1979."

Returning to Jedda, Saudi Arabia, to complete his studies, bin Laden spent a great deal of time raising money and recruiting volunteers for Azzam's Office of Services, which was on a worldwide mujahideen recruitment drive. In 1982, a year after his graduation, he decided to commit himself full-time to the struggle and arranged to ship into Afghanistan scores of construction vehicles from Saudi Arabia. "We transported heavy equipment from [Saudi

Arabia], estimated at hundreds of tons altogether, that included bulldozers, loaders, dump trucks, and equipment for digging trenches. When we saw the brutality of the Russians bombing mujahideen positions . . . we dug a good number of huge tunnels and built in them some storage places, and in some others we built a hospital. We also dug some roads." On rare occasions bin Laden would visit the front lines, but his prime contribution was organizing Saudi volunteers.

In 1984, working with Azzam, he established a sort of indoctrination center to help prepare mujahideen on their way to battle and to direct them to the various units at the front. To house the facility, which they called Beit-al-Ansar, "the House of the Faithful," they rented a house outside Peshawar in University Town. Located amid sweet-smelling bougainvillea on a quiet backstreet known as Syed Jalaluddin Afghani Road, it became a crossroads for Arabs throughout the region looking for adventure and jihad. Once checked in, they would join bin Laden in simple meals and sleep on thin wooden pallets stretched across the floor.

By 1986, bin Laden was itching to get more heavily involved in the actual fighting, and he began building his own guerrilla-training facilities inside Afghanistan, eventually establishing six camps. The graduates—Arab mujahideen, some with Syrian and Egyptian military experience—then became part of bin Laden's private military unit and launched their own battles against the Russians. As Arabs around the Middle East heard of his Beit-al-Ansar house and camps, more began joining him in the fight. In an effort to keep track of the mujahideen as they transited from Beit-al-Ansar to camp, to the front, then back to Beit-al-Ansar, bin Laden set up a tracking system he called "The Base"—"Al Qaeda" in Arabic—a term that later came to connote his terrorist enterprise.

In 1989, as the Afghan war was winding down, Azzam was killed in Peshawar by a car bomb and bin Laden moved back to

Saudi Arabia. Soon Saddam Hussein began making his move against Kuwait and bin Laden asked Saudi King Fahad to support him in his effort to resurrect his mujahideen army to fight Iraq's forces. When he was turned down and the Americans were allowed to set up bases in Saudi Arabia instead, bin Laden was outraged. Like his mentor Azzam, he had a burning desire to see not only Palestine, but all Muslim lands, freed of Western occupation. As his relations with the royal family quickly deteriorated, his house was searched and he was forbidden to leave the country. But he eventually managed to escape to Pakistan and then Afghanistan, where he again joined up with many of his former mujahideen.

With the war over, the various Afghan parties began to squabble and factionalism broke out, leaving bin Laden frustrated. In late 1991, only months after arriving, he decided to leave. Now running out of places to go, he rented a private jet, loaded up a number of his close associates, and flew to Sudan, where he was welcomed as a special guest and spent most of his time assisting the government in road construction. The pressure from the Saudi government continued, however; his assets were frozen, and in 1994 they withdrew his citizenship, an act made all the more bitter because they widely publicized the action. Pressure also came from the American government to expel bin Laden, and in the spring of 1996 he again began making preparations to return to Afghanistan.

About the same time, beginning on April 11, 1996, a series of shock waves rumbled through the Muslim world as a result of Israel's massive bombardment of Beirut and southern Lebanon, which Israel had by then been occupying for fourteen years. Known as "Operation Grapes of Wrath," it was the first time Israel had attacked Beirut since Ariel Sharon's ill-fated 1982 invasion of Lebanon. According to Israeli writer Israel Shahak, the real purpose of the attack was to capture as much Lebanese territory as possible.

"It is quite obvious," wrote Shahak, "that the first and most important Israeli aim to be established in the 'Grapes of Wrath' is to establish its sovereignty over Lebanon—to be exercised in a comparable manner to its control over the Gaza Strip."

Two days after it began, on April 13, ambulance driver Abbas Jiha from the village of Mansouri was busy rushing patients wounded in the fighting to a hospital in the town of Sidon. On his return to Mansouri, panic had broken out and explosions were taking place. People began pleading for him to take them to Sidon. Jiha quickly squeezed four of his children into his ambulance along with ten other people, including a family, and began driving toward Sidon.

Suddenly, an Israeli helicopter began chasing his ambulance. Minutes later, two missiles were fired, one of which exploded through the rear door, engulfing the vehicle in fire and smoke and hurling it sixty feet through the air. Thrown clear, Abbas Jiha began running toward the flaming heap of twisted metal. "My God, my God," he screamed, shaking his fist at the sky, "my family has gone." In all, six people were killed, including Jiha's nine-year-old daughter and his wife.

Israeli officials later admitted the ambulance had been targeted but claimed, falsely, that the vehicle was owned by Hezbollah and was transporting one of the group's fighters. Jiha had no connection with terrorist groups, and the thought that Israel could target an ambulance packed with innocent people, including many children, outraged Muslims throughout the Middle East.

On April 18, one week into Operation Grapes of Wrath, a reporter for London's newspaper *The Independent* was traveling in southern Lebanon with a United Nations convoy. Robert Fisk, Britain's most highly decorated foreign correspondent, spent a quarter of a century covering the Middle East and was the recipient of the British International Journalist of the Year Award seven times, including for 1996. As the vehicles were approaching the small village of Qana, Fisk could hear the sound of artillery, he recalled.

The convoy had stopped at Qana that morning and noticed it was crowded with about eight hundred refugees. They had been transported there for their safety by armored UN vehicles from nearby villages that had come under Israeli bombardment. When the convoy finally arrived in Qana shortly after two in the afternoon, fire was everywhere and proximity shells were bursting in the air. Antipersonnel weapons designed to explode about two dozen feet above ground, they would shower down razor-sharp shrapnel, butchering anyone beneath.

"It was a massacre," wrote Fisk in a front-page story. "Israel's slaughter of civilians in this terrible 10-day offensive—206 by last night—has been so cavalier, so ferocious, that not a Lebanese will forgive this massacre. There had been the ambulance attacked on Saturday, the sisters killed in Yohmor the day before, the 2-year-old girl decapitated by an Israeli missile four days ago. And earlier yesterday, the Israelis had slaughtered a family of 12—the youngest was a four-day-old baby—when Israeli helicopter pilots fired missiles into their home."

The Israeli government later claimed the attack on the UN refugee camp at Qana was a mistake. But a formal, top-level United Nations investigation came to a different conclusion. "It is unlikely" that Israeli gunners simply erred, said the report, and demanded that Israel pay $1.7 million in damages. "Contrary to repeated denials," said the report, "two Israeli helicopters and a remotely piloted vehicle were present in the Qana area at the time of the shelling." Amnesty International also conducted an investigation of the massacre, and they concluded "that the IDF [Israeli Defense Force] intentionally attacked the UN compound."

Arieh Shavit, a columnist for the Israeli daily newspaper *Ha'aretz*, noted: "How easily we killed them [in Qana] without shedding a tear. We did not denounce the crime, did not arrange for a legal clarification, because this time we tried to deny the abominable horror and move on." And the international edition of *Time* magazine noted, "Around the Middle East . . . Qana is already a byword for martyrdom. The southern Lebanese village figures as a shrine drawing up to 1,000 pilgrims a day: busloads of schoolchildren, Cabinet ministers from Beirut, even a daughter of Iran's President Ali Akbar Hashemi Rafsanjani. Black banners overlooking rows of graves decry the 'barbarity' of Israel."

While largely ignored by the American press, the massacre at Qana was front-page news in London, much of Europe, and throughout the Middle East, where the story continued for days. Already burning with hatred for America and Israel, the pictures of headless Arab babies and other grisly photographs that appeared throughout the media were likely the final shove, pushing bin Laden over the edge and leading him to dedicating his life to war against what he would call the Israeli–United States alliance. From then on, he would often use the massacre at Qana as a battle cry, and it would become the match lighting the fuse that would eventually lead to the World Trade Center on a Tuesday morning five years later.

CHAPTER 7

THE FARM

Determined to reverse the CIA's decline, George Tenet sent a warning to all employees soon after taking over. Later he would call it the most important thing he would ever say to his workforce. Without radical change, he cautioned, "we will no longer be relevant ten years from now." Tenet then telegraphed an unmistakable signal. He ordered workers to place a painting of Richard Helms, the controversial former director who had a particular fondness for covert operations, over his private dining area. At his morning meeting with senior agency executives, Tenet would regularly open with the simple question "Who did we recruit last night, and what difference will it make?"

To rebuild the Directorate of Operations and its Clandestine Service, Tenet reached back in time, persuading a retired DO chief to reclaim his seventh-floor office. A fifty-seven-year-old former Marine infantry officer who served two tours in Vietnam, Jack G. Downing was the poster-boy spy. Educated at Harvard, he spoke fluent Russian and Chinese and had the unique distinction of being the only person to serve as CIA station chief in both Beijing and Moscow. He was "a world-renowned operator," Tenet said, "who reads Chinese poetry for kicks."

"There was a reluctance to take risks," Downing said of the

agency when he returned. He decided to change that attitude—and to begin at The Farm. Starting immediately, each recruit would be required to bail out of a plane, commando-style, at 1,200 feet. "Ordinary people are not inclined to jump out of an airplane," Downing said, "and we are not looking for ordinary people." Soon, the muffled booms returned to The Farm and Harvey Point as the number of clandestine officers—and bomb-training exercises—began increasing.

By 1999, the number of recruits, mostly between the ages of twenty-seven and thirty-two, had jumped to 120 and was expected to rise to 180. At an average cost of $450,000 to train a case officer, rebuilding the Clandestine Service involved a significant investment. But Tenet believed it was worth every penny. "At the end of the day," he said, taking a swipe at NSA and the other technical spy agencies, "the men and women of U.S. intelligence—not satellites or sensors or high-speed computers—are our most precious asset."

Downing also began placing a major focus on the marriage between humans and machines to revolutionize intelligence collection and created a new unit to exploit it called the Technology Management Group. Picked as its first chief was Hugh Turner, fifty-four, a veteran case officer who was fluent in both Arabic and Turkish and won the Silver Star with the Green Berets during the Vietnam War. Turner's most important asset was the ultrasecret Special Collection Service, a unique hybrid of technical eavesdropping specialists from the National Security Agency and clandestine operators from the CIA. The joint organization was designed to penetrate foreign targets, from embassies to terrorist meeting sites, with sophisticated listening devices. It was a job made all the more difficult as communications became ever more complex with the growing use of encryption, fiber-optics, and the Internet.

"Yesterday's code clerk is today's systems administrator," said one very senior CIA official. The easiest way to a large amount of secrets is to get into foreign databases, and the best way to do that is to recruit—through bribes or other offers—the people who manage the systems. Also, by bribing someone to plant bugs in the keyboards or other vulnerable parts of a computer network, NSA could intercept the messages before the cryptographic software has a chance to jumble the text.

The chief of the SCS alternates between NSA and CIA officials. SCS is headquartered in a heavily protected compound of modern buildings on Springfield Road in Beltsville, Maryland, a few miles south of NSA. There, in what is known as "the Live Room," the electronic environment of target cities is re-created in order to test which antennas and receivers would be best for covert interception. Elsewhere, bugs, receivers, and antennas are fabricated into everyday objects so they can be smuggled into foreign countries. "Sometimes that's a very small antenna and you try to sneak it in," said former CIA Director Stansfield Turner. "Sometimes the signal you're intercepting is very small, narrow, limited range, and getting your antenna there is going to be very difficult."

While in some places NSA or SCS has compromised a nation's entire communications system by bribing an engineer or telecommunications official, in others much of the necessary eavesdropping can be done from special rooms in U.S. embassies. But in difficult countries, clandestine SCS agents must sometimes fly in disguised as businessmen and covertly implant the necessary eavesdropping equipment. He or she might bring into the target country a parabolic antenna disguised as an umbrella. A receiver and satellite transmitter may be made to appear as a simple radio and laptop computer. The SCS official would then camouflage and plant the equipment in a remote site somewhere along the microwave's narrow beam—maybe in a tree in a wooded area or in the attic of a rented farmhouse. The signals then captured by the equipment would be remotely retransmitted to a geostationary satellite, which would then relay them to NSA. At other times, no other solution is possible except climbing a telephone pole and hardwiring an eavesdropping device.

The SCS will also play a key role in what is probably the most profound change in the history of signals intelligence—the eventual switch from focusing on information "in motion" such as communications signals, to information "at rest," such as computer databases. Since the first transatlantic intercept station was erected on Gillin farm in Houlton, Maine, just before the close of World War I, signals intelligence has concentrated on intercepting signals as they travel through the air or space. But as technology makes that increasingly difficult and cost-prohibitive, the tendency, say senior intelligence officials, will be to turn instead to information "at rest"—the vast quantity of information stored on computer databases, disks, and hard drives. This may be done either remotely through cyberspace or physically by the SCS.

In a large sense, the changing philosophy represents the American spy world turned full circle, back to where the best way to get secrets is to steal them from where they are stored. Only this time, it may be a single hard drive containing critical information.

In 1999, Downing retired for the second time and Tenet picked the departing official's deputy, James L. Pavitt, to replace him. Like Tenet, Pavitt was an enthusiastic booster of the Clandestine Service who would speak proudly of "his" spies. "My spies save the world a little bit every day," he said. "What in fact they do, day in and day out, is recruit spies and steal secrets. They steal secrets to help protect our country . . . I have thousands of people who work for me around the world."

Ramrod straight with a shock of snow-white hair, Pavitt first began practicing his tradecraft in 1964 as a freshman at the

University of Missouri. "I'll probably get indicted for this," he said, "but I was able to take a Missouri driver's license and change that middle number that allowed me to get into wherever it was to get a six-pack of beer. I was so proud of myself, but little did I know that what I was doing then was what I was going to be doing for the rest of my career . . . It's a long way from Wallen's Springs, where I used to go and drink beer as a freshman."

Eventually majoring in history, Pavitt's hero during his senior year was Robert F. Kennedy, who was then running for the White House on a promise to pull America out of its deadly quagmire in Vietnam. "I was an idealistic young man given over to the hope that I would not die in Vietnam," he said, "convinced that perhaps what we were doing in Vietnam was not right."

On June 8, 1968, he received his diploma in the university's packed and screaming stadium. "I remember the excitement," he said. "I remember going home and then getting a phone call in the middle of the night. And it was a call from a friend who said that I have some terribly bad news to tell you, it was not that a member of my family had been killed but rather that someone who was my idol had been shot dead in a hotel lobby in Los Angeles, and that was Senator Robert Kennedy. And I remember to this day that on the day I graduated, the man who was for me at that time a hero, someone who represented something that was good not bad, peaceful not war, had been shot down."

A Phi Beta Kappa key holder, Pavitt had planned to be a history professor, but a year into his Ph.D. program he was drafted into the army, trained in the blacker arts of intelligence collection, and then posted to Berlin during the height of the Cold War. "I had been trained to do all sorts of things, and had I in fact gone to Vietnam instead of Berlin," said Pavitt, who speaks German, "I'm sure I never would have returned." Following the army, he continued to hone his skills at deception, but instead as a speechwriter on

Capitol Hill. "I wrote a speech for the congressman [Harold Donahue of Worcester, Massachusetts] once on health care financing, and if you read it you did not have a clue whether the Congressman was for or against it. And it was with that I decided to do something else, and I joined the CIA."

Since that day in 1973, Pavitt had been carefully climbing the agency ladder with clandestine assignments in Austria, Germany, Malaysia, and Luxembourg before eventually being named, in 1992, to the National Security Council as the top intelligence officer during the first Bush administration. A year later, with the election of Bill Clinton, George Tenet would take his place.

In 1995, as Tenet became the agency's deputy director, Pavitt took charge of a new counterproliferation division within the DO. Its job, in addition to secretly tracking the transfer of weapons of mass destruction, was to actively halt or disrupt the deadly shipments of the same. According to one former CIA official, this involved such risky missions as arranging the hijacking of ships transporting the materials to and from North Korea as they passed through the pirate-filled waters of the Straits of Malacca. Finally, in August 1999, Tenet named Pavitt to be the Deputy Director of Operations and head of the Clandestine Service—the country's master spy. "I run America's espionage service," Pavitt would later proudly boast. "I run the spy service of America."

But when Pavitt walked into the sixth-floor conference room for the first of his weekly DO meetings, the Clandestine Service was still struggling to recover from nearly a decade of neglect. Sitting at the head of the long conference table, Pavitt was surrounded by the ghosts of America's secret past. Along the gray, sound-absorbing walls were the photographs of the men who, as deputy directors of operations, had directed America's Clandestine Service for nearly half a century: from the black-and-white snapshots of Allen Dulles, pipe in hand, rimless glasses, an expression both knowing and inquisitive, to the sober, official color photo of his most recent predecessor, Jack Downing, square-jawed and silver-haired in front of the Stars and Stripes.

As he sat, waiting for his new staff to arrive, Pavitt may have wondered how his picture might be viewed years from now. Would he be among the legendary or the forgotten? The famous or the infamous? For all his successes, Dulles was ultimately fired by President Kennedy for his role in the Bay of Pigs disaster. Frank Wisner, Dulles's successor, committed suicide. Richard Helms, who left the agency as Pavitt was just arriving, would receive a suspended prison sentence for withholding from Congress information on the CIA's covert operations in Chile. And Clair George would be indicted for his role in the Iran-contra scandal.

Soon Pavitt's division chiefs—Europe, Africa, East Asia, the Near East—began filing in. Long known as the "barons," they would take their specific seats around the table according to strict tradition and territoriality. His chief of counterintelligence would sit at the opposite end of the table, and the heads of the lesser staffs would occupy stiff chairs along the wall. By then Pavitt's secret kingdom had shrunk to about 5,000 people, with less than a thousand actual case officers engaged in overseas missions. And the DO was running no more than ten to fifteen operations at any time around the world.

Nearly three years later, in April 2001, Pavitt sat in his seventh-floor office overlooking an endless expanse of leafy green treetops, reflecting about the past and worrying about the future. Arty prints covered the walls: a Toulouse-Lautrec, a poster from a turn-of-the-century international hygiene conference with a giant eyeball staring down from the center, an antique map of Russia. On his desk—a thick sheet of glass supported by silver steel legs—was a silver cup with an assortment of Mont Blanc pens as thick as Cuban cigars. And on the wall behind him was a clock with the ominous words "Last Flight Out."

"Our resources were perilously depleted earlier in this decade," he said, "when people, and some in the intelligence business, thought that the end of the Cold War meant the end to danger and uncertainty in this world." With a flash of anger, Pavitt growled. "For too long we accepted the perspective that, well, we could always do more with less. What unadulterated horseshit— do more with less. And you had crazies around this [intelligence] community say if you can't do more with less, you can do better with less. We drew a line in the sand and said that is wrong . . . It doesn't cost a lot of money to run America's spy service if you look at what it costs to spot, assess, develop, and recruit spies to steal secrets."

In fact, said Pavitt, his life had become much more complicated over the past decade. "We worry about all sorts of places. Who are getting delivery systems, nuclear, biological, or chemical capabilities, or trying to," he said. "Terrorism has become a much, much, much larger problem. Organized crime, narcotics—all issues we have to worry about—have grown significantly since the end of the Cold War. The only thing that hasn't grown significantly are the resources I have to work with."

Continuing Downing's efforts to rebuild the Clandestine Service, and reinvigorating the agency's presence overseas, Pavitt began the largest recruitment drive for new case officers in its history. From 1998 to 1999, the number of job offers jumped 52 percent and, with additional money from Congress, five hundred new case officers were hired. He also continued to revitalize The Farm, which once doubled as the private hunting preserve for senior officials on weekend getaways. "The quail shooting has been banned," said Pavitt. "I've got people, extraordinary young men and women with extraordinary backgrounds, signing up to be intelligence officers. They've got good foreign-language skills, average age is about thirty, they've got good overseas experience, advanced degrees. I pay them $45,000, I challenge them, I push them, I make them jump out of an airplane five times just to make them do something they think they can't do. And then I send them off to places around the world where life is dangerous."

"Needless to say," said Pavitt in the spring of 2001, "at the start of the twenty-first century my operational agenda is running higher than ever, higher than anyone expected in the aftermath of the Cold War. Somalia, Haiti, Bosnia, Rwanda, Burundi, Iraq, Kosovo, East Timor, I could go on and on and on and on."

But while the Clandestine Service focused on building up its numbers, there was little attention paid to changing the downward spiral of its performance. Even though hundreds of new recruits were being pumped through The Farm on their eighteen-month training cycle, the instruction by September 2001 was still basically the same as it was during the middle of the Cold War. Rather than focus on penetrating terrorist organizations, the emphasis remained directed toward recruiting foreign-embassy officials at cocktail parties. According to a Clandestine Service officer who went through The Farm shortly before 2001, little that was taught at The Farm was relevant to the targets the United States was facing in the post–Cold War world. And many of the instructors were retired with only Cold War experience. One course involved ways to recruit an agent, according to an interview with a case officer who went through the program in the late 1990s:

They have the three sets: a bump, where you try to meet someone you don't know, you haven't been introduced to yet. And then there's the embassy meetings; and then there's meeting someone through someone else. And there is always a set way that that's done. But it was usually in the traditionally way—it was nothing creative, nothing to really meet the demands of today's intelligence.

I was supposed to meet someone at a bagel store. I was given his description, but I'd never met him before. My job was bump into him as if it was a natural incident. Start up a conversation, and then from then on your goal was to get another meeting. Usually it's places in Williamsburg [Virginia]. It went okay. Again, the goal was to stay under the radar. So if we didn't do anything that annoyed one particular person, they [the instructors] wouldn't make your life miserable.

They gave you some ideas and then there was some room for your own creativity. But after a while you pick up on patterns, you know what certain instructors like, and you knew what worked, and you just learn that thinking so much outside the box isn't rewarded. I think they're still struggling to find their identity, because after the Cold War, their strategy changed, the roles changed, and they still can't identify what their role is.

The one thing they really did not like was when I asked why certain things happened. They just couldn't answer it. Everything was, "What are you going to do, it's the way it has been done." And I just said, "Why does it have to be done that way?" They engineered something really bad. "Well, why is it done that way?" It's not a culture that promotes innovation.

According to the DO officer, there was virtually no focus on infiltration of Middle Eastern terrorist organizations, or even on recruiting potential terrorist sources:

It was still very traditional. Even after the African Embassy bombings, the only new thing they incorporated was maybe a direct threat to the embassy, or to American personnel and how to handle that administratively. But even those exercises depended on a walk-in. And how often do you get that lucky?

It wasn't: Here's this group, let's try to design some operation to penetrate that group. It was never like that. Everything was always passive. Or a lot of the exercises were designed so that the person you met had a cousin who knew someone who is a member of a group that is very anti-American. It was almost handed to you. And then of course you have a natural broker to introduce you to the person you want to meet in this anti-American group. It wasn't that imaginative—everything was very prescribed.

I think a lot of it is risk: What if that person died, and then who's going to have to assume responsibility for that? I found them very risk-averse. And the one thing I learned throughout the whole place was you advance by staying under the radar, by not taking a political stance. And just making friends with the right people. And that's how you advance. You don't voice unpopular opinions.

Many in this officer's class were in their late twenties and early thirties. "They attempted to recruit older people with more life experience, and they realized that it backfired because we weren't as controllable," the person said. "So in successive classes we found that the age had dropped, the requirements had dropped for language. I was just surprised, because some of them were just out of college with no work experience. We kept noticing that the newer people, they were much younger and usually they tend to come straight from college. And then we sort of realized that the pendulum had swung in the other direction."

The vast majority of DO officers fresh from The Farm were still being sent under light diplomatic cover to comfy embassy jobs around the world, from Rio to Rome, posing as State Department employees. There they would attempt to recruit other diplomats, government officials, or potential sources at cocktail parties and other functions. It was the way it had always been done—tradition. Like the rigid order in which the division chiefs sat around the DO conference table, and even parked their cars according to the prescribed pecking order.

The agency case officers, however, were unlikely to bump into an Al Qaeda source in a bagel shop in Virginia, or a coffee shop along Vienna's Ring Road. And the threats were not coming from Rio or Rome, or even from Moscow. They were clearly coming from terrorist organizations within the Middle East—violent groups that over the decade had left a long trail of death and destruction, from the first World Trade Center bombing to the attack on the American embassies in East Africa to the assault on the USS *Cole*.

Yet little thought seems to have been given to attempting to penetrate Al Qaeda with agency employees—cleared American citizens with Middle Eastern appearances, knowledge, and language abilities specifically recruited and trained to bore into the organization. Not only was Al Qaeda never penetrated by CIA officers, it appears that the agency never once even tried to infiltrate the group. The philosophy was, and still is, that groups like Al Qaeda are too tough—or too dangerous—to penetrate using agency personnel, so why even try. "You've got the close family, tribal ties," said a senior CIA official in a December 2003 interview. "It's a whole different ball game as far as penetrating Al Qaeda."

In an agency that constantly boasted of risk-taking and derring-do, there seemed to be little of it. In reality, working for CIA was a very safe occupation. On average, the CIA loses slightly over one person a year in the line of duty—seventy-nine since the agency was formed in 1947. By comparison, forty-one New Jersey law-enforcement officers died in the line of duty in 2001 alone.

Another reason for the agency's failure to use its own people to try to penetrate the terrorist organizations may have been a reluctance to dirty its own hands. Throughout his career, J. Edgar Hoover refused to allow FBI agents to work undercover, feeling they were above such things. Only after he died did the bureau begin using agents to penetrate and infiltrate groups such as the Mafia, and the results were often spectacular.

One official who spent much of the 1990s in the Clandestine Service and still works for the agency said the CIA is so tied to American embassies around the world, it was almost as if they were connected by umbilical cords. That Clandestine Service officers would be sent to live in caves or infiltrate Al Qaeda was out of the question. "You're asking them to leave the mother ship, and the mother ship is the embassy, and the embassy provides all the nurturing we would ever need," the person said in a late 2003 interview. "We get a commissary and we get cable television and we get rent-free housing and all the utilities paid for, and we get cars to drive around in, and we get to go on the cocktail circuit and be witty and charming and everybody loves us. Don't ask us to leave the mother ship—that is the issue. We're just tied to this embassy structure—this cocktail-circuit structure with an umbilical cord. Since the Cold War we really didn't know what we were doing, but we continued to trudge along, saying Russia's still the target and everything else is not important."

Another former agency officer who worked in the DO during the 1990s and into the new century thought the reason the agency refused to attempt to penetrate Middle Eastern terrorist groups was the CIA's need for total control over its officers. "I think the biggest issue is control—can you control your employees," the person said. "You can't communicate with them for a couple of months, and who knows what's going on, and again it's this mentality of being risk-averse—if something happens, who's going to pay for it? I don't want to be accountable." The person added, "I don't think they went out and recruited Middle Eastern types—they just relied on applications."

In interviews with numerous CIA operations and case officers who spent years in the Clandestine Service, and who were serving at headquarters and overseas assignments in September 2001, there was great anger and frustration that many of the agency's past problems had never been corrected. They were also very critical of the agency leadership, the absence of professionalism within the Clandestine Service, and the lack of seriousness when it came to the war on terrorism. While some of the officials eventually quit the agency in sadness and disgust, others continue to work there.

By September 2001, promotions continued to be based primarily on the recruitment of agents—local residents or officials—regardless of the quality of intelligence they were providing. "One case I ran for a long time, and kept trying to turn it in," said one case officer at an overseas station. Despite complaining to the chief of station that the agent was providing useless intelligence, the officer was forced to continue running him:

> They didn't want to terminate it. This is one of the reasons that I left—because I went into the agency with a sort of grand sense of mission, really wanted to serve. But there was not a lot of emphasis on the quality of your recruitment. It all was kind of like a big game—

you have to get a certain number of recruitments. And I was developing a couple of cases, and I had sort of made a decision that if I didn't feel like a recruitment was worth it, I wasn't going to pursue it. Worth it meaning that I didn't feel that we were really going to get valuable intelligence from this person. And routinely my immediate boss would say to me, "Well, you can make it look good to headquarters—it's good for you to get just as many scalps as you can."

And all of us were kind of trained in a way to make things sound good to headquarters. But headquarters, meanwhile, was a big void. There's nobody at the helm back there, really. So it's all kind of this elaborate game where the chief of station is looking out for himself and his station, his little fiefdom, which he wants to look good.

Another case officer who also served in the Directorate of Operations before, during, and after September 2001 agreed. The officer said that despite the shuffle at the top with the arrival of Tenet and Pavitt, by September 2001 nothing much had changed in terms of the excessive focus on recruitments, many of which were phony:

I saw a lot of backbiting and backstabbing and a lot of self-promotion, and a lot of fabricating of cables overseas that turned into nothing. And the reason why they were portraying these cases as active cases was because they were getting promotions based on how many cases they ran.

They were either making them up out of whole cloth, or sending cable after cable saying this person is so wonderful and he's doing this and he's doing that and he's recruited and he's agreed to X, Y, and Z, and then when the case gets turned over to somebody else, the person that was supposedly the recruitment sits down with this other person, saying, "You're who? I never agreed to work for the CIA, what are you talking about?"

There's a warm turnover, which is when officers are together and they are introduced together, and there are cold turnovers, when for whatever reason they can't have that introduction. So basically the next person calls them up—can you meet me, I'm Joe Blow's best friend, and now I'm your best friend. So in a lot of these cases it would be a cold turnover. The reason that would happen was that promotions were tied to recruitment number.

Still another case officer, who was working at the agency during that same time period, was shocked at how amateurish the recruitment operations were:

It's absolutely appalling. We knew this wasn't the way to do business. We knew that times had changed. But you still do a little role-playing—it was silly. To go to little parties. I had a boss whose goal was to see how many business cards you were able to take back. And you'd get little kudos for how many cards you would get. I would just go up to people and say, "I'm having a contest, I need business cards," and I would come back with thirty business cards. And my boss would say, "That's fantastic."

But you know none of these people had anything useful. It didn't matter, it was just numbers. It's all quantity—It's just how many reports, how many numbers. As much as they say that it's not, it really is. So the people you end up getting and learning a lot about are worthless. I used to make cases and cases and complain and complain and say these people are worthless, they're taking your money, they're taking your time, they're taking your resources. It just didn't matter.

It's such a numbers game, it was shocking. I had one case I was running and I knew it was bad—he wasn't a bad guy, he was just giving us crap. And nobody cared. I said let's just get rid of this—take the money and put it toward a more useful program. But they won't because it looks good. It could be two thousand dollars a month, it could be five thousand dollars a month. And there were so many cases like this. People liked to joke, "It's like spending three thousand dollars to have coffee with somebody. It's like a three-thousand-dollar coffee day."

I was in one domestic office where the person who put out the most reports got a paper crown from Burger King and a little prize, like a gift certificate at an Olive Garden restaurant. They would cut their reports so they would have more numbers or they would just put out crap, and no one would care, just so they could say I got the dinner this month. And it was a way to get promoted. Can you imagine people running around with Burger King crowns on—giving them an Olive Garden gift certificate? I think it is so ingrained.

The decision to keep CIA employees at arm's length from the terrorist organizations was a serious mistake. At the same moment the CIA was convinced Al Qaeda was impenetrable, a number of American citizens and other westerners were secretly joining Al Qaeda in Afghanistan—and being welcomed with open arms. Among them was John Walker Lindh, who eventually, without even trying, began to hear bits and pieces of the September 11 plot against the United States. A twenty-year-old college dropout from Marin County, California, whose only preparation was to grow a beard, study the Koran, and learn a little Arabic.

In May 1996, Israel's Grapes of Wrath invasion of Lebanon came to its violent conclusion with the massacre at Qana. At about the same time, bin Laden moved back to Afghanistan. For his hideout, he picked a site deep in the remote and rugged Hindu Kush mountain range in the eastern part of the country. Then under the control of Yunis Khalis, an influential warlord who would later join the Taliban, it was an appropriate choice. "Kush" in Persian is derived from the verb "to slaughter." Almost impenetrable, the chain of cloud-piercing peaks and deep stony valleys is nearly a thousand miles long and two hundred miles wide, with over two dozen perpetually snow-covered summits more than four miles high.

As bin Laden was planning his move to the remote mountains of Afghanistan, where communications would be a serious problem, his man in London, Khalid al Fawwaz, had a solution. "To solve the problem of communication," he wrote to bin Laden in 1996, "it is indispensable to buy the satellite phone." Bin Laden agreed, and al Fawwaz, who would later be charged with conspiring with bin Laden to murder American citizens abroad (he is awaiting extradition from England), turned to a student at the University of Missouri at Columbia, Ziyad Khalil. Khalil had become a spokesman for the rights of Muslim students at the university and he agreed to help al Fawwaz purchase the $7,500 satellite phone, although there is no evidence that he knew he was procuring it on behalf of bin Laden. After doing some research, Khalil then bought the phone from a firm on New York's Long Island.

Over the next two years, the phone was used for hundreds of calls, to London, Iran, Saudi Arabia, Pakistan and Sudan. Bin Laden's telephone number—00873-682505331—also turned up in the private phone books and date-planners of terrorists in Egypt and Kenya. It was even used to disseminate a February 1998 declaration of war which declared that American civilians should be killed. From 1996 through 1998, Khalil ordered more than 2,000 minutes of telephone airtime for bin Laden's phone.

In a lucky break, NSA obtained bin Laden's phone number and was able to secretly eavesdrop on it as the signals transited communications satellites.

Hidden away with a small circle of supporters in the caves of the Hindu Kush, bin Laden had the motive for his war, but what he lacked was the means to carry it out. Within a month he would have his answer. For nearly a decade, the United States had largely been immune from major, organized terrorism overseas. But that was about to change.

On June 25, 1996, a monstrous explosion ripped through the Khobar Towers, a high-rise housing complex in Dhahran, Saudi Arabia. It was home to the USAF 4404th Wing—an occupying force in the eyes of many Muslims. A later investigation by the Defense Special Weapons Agency determined that the truck bomb was the largest terrorist device ever directed at Americans up until that time. Estimated to have the explosive force of 20,000 pounds of TNT, it was bigger than the bombs used in Oklahoma City, the World Trade Center, and even the Marine Corps compound in Beirut, which was estimated to be about 12,000 pounds of force. In all, nineteen Americans were killed and 372 were wounded.

After a long investigation, the Justice Department charged fourteen members of the Saudi Hezbollah with, among other things, use of weapons of mass destruction against American nationals.

Although bin Laden, according to the Justice Department, had nothing to do with the attack, it appears to have had a major impact on him. Soon afterward, he frequently pointed to the operation with pride. Bin Laden would tell a reporter from CNN, "We look upon those heroes, those men who undertook to kill the American occupiers in Riyadh and Khobar. We describe those as heroes and describe them as men. They have pulled down the disgrace and submissiveness off the forehead of their nation."

For bin Laden, dripping with hatred and looking for a way to fight back, the massive bombing at Khobar Towers may have provided him with the answer. The problem was lack of knowledge and experience with international terrorism. As bin Laden sought to expand Al Qaeda from a local guerrilla organization into an international terrorist network, he needed someone with both technical know-how and international experience. The man with the perfect résumé was Khalid Shaikh Mohammed.

Following the arrest of Abdul Hakim Murad on January 7, 1995, as he and Ramzi Yousef were cooking chemicals for Bojinka in the Philippines, Yousef managed to escape back to Pakistan. But just a month later, he was located, arrested, and brought to the United States. His uncle, Khalid Shaikh, however, was far more careful—constantly using different aliases—and managed to elude the worldwide manhunt that followed an indictment for his role in the 1993 bombing of the World Trade Center.

After remaining in the Philippines for a number of months, Khalid Shaikh departed for the wealthy Gulf state of Qatar in late 1995. There, under an assumed name, he was provided living accommodations on a large farm outside Doha, the capital. It was owned by Interior Minister Abdullah bin Khalida Thani, a member of the Qatari royal family. Hearing of plans by the United States to request Qatar's foreign minister to hand Khalid Shaikh over to U.S. officials, Khalid Shaikh fled Qatar, once again escaping capture. From Qatar, Khalid Shaikh flew into the welcoming arms of Osama bin Laden in Kandahar, Afghanistan.

To some extent they were an odd team—the rail-thin ascetic used to flowing white robes and quoting the Koran, and the chubby high-flyer with a fondness for white tuxedos and ladies of the night. Their common denominator was a shared hatred for Israel and the United States. Al Qaeda would also reflect a similar mix among its members—worshipers and womanizers, drinkers and devotees. The glue that kept them together was their deep-seated belief that the United States and Israel had declared war on the Muslim world, and that it was time to defend both their religion and their homelands.

Now, with Khalid Shaikh, a terrorist mastermind, directing Al Qaeda's worldwide operations, bin Laden had his "know-how" and decided it was time to launch his war. On August 23, 1996, he issued his call to action: "My Muslim Brothers of The World . . . Your brothers in Palestine and in the land of the two Holy Places [Saudi Arabia] are calling upon your help and asking you to take part in fighting against the enemy—your enemy and their enemy—the Americans and the Israelis. They are asking you to do whatever you can, with your own means and ability, to expel the enemy, humiliated and defeated, out of the sanctities of Islam."

"It should not be hidden from you," he wrote, "that the people of Islam had suffered from aggression, iniquity and injustice imposed on them by the Zionist-Crusaders alliance and their collaborators; to the extent that the Muslims' blood became the cheapest and their wealth as loot in the hands of the enemies. Their blood was spilled in Palestine and Iraq. The horrifying pictures of the massacre of Qana, in Lebanon, are still fresh in our memory . . . the people of the cross [Americans] had come with their horses [soldiers] and occupied the land of the two Holy

Places [Saudi Arabia]. And the Zionist Jews fiddling as they wish with the Al-Aqsa Mosque [in Jerusalem]."

Turning his attention to the United States, he said we "hold you responsible for all of the killings and evictions of the Muslims and the violation of the sanctities, carried out by your Zionist brothers in Lebanon; you openly supplied them with arms and finance. More than 600,000 Iraqi children have died due to lack of food and medicine and as a result of the unjustifiable aggression [sanctions] imposed on Iraq and its nation. The children of Iraq are our children. You, the USA, together with the Saudi regime, are responsible for the shedding of the blood of these innocent children."

With his new terror chief in mind, bin Laden sent out a dangerous and explicit warning: Unless the United States changes its anti-Muslim policies within the Middle East, his organization will begin carrying out terrorist actions within the United States, similar to the earlier attack on the World Trade Center. "I say if the American government is serious about avoiding the explosions inside the U.S.," said bin Laden, "then let it stop provoking the feelings of 1,250 million Muslims. Those hundreds of thousands who have been killed or displaced in Iraq, Palestine, Lebanon, do have brothers and relatives. They would make of Ramzi Yousef a symbol and a teacher. The U.S. will drive them to transfer the battle into the United States. Everything is made possible to protect the blood of the American citizen while the bloodshed of Muslims is allowed in every place. With this kind of behavior, the U.S. government is hurting itself, hurting Muslims and hurting the American people."

It was an articulately delivered warning—halt your war on the Muslim people or we will launch a war on your people. And it will be America's own actions that will provide him with his troops "to transfer the battle into the United States." In this war, bin

Laden said, civilians are fair game. "Regarding the American people, they are not exonerated from responsibility, because they
chose this government and voted for it despite their knowledge of
its crimes in Palestine, Lebanon, Iraq and in other places." Finally,
when asked what his future plans were, bin Laden gave an ominous answer: "You'll see them and hear about them in the media,
God willing."

The wake-up alarm went off six months later. On August 7,
1998, the concussion of a mighty truck bomb blew out a high wall
of windows in the American embassy in Nairobi, Kenya. Twinkling
shards of glass, like ice crystals in a sudden winter storm, rained
death and mutilation on innocent passersby below. The rear half of
the embassy was torn away like the back of a cardboard cereal box,
and another three-story building, the Ufundi Cooperative House,
home to a secretarial school, was gutted. Dismembered body parts
in small crimson puddles covered the area, broken bodies hung
from rebar and cement on exposed upper floors of the embassy, and
another fifteen people who happened to be in a passing bus were
incinerated in their seats.

At almost the same moment, four hundred miles to the south
in the Tanzanian capital of Dar es Salaam, a bomb planted in a
gasoline tanker exploded near the entrance of the American
embassy, destroying the front of the building and bringing further
death and injury.

"The war has just begun," said bin Laden.

In a little-publicized interview in Arabic, bin Laden
explained the reason for targeting America's embassies in East
Africa. "The Nairobi embassy was actually six embassies combined in one," he said. "The brutal U.S. invasion of Somalia kicked
off from there. Some 13,000 from among our brothers, women,
and sons in Somalia were killed. . . . For the past few decades, plots
have been hatched to partition Sudan from there. These plots are

hatched in Nairobi. As is widely known, the U.S. embassy in Nairobi is the agency that is doing this. The greatest CIA center in eastern Africa is located at this embassy. Thanks to God's grace to Muslims, the blow was successful and great. They deserved it. It made them taste what we tasted during the massacres committed in Sabra, Shatila [Lebanon], Dar Yasin [Palestine], Qana, Hebron [Israel], and elsewhere."

Despite the fact that the NSA was able to monitor bin Laden's satellite phone, the agency was never able to pick up any clues to the plot. Yet the phone was used by bin Laden and his top lieutenants to help orchestrate the bombings.

In October 1997, Ibrahim Eidarous, currently awaiting extradition from England as part of the embassy bombing conspiracy, sent word from London to Afghanistan asking Ayman al-Zawahiri, bin Laden's right-hand man, to call 956375892. This was a mobile phone in London belonging to yet another alleged embassy bombing co-conspirator, Abden Bary, who is also awaiting extradition from London. The following day, the satellite phone was used to make several calls to that phone number in London. According to intelligence officials, bin Laden also used the phone for nonsensitive calls, such as to his mother.

NSA would not have another opportunity. Following a U.S. cruise missile attack on one of his training camps, bin Laden never used the phone again. Although he certainly knew all along that the phone could be monitored, until then he may not have realized that it could also act as a homing device for cruise missiles.

Anger at Israel and America for their perceived anti-Muslim policies, as bin Laden predicted, penetrated deep inside Muslim communities all over the world—including within the thin plaster walls of a four-story apartment building at 54 Marienstrasse in Hamburg, Germany. The boxy, modern structure was located in the Harburg section of the waterfront city, a cosmopolitan area of briefcase-clutching middle managers and Portuguese bakeries selling warm, sugarcoated malassada and custard pies. One of the residents, occupying a three-bedroom, first-floor apartment, was Mohamed Atta. In 1999, he graduated with high honors and a degree in civil engineering and urban planning from the nearby Technical University of Hamburg–Harburg.

Atta's flat resembled something a college debating society or a war council might use. A small circle of Arab friends from different countries and with different degrees of religious commitment would gather regularly and discuss the growing threats facing Muslims around the world. Always at the top of the list was the Israeli-American axis. Among the group was Ziad Jarrah, a student who grew up in war-torn Lebanon and graduated from school in Beirut days before Israel renewed its bombing campaign of the city. As Operation Grapes of Wrath once again brought fear and misery to his friends and relatives in Lebanon, Jarrah left for college in Germany barely a week ahead of the first bombs.

Already fluent in Arabic, English, and French, Jarrah enrolled in a German-language course at the University of Greifswald, near the Baltic Sea. In 1997, he transferred to the University of Applied Science in Hamburg, where he studied aircraft engineering. Almost every week, he would drive to the German industrial city of Bochum to spend the weekend with his girlfriend, a medical student, where his name was next to hers on the mailbox of her small dormitory room. An above-average student for two years at the university, by 1999 he had begun spending more and more time in Bochum and also in the Harburg section of Hamburg, hanging out at 54 Marienstrasse.

Atta met a number of his friends, including Jarrah, at the Al Quds mosque in downtown Hamburg. A worn three-story building on Steindamm Street near the main train station, it was sandwiched between a bodybuilding parlor and a Turkish coffee shop. While many Muslims kept their rage against Israel and the United States unseen and sealed up inside, like a shaken soda bottle with a tight cap, others found a welcome outlet in the fire-spewn rhetoric echoing from a few local mosques and in small clusters of friends. Finally, they could pry off the cap, vent their anger—for some built up over decades—and find supportive voices offering agreement, reinforcement, and even divine salvation.

"The Jews and crusaders must have their throats slit," said Al Quds's Imam Mohammed al Fizazi in a videotaped sermon around that time. It was in this mosque that Mohamed Atta signed his last will and testament shortly after Israel's Grapes of Wrath bombing campaign against Lebanon began. Many believed that Israel and America had long before declared war on them—Grapes of Wrath and the massacre at Qana being only the latest outrage. For some, it was time to sign up and join the jihad to defend their families, their countries, their religion. To them, Osama bin Laden was a hero, someone who dedicated his life and his fortune to helping push the Russians out of Muslim Afghanistan—a solitary moment of glory in an era of constant encroachments by the West. Bin Laden was their General George Patton, with a walking cane instead of a riding crop.

One of Atta's roommates at 54 Marienstrasse was a slight, round-faced immigrant, Ramzi Binalshibh. On September 22, 1995, he stepped off a ship in Hamburg with one suitcase and a plea for political asylum, claiming illegal detention and torture in his native Sudan. In fact, he was born on May 1, 1972, in San'a, the capital of Yemen, and he grew up in the sandswept village of Amad in the eastern Yemeni province of Hadramaut.

A sweltering, remote land sandwiched between the turquoise Arabian Sea and the rolling sand-waves of the Ar-Ruba' al-Khali desert, it is also where Osama bin Laden's father spent his youth.

Ironically, nearby is the celebrated city of Shibam. It is known as "the Manhattan of the desert." Its five hundred five- to seven-story ancient buildings are considered the first skyscrapers in the world. Half a millennium old, they are crammed into an area of perhaps only five hundred square meters. Once the capital of Hadramaut, and now a town of about 7,000, the age-old skyscrapers are made of mud bricks and wooden superstructures on stone foundations.

The fourth among six brothers, Binalshibh graduated from a secular high school with honors and won a scholarship to study economics and political science in Germany. But the death of his father when he was sixteen required him to change his plans, and he instead took courses in English and went to work for a private commercial bank in Yemen. "He maintained a simple life in Yemen, with our mother, who took care of the family since our father died," said his brother, Ahmed Binalshibh.

Another member of Atta's small circle of friends was Marwan al-Shehhi, who arrived in Germany on April 28, 1996, shortly after Jarrah. Born on May 9, 1978, in Ras al-Khaimah, part of the oil-rich United Arab Emirates, he had a scholarship and received a generous monthly allowance from home. After taking some German prep courses in Bonn, he switched to the Technical University of Hamburg–Harburg, where Atta was attending. Also attending the school, studying for a degree in electrical engineering, was Said Bahaji, who became another of Atta's roommates. He was born in Germany's Lower Saxony in 1975 and moved to Morocco, the birthplace of his father, in 1984. After high school, he moved back to Germany in 1995 and enrolled in college.

By the end of the summer of 1999, the group was convinced that it was time to put a period at the end of the long discussions and turn instead to action. A critical player in that decision was Mohammed Haydar Zammar, a three-hundred-pound tanklike figure who spent much of his time sounding the battle cry of war to anyone who would listen. "We cannot just sit and do nothing," he exclaimed, blasting the actions of the United States and Israel against the Palestinians and other Muslims. A battle-hardened veteran of the wars in Afghanistan and Bosnia, in 1996—the year of Israel's Grapes of Wrath campaign and the Qana massacre—he flew to Afghanistan and pledged his allegiance to Al Qaeda.

"The group's discussions became increasingly virulent," said Kay Nehm, Germany's lead federal prosecutor. "The members' hatred focused on 'world Jewry' and the United States of America. To defeat these was seen as the central objective of the jihad." The prosecutor added, "By October 1999 at the latest, the members of the group under Atta's leadership had decided to participate in a jihad through a terrorist attack on America and kill as many people as possible."

On October 9, 1999, the group gathered at the Al Quds mosque to celebrate the wedding of Atta's roommate, Said Bahaji. It was an unusually festive occasion with a great deal of laughter. Tables were covered with lamb, baked plums, eggs, almonds, unleavened bread, small round Moroccan sweet cakes, and pitchers of lemonade. Ramzi Binalshibh was sitting cross-legged on the floor when he apologized for interrupting. Then he made a short tribute to his close assembled friends. After denouncing the United States and Israel, he said, "The goal of every Muslim is to free the Islamic lands of every oppressor and tyrant! . . . And when these tyrants attack you, you will become a wave of fire and blood!" A short while later, Marwan al-Shehhi led the guests as they joined in an old Arab fighting song: "We will be filled with glowing enthusiasm," they sang, "and we will crush the thrones of the oppressors!"

It was as if they were heading off to war, and by then they secretly knew they were. Encouraged by Mohammed Haydar Zammar, the Al Qaeda recruiter, the four friends had secretly submitted their application to attend one of bin Laden's training camps and then volunteered to fight in Chechnya. Although they considered the Israeli-American aggression in the Middle East to be the greatest threat, the principal military effort being waged by the latter-day mujahideen was against the Russians in the break-away former Soviet republic. At the time, the idea was simply to go off and earn their jihad stripes and then see where life took them.

When he joined forces with bin Laden in 1996, three years earlier, Khalid Shaikh Mohammed had suggested bringing the war to America through the use of a spectacular form of aviation terrorism—suicide pilots who would crash planes into government buildings. At first he mentioned crashing a plane into the CIA headquarters just across the Potomac River from Washington. But bin Laden had his sights set considerably higher. "Why do you use an ax when you can use a bulldozer?" he said. After a discussion about hijacking five passenger jets on each coast, the two settled on a total of four planes, a much more manageable number—and bin Laden had four pilot candidates in mind. They were tough, dedi-cated, and willing to die for the cause. Two were from Saudi Arabia, Khalid Almihdhar and Nawaf Alhazmi, both hardened veterans from the bloody fighting in Chechnya and Bosnia. Two others were from Yemen.

But whereas the two Saudis successfully received visas to the United States in April 1999 from the American embassy in Jeddah and were undergoing training, the two Yemenis were turned down, leaving them short two pilots. By the fall, however, they had the solution to their problem. Among the applications received for guerrilla training at the camps were four from Germany that looked enormously promising—most were Western-educated, spoke English very well, had technical training, and were dedi-cated to the cause. On November 29, 1999, Mohamed Atta flew to Istanbul and then boarded Turkish Airlines Flight 1662 to

Karachi, Pakistan, on his journey to Afghanistan. For security, the others departed on different days and took different routes.

When they arrived in Kandahar, according to a senior intelligence official who has access to the interrogation reports of Khalid Shaikh and others, they were welcomed with open arms. "They wanted to go off and do jihad, and their destination was Chechnya during the fall of '99," he said. "They show up in the camps and they're manna from heaven, because they have lived in the West, they have good passports, they have good technical skills, speak English in varying degrees, and they were right at a time when this plot is being formulated, and they go, 'Wow.'" In an unusual honor, they were invited in for a personal one-on-one meeting with bin Laden.

As the Hamburg four underwent intensive training at the camp, Khalid Shaikh was in the middle of planning another spectacular attack against the United States. Having previously hit at the State Department with the embassy bombings, he now intended to send the same message to the Pentagon, with a massive suicide bombing of a U.S. naval ship. Both Almihdhar and Alhazmi were scheduled to take part, and they were spending their days training for their roles in that as well as the air attacks.

In late December, however, plans were made to send them to the Malaysian capital of Kuala Lumpur for a secret and important meeting the following month, a meeting that may have dealt with both plots, the USS *Cole* and September 11. The travel arrangements for Almihdhar and Alhazmi's trip were being put together at a safe house in Yemen used by Al Qaeda for logistics, and as a sort of clearinghouse for information to be passed on to bin Laden.

The building was owned by Almihdhar's father-in-law, Ahmed Al-Hada, a Yemeni and a follower of bin Laden. In a lucky break, the CIA had obtained the address and phone number as a result of an interrogation of one of the terrorists involved in the embassy bombing in Nairobi. NSA put the phone on its watchlist and began listening. Then, in late December, details of the meeting in Kuala Lumpur were mentioned on a cell phone call to the house, along with the name "Khalid Almihdhar" and Alhazmi's first name, "Nawaf." NSA was able to intercept the call and passed the details to a special CIA unit called Alec Station.

As Almihdhar's name flowed into the agency's giant ear, America's spy world was getting the first tiny piece of a large and complex puzzle. It was a sudden and lucky break for the U.S. intelligence community—an organization set up following the attack on Pearl Harbor to never allow another surprise attack. Now the question was whether they would be able to complete the puzzle in time.

CHAPTER 8

KANDAHAR

In 1996, the Directorate of Operations named Gary Schroen, a veteran case officer with twenty-six years in the Clandestine Service, to be chief of station in Islamabad, Pakistan. Stocky and graying, with a touch of the Midwest in his speech, he was an old Afghan hand who had twice before served tours in Islamabad and was fluent in Dari, which was spoken in Afghanistan.

With the end of the Soviet Union and the Cold War, Afghanistan had once again reverted to its position as an odd little country with a strange-sounding name. The only people still talking about it were a handful of retirees who would get together for long lunches in out-of-the-way restaurants in northern Virginia. There they would reminisce about the "good war," the one they won, the one that can never be taken from them. In an agency where victories are rare, and acknowledging them even rarer, the time they beat the Russians in the snowcapped ridges and craggy pinnacles of Afghanistan is the CIA's Normandy.

On the evening of February 15, 1989, a high-priority "Immediate" message from the CIA's station in Islamabad, Pakistan, clanked out on a teletype in headquarters. It was just two words, made from X's, but they covered the entire page: "WE WON." The last Russian soldier had crossed the Termez Bridge into Uzbekistan. For the case officers in the DO, the sound of corks popping from bottles of young champagne replaced the bang of deadly mortar rounds.

With the American embassy in Kabul abandoned following the war with the Soviets, the CIA had a serious problem. In countries without U.S. embassies, the agency is virtually deaf and blind because nearly all Clandestine Service officers are hidden under the light cover of embassy diplomats. Without an embassy, the CIA was out in the proverbial cold.

Placed in charge of "Kabul station" in Islamabad during an earlier tour in the late 1980s, Gary Schroen's first mission was to act as paymaster for the four dozen or so former Afghan commanders still on the agency's payroll. One of those, Ahmed Shah Massoud, alone received a hefty $200,000 a month from the agency. But this was to be kept secret from the Pakistani ISI because he was also getting bags of cash from them.

Initially, the CIA targeted its highly paid Afghan agents against Muhammad Najibullah, the Soviet puppet left in charge of Afghanistan when the Russians pulled out. During secret meetings, preppy CIA officers would spread out satellite photographs in front of bearded Afghans and Pakistani intelligence officials wearing salwars. Jabbing their fingers, they would point out specific locations, such as Sarobi Road in Kabul, and explain where to place the explosives and how to set up the machine-gun nests to ambush Najibullah's convoys.

In retrospect, one now wonders how much better off the United States would have been had the CIA stopped with the ouster of the Soviet military and simply left Muhammad Najibullah in office. But under the Reagan and George H. W. Bush presidencies, the CIA's budget and secret mandate for covert action was considerable, as were their marching orders.

In the long CIA war to replace the Afghan leader with their

own puppet, thousands were killed and maimed. Many of the proxies used to fight the battles were Islamic fundamentalists. Terror tactics were often employed. At one point, Najibullah warned, "If fundamentalism comes to Afghanistan . . . Afghanistan will be turned into a center for terrorism." He was right, but in the monochromatic world of the Reagan and Bush administrations, all that mattered was overthrowing pro-Communist leaders. Worrying who came after them was beyond their field of intellectual vision.

Thus, in 1992, the CIA succeeded. Najibullah was ousted. Like a child's toy, the United States wanted Afghanistan only because the Russians wanted it; and when the Russians were gone, so were the United States and the CIA. But the victory would rapidly prove Pyrrhic.

What the CIA left behind, in the hands of feuding warlords, was a country in violent chaos, armed to the teeth with everything from Swiss antiaircraft cannons to American Stinger surface-to-air missiles. Of the 2,300 missiles delivered to the anti-Soviet mujahideen during the war, 600 still remained missing. According to some estimates, Afghanistan by then contained more personal weapons than all those in India and Pakistan combined. More such weapons had been smuggled, dropped, and trucked into Afghanistan during the 1980s than to any other country in the world.

When the CIA ousted Najibullah, they walked away and left the door wide open for Osama bin Laden and the Taliban, a group of radical Islamic fundamentalists, to walk right in. Bin Laden arrived by chartered Ariana Afghan Airlines jet in May 1996, and by the summer of that year the Taliban, promising an end to warlordism and a return to law and order, was building up its forces to take over the country.

Now in 1996, with bin Laden becoming a threat, the CIA had returned after its four-year absence and Gary Schroen was trying to pick up the pieces. In September 1996, Schroen began by attempting to reactivate his covert relationship with Ahmed Shah Massoud, the fearsome Afghan guerrilla commander who had helped force the Soviets, and later Najibullah, out of the country. Following Najibullah's ouster, Massoud became the defense minister in the weak and crumbling Kabul government.

Schroen asked Massoud for his help in developing intelligence on bin Laden from his contacts in Afghanistan. But unlike in the war years, Schroen no longer had large bags of American dollars to offer him. Instead, he suggested to Massoud that if he could help recover some of the six hundred missing Stinger missiles, the CIA would pay him handsomely for them. Massoud was unenthusiastic but said he had eight of his own he could return and agreed to see what he could do to help with bin Laden.

But by then it was too late.

On September 25, less than a week after Schroen's visit, Taliban forces financed largely by bin Laden made an aggressive push on Kabul. The next day, Massoud and his loyalists fled to the Panjshir Valley in the far northern part of the country. By nightfall, the Taliban was in control and bin Laden was more protected than ever. Once again, the news caught the CIA by surprise. The United States was left not only with the Taliban and bin Laden, but with the possibility that they were armed with many of the more than six hundred missing Stingers—each one capable of taking down a passenger jet. Some reports indicated that Mullah Mohammed Omar, leader of the Taliban, had at least fifty-three of the deadly weapons himself.

Seeing a possible disaster in the making, headquarters authorized Schroen to arrange a meeting with Taliban leaders, fly to the Afghan city of Kandahar, and negotiate for the return of the missiles. This would have meant providing the cash-strapped fundamentalists with between six and eight million dollars. Accompanied by other embassy officials, Schroen arrived on a chartered United Nations plane in February 1997. Leaving the airport, they traveled through the bleached and barren landscape of southern Afghanistan, passing mud-and-wattle buildings dusted with cinnamon-colored sand blown from the vast desert plains.

Rickety local jitneys crowded with bearded men in pancake hats filled the streets as they arrived in Kandahar. The second-largest city in the country, it sits at an important crossroads, the point where the main road from Kabul branches northwest to Herat and southeast to Quetta in Pakistan. They passed by the large octagonal Mausoleum of Ahmed Shah Durrani, with its coffee-colored brick exterior, delicately tiled in blue, green, yellow, and brown. Capped by a blue dome, it was built in honor of Durrani, considered the father of Afghanistan, who led Pashtun tribes to conquer lands from Mashad in Iran to Srinagar in Pakistan and created the first modern Afghan state in the eighteenth century.

The visit did not go well. Mullah Omar refused permission to meet with them and sent them instead to a local governor, who rejected the offer. By then bin Laden had fully moved to Kandahar and was living in a compound near where Schroen was staying, while organizing local construction projects.

It was a wilderness of mirrors. The CIA was after bin Laden, who was protected by the Taliban. The Taliban, in turn, received considerable covert military and financial support from Pakistan, which received considerable aid and support from the United States.

But it was loose missiles that remained the highest priority for the CIA in 1997. The image of an American passenger jet blown out of the sky by one of the agency's Stingers was something no one wanted to contemplate. So, shortly after his failed mission to Kandahar, CIA station chief Schroen boarded another United Nations supply flight and hitched a ride to Taloqan in the remote far north, the redoubt of Ahmed Shah Massoud.

Once the battleground for Genghis Khan, Taloqan means

"Lake of Blood." It was a bustling town with wide avenues lined with trees and packed with horse-drawn taxicabs, firewood-laden donkeys, and colorfully painted trucks belching clouds of blue-gray exhaust. Sitting at the heart of the city was a sprawling bazaar that sold bubbling water-pipes, carved white tobacco pipes, and hand-woven carpets. Taloqan also provided access to nearby Tajikistan, the former Soviet republic, where Massoud would obtain shipments of arms and supplies.

Again Schroen asked for Massoud's assistance in rounding up the missing weapons. He also asked for his help in providing intelligence on bin Laden, but given his distance from both Kabul and Kandahar, in addition to the fact that they were enemies, there was little likelihood that much information would be forthcoming. And again, except for some secure communications gear, the agency would provide him no money without producing some Stingers. Having lost his battle-scarred country and now reduced to life in a mountain hideout, Massoud wanted more from the CIA. Nevertheless, he agreed to help with the missiles in the hope that it would lead to greater support later on.

In addition to bin Laden, the CIA's Counterterrorism Center was also very interested in finding another person, one who topped the agency's own Most Wanted list: Mir Amal Kasi. He achieved that ranking on the bitterly cold morning of January 25, 1993, when he parked his pickup truck near the entrance to CIA Headquarters in Langley, Virginia, and stepped out with an AK-47 assault rifle. At the height of morning rush-hour traffic, Kasi took aim at cars stopped at a red light, waiting to turn down the agency's access road.

The first shot smashed through the rear window of a Volkswagen Golf driven by twenty-eight-year-old Frank Darling, an agency Clandestine Service employee. "Oh my God," he yelled to his wife of three months, Judy Becker-Darling, who was sitting next to him. "I've been shot. Get down!"

At that moment, Kasi pumped a round into another car, this one driven by agency analyst and physician Lansing Bennett, sixty-six, killing him. He then walked between the double line of cars, rapidly snapping the curved steel trigger on the rifle, wounding two CIA employees and an agency contractor before returning to the VW Golf.

Judy Becker-Darling was hunched under the dashboard and heard what sounded to her like balloons popping. When she briefly lifted her head up, she saw that she was looking down the barrel of a gun. "Get down," her husband yelled again. Bang, bang, bang—Kasi fired three more shots, hitting Frank Darling in the leg, groin, and head and instantly killing him. "I hope he runs out of bullets," prayed his wife, who saw the image of a gun brush past her window. Then she looked over at her husband. "When I picked my head up, Frank was shot in the head."

"I shot approximately ten rounds, shooting five people," Kasi later said. "I aimed for the chest area of the people I shot." He stopped, he said, only because "there wasn't anybody else left to shoot." Then he climbed back into his truck and, after a short while, returned to his apartment a few miles away. The next day, he boarded a plane to Pakistan.

As to the reasons for the sudden burst of violence, Kasi blamed America's Middle East policies, saying he wanted to "teach a lesson" to the United States. "Like a suicide bomber," noted *The Washington Post*, "Kasi was willing to sacrifice his life to protest U.S. foreign policy, which he believed was hurting Muslims worldwide." Kasi's roommate told the police that Kasi would get incensed watching CNN when he heard how Muslims were being treated. Kasi had said he was going to do "something big" at the White House, the Israeli embassy, or the CIA, but at the time his roommate did not think he was serious.

Kasi pointed specifically to the bombing of Iraq by U.S. aircraft and the "killing of Palestinians by U.S. components," apparently referring to Israel. "Several days before the shooting," he said, "I decided to do the shooting at the CIA or the Israeli embassy but decided to shoot at the CIA because it was easier because CIA officials are not armed." Kasi added that he was "upset with the CIA because of their involvement in Muslim countries."

It was an early warning of the violent level of hatred building among Muslims around the world caused by America's fatally flawed Middle East policies. In Pakistan, Kasi's actions were greeted with cheers, and only weeks later the first World Trade Center bombing would take place.

Because it was believed that Kasi had fled to the Afghan-Pakistani area, DO case officers from the Islamabad station renewed contact with GE/Senior—the cryptonym for a group of Afghan tribal warriors who had served on the agency payroll during the war against the Soviets. They agreed to again work for the agency, now as manhunters on the trail of Kasi, and were assigned a new cryptonym, FD/Trodpint.

The group quickly became one of the best-financed and most heavily armed posses in history. They were supplied with boxloads of AK-47 assault rifles, deadly mines, electronic surveillance equipment, encrypted communications gear, heavy-duty trucks and motorcycles, mobile beacons to pinpoint locations, and hundreds of thousands of dollars in cash.

If FD/Trodpint was able to locate Kasi in Pakistan, the instructions were to immediately notify the CIA station in Islamabad, which would, working with Pakistani authorities, arrange the arrest. But if he was spotted in Afghanistan, the capture would be far more complicated. Without a cooperative arrangement with the Taliban, the agency would have to conduct a secret exfiltration of Kasi and possibly the whole team. That would require locating a usable landing strip, and FD/Trodpint managed to find one in an isolated section of the desert outside Kandahar.

The CIA then closely examined the site with high-resolution satellite imagery and found it acceptable. But the one thing they could not determine was whether the sand was hard-packed enough to accommodate the weight of a sizable aircraft. To answer that question, the agency approved a highly secret covert operation in which a team from the agency's Special Activities Division, made up mostly of veterans of military special-operations units, would make a lightning-quick dash into Afghanistan from Pakistan. Flown low to the ground and in the dead of night, the team landed at the site undetected. After quickly testing the hardness of the soil and rechecking the satellite coordinates, they zipped back to Pakistan with the positive results. The trip also served as a trial run should Kasi be located in Afghanistan.

But the team of tribal Afghans who made up FD/Trodpint were never able to locate Kasi. Instead, it was the temptation of the CIA's multimillion-dollar reward that led an informant to the U.S. consulate in Karachi, Pakistan, in May 1997. Introduced to the CIA's chief of base, who reported to Islamabad, the Pakistani offered his bona fides—Kasi's application for a Pakistan driver's license. Although he was using an alias, the document contained both Kasi's photograph and his fingerprint.

The man said that a local tribal leader in Kasi's native Baluchistan, a province in Pakistan alongside the Afghan border, had been protecting and working with the fugitive for the past two years but was now ready to turn him in for the reward. Eventually, a plan was worked out to have Kasi's associate take him along on a business trip in June to Dera Ghazi Khan in central Pakistan. The CIA station in Islamabad coordinated the operation with the

Pakistani intelligence service, which agreed to transport a team of CIA and FBI agents to Multan, near the meeting location, and then to the Shalimar Hotel, where Kasi was to be staying.

About 4:00 A.M. on June 15, 1997, two FBI special agents from the elite Hostage Rescue Team—Special Agent Brad Garrett, who had been assigned the case minutes after the shooting took place, and CIA Islamabad station chief Gary Schroen—approached the hotel wearing traditional Pakistani clothes to hide their jeans and weapons. "It was surreal," recalled Garrett. "It's dark. It's dusty. I felt like I was in a David Lynch movie. We're actually starting to sweat it." Then he began getting concerned. "What if we end up killing him? Or killing the wrong person? Or one of us gets killed?"

In the dark morning, Kasi's associate knocked on his door in the $3-a-night hotel and yelled that it was time to get up. Upon hearing a response, Garrett kicked in the door, grabbed the man, and pinned him to the floor. But now he wasn't sure he had the right person. The individual struggling to get up had a beard and was heavier than he thought. "Turn him over," he ordered several of his fellow agents as he continued to straddle him. Then Garrett grabbed Kasi's left thumb and pressed it against a flip-open ink pad. With his free hand, the FBI agent pulled a magnifying glass out of his bag, studied the print, and compared it with a sample he had brought along. "It's a match," Garrett shouted triumphantly. The team rushed Kasi to the airport, where a CIA helicopter was waiting for them. Gary Schroen grabbed up his secure telephone and passed the good news to headquarters.

On the trip back to the United States, Kasi stated his reasons and offered no regrets. "He was very up-front about what he did. He didn't try to blame it on anyone. He didn't try to hide it," said Virginia prosecutor Robert Horan, Jr. "It wasn't personal. It wasn't like hating individuals. It was more institutional," noted Garrett, adding that back home Kasi had become a hero.

With Kasi captured, the decision was made to turn control of
FD/Trodpint, the heavily equipped team of Afghan anti-Soviet
warriors turned "bounty hunters," over to the unit then trying to
track down Osama bin Laden. Unlike Kasi, however, bin Laden
was only a suspect in a number of past terrorist events; he had not
yet been indicted, although a grand jury in New York was—or
would be—investigating him about that time. Thus, once
FD/Trodpint found him the plan was for the Afghan tribal team
to kidnap him and hold him in a cave near Kandahar for about a
month while the proper legal papers were obtained. Then he
would be exfiltrated using the same landing strip planned for
Kasi's removal.

But in reality, given the great security with which bin Laden
constantly surrounded himself, it is unlikely that the Afghan tribal
team would ever have been able to capture the Saudi without a
major battle. And it is unlikely that the former guerrilla fighters
would have cared whether they captured bin Laden dead or
alive—whichever happened to be easier. Thus, the plan was likely
looked at by officials back at Langley as little more than a fig leaf
to protect them from charges of planning an assassination.

By the spring of 1998, the danger to the United States posed by
bin Laden was clear for everyone to see. In February, he issued his formal declaration of war: "Jihad Against Jews [Israel] and Crusaders
[America]." "We issue the following fatwa to all Muslims," he wrote.
"The ruling to kill the Americans and their allies—civilians and military—is an individual duty for every Muslim who can do it in any
country in which it is possible to do it."

Then, in late May, he appeared on prime-time network news
across the country, telling ABC's John Miller, "We predict a black
day for America and the end of the United States as United States,
and will be separate states, and will retreat from our land and collect the bodies of its sons back to America. Allah willing."

Despite the growing dangers, the CIA's best hope for capturing bin Laden rested with their small group of tribal warriors. But many on the FD/Trodpint "bigot list"—those officials cleared and with the "need to know" for the operation—were beginning to raise questions. The highly paid mercenaries claimed to have had a shoot-out with bin Laden's bodyguards, killing several as their main target escaped. But a number of doubts were raised about the account, with suggestions that the event may have been made up to justify their continued employment. The major problem was the agency's lack of on-site knowledge—the failure to place its own people in the field with the team.

The lapse was part of a historic reluctance by the agency to develop a capability to infiltrate hostile and potentially hostile organizations with its own trusted and trained employees. The CIA unit with the greatest resources for such an operation was the little-known Office of External Development (OED), probably the most secret part of the secret agency.

OED was in charge of the agency's "non-official cover" (NOC—pronounced "knock") program, which was made up of employees who work completely undercover. In countries where they are posted, they conduct their secret operations without any overt connection to the U.S. embassy or U.S. government.

They were also the CIA officials who traditionally took the greatest risks because they operated without diplomatic cover. If they got caught passing money or receiving documents from a recruited spy, they could quickly be arrested, sentenced to a long prison term, and the CIA would deny any connections. It was the OED that had the best capabilities to recruit and develop personnel—NOCs—to penetrate Al Qaeda in the years prior to 2001.

Yet throughout those years, that capability was largely squandered and little attention was paid to developing such personnel. Not only was Al Qaeda never penetrated by a NOC—or by any other agency personnel, for that matter—it appears that the CIA never once even tried to infiltrate the group with its own highly trained officers. "As of late 1999, no program to insert NOCs into an Islamic fundamentalist organization abroad had been implemented," said one former DO official. Another former DO officer who served in the Middle East added, "NOCs haven't really changed at all since the Cold War. We're still a group of fake businessmen who live in big houses overseas. We don't go to mosques and pray."

"We would almost never in any operation do that, put an agency officer into one of those organizations," said a senior intelligence official in an interview in December 2003. Seeming surprised even at the question, he added: "The risk that the individual would be identified and then be available for exploitation is just so great that that's not the operating method of this organization. . . . That's not the MO of this organization, not just with regard to counterterrorism, but it's just rare that you would do that—it's not that we don't have people with all different kinds of covers, and all different kinds of approaches to penetrating lots of different organizations, but just rarely would we take a staff officer and do something like that."

Instead, he suggested, the agency would recruit someone local to penetrate the organization. But then you always have the problem of whether that person is telling the truth, as with FD/Trodpint, and who he or she is really working for. "An asset, yes, somebody recruited to do that, yes. But a staff officer—probably not the way you want to do business," he said.

The philosophy was, and still is, that groups like Al Qaeda are too tough—or too dangerous—to penetrate using agency personnel, so why even try. "You've got the close family, tribal ties," said a senior intelligence official in a December 2003 interview. "It's a whole different ball game as far as penetrating Al Qaeda."

Rather than risk using its own officers, the agency depended instead on friendly foreign intelligence organizations, such as Pakistan's Inter-Services Intelligence Directorate (ISI), and opposition groups in Afghanistan. During the CIA's covert proxy-war against the Soviets in Afghanistan, the ISI proved very helpful to the agency. Throughout much of the 1980s, a ceaseless stream of khaki-shirted CIA specialists, carrying operational plans in locked briefcases, made pilgrimages to the organization's secret headquarters in Rawalpindi.

But by the late 1990s, the ISI had become riddled with officers and agents sympathetic to Al Qaeda and the Taliban regime in Afghanistan. Many ISI officials played major roles in setting up, funding, and directing the Taliban government and its intelligence bureau, Istihbarat. Pakistan benefited by using these groups as talent pools for guerrilla fighters in an attempt to spark an uprising in India-occupied Kashmir, an area long claimed by both countries. Thus, much of the intelligence the CIA obtained from the ISI on bin Laden and Al Qaeda was tainted or compromised.

Finally, the CIA turned to the Taliban's chief opposition group in Afghanistan, the Northern Alliance, made up of rebels from a variety of ethnic and religious backgrounds with the common goal of toppling the regime. But since these groups had been at war with Al Qaeda and the Taliban for years, they were hardly in a position to provide useful intelligence on the long-range plans of the groups, especially as they related to future terrorist strikes against the United States.

The one group within the CIA's Clandestine Service that is in the best position to penetrate organizations like Al Qaeda is the NOC program (recently renamed the "Non-Traditional Platform" program). It is wrapped in mystery, and little has ever been written about it; even within the CIA, few employees know anything but the barest details. It has also remained very small, selective, and remote; NOCs speak of agency personnel as "insiders," while they speak of themselves as "outsiders." At its height during the 1990s, there were only about 150 NOCs compared to about 2,500 DO case officers.

But throughout the 1990s, even within this select group, there was little innovation, growth, or redirection toward Middle East terrorism. Within the upper reaches of the agency and the DO, many officials looked at the program with a jaundiced eye, including James L. Pavitt, the chief of the Clandestine Service. He always seemed skeptical about the group and never expanded it beyond its traditional direction. Pavitt felt the NOCs were more expensive to maintain, and created more problems than the traditional DO case officers who worked out of embassies. Creating cover was more difficult for the NOCs, as was communication with them and establishing separate accounting procedures. Thus, the program basically languished when it might have been used to penetrate Al Qaeda, in the same way that the FBI was redirected to penetrate the Mafia.

One of those who spent the 1990s as a NOC said the often-heard complaints from the CIA's senior management usually came from people who had little real understanding of the NOC organization. "We were always told," he said, "from the inside perspective, that we were too expensive—we were more expensive to put into the field, to maintain, to care and feed. And from our own internal organization we were told we were no more expensive because the agency pays Department of State for cover slots [for undercover DO case officers], they pay for housing, and they pay for all these things. So if you subtracted all those costs, we were equivalent in what we cost."

While recruits for the CIA's Clandestine Service—the Directorate of Operations—usually came from applications submitted to the agency, recruiting for the NOC program was far more secret and selective. They were usually developed as a result of blind ads placed by agency cover companies masquerading as executive search firms looking for people with international business experience. According to the former NOC in a January 2004 interview, "The typical advertisement would request—it wouldn't ask for anything about U.S. citizenship, but it would request experience on international projects, either residence abroad or birth abroad, education at foreign universities, native capabilities in certain languages, things like that. And there's an amazing diversity of people highly qualified that are foreign born that are here in the U.S."

It was by answering such an ad that the NOC himself, a person with an MBA and prior business experience in the Middle East, was recruited. "I had seen an ad from an ostensible headhunting firm advertising for international business positions," he said. "It was in *The Wall Street Journal* or *Barron's*, and I dashed off a résumé. At the time I came in, they had accumulated somewhere on the order of 18,000 résumés and responses for every class. And my class ended up being three people." And out of the three, he was the only one to graduate.

While people with extroverted personalities often do well as case officers in the DO's Clandestine Service, self-motivated introverts often do better in the NOC program. "You want to be under the radar, you don't want to be recognized, and any recognition or awards were truly embarrassing to me, and I think that's a very natural fit for that kind of career," said the NOC. "You don't want to have anyone single you out for any reason. And it allows you to operate very well without suspicion and move very seamlessly. The only time I've been up before a few people was at my wedding, and it scared me to death."

For normal DO Clandestine Service case officers, the training lasted fifty-two weeks, with eighteen of those weeks spent undergoing operational training at The Farm. But the NOCs were often isolated from their counterparts, who would end up assigned to an embassy in an undercover position. "At the time you learned everything that an inside officer learned, much of which is not going to be useful to you once you actually finished," said the NOC. "But it was all done in safe houses and unofficial facilities around the Northern Virginia area. It was for security, so people at The Farm wouldn't know who we were."

The process was very selective. "They started with 18,000 résumés collected," he said. "They probably contacted 500, then brought in for polygraphs and psychological testing and everything else about 100, and made offers to a dozen or so, and got three of us in there, and one cranked out of the machine at the other end. A couple of dozen instructors, support people. It was a very expensive undertaking."

Once the training was completed, the NOCs were placed within the CIA's area divisions, such as East Asia (EA) or Near East (NE). "When I came in [in the early 1990s], the routine was for the NOC Operations Branch to go out into the divisions and try to sell you," the NOC said. "Here I've got an MBA that speaks Japanese and has experience with international clients in the Middle East. And they'll go to different divisions and try to put you with people—like an in-house search firm." But because the NOC Operations Branch would occasionally be left with NOCs they were unable to "sell," the policy has recently changed. "During the past three or four years," said the NOC, "they started interviewing people and, before bringing them on, would take that résumé to the area divisions, so you didn't come on unless you had a sponsor."

After receiving an assignment to a location—for example, Singapore—the NOC would be embedded in a company, which could range from a large multinational business to a small few-person investment banking firm. In either case, the CIA would have to first get the approval of the company's chief executive officer. "The cover provider is always witting," said the NOC. "For example, IBM—I don't know if IBM covers people or not, but at IBM it might be the CEO and the general counsel, and then the person you report to directly. So there may be three people. And they've generally kept the rule of maximum of five witting people in an organization.

"I worked for what was called a boutique investment banking firm," he said, "and the firm was actually just one fellow who had managed to have done a great job of selling himself to the NOC cover branch and had negotiated a very big fee, and wanted representation in [a foreign city]. So I went over and opened an office and tried to drum up business. It's a great cover, because if you're in the business of moving money around you can ask any question you want, and if people are interested in having a piece of that money, they're going to answer your questions. And it opens a lot of doors.

"I would be in an office from eight in the morning until six at night, and then work in operational activity at lunchtime or in evenings or weekends, and typically, forty to forty-five hours a week working for the company and then another twenty-five or thirty hours a week doing operational activities. Either handling recruited assets or out there developing sources that people had— the station said we need an asset in this area in which you have particular access through your job or your social standing. 'Trolling' is the word used a lot—targets of opportunity."

Sometimes the NOC would "pitch" a possible asset himself and then run the person as a case officer would, and at other times he would simply find people for operations officers at the embassy to pitch.

"[I have to consider], can I bring this person to the point

where they can give me information and I can get them bound to me without turning them over to someone else?" said the NOC. "And that's a good way to do it, in which way you can continue on in your own persona—but you have to weigh that risk against the possibility that someday this guy's not going to believe what I'm telling him. Or do you introduce them to a friend, or arrange a chance meeting, or make available information that allows some-one else to approach them? And if you've spent six months, and you know that this guy is a dog breeder and he can be found at this place, and here are his interests and here's his political leanings, and things like that—it could be easy to set up someone else to be there at the right place at the right time with the right interest to take that over, and not have any visible connection between us."

Once the asset was recruited, a great deal of time and consid-eration was given to selecting meeting sites and locations for dead drops. The routes were designed to detect whether the NOC was being followed. "We used to have to put in plans for all of our sur-veillance-detection routes, where we were going to asset meet-ings," said the NOC, "and the CI chief would review them, and the ops chief would review them, things like that. And one time I had inadvertently mixed up the names of two subway lines, and I got a note back from one of these guys saying we're doing a thorough review of this because you purported to be at this station at this time and it's not on the line you said it was on. And for me it was an innocent error. I took a two-hour route and I stopped here, and here, and here. If you're familiar with the city and you're familiar with patterns, it's like an eight-hour route. They review them before the meetings. Some would want to see it and some wouldn't—it depends on the station and how junior the per-son was."

As the NOC quickly learned, even the best-planned surveil-lance-detection routes occasionally ran into problems. "I had a

couple of hairy instances," he said. "One of them, we were termi-
nating a fellow in [a friendly Asian country]. Letting him go, he
wasn't useful anymore. Very nice guy. My cover there was as a visiting businessman from Hong Kong. So he had very graciously
agreed to meet out near the airport.

"Because they had been having terrorist incidents, there were
a lot of roadblocks and tightened security. I had run the route two
or three times before meeting the fellow, and there were roadblocks at various places, but they seemed to be rather static and not
changing daily or regularly. And I had also gone into the station
and asked for an update on that, and everything seemed good. I
had about 50,000 dollars . . . since I was paying out this fellow's
escrow account, and I had not much else in my bag. Often, the
escrow account protects someone from trying to live outside their
means; we hold it in an escrow account for them. So I was cashing
him out. So it was a pretty sizable amount in cash, in big bundles.

"I had gone through three or four hours of surveillance
detection to get there. And [then] I turned one of the final corners
in the last ten or fifteen minutes before I was supposed to meet
him and I came across a roadblock that would have meant a very
thorough search of my bag. So I made some quick changes to the
rest of the route to get to where I needed to go. But I was within
twenty-five feet of going through that, and managed to avert that,
but it was because of area knowledge and thorough preparation
beforehand."

Traveling with large amounts of money to pay assets was
always a major difficulty for NOCs, who were not allowed to get
money from the embassy or even go anywhere near it. Ironically,
the more the international community tightened up on the movement of cash to fight terrorism, the harder it became for the NOCs.
"We weren't allowed to go into the station, we weren't allowed to
have personal meetings in country with anyone from the station,"

said the NOC. "Money movement out to NOCs in the field is a huge problem. The sophistication with which banks and law-enforcement agencies try and track money movements, try to deter criminal activities, also keeps you from getting big sacks of cash. And there's been a lot of attention paid to how you get big sacks of cash or their equivalent to people in the field. And that's a very thorny issue."

The biggest difference between DO case officers and the NOCs is their lack of diplomatic immunity. When case officers assigned to the DO's Clandestine Service travel, they carry diplomatic passports, and if they get caught and arrested passing money or receiving documents from an asset, the worst that can happen is that they would be declared persona non grata and tossed out of the country. But the NOC is forbidden from revealing his relationship with the CIA, and the best he or she can hope for, especially in a hostile country, is to eventually be exchanged or "exfiltrated"—snatched—by the agency and brought to safety.

Despite the risks, actual arrests are fairly rare. A close call happened in Saudi Arabia during the 1990s. "The fellow was about to recruit someone, and it turned out that we had gotten other reporting that this guy was working for Saudi intelligence, and they were getting fairly close to arresting our fellow," said the NOC. "We spirited him and his family away to a neighboring country in the dead of night, and they were airlifted from there. That was early nineties. But it is relatively rare for a lot of different reasons. Number one, you're very well trained and very well prepared and you typically don't come up on the radar. If you've got a hundred thousand expatriate businessmen in the country, like Japan or China, they can't watch everybody no matter how hard they try. If you stay under the radar fairly well, and if you don't screw up or someone else doesn't screw up for you, you're in pretty good shape."

If a friendly country wants to get rid of someone they suspect as a CIA spy, there are a number of ways they can go about it. "Liaison [the local country's intelligence service] will come in and put a photograph down—the chief or somebody. The locals will come in and say we think this guy's a criminal, what do you think? And the [CIA] chief [of station] will send you a message saying you need to go home, we'll straighten this out.

"If the liaison service want to be hostile and want to make a point, then they do. In Tokyo, a couple of times they went in and tore up offices and dumped over files belonging to two or three unrelated NOCs at the same time because they thought they were NOCs—and they were correct. Making the point that we could do this if we wanted to. And when you tear up three offices of seemingly disconnected, unconnected people in the same day, you're making a point there. I think that's about as muscular as they got. But that's still pretty benign. They haven't detained anybody, haven't made a big scene about it, they've gone very privately and said we understand what you're doing, you need to stop."

Some NOCs spend their entire careers without ever setting foot in the CIA's headquarters building. "From the time I became a NOC, I wasn't allowed anywhere near headquarters," said the NOC. On the rare occasions they do have to go into the agency offices, they would use an alias and put on a disguise. About once a year, many of them get together for meetings to discuss common problems and exchange ideas on different techniques.

"You'll come back here for a conference once a year—to Denver or San Antonio or Minneapolis or some place and get together as a group and talk about techniques and updates," said the NOC. "Sometimes it's in a secure place, sometimes someone's working on agency programs as a contractor—TRW or Lockheed—someone from the agency will come in and say they need a meeting room, not really explain what it's for, but they'll host a meeting and everyone will come in in alias and spend a week on a business meeting there, ostensibly meeting with that company. And the management will come out and talk to you about various things. They'll bring out the administrative people to talk to you and things like that."

One of the major irritants for the NOCs who were very successful in their cover jobs was giving back the money they earn over their government salary. "You don't get any more than a government paycheck, and for many months you don't even get that if you're out of sight, out of mind," said the NOC. "I had a four-month TDY to a place, and when I got back and talked to my wife for the first time, she hadn't been paid the entire time I had been gone. That's obviously quite disturbing, more so to younger people who are closer to the edge than I am, but the money you get from your company, you pay back the difference between one salary and the other. Sometimes very painfully, depending on certain issues. There are a few people who turned back seven-figure commissions for arranging very large deals, and I'm sure that must have been very painful to them. And the company on occasion must have gone to higher-ups at the agency and said, this guy really earned this, how can I make this happen. And the answer is it can't. It's not going to happen."

But, he said, the biggest problem throughout the post-Cold War period was not complaints about money, but a serious lack of enthusiasm for the NOC program by the agency's top leadership. "It went from miserable to horrible in relative terms. It's been kind of stuck at horrible for the past ten years," he said. Even DO case officers in the field would often look down at the NOCs and view them not as highly trained fellow agency employees, but simply as locally recruited spies, or "assets." "Internal to the NOC program, you were told you guys are the best, that's why we're keeping you separate, and all these things, and you'll handle the most sensitive cases and all this," he said. "Once you got into the field, it was very different—you got the last choice of cases and the least attention and the most administrative problems. And they had to train the case officers who worked with us to quit saying they were our handlers, because we weren't assets, we weren't there for their pleasure."

According to another senior intelligence official familiar with the NOC program, "They [senior CIA officials] looked at it as a second-class operation, traditionally. They look down at the NOC program. That's why they shuffle these guys around. . . . I think part of it is out of sight, out of mind." Like their DO counterparts, the NOCs report to the CIA chief of station in whatever country they are assigned. But unlike the DO case officers, they seldom actually meet with the chief of station, for reasons of security.

Even the critical decision of matching the right experienced NOC to the right country and position was handled haphazardly. "In my time, there was this very nice man—but he was also the doddering old grandfather type who forgot why he came to see you and should have retired twenty years before," said the NOC. "He would come out and have a discussion with you and he would go back in and represent you. I remember distinctly this guy coming out, and he had Mexico City written on an index card, and I think it was to remind him that there was a need in Mexico City. And he came out and he said Mexico City, and we talked for a long time and we determined that that was not the right place for me and that there was a greater need for me in [an important country in another part of the world] and that I should go into the language program there and go off to [that country]. And two weeks later I got a message saying I was all set to go to Mexico City. And I'm sure what he did was he got back and he took his card out and he said, 'Oh, Mexico City,' and went to work on that."

By the end of the decade, the fact that morale within the agency was bottoming out was a secret senior officials wanted to keep from the public. "There was a lot of conscious ignorance about the outflow of talent in the late nineties," he said. "There were articles in the newspapers about people leaving in droves, and we got messages on a weekly basis saying people are not leaving in droves. And we'd all look at each other and say, 'Well, I know four people who have left, and if everyone knows four people who have left, I'd call it a drove. People are definitely leaving.' Unfortunately, they were good people. A lot of very good people left, and we were told there's not really a problem, morale is good. Very different from the bottom-up perspective."

The former NOC said he didn't understand why the agency never tried to penetrate Al Qaeda with the program, and said it could have been used like the FBI uses undercover agents to penetrate the Mafia. "Is it any riskier than putting a guy into the mob in New York?" he asked. "There are people that will do that, and we just haven't asked them to. . . . It requires a lot of dedication and sacrifice on the parts of the particular people involved in it. You can parallel the NOC and the embassy-covered operations officer to law enforcement, where you have people in uniform and you have an undercover agent. The person in uniform projects strength and protection and all these things, so that people are deterred. So that if someone wants to approach you and give you something, they know where to find you, because you're wearing a uniform. But the undercover guys are the ones that are out there, not only collecting information about what's going on, but able to understand and anticipate what's going to happen. There's no reason the intelligence community operations side can't operate the same way."

Speaking about his experience in the Middle East, he noted that he had met a number of Americans who had converted to Islam, changed their names, and integrated into the culture in Saudi Arabia and other locations. "People really do truly convert and integrate into that society," he said, "and there's no reason that we can't have—even starting from a purebred white—a guy that does that. But we also have the large number of people who are from the region who are patriotic Americans who you could ask and they've got a leg up on doing some of this. It's very common in law enforcement, and it's dangerous and people get killed, but the benefits are very great."

He added, "The agency is only a step away from where they could be. In my own particular instance, in the mid to late nineties, I was going in and out of [a dangerous foreign country hostile to the United States] in alias. And there were a number of times when I had skirmishes at the border that were ugly and that were potentially very damaging and dangerous, and you're trained well, you know what you're doing, and everyone understands the risk before they do these things. And so there's no reason why you can't just carry that one step further because you've got guys who realize this is for the greater good. And anyone out there on the front lines today that's got a weapon in their hand is willing to make the ultimate sacrifice. It's a different form of it, but there's no shortage of people ready to make that sacrifice."

The NOC said he left the CIA at the dawn of the new century because of the lack of risk taking and innovation he found within the agency in general and the NOC program in particular. "Did you ever hear the phrase that they were looking for the real CIA?" he asked, rhetorically. "Because it couldn't be what we see here, because this is too mundane and well within the ordinary, and so they must have a really supersecret place somewhere doing all that good stuff that you've heard about. This must be a cover. And I've heard about that. And that really is one of the reasons I left. I went to [a company in private industry] from the agency, and in talking to people there they said, 'Why did you leave?' and I said, 'I wanted the chance to be creative, innovative, take risks, and do something new.' And the agency should be the place that people go to do those things, rather than flee from it in order to do those things."

He added, "We're not the Department of Agriculture, we're the CIA, we need to be doing things in a different way, and if I can't get you because it's four P.M. and you've gone home and that's really all you care about, then you need to be working at the Post Office. The Post Office serves a wonderful purpose, but it's different. They have perfected the bureaucracy at CIA such that you don't have the climate of esprit de corps that you had in the sixties and pre-'75 era. It's now another—slightly different—but another government institution. And for all the criticisms and faults that it had pre-'75, I think you did have a real feeling that people were accomplishing things, they were dedicated to their work, it wasn't just a job. And today I think it's just a job, which is a shame."

As the threats from bin Laden began to grow, the CIA's Counterterrorism Center in January 1996 established a separate unit with the sole mission of collecting intelligence on the Al Qaeda leader and disrupting his network. In an unprecedented action, the unit became a separate CIA "station"—the only one focused on a single individual rather than a country.

Code-named Alec Station, after the son of its founder, the organization was located within the Counterterrorism Center's warren of cubicles and offices on the first floor of the New Headquarters Building. It began with ten to fifteen case officers and analysts, plus a few FBI agents and analysts. While the chief of the station was from the CIA, his deputy was from the FBI. Three years later, the FBI also created a bin Laden unit at its downtown Washington headquarters.

In addition to its own piece of real estate at CIA headquarters, Alec Station also had the firm backing of the White House. National Security Advisor Anthony Lake had personally approved the creation of the unit, and months earlier President Clinton had signed Presidential Decision Directive 39, titled "U.S. Policy on Counterterrorism." It was a secret order that instructed the CIA to undertake "an aggressive program of foreign intelligence collection, analysis, counterintelligence, and covert action." Authority was granted to capture—"render," in legalese—terrorist suspects "by force . . . without the cooperation of the host government" and bring them to the United States to face justice.

By the summer of 1998, bin Laden was dividing much of his time between a small compound in downtown Kandahar and a much larger one in an isolated part of the desert about three miles from the airport. Known as Tarnak Farm, it was where many of his followers, as well as some family members, were housed. He would also spend some nights there with one of his wives. The walled facility of about one hundred acres had previously served as a government agricultural cooperative and contained about eighty living quarters, many made of baked mud or concrete, and a six-story office building. Eventually, bin Laden also built a training camp for mujahideen within the ten-foot crumbling brown walls of the compound.

The CIA had never developed a capability to infiltrate Al Qaeda with its own trusted officers. Nor did the agency develop any NOCs who could blend in and collect intelligence on the ground in Afghanistan, or supervise the agency's FD/Trodpint team of tribal fighters. Thus, the agency was left with only a few dozen veteran mujahideen from a war that had ended a decade earlier, a group that had already raised skepticism regarding its veracity and was ridiculed by a number of senior officials. The ridicule increased when officials discovered that the clan lived on a CIA-rented vineyard growing grapes.

Nevertheless, the scheme that called for FD/Trodpint to kidnap bin Laden was the best they could come up with and the decision was made to develop a plan to capture him in the middle of the night from Tarnak Farm. But because the tribal team could not see over the ten-foot wall of bin Laden's desert compound, the CIA turned from their horseback mercenaries to the highly secret space-borne spies of the National Imagery and Mapping Agency (NIMA) and the National Reconnaissance Office (NRO).

Orbiting in the heavens around the earth was a constellation of spy satellites, each costing more than a billion dollars. Eavesdropping from 22,330 miles in space, a point where they can "hover" over one spot, are several signals intelligence satellites. The Vortex/Mercury systems listen in on microwave communications, including telephone calls; and the Magnum/Orion satellites suck in a variety of other frequencies.

Also orbiting high in the heavens are imaging satellites, including two Advanced Crystal and a newer Enhanced Crystal with optical and infrared sensors. Three Lacrosse/Onyx imaging radar satellites have the capability to see at night and through clouds. Weighing about 15 tons apiece, the Crystals are similar to the Hubble Space Telescope with two-and-a-half-meter mirrors, only pointed down to earth instead of into deep space. From hundreds of miles above, orbiting from pole to pole, they were capable of seeing objects on the ground as small as ten centimeters across—about four inches—during the day. The Lacrosse satellites could "see" about two to three feet at night.

Twice a day, each of the school-bus-size spacecraft would pass overhead for about three minutes, peering down into Tarnak Farm. Even if not directly above, the sophisticated slant-range capability of the camera system would allow for quality imagery one hundred miles to the left or right of its ground track. As the NRO's orbital engineers kept the satellites flying, imagery analysts from NIMA used powerful computers to turn the digital pixels into an interactive 3-D visualization of the back alleys and dusty passageways within the compound. This would give the agency a "fly-through" ability to virtually walk the streets of Tarnak Farm.

While the imagery was not detailed enough to actually spot bin Laden by appearance, and the brief fly-over time did not allow a capability to track his movements, the pictures clearly showed many families, children, women, and other innocent people constantly moving within the compound and in and out of its buildings.

Because there was no way to guarantee a successful surgical operation, and every likelihood that a raid by a motley collection of hired guns not known for their moderation could turn into a bloody massacre, the CIA's FD/Trodpint kidnapping operation was stillborn. It was rejected by senior officials at both the CIA and White House and never even reached the desk of President Clinton.

The realization that bin Laden had declared war on the United States became obvious to everyone at least by August 7, 1998, when the American embassies in East Africa were blown up. Once again, the CIA was caught totally by surprise. Because the agency had spent most of its time and money on its band of Afghan soldiers of fortune, and no effort trying to actually penetrate the group, in Afghanistan or elsewhere, it picked up not a whisper of the long-planned and complex plot. The attacks followed two years of public threats by bin Laden, including a clear declaration of war only months earlier on network American television.

The surprise attack was a massive blow to an agency established following World War II specifically to prevent such surprises. George Tenet acknowledged as much in his confirmation hearings. The business of the intelligence community, he said, is "not to observe and report, but to warn and protect."

For decades, pressing the government's alarm bell has been the responsibility of a single CIA official with the title National Intelligence Officer for Warning. Such a concept began in 1953, when then CIA Director Walter Bedell Smith established a twenty-four-hour-a-day warning center known as the National Indications Center. The organization's mandate was to monitor the world's largest military forces and provide early warning of any mobilizations. It was created on the heels of the intelligence community's spectacular failures to warn of the Berlin blockade, the North Korean invasion of the South, and the Chinese entry into the Korean War.

But more intelligence failures followed, including the Soviet invasion of Czechoslovakia, the Arab-Israeli War of October 1973, and the surprise overthrow of the Shah's government in Iran by the Ayatollah Ruholla Khomeini in 1979. This led to the establishment of the National Warning Staff and the National Intelligence Officer for Warning (NIO/W) as the single person with his or her finger on the buzzer. Since 1996 through at least 2004, that person was Robert D. Vickers, whose background was in imagery analysis.

In a little-known action in the mid-1990s, however, responsibility for terrorist warnings was removed from the NIO/W and placed in the lap of the head of the Counterintelligence Center, Jeff O'Connell.

In retaliation for the embassy bombings, Clinton ordered a cruise missile attack on a bin Laden camp at Zhawar Kili in eastern Afghanistan. It was a place bin Laden had occasionally used to meet with members of the international press, or to issue statements, such as his declaration of war against "Jews and Crusaders." The CIA had received intelligence that a meeting was to take place there on August 20 and that bin Laden might be among those attending. But retired Marine General Anthony C. Zinni, responsible for the Middle East and Central Asia as chief of the Central Command at the time, said "the intelligence wasn't that solid" and the odds of hitting bin Laden with a cruise missile "was a long shot, very iffy."

When the smoke cleared following the hit by sixty-five U.S. Tomahawk cruise missiles, costing about $750,000 each, there were about twenty-one people dead and scores wounded, most Pakistani. Bin Laden and top members of Al Qaeda were not among them. Another thirteen missiles streaked over the Indian Ocean and came down on a pharmaceutical factory in the Sudanese capital of Khartoum. Known as the al Shifa plant, the CIA had claimed that intelligence showed that it was owned by bin Laden and was producing chemical weapons, neither of which proved to be true.

In fact, the CIA's intelligence on Sudan was so bad that just two years before, the agency was forced to formally withdraw more than one hundred of its intelligence reports on the country after reaching the conclusion that their key source was a fabricator. In addition, the United States had closed its embassy in Sudan— and without an embassy, the CIA is without spies.

Thus, their information came from a mix of defectors and opposition groups, neither of which are traditionally very reliable, and several foreign liaison relationships. The agency had obtained a soil sample from outside the plant, revealing the presence of Empta, a chemical used to make VX nerve gas. But this also later proved suspect. Eventually, even officials within the State Department and CIA began admitting the obvious. "As an American citizen, I am not convinced of the evidence," said one administration official who acknowledged that the intelligence may have been a mistake.

In the end, the only winner was Osama bin Laden. All along his goal, and that of his top leadership, was to draw the United States deeper and deeper into the sinkhole of a war in the Middle East. Ayman al-Zawahiri, bin Laden's close associate and confidant, argued that Al Qaeda should bring the war to "the distant enemy" in order to provoke the Americans to strike back and "personally wage the battle against the Muslims." It was that battle that bin Laden and al-Zawahiri wanted to spark. As they made clear in their declaration of war "against Jews and Crusaders," they believed that the United States and Israel had been waging war against Muslims for decades. Now their hope was to draw the Americans into a desert Vietnam, with bin Laden in the role of North Vietnamese President Ho Chi Minh.

"I think that raid really helped elevate bin Laden's reputation in a big way, building him up in the Muslim world," said Harlan Ullman, a defense analyst at Washington's Center for Strategic and International Studies. "My sense is that because the attack was so limited and incompetent, we turned this guy into a folk hero."

In an address to the nation explaining his military response in Afghanistan and Sudan, President Bill Clinton declared: "A few months ago, and again this week, bin Laden publicly vowed to wage a terrorist war against America." About the same time, he signed a Top Secret "Memorandum of Notification" authorizing the agency to use lethal force if necessary to capture bin Laden and his top deputies.

Yet it was not until December 1998, four months later, that Director of Central Intelligence George Tenet finally came to the same conclusion and declared war on bin Laden. In an internal memorandum to senior CIA managers, he exclaimed: "We must now enter a new phase in our effort against bin Laden . . . We are at war . . . I want no resources or people spared in this effort, either inside [the] CIA or the [intelligence] community."

By then it was becoming more and more clear that bin Laden had his eyes on the ultimate prize—the United States. On December 1, an intelligence community assessment of bin Laden warned, "UBL is actively planning against U.S. targets . . . Multiple reports indicate UBL is keenly interested in striking the U.S. on its own soil . . . Al Qaeda is recruiting operatives for attacks in the U.S. but has not yet identified potential targets." Soon thereafter, another report cautioned, "The intelligence community has strong indications that Bin Laden [sic] intends to conduct or sponsor attacks inside the United States."

But the "wartime" CIA looked a lot like the "peacetime" CIA. Tenet's "declaration of war" was so low-key that not even the assistant director of the FBI's Counterterrorism Division had even heard of it. Neither had senior officials in the Pentagon or the U.S. military. And despite his order that "I want no resources or people spared in this effort," Tenet never even bothered to increase the personnel strength of the Counterterrorism Center (CTC) following his "declaration of war." Nor did he increase the numbers after the December 1999 Millennium terrorism attempt, or after bin Laden's deadly October 2000 attack on the USS *Cole*.

The failure to translate words to actions greatly angered many within the CTC. One former CTC chief said his organization, in the years leading up to the fall of 2001, constantly lacked adequate people, money, and authorization to undertake appropriate operations against Al Qaeda. He recalled a conversation with Deputy Director of Operations James Pavitt, who said "there were not enough personnel to go around and that CTC was already well-supplied with staff compared to other CIA divisions." The feeling was the same within the bin Laden unit—Alec Station— according to a former chief of that organization. "We never had enough officers from the Directorate of Operations," he said. "The officers we had were greatly overworked. . . . We also received marginal analytic support from the Directorate of Intelligence."

"In hindsight," Tenet now admits, "I wish I had said, 'Let's take the whole [bin Laden] enterprise down,' and put five hundred more people there sooner."

But while Tenet can be blamed for not putting money and people where his mouth was, the real problem is simply the nature of the post–Cold War world. During the half-century when Moscow sat fixed at the center of a giant bull's-eye of intelligence targets, prioritization was easy. The only question was how to divide people and resources between the Soviet military, diplomatic missions, and satellite countries. But when the Soviet Union collapsed, the giant bull's-eye disappeared and was replaced by a shooting gallery with black silhouette targets popping up everywhere—in back, in front, behind rocks, under bushes. The public, the press, and the Congress were requiring the intelligence community to see everywhere at all times, which was not only impossible but also irrational.

Targeting went from a steady state to wild surges. With North Korea becoming a growing threat, much of the intelligence community trained its eyes, ears, and human agents in that direction. But that left India and Pakistan wide open, and the spy world was caught red-faced when India suddenly exploded its underground nuclear weapon. As more resources were redirected toward the subcontinent to make sure that didn't happen again, a crisis would break out in another part of the world and the intelligence community would come up short and have to again surge in another direction. When American forces suddenly went into Haiti, NSA had only one person fluent in the local Haitian Creole dialect. Likewise with Somalia, Rwanda, Bosnia, and on and on.

"As I declared war against Al Qaeda in 1998," said Tenet, "in the aftermath of the East Africa embassy bombings—we were in our fifth year of round-the-clock support to Operation Southern Watch in Iraq. Just three months earlier, we were embroiled in answering questions on the India and Pakistan nuclear tests and trying to determine how we could surge more people to countering weapons of mass destruction proliferation. In early 1999, we surged more than eight hundred analysts and redirected collection assets from across the intelligence community to support the NATO bombing campaign against the Federal Republic of Yugoslavia."

Tenet also points a finger of blame at Congress for not giving him all the money he asked for. "Senator Kyl once asked me," Tenet said, "'How much money are you short?' 'I'm short $900 million to $1 billion every year for the next five years' is what I answered. And we told that to everybody downtown for as long as anybody would listen and never got to first base. So you get what you pay for. . . . And everybody wonders why you can't do all the things people say you need to do. Well, if you don't pay at the front end, it ain't going to be there at the back end."

But lack of funding is often a cop-out for other failures, such as moving more quickly from a Cold War mentality within the Clandestine Service to a real-world paradigm. That is a matter not of money but of leadership. Beyond retooling and rebuilding the CTC and the CIA, Tenet was faced with a major problem when it came to reorganizing the entire intelligence community to fight terrorism. Few realize that the Director of Central Intelligence has real direct control over only 15 percent of America's total spy world. The man who controls the other 85 percent is Secretary of Defense Donald Rumsfeld, and he indicated early on in his current job that he expects to remain in control. Yet he was far more concerned with downsizing the Pentagon than reorganizing and reinvigorating the intelligence community.

Rather than wage a smart intelligence war—increasing linguists and analysts, recruiting Americans whose appearance and background fit the part, and then developing creative ways for the Clandestine Service to penetrate Al Qaeda—Tenet simply turned again to the knuckle draggers: covert action. It was a route he himself had warned against at the time of his move into the director's office. Using secret wars to prop up failed foreign policy leads only to disaster, Tenet cautioned. History books are filled with examples, from the Bay of Pigs to Vietnam to the Iran-contra scandal. Now the CIA would again be used to substitute for America's failed and destructive Middle East policies.

The latest plan involved stationing two Los Angeles–class attack submarines, armed with cruise missiles, deep under the waves of the Arabian Sea off the coast of Pakistan. At the same time, Alec Station would continue to use its FD/Trodpint team to try to spot bin Laden and determine when he was in a location that was targetable by the missiles.

But after the team sent word that bin Laden had been spotted back at Tarnak Farm, again Clinton, Tenet, and the rest of the senior officials who made up what was known as the "Small Group" were faced with the same dilemma as before. How could they take out an individual with a cluster of highly explosive cruise missiles without killing dozens of innocent civilians, including women and children, nearby? Other questions involved the legality of assassinating someone who at that time hadn't even been indicted for a crime, and the certainty of the identification, especially since Tenet was unable to get a second independent positive ID. Without that, he told the group, he could not recommend the strike.

If bin Laden's goal was to create a sense of panic within the upper reaches of the American government, he appeared to be succeeding, as senior officials seemed to leap in desperation from plan to plan. During a December 1998 visit to Washington, Pakistani Prime Minister Nawaz Sharif was asked for help in capturing bin Laden. He suggested that the CIA train a group of his commandos who could be stationed along Pakistan's border with Afghanistan and placed on the ready to help capture bin Laden.

Clinton agreed, but senior administration officials knowledgeable of the deal soon realized that what Sharif really was after was an elite commando unit for his own purposes. Always worried about a possible coup, the team could act as his personal bodyguards, trained and paid for by the CIA.

Weeks later, the CIA discovered that someone who *might* be bin Laden was falcon hunting in western Afghanistan with what appeared to be members of the royal family from the United Arab Emirates. To some in Alec Station, the attitude was "Let's just blow the thing up. And if we kill bin Laden, and five sheikhs are killed, I'm sorry." But both Tenet and the White House realized the international furor that would develop, especially if they made a mistake—which was likely because their only ground source was FD/Trodpint—and vetoed the plan.

Increasingly under Mike _____, its CIA chief, Alec Station began taking on the feel of the king's executioner. After the decision against blowing up the Tarnak Farm and the hunting camp, Mike unleashed a blast of angry e-mails to an assortment of officials. Some saw him as an unkempt, tactless, annoying manager who had little understanding of the international ramifications of some of his suggestions. Killing innocent women, children, and members of royal families in harebrained, and likely to fail, cruise missile assassinations was the best way to increase, not decrease, hatred and terrorism directed at the United States.

Complaints began coming in, even from the White House. Mike later acknowledged that many even within his own agency believed he and his unit had gone off the deep end. "The rest of the CIA and the intelligence community looked on our efforts as eccentric and, at times, fanatic," he said. In 1999, after three years as head of Alec Station, Mike transferred to another job at CIA headquarters.

As his replacement, Tenet picked one of his fast-rising executive assistants, Rich _____. Around the same time as the shakeup in Alec Station, Tenet also changed the guard at the top of the Counterterrorism Center. Jeff O'Connell was sent to Tel Aviv to become chief of station and was replaced by Cofer Black, who had previously served as chief of station in Khartoum, Sudan. While there he became the target of an abortive murder or kidnap plot by Osama bin Laden, so he had a personal as well as professional reason to go after him. Tenet wanted "action," and he thought Black could get it for him.

Bespectacled and chunky, Black was a throwback to the old days of covert action. His vocabulary overflowed with the macho jargon of war. Black became the top person within the intelligence community charged with sounding the alarm before a terrorist attack—the lookout on the bridge of the *Titanic*.

Despite the change in leadership, the atmosphere within Alec Station remained highly charged and hell-bent to capture or kill bin Laden at almost any cost. But there were also internal frictions. Some DO case officers in the field resented the fact that of the two dozen people working in Alec Station, more than two-thirds were female and that most came from the DI—the Directorate of Intelligence, which is the analytical side of the agency. The DO, they believed, was a man's world and they did not like to "take direction from the ladies of the Directorate of Intelligence," said one manager in Alec Station.

And there was bitterness also between the FBI agents assigned to the unit and the CIA officials. They were two separate breeds, with different career paths, different objectives, different responsibilities, and different personalities. The FBI agents were interested not only in gathering intelligence but also collecting evidence for current or future cases, things the spooks had little interest in. Some of the CIA managers, on the other hand, who looked at their job as covert operators—plotting coups, paying off tribal warriors, arranging the shipments of explosives—wanted no interference from the G-men and -women.

The epicenter of the clash between the two cultures was the relationship between Rich and John P. O'Neill, the flashy, outspoken chief of the FBI's National Security Division in New York.

Born in Atlantic City, New Jersey, in 1952, O'Neill spent much of his special-agent career as a latter-day Eliot Ness, busting members of the Mafia in Chicago, before moving on to head the bureau's Counterterrorism Division in Washington prior to New York. He wore wide-lapeled double-breasted Valentino suits and silky black "gangster socks," was married but lived with another woman, and hung out with journalists at Manhattan's celebrity-studded watering hole Elaine's.

As the person in charge of counterterrorism and counterespionage for the New York area, he had regular dealings with Rich and other CIA officials in Alec Station. "They despised the FBI and they despised John O'Neill," said one FBI friend of O'Neill with knowledge of the clash, "because of his personality, because of his style, because he was John, because they couldn't be John."

But it was also O'Neill's ego, sharp elbows, and abrasiveness that got under the skins of the spooks at Alec Station. "If you get a guy that becomes a little bit too flashy or too full of himself, then sometimes he will promote himself at the expense of the agency," said one of his colleagues. "By that, usually what happens is that an individual starts giving out information, or he starts doing favors that he shouldn't be doing—he's compromising himself, as far as being an FBI agent. So I think there was, sometimes, concern and worry about that with John."

A CIA official acknowledged the problem. "The working relationships were difficult at times," he said. "This had been a long-term, sort of systemic type of problem. There's an underlying difference in mission between law enforcement and intelligence, and that affects the way the two organizations operate. You also have a difference in—'It's our stuff, it's our information, it's not your stuff and your information, and we're concerned about how you're going to use it,' just generally."

But the most serious problem was Rich's lack of management,

his myopic obsession with bin Laden, and his focus on the fun and adventure part of the job. While jetting off to secret meetings from Paris to the Hindu Kush, he overlooked the day-to-day routine of ensuring that critical information was shared, never followed up on important clues, and lost track of key members of Al Qaeda.

"Rich was seen by some of his colleagues as typical of the unyielding zealots the unit had seemed to produce one after another since about 1997," noted *The Washington Post* managing editor Steve Coll. "The bin Laden team seemed to think theirs was the only national security problem that mattered, some of their colleagues felt. They talked about the Al Qaeda threat in apocalyptic terms. And if you weren't with them, you were against them."

Instead of engaging in the difficult and tedious work of recruiting and developing a network of sources to penetrate Al Qaeda in Europe, Asia, Africa, and elsewhere, Rich and Cofer Black spent much of their time on covert operations. They flew to Tashkent, the capital of the former Soviet republic of Uzbekistan, which borders Afghanistan to the north, and financed a strike force led by Uzbek military commanders.

The idea was to use them to kidnap bin Laden, but there was almost no likelihood that such an operation would ever be feasible. Uzbekistan was over a high mountain range and far away from bin Laden's heavily defended base in southern Afghanistan, and triggering a war with the Taliban was not in their best interest.

Nevertheless, the brutal and corrupt leader of the country, former Communist boss Islam Karimov, was happy to accept the CIA's bags of money to keep his torture chambers running. And the commando training would be useful to continue the repression of women and religious minorities. Amnesty International called the country's record in human rights "dire," with thousands of political prisoners in jail indefinitely and crackdowns on religious dissent and women. "Unfair trials, torture and ill-treatment were routinely associated with these cases," said the report. "Torture was 'systematic' in Uzbekistan." According to a forensic report commissioned by the British embassy, two prisoners were even boiled to death.

Another recipient of large bags of CIA cash was Ahmed Shah Massoud. The charismatic leader of the Northern Alliance, his principal income came from selling large amounts of quality heroin and opium to European and American drug kingpins. Rich and other DO case officers would fly in to airfields near Massoud's mountain hideout with briefcases packed with a quarter of a million dollars.

But by December 1999, Massoud's quixotic quest to retake Afghanistan from the Taliban had become a fantasy. And, far away from his archenemy bin Laden, he could also provide little useful intelligence. Nevertheless, apparently more out of emotion than logic, Alec Station continued to invest enormous energies and hopes that, with U.S. help, Massoud would someday overthrow the Taliban and capture bin Laden. Nothing could be further from reality.

While one part of the CIA was bankrolling Massoud's group, another part, the CIA's Counter-Narcotics Center, was warning that he posed a great danger. His people, they warned, were continuing to smuggle large amounts of opium and heroin into Europe. The British came to the same conclusion. White House counterterrorism expert Richard Clarke called Massoud's Northern Alliance "not a very good group of people to begin with. They're drug runners. They're human rights abusers. They're an ethnic minority. It's just not something that you're going to build a national government around."

As Alec Station squandered its time and money building its secret army, George Tenet, Cofer Black, and Rich were forced to admit the embarrassing truth. After four years and hundreds of millions of dollars, Alec Station had yet to recruit a single source within bin Laden's growing Afghanistan operation. It was more than embarrassing—it was a scandal.

On December 3, Black's Counterterrorism Center made a presentation at the White House to the Small Group, the Clinton administration's most senior national security officials. "At this time," the briefer said, "we have no penetrations inside [bin Laden's leadership]." In fact, as they later admitted, prior to September 11, 2001, "the CIA had no penetrations of Al Qaeda leadership, and the Agency never acquired intelligence from anyone that could be acted upon."

It was George Tenet's biggest secret. Not only was Al Qaeda never penetrated, neither the Counterterrorism Center nor Alec Station ever picked up a single piece of usable intelligence on bin Laden or his organization, the country's greatest threat.

It was a dangerous time to be without intelligence. Within days, the 9/11 plotters began their operation.

Osama bin Laden and Khalid Shaikh Mohammed had agreed that four aircraft would be hijacked within the United States and then flown into major targets in New York and Washington. Khalid Almihdhar and Nawaf Alhazmi, both tested veterans of wars in Chechnya and Bosnia, had been selected to be the first two pilots. Mohamed Atta and his Hamburg team would also be pilots.

Then, that same month, the single clue appeared. NSA intercepted the telephone call to the Al Qaeda safe house in Yemen mentioning Khalid Almihdhar and the meeting in Kuala Lumpur, Malaysia. After an analyst wrote up a report, it was promptly sent off electronically to both FBI headquarters and the CIA. But the FBI dealt primarily with domestic terrorism matters and depended on the CIA for intelligence overseas. That left only Alec Station standing between the hijackers and the lives of 3,000 people.

The NSA intercept indicated that "Khalid," "Nawaf," "Salem," and others were going to be traveling to Kuala Lumpur. CIA analysts later determined that "Khalid" was Khalid Almihdhar. "We knew that some guys that looked as though they were Al Qaeda—associated were traveling to KL," said a senior intelligence official in a December 2003 interview. "We didn't know what they were going to do there. We were trying to find that. And we were concerned that there might be an attack, because it wasn't just Almihdhar and Alhazmi, it was also eleven young guys—which was a term that was used for operatives traveling. We didn't have the names of the others, and on Alhazmi [who would also take part in the 9/11 attack] we only had his first name, 'Nawaf.' So the concern was: What are they doing? Is this a prelude to an attack in KL—what's happening here?"

In late December 1999, Khalid Almihdhar was in Yemen and Nawaf Alhazmi was in Karachi, Pakistan. Nawaf planned to leave Karachi for Kuala Lumpur on January 2, and Almihdhar would leave Yemen around the same time and change planes in Dubai. Later, however, Nawaf altered his plans so he would arrive in the Malaysian capital on January 4. CIA officials, working with their Pakistani intelligence counterparts, planned to have Nawaf's passport scrutinized as he passed through the Karachi airport on that date.

But officials in the CIA's Islamabad station and its Karachi base never considered the possibility that Nawaf might again change his schedule. Thus, they never bothered to have alternative flights placed under surveillance. As a result, when Nawaf decided to keep to his original schedule and depart Karachi on January 2, no one was watching. By the time Pakistani intelligence agents were in place two days later, Nawaf was long gone. Nawaf apparently flew to Singapore for two nights and continued on to Kuala Lumpur on the fourth.

CIA officials had more luck with Khalid Almihdhar. As planned, he boarded a plane on January 5 at Sana'a's hulking international airport, leaving behind the sharp smell of wood fires drifting across Yemen's dry, rocky landscape in winter. Landing at Dubai, the flashy business capital of the United Arab Emirates, he was in the process of transferring to his flight to Kuala Lumpur when he was pulled aside by customs officers. At the request of the American embassy, they took his Saudi Arabian passport and secretly photocopied it before letting him go on his way. UAE officials then passed the copy to the CIA station chief in Dubai, who faxed it on to Alec Station.

What was striking was that Almihdhar's passport had a multi-entry visa in it for the United States. It was a worrisome fact that he was associated with Al Qaeda and was on his way to what appeared to be a major terrorist meeting. Seeing that the visa had been issued in Jeddah, Saudi Arabia, in April 1999, analysts in Alec Station requested that the embassy there fax them a copy of Almihdhar's visa application, which indicated that his ultimate destination was New York. That Almihdhar, a member of Al Qaeda, had intentions of traveling to the United States, and in particular New York, was obviously something in which the FBI would have been very interested.

When Almihdhar arrived in Kuala Lumpur on January 5, the Malaysian security service, Special Branch, placed him under constant visual surveillance on behalf of the CIA. That same day, Alec Station notified officials around the world that "we need to continue the effort to identify these travelers and their activities . . . to determine if there is any true threat posed." The cable added that the FBI had been notified. It also said that copies of Almihdhar's passport and visa were given to the bureau. But this is a point FBI officials vigorously deny. It is a critical issue. An Al Qaeda member was headed for the United States, quite possibly New York, and Alec Station had a copy of his passport and visa.

The issue of whether Alec Station passed the critical Almihdhar passport and visa photocopies to the FBI remains white-hot. "We have documents within the agency that said a photocopy of the passport was sent to the bureau," said a senior intelligence official. "The bureau says they don't have any record of getting it. It was sent from Alec Station—the operator who was working the case, the person who was organizing the whole operation. The point is we have the message that says that was done. What we say about it is there is no reason in the world that she would create a contemporary e-mail and then not do it."

But FBI officials familiar with the issue are just as adamant, and angry, that nothing was passed. "They refused to tell us because they didn't want the FBI, they didn't want John O'Neill in particular, muddying up their operation," said one in a December 2003 interview. "They didn't want the bureau meddling in their business—that's why they didn't tell the FBI. Alec Station worked for the CIA's CTC. They purposely hid from the FBI, purposely refused to tell the bureau that they were following a man in Malaysia who had a visa to come to America. The thing was, they didn't want John O'Neill and the FBI running over their case. And that's why September 11 happened. That is why it happened. . . . They have blood on their hands. They have three thousand deaths on their hands."

Congressional investigators came down on the side of the FBI. "The weight of the evidence does not support [the CIA's] assertion."

"I know someone who did lie," said an FBI official, "and said she brought documents down to the FBI, and you check the visitors logs and she had never got into the building. . . . She lied about her role. She was a DI person, not an operations person. She lied to the Joint Committee about saying that she went to the FBI saying she brought them information about Almihdhar. And we checked the visitors logs and she was never in the building—[the] headquarters in Washington. Then she said she gave it to somebody else, she said 'I may have faxed it down—I don't remember.'"

When Almihdhar and Alhazmi arrived in Kuala Lumpur in early January 2000, the Malaysian security service, Special Branch, placed them under constant visual surveillance on behalf of the CIA. From the airport, they traveled twenty miles south to Evergreen Park, a secluded, palm-rimmed condominium complex next to an eighteen-hole golf course designed by Jack Nicklaus. The home was the weekend getaway for Yazid Sufaat, who earned a degree in biological sciences from California State University, Sacramento, in 1987. His wife also graduated from the school, with degrees in medical technology and biochemistry.

Although the intelligence service was not able to listen in on what was taking place, the activities of the men seemed suspicious. "We were able to watch what they were doing," said the senior intelligence official, "but we never knew what they said at that meeting. We were just able to track them, we didn't know what they were talking about—they acted suspiciously, they were making phone calls outside the apartment, so it looked a little dirty." Yazid Sufaat was later arrested by Malaysian authorities, who said he had ties to Riduan Isamuddin, a major local terrorist also known as Hambali. They believe that Sufaat was simply a foot soldier who provided housing and false identification letters and helped obtain explosives for members of Al Qaeda.

In Washington, the Kuala Lumpur operation was being followed at the highest levels of the intelligence community and the White House. Updates were circulated to senior officials on January 3 and 5. Rich, the chief of Alec Station, apparently gave briefings on the developments to senior CIA officials. The updates were usually reviewed every day by both Tenet and President

Clinton's national security advisor, Sandy Berger. On January 5 and 6, FBI Director Louis Freeh and other top bureau officials were also briefed. As part of the turf battle, they were told that the CIA was the lead agency for the operation and that if an FBI angle to the case happened to develop, they would let the FBI know. In other words, don't call us, we'll call you.

Aside from the issue of whether the CIA told the FBI about the visa, Alec Station was clearly seeking to keep the FBI at arm's length from the operation, according to a senior intelligence official. "We said to the bureau," he said, "the guys are here [Kuala Lumpur], this is how many people are involved, we're tracking them, but it doesn't look like this has become a criminal matter that should be worrisome to you." On January 7 and 10, they notified operations officers working on the case in Asia that they had run database searches on the few names that had turned up but thus far no "hits" had developed.

But inexplicably, Alec Station never asked NSA to run the names through its much larger database. And the NSA never bothered to take the initiative when they first obtained the intercepts. If they had, its analysts would quickly have identified "Nawaf" as Nawaf Alhazmi. Then someone could have asked the State Department to run a check on the name. That would have produced the disturbing news that he also had a visa for the United States issued in Jeddah on almost the same day as the one issued to Almihdhar. Thus, at this point, two dangerous members of Al Qaeda were set to come to the United States, but because of turf battles and sloppy work, no alarms had been sounded by Alec Station.

On January 8, Malaysian Special Branch officers following the suspected Al Qaeda members saw three of them suddenly go to the airport and board a flight for Bangkok, Thailand. They quickly notified the local CIA station chief, who asked the

Bangkok station for help. The next day, a Sunday, officials in Alec Station sent a message marked "NIAC [for Night Action Required] Immediate"—the second-highest priority under Flash—to Bangkok to emphasize the importance of the operation. NIAC Immediate messages are required to be acted upon no matter what time of day they are received.

From the flight manifest, Special Branch was able to determine that one of them was named Khalid Almihdhar and that another had the name Alhazmi. But no one yet had connected the name "Nawaf" with "Alhazmi." For the third person, all they were able to get was part of a name—"Khallad." It was the Arabic word for "silver." In reality, Khallad was Khallad bin Attash, a Yemeni and hardened member of Al Qaeda who had lost his leg training in bin Laden's Afghanistan camps and had replaced it with a silver prosthetic leg. He had just come from a failed attempt to sink a U.S. warship, USS *The Sullivans*, in Yemen's harbor, but it would be an operation that would eventually succeed nine months later against the USS *Cole*, killing seventeen American sailors.

For Alec Station, things went from bad to worse. Despite the importance of the operation, Rich had never bothered to write up and distribute an intelligence report on it—what is known as a TD, or Telegraphic Dissemination. "A TD would have gone to a lot of people," admitted the senior intelligence officer, "but we didn't do that." As a result, when the three members of Al Qaeda arrived in Bangkok, no one had been alerted to watch for either Khalid Almihdhar or Nawaf, the two names they had. And by the time the alert from Kuala Lumpur with the newly acquired names reached the CIA station in Bangkok, the plane had already landed and the passengers had disappeared into the crowded streets of the city.

It was a serious blunder. It was later discovered that the purpose of the meeting was for Khallad bin Attash to rendezvous with two other Al Qaeda members who were to pass him a wad of cash, a portion of which would go to Almihdhar and Alhazmi for their American 9/11 terrorist operation.

Despite losing the key suspects, Rich told senior CIA officials four days later, on January 12, that the surveillance in Kuala Lumpur was continuing. Two days later, he again told his superiors that they were continuing to track the Al Qaeda suspects, but by then Alec Station had no clue where Almihdhar, Alhazmi, and Khallad were and all tracking had ceased.

The agency then asked the Thai intelligence service to put the names on its watchlist and also, belatedly, asked NSA to include the names on its expansive watchlist, but the results were disappointing. Alec Station made no further attempts to locate the missing suspected terrorists.

The sole purpose for setting up Alec Station was to keep track of bin Laden and members of Al Qaeda—and most important, to keep them out of the United States. Yet after NSA managed to pick up the first clue, and after a successful worldwide operation that tracked Khalid Almihdhar and Nawaf Alhazmi to Kuala Lumpur, and discovered that at least Almihdhar had a multi-entry visa to enter the United States, Rich completely dropped the ball.

More important, despite the likelihood that Almihdhar was headed for the United States, and possibly New York, Rich never even bothered to submit his name to the State Department's terrorist watchlist—TIPOFF. It was a dangerous oversight. "What we had was an Al Qaeda guy, all his passport information, and a visa to the U.S.," said the senior intelligence official. "If you look at the State Department standard for watchlisting, that met it, not a question about that. And we didn't do that."

TIPOFF is an intelligence database that receives information on suspected terrorists from U.S. law enforcement, intelligence, and other agencies. By 2001, it contained more than 70,000 names of suspected terrorists who were either members of foreign terrorist organizations, known hijackers, car bombers, assassins, or hostage-takers. It was designed to enhance border security by using secret intelligence and law-enforcement information to identify terrorists. When a Customs officer submits a name into the database, if the name is on the TIPOFF watchlist, a double zero—00—will appear on the officer's computer. Consular officers must certify that they have checked the TIPOFF systems before issuing visas, and are liable to criminal penalties if they do not. There are no criminal penalties for failure to submit the names of suspected terrorists, however.

Not only did Alec Station not submit Almihdhar's name, it was later discovered that the agency was chronically delinquent in its submission of such information. Around the same time, the agency was sitting on at least fifty-eight other suspected terrorists without submitting their names. "Sometimes you're focusing on a question, one question—What were they up to in KL?" said the senior intelligence official. "And you miss another question, which is: What should I do about these guys, what's the opportunity that I have here?, and they [Alec Station] didn't focus on that."

Thus, on January 15, 2000, the first two members of the 9/11 plot, including its leader, Khalid Almihdhar, boarded a United Airlines jet in Bangkok, flew to Los Angeles, and were admitted to the United States with a smile and a wave. They eventually moved into an apartment in San Diego and began their plotting.

At Alec Station, CIA officials assumed the Al Qaeda members were still in Bangkok but never made any follow-up inquiries or pressed the Thai government for more information. Incredibly, the matter was completely dropped. Every now and then, an NSA intercept would turn up with some personal information relating to Almihdhar or Alhazmi, but nothing to indicate where they were or what they were doing. As for Rich, once the Al Qaeda members dispersed and things began falling apart, he simply paid no attention.

Like a train wreck in slow motion, in February the CIA's Kuala Lumpur station was reminded of the Al Qaeda trip to Bangkok by another matter and decided to query their station in that city. A month went by without a response. Then, on March 4, the CIA Bangkok station finally sent word back to Kuala Lumpur that Nawaf Alhazmi—they finally had obtained his full name—had departed for Los Angeles nearly two months earlier. Although the Thai intelligence service apparently gathered the information from flight manifests on the day of departure, they never bothered to pass it on—and worse, the CIA didn't bother to ask for it until months later. The day after the Bangkok station transmitted the details to Kuala Lumpur, Alec Station was notified.

But once again CIA officials in Alec Station failed to pass on the critical information to either FBI investigators or the State Department's watchlist office, even though it was now clear that at least one Al Qaeda member had flown to the United States following an important and secret terrorist summit meeting. Also, although there was no record of Almihdhar's departure, it might have been assumed that since he and Alhazmi were traveling together, and both had visas for the United States, he was likely on the same plane—which he was—or had already flown to the United States separately. Finally, Thai intelligence also reported that Khallad bin Attash, the Al Qaeda paymaster and mastermind of the upcoming attack on the USS *Cole,* had departed for Karachi, Pakistan, on January 20, again without anyone being alerted.

"The folks in Alec just missed it, they missed the significance of it, they didn't read it, they just missed it," said the senior intelligence official. "It was an operational message, and our guys just missed it. Not only was it not told to the FBI, we didn't internalize it, we didn't understand what it meant, or didn't take it on board. The long and the short of it is we missed it, so we missed another opportunity then to watchlist these guys. At the end of the day, we didn't penetrate the plot, we just didn't."

After arriving in Los Angeles, Almihdhar and Alhazmi settled in San Diego. They moved into apartment 127 of the Parkwood Apartments, a townhouse complex near a busy commercial strip on Mount Ada Road in Clairmont. There they bought season passes to Sea World, dined on fast food, frequented strip clubs, and took flight lessons at nearby Montgomery Field. All under their real names. They also opened a $3,000 checking account at the Bank of America; obtained driver's licenses, Social Security cards, and credit cards; and bought a 1988 Toyota Corolla for $3,000 and registered it—all with their real names. Alhazmi was even listed on page 13 of the 2000–2001 Pacific Bell White Pages: "ALHAZMI Nawaf M 6401 Mount Ada Rd. 858-279-5919."

Eventually, they moved into a room rented to them by Abdussatter Shaikh, a local businessman—who also happened to be a part-time FBI informant. "He stayed at the home of a source of ours," said an FBI counterterrorism official. "Had we known about them, we could have tasked our source. If we had been told about them, we would have followed them and said, hey, these guys are going to aviation school." There could not have been a more ideal situation for putting the pieces of the 9/11 puzzle together—had anyone been looking for them.

But as additional members of the 9/11 team made their way into the United States during the spring and summer of 2001, the chief of Alec Station was still obsessed with his unproductive covert-action schemes. That spring he decided to spend a few days in Paris, bringing another briefcase packed with a quarter of a million dollars in cash to Ahmed Shah Massoud, who was also enjoying April in Paris. Back in Afghanistan, Alec Station still had not picked up even one piece of actionable intelligence or made a single penetration of bin Laden's organization.

Other Americans, however, had—and with very little difficulty. On a number of occasions, they had even met personally with bin Laden and been told that he had multiple suicide missions planned for the United States.

Among those on the inside of Al Qaeda's al Farooq terrorist camp were eight newly arrived native-born Americans in their twenties, including John Walker Lindh. Twenty years old, Walker Lindh grew up the middle of three children in the affluent northern California community of Marin County. Pale and wiry, with a boyish face hidden beneath a jet-black beard, his father worked as a government lawyer and his mother was a health-care aide.

He was the all-American boy. "I remember playing football, basketball, soccer, catch, stuff like that," recalled his childhood friend Andrew Cleverdon. Walker Lindh was musical, took easily to languages, and was very studious. At age twelve, he saw the movie *Malcolm X,* and became fascinated by its depiction of Saudi Arabia, Mecca, and the annual ritual of the hajj. In 1997, he converted from Catholicism to Islam, began using the name Sulayman al-Lindh, and joined a mosque in Mill Valley, California. A year later, on a quest to understand his new religion, he arrived in the Yemeni capital of Sana'a and began studying Arabic, the Koran, and Islam at Al-Iman University.

In October 2000, Walker Lindh left for Pakistan and enrolled in an Islamic fundamentalist school—a madrassa—in Bannu, a desert town close to the Afghan border. Located off an alleyway, behind dented, blue-painted metal doors, the small institution had about forty students. There, Lindh spent his days sitting rigid while reciting and memorizing the Koran. Near a book cupboard, headmaster Mohammed Iltimas Khan would sip cups of tea sweetened with buffalo milk; and in the courtyard boys chanted Koranic verses.

By April 2001, after about six months at the madrassah,

Walker Lindh had become very sympathetic to the Muslim struggle around the world and decided to join the Islamic Jihad. The
next month he left for Peshawar, about eighty miles from Bannu
in Pakistan's northwest. Using the nom de guerre Abdul Hamid,
he met with recruiters for the Harkat-ul-Mujahideen (HUM)
("Movement of Holy Warriors"). One of Pakistan's largest and
most feared terrorist organizations, it is believed to be responsible
for terrorist attacks and unsuccessful assassination attempts on the
life of President Pervez Musharraf.

With little difficulty, after several days of interviews, he was
sent to a training camp in Mansehra, a small town in the mountains of northern Pakistan, about ten miles from disputed Kashmir,
where most of the fighting was taking place. Walker Lindh joined
about four hundred other volunteers, mostly Pakistani, who were
undergoing rugged training in the use of pistols, Kalashnikovs,
explosives, and guerrilla tactics.

But it was in Afghanistan, not Kashmir, that Walker Lindh
wanted to fight. "We train volunteers in the most basic skills they
need in Afghanistan," said one of Walker Lindh's instructors in
the HUM camp. "One doesn't need advanced guerrilla training to
go to Afghanistan, because the war there is not so difficult. The
enemy is in front of you and you're shooting at him. But war in
Kashmir is the most difficult. You need advanced training to fight
there. You face the enemy on all sides in Kashmir. . . . We sent him
to our Peshawar office and they arranged his trip to Afghanistan."

In late May 2001, Walker Lindh arrived in Kabul and made
his way down to the Darul-Aman district in the southwest part of
the city. Once a locus of power and prestige, by then it resembled
a moonscape of giant craters, relics of endless shelling of the city
during the battle for Kabul in the early 1990s.

Near the Kabul Museum, Walker Lindh entered the
mujahideen recruitment center and presented his letter of intro-

duction from the HUM. Then he told recruiters that he was an American and that he wanted to go to the front lines to fight. But because his Afghan-dialect language skills were deficient, he was rejected. His Arabic, however, was quite good, and he was advised to join with the Arabs of Al Qaeda and to go to one of their training camps.

Accepted into Al Qaeda, Walker Lindh was sent for several days to a bin Laden guesthouse in Kandahar. He was then put on a bus with about twenty other trainees, mostly from Saudi Arabia, and driven southwest through the flat desert plain toward the low, broken ridges of the Rod Para Mountains.

It took about an hour to cover the thirty miles to the remote town of Meivand, and then another hour was spent driving over unmarked sandy tracks that eventually disappeared altogether. Eventually the bus came to Al Qaeda's al Farooq training camp, a massive facility consisting of more than fifty buildings, including a hospital, that sat on the floor of a hidden canyon. A large cave complex was used for storage and housing, and despite its remote location, the terrorist school had a running water supply and underground electrical wiring.

At the time Walker Lindh arrived, around the first of June, five other Americans were in their third week of training and two other Americans would arrive within days. Like Walker Lindh, they were all native-born U.S. citizens in their twenties who had grown up in a middle-class suburban environment near Buffalo, New York. One was a youth counselor, another had been voted the "friendliest" in his high school class and was a soccer team co-captain, and most were married with children. Unlike Walker Lindh, they were of Yemeni ancestry.

Although Walker Lindh never met the other Americans during the seven-week course, he knew they all took part in training and instruction in the use of weapons. These included Kalashnikov rifles, 9mm handguns, M-16 automatic rifles, and rocket-propelled grenade launchers. In the evening, the recruits gathered at the camp mosque and listened to guest speakers. On various occasions, one of those would be Osama bin Laden. After the lecture, trainees would line up for a handshake and bin Laden would thank them for volunteering.

It is clear that Lindh was able to acquire information on bin Laden's future plots. At one point in June, Walker Lindh was told by one of his instructors that "bin Laden had sent forth some fifty people to carry out twenty suicide terrorist operations against the United States and Israel." Lindh told investigators that the first phase was originally planned to have "consisted of five attacks," as opposed to the four that were actually carried out. He said a "close associate" of bin Laden told him "there should have been five planes used" on September 11, "the fifth targeting the White House." The information confirmed the FBI's theory that Ramzi Binalshibh was originally scheduled to be the pilot of a fifth attack, but this was thwarted when, after four tries, he still could not get a visa to enter the country.

Lindh also said he had heard that "fifteen more operations were pending." Lindh was also approached by one of the instructors, who inquired if anyone would be interested in taking up jihad in either the United States or Israel. Lindh turned down the offer, saying he had come to Afghanistan to help the Taliban against the Northern Alliance.

Occasionally, bin Laden was accompanied by Ayman al-Zawahiri, leader of Egyptian Islamic Jihad, and during one visit to the camp he announced the merger of al-Zawahiri's terrorist group and Al Qaeda. A number of the Americans from the Buffalo area were present at the announcement. One of them, twenty-eight-year-old Sahim Alwan, had a private meeting with bin Laden, who, sitting on pillows on the floor, asked him how

American Muslims viewed suicide operations. "We don't even think about it," Alwan said. Bin Laden smiled, said Alwan.

Around the same time, bin Laden decided to put the United States and Israel on notice. On June 21, Bakr Atyani, a correspondent for the London-based Middle East Broadcasting Company, met at a predesignated spot and was placed in a car with blackened windows. He was driven to bin Laden's desert compound outside Kandahar and brought into a mud-walled room. There, sitting on low cushions, surrounded by several men in beards and turbans, was Osama bin Laden.

Keeping to his agreement with Mullah Omar not to talk to the press, bin Laden greeted Atyani with pleasantries but did not say anything substantive. Instead, he simply smiled and nodded agreement as his top aides, including al-Zawahiri, issued a chilling warning. "The coming weeks will hold important surprises that will target American and Israeli interests in the world," they told Atyani. The journalist later said, "I am 100 percent sure of this, and it was absolutely clear they had brought me there to hear this message."

To reinforce his warning, bin Laden released an Al Qaeda–made videotape showing terrorist training exercises. Opening with shots of the USS *Cole* following its attack by suicide bombers eight months earlier, the tape went on to show scenes of soldiers shooting at a movie-screen image of former President Bill Clinton. On the tape, bin Laden declares: "To all the mujahideen, your brothers in Palestine are waiting for you, it's time to penetrate America and Israel and hit them where it hurts most." Bin Laden later met privately with one of the Americans training at his camp and asked him to take several copies of the tape and deliver them to addresses in Pakistan.

In view of the constant references to a dual attack in the United States and Israel, it is likely that the original plan called for simultaneous strikes against both countries. The plot may have involved blowing up an Israeli El Al airliner as well as the main Tel Aviv train station, killing hundreds of people.

Around the same time that members of the 9/11 team were flying coast to coast on test runs, and eight Americans were training at bin Laden's al Farooq terrorist camp, British Al Qaeda member Richard Colvin Reid was looking for weaknesses in Israeli security. Born in 1973 in England's rural Kent County, Reid was the son of a British Catholic mother and a Jamaican Protestant father.

After dipping in and out of petty crime during his teenage years, he ultimately wound up in the Blunda Jail, known for its rough company. During a three-and-a-half-year sentence, in which he began associating with a number of Pakistani inmates, Reid converted to Islam and was released in 1996. "He was eager to know Islam, to learn Arabic, to be an active member of this community," said Abdul Haqq Baker, the imam of the Brixton Mosque, where Reid spent much of his time.

Another person who spent a great deal of time in the converted Victorian row house was Zacarias Moussaoui, a French student who would later be linked to the September 11 attacks. Although it is not known whether the two were acquainted at the time—Moussaoui frequented the mosque from 1996 to 1997—both also were familiar faces at the Finsbury Park Mosque in North London. The mosque was known as a haven for fundamentalists, and its leading cleric was Abu Hamza, who had lost an eye and both hands—replaced by metal hooks—during anti-Soviet fighting in Afghanistan.

A central focus of the Brixton Mosque is the American-backed Israeli oppression of the Palestinians, and it was a cause that Reid became passionate about. His view was summed up by the mosque's imam, Abdul Haqq Baker: "The U.S. and Israel are the enemy, and good Muslims must take up the battle against the enemy." In 1999, Reid went to Pakistan supposedly for educational reasons, but, U.S. officials believe, in reality it was to attend one of

Osama bin Laden's guerrilla-training schools across the border in Afghanistan.

In early July 2001, shortly after bin Laden's warning, Reid flew from Karachi, Pakistan, to Amsterdam, and on July 6 he applied for a new passport at the British consulate there. The document quickly issued to him was without any of the suspicious entry and exit stamps contained in his old passport.

On July 12, Reid went to Amsterdam's airport and boarded an Israeli El Al flight for Tel Aviv. He said that because security did not check the insides of his shoes, he thought a suicide mission might be successful if a shoe bomb was used. Once he arrived in Tel Aviv, he traveled to a number of major cities, including Jerusalem, Haifa, and Bethlehem, looking for potential bombing sites. According to FBI reports, "His trip to Jerusalem further emboldened him to attempt an act against the West when he witnessed the many checkpoints and travel restrictions on Muslims." Reid also became incensed during a visit to the Aqsa Mosque, the location of the Dome of the Rock. "It angered him to see 'Jews with guns' inside the mosque," said an FBI report.

Ten days after he arrived, he crossed the land border by bus into Egypt, spent a week in Cairo, and then flew to Istanbul, Turkey, before returning to Karachi on August 7. From there he may have slipped into Afghanistan.

Following the trip, according to federal investigators, Reid "reported to an associate in Afghanistan that the reception area of the Tel Aviv train station would be a particularly good bombing target, especially on a Saturday night, because it could be entered without being searched and contained at least a hundred people at the arrival time of any given train." This scouting trip was made at the same time that members of the 9/11 terrorist cells in the United States were also conducting test flights.

An Al Qaeda computer later found in Afghanistan contained

an identical itinerary, complete with matching dates, as part of an Al Qaeda reconnaissance mission. But it was for a person by the name of Abdul Ra'uff, which was Reid's nom de guerre from his days at the camp in Afghanistan. John Walker Lindh used the pseudonym Abdul Hamid at the camp.

Once back in Pakistan, or possibly Afghanistan, Al Qaeda associates began working on the sophisticated shoe bomb. First the soles of a pair of rugged ankle-high hiking shoes were sliced off with a knife. They were made with waffle-patterned cushioning cells to soften a person's walk and improve traction. High explosives were then packed into the cells on the inside of the soles.

Detonating cord, containing a small quantity of high explosive and designed to expand the explosion throughout the packed cells to ensure complete detonation, was then laced through the shoes and an improvised detonator was filled with a quantity of a noncommercial explosive. Next a safety fuse containing black powder was connected to the detonator and made accessible through a small hole in the inner soles of the shoes. Finally, the soles were glued and tightly resewn back onto the shoes. Because the plastic explosives needed to be detonated to explode, Reid would be able to walk in the bomb-laden shoes without a problem.

Later, the decision was made to delay the shoe-bomb attack, possibly as part of a second wave of bombings, and the target was changed from Israel to the United States. "America is the problem," Reid would later say, explaining the change. "Without America, there would be no Israel." His motivation to become a suicide bomber for Al Qaeda, he would later admit, was primarily America's support for Israel and its treatment of Muslims throughout the Middle East. When asked why he turned to violence, he said, "People tried peaceful methods for seventy years." As Al Qaeda plotted another airline bombing during the summer of 2001, Alec Station had no clue.

The Middle East Broadcasting Company report of bin Laden's warning and the accompanying video hit Tenet and Alec Station like a thunderclap. They knew that shortly before the embassy bombings he had allowed in a reporter from ABC News and offered a similar warning. Despite all the time and money they had spent on FD/Trodpint and the other covert operations, they never picked up a clue. And without ever having penetrated bin Laden's organization, they had nowhere to go.

Had they simply followed the path taken by Walker Lindh or the other Americans at that moment in bin Laden's training camp, they would have known that his plan involved multiple suicide operations within the United States and Israel. But Tenet would later claim that such a penetration was too hard for the CIA.

Within hours of the news report, and for much of the summer, CIA and NSA warning alerts began flashing as the "chatter"—phone calls and e-mails throughout the Middle East and elsewhere—filled with talk of jihad and attacks. "Unbelievable news coming in weeks," said one intercept. "Big event—there will be a very, very, very, very big uproar," said another. "There will be attacks in the near future," said a third.

Much of the chatter was no doubt generated by comments made by energized and excited people long anti-American. Others may have been part of a deliberate disinformation program to throw the U.S. intelligence community off guard. With so many alerts, no one would be able to tell which was real and which was not.

At the State Department, a "Worldwide Caution" was issued regarding the risk of terrorist attack and specifically mentioned groups linked with bin Laden and Al Qaeda; U.S. military forces throughout the Persian Gulf were placed on a heightened state of alert; a Marine Corps contingent in Jordan cut short its training session and returned to its ships; the U.S. Fifth Fleet sent its ships out to sea from ports in Bahrain.

It was clear that Alec Station and the rest of the intelligence community assumed that the attack was going to take place overseas. Nevertheless, on July 5, as the hostile chatter grew following bin Laden's warning, White House counterterrorism coordinator Richard Clarke met in the Situation Room with top domestic law-enforcement officials from the FBI, Federal Aviation Administration, the Customs Service, the Immigration and Naturalization Service, and other agencies. But without any intelligence as to when and where an attack might take place, all that was done was the issuance of several new security advisories, including an FAA warning concerning the risk of aircraft hijackings conducted to free terrorists locked in American prisons.

Five days later, on July 10, the CIA's Counterterrorism Center prepared a briefing paper and issued it to senior Bush administration officials. It apparently made no mention of Bakr Atyani's Middle East Broadcasting Company report and instead, using Atyani's exact language, tried to make it sound as though the information came from its own intelligence activities. "Based on a review of all-source reporting over the last five months," it said, "we believe that [bin Laden] will launch a significant terrorist attack against U.S. and/or Israeli interests in the coming weeks." It was old open-source news made to sound like a brilliant piece of intelligence work.

As the number of warnings and alerts continued to grow throughout the summer, Counterterrorism Center boss Cofer Black sounded the terrorism alarm. Addressing a counterterrorism conference, he seemed resigned to the fact that there was nothing anyone could do about it. By then he began realizing that this time it might actually be the big one—an attack within the United States. But he had no intelligence. None. "We are going to be struck soon," he said. "Many Americans are going to die, and it could be in the U.S." Yet no precautions were ever taken within the United States, only overseas.

On August 6, the growing concern over a possible Al Qaeda attack on U.S. soil reached the highest level. On that date, President George W. Bush read in his President's Daily Brief (PDB) a two-page CIA report entitled: "Bin Laden Determined to Strike in US." It was clear that time was getting short. The PDB warned that the FBI had intelligence indicating that terrorists might be preparing for an airline hijacking in the United States and might be targeting a building in lower Manhattan.

The report also warned that a group of bin Laden supporters was in the United States planning attacks with explosives and that bin Laden was determined to "retaliate in Washington" for the United States' 1998 missile attack on his facilities in Afghanistan. According to the PDB:

> Clandestine, foreign government, and media reports indicate Bin Laden since 1997 has wanted to conduct terrorist attacks in the US. Bin Laden implied in US television interviews in 1997 and 1998 that his followers would follow the example of World Trade Center bomber Ramzi Yousef and "bring the fighting to America."
>
> After US missile strikes on his base in Afghanistan in 1998, Bin Laden told followers he wanted to retaliate in Washington, according to a [foreign intelligence] service.
>
> An Egyptian Islamic Jihad (EIJ) operative told an [agent of a foreign intelligence] service at the same time that Bin Laden was planning to exploit the operative's access to the US to mount a terrorist strike.
>
> The millennium plotting in Canada in 1999 may have been part of Bin Laden's first serious attempt to implement a terrorist strike in the US. Convicted plotter Ahmed Ressam has told the FBI that he conceived the idea to attack Los Angeles International Airport him-

self, but that Bin Laden lieutenant Abu Zubaydah encouraged him and helped facilitate the operation. Ressam also said that in 1998 Abu Zubaydah was planning his own US attack.

Ressam says Bin Laden was aware of the Los Angeles operation.

Although Bin Laden has not succeeded, his attacks against the US Embassies in Kenya and Tanzania in 1998 demonstrate that he prepares operations years in advance and is not deterred by setbacks. Bin Laden associates surveilled our Embassies in Nairobi and Dar es Salaam as early as 1993, and some members of the Nairobi cell planning the bombings were arrested and deported in 1997.

Al-Qa'ida members—including some who are US citizens—have resided in or traveled to the US for years, and the group apparently maintains a support structure that could aid attacks. Two Al-Qa'ida members found guilty in the conspiracy to bomb our Embassies in East Africa were US citizens, and a senior EIJ member lived in California in the mid-1990s.

A clandestine source said in 1998 that a Bin Laden cell in New York was recruiting Muslim-American youth for attacks.

We have not been able to corroborate some of the more sensational threat reporting, such as that from a . . . [redacted portion] . . . service in 1998 saying that Bin Laden wanted to hijack a US aircraft to gain the release of "Blind Shaykh" 'Umar 'Abd al-Rahman and other US-held extremists.

Nevertheless, FBI information since that time indicates patterns of suspicious activity in this country consistent with preparations for hijackings or other types of attacks, including recent surveillance of federal buildings in New York.

The FBI is conducting approximately 70 full field investigations throughout the US that it considers Bin Laden-related. CIA and the FBI are investigating a call to our Embassy in the UAE in May saying that a group of Bin Laden supporters was in the US planning attacks with explosives.

But Bush had just begun a month-long vacation at his ranch in Crawford, Texas, and the report seemed to have made little impression on him. He pressed no alarm bells and the most important topic on his agenda seemed to be his golf game. The next day, he was playing golf at the Ridgewood Country Club in Waco, Texas, when he ran into a group of reporters. "No mulligans, except on the first tee," he said as the reporters laughed. "That's just to loosen up. You see, most people get to hit practice balls, but as you know, I'm walking out here, I'm fixing to go hit. Tight back, older guy—I hit the speed limit on July 6th."

In late summer, 2001, an FBI agent assigned to Alec Station decided to take a second look at the file of cables and images generated in Kuala Lumpur, Malaysia, during the month of January 2000. To his astonishment, he discovered photographs of two suspected Al Qaeda men, Almihdhar and Alhazmi, and the fact that they had been issued multi-entry visas and that they had probably already entered.

Thus on August 23, 2001, one year and eight months after NSA snatched the first piece of the puzzle from the safe house in Yemen, the names of Khalid Almihdhar and Nawaf Alhazmi were finally submitted to the State Department. But there seemed little alarm at the highest levels of government.

That same day, Bush took a trip to Crawford Elementary School, where the children peppered him with questions. During the session, he spoke of his afternoon schedule. He had a meeting with his national security advisor, Condoleezza Rice, followed by a call to the president of Argentina, lunch with the first lady, a visit with the family pets, a call to his personnel office, and a tree lesson. "We've got a horticulturist coming out from Texas A&M to help us identify the hardwood trees on our beautiful place," he said.

The next day Almihdhar and Alhazmi were placed on the TIPOFF watchlist, alerting INS in case they tried to enter the country. By then, they had already been here for nearly two years, and September 11 was only eighteen days away.

In all, the nineteen hijackers entered the United States a total of thirty-three times, through more than ten different airports, without ever being stopped or detained. "The innovation Al Qaeda introduced is 'clean operatives,'" said Doris Meissner, Immigration and Naturalization Service (INS) commissioner up until 2000, "who can go through immigration controls undetected." That is because they had no criminal records, no known terrorist connections, and had not been identified by intelligence methods for special scrutiny. She added in January 2004, "Even under the best immigration controls, most of the September 11 terrorists would still be admitted to the United States today."

On August 28, the department's Bureau of Diplomatic Security was contacted and asked to supply the FBI with visa information, but was not asked to help locate the suspected terrorists. Nor was any other information provided that might have indicated that there was a high priority or an imminent danger. It was simply routine, one of about fifty a day it normally receives. The INS therefore never bothered to search its database and simply provided the FBI with the address listed on Almihdhar's immigration form.

Like the CIA and FBI, the NSA was also desperately trying to find terrorists during the summer of 2001. By then, life had become considerably more difficult for the agency than it had been during the Cold War. Everything had changed. Instead of a stationary target, Al Qaeda was in constant motion around the world, with no uniforms or diplomatic passports to help keep track of them.

Unlike the old Soviet Union, with its fixed army, navy, and air force bases, bin Laden spent much of his time living in caves, and his training camps could easily be abandoned and reestablished somewhere else almost overnight. Where the Russians were always talking, Al Qaeda seldom communicated electronically, and when they did it was often with a phone card and a random phone, or an e-mail sent from a public library or Internet café. For their most important information, however, Al Qaeda preferred messengers over transmitters. And while NSA was overflowing with people who spoke Russian and the various Slavic dialects, those completely fluent in Hazzar, Urdu, Pashto, Uzbek, Dari, Farsi, Tagalog, and even Arabic—the languages of their new targets—were negligible. There were not many colleges teaching courses in such subjects and priming the pump.

A focal point for the terrorist warnings that summer was the National Security Agency's National Security Operations Center, which was at the very heart of the agency's worldwide eavesdropping activities. Located in Room 3E099 on the third floor of OPS 1, the windowless, war room–like command center was manned round-the-clock by five rotating teams of civilians and military personnel. Waist-high cubicles separated target areas, such as transnational and regional threats; large video screens covered the walls; and computer monitors glowed like electronic candles in the dim light. On the top of the wall, clocks ticked off time in such places as Bosnia, Moscow, and Iraq. Red lights began flashing the moment a visitor without the proper security clearances entered the room.

In addition to the spike in worrisome communications traffic, many of the messages indicated that bin Laden and Al Qaeda intended to strike against American interests in the very near future. In May, intelligence was received that supporters of bin Laden were planning to carry out a terrorist operation within the United States using high explosives. They were planning to enter, said the report, via Canada, the longest undefended border in the world.

"Throughout the summer of 2001," said NSA Director Michael V. Hayden, "we had more than thirty warnings that something was imminent." But the "chatter," as it is called, contained no details on exactly what, where, when, or how an attack might take place. Most often it consisted of intercepts of terrorists overheard talking to each other in general terms about the impact that an attack might have—hundreds killed, for example—without mentioning the precise target or date of the attack.

Some within the intelligence community were startled at the sudden increase in chatter, calling it "unprecedented." "The chatter level went way off the charts," said Porter J. Goss. In June, the intelligence community issued a terrorist threat advisory warning U.S. government agencies that there was a high probability of an imminent terrorist attack against U.S. interests by bin Laden's organization. "Sunni extremists associated with Al Qaeda are most likely to attempt spectacular attacks resulting in numerous casualties," it said.

Possible locations for the attacks included the Arabian Peninsula, Israel, and Italy. Similar reports indicated that Al Qaeda expected near-term attacks to have dramatic consequences on governments or cause major casualties. But these reports, like the dozens of others obtained during the summer, were vague in terms of timing, locations, and means.

According to a senior intelligence official who is among those charged with determining the causes of the September 11 attacks and the American intelligence community's response, the conflict between Israel and Palestine was always at the heart. "It's central," he said. "It's not the only thing, but it's the central thing."

As warning messages flashed out of NSA to the White House at the end of August, no one noticed a small group of Middle Eastern men checking into the nearby eighty-room Valencia Motel. Located in the NSA "company town" of Laurel, Maryland, it was just a few miles away from the agency's front gate. Moving into Room 343, a small living room–kitchenette suite, was Khalid Almihdhar and his team of terrorists as they began the final preparations for their attacks.

Never disguising their presence, they checked in using their real names, paid the weekly rent of $308 with a credit card, ate at a local pizza parlor, visited an adult bookstore, shopped at the Giant supermarket, washed their clothes at the Sunshine Laundry, and bought weekly memberships at Gold's Gym in nearby Greenbelt. Team member Hani Hanjour, who had a pilot's license, went up with instructors several times at the nearby Freeway Airport in Bowie, and both Mohamed Atta and Ziad Jarrah, the student from war-torn Beirut, came to visit.

As millions of intercepted communications from around the world funneled into the agency's giant satellite dishes, Almihdhar was communicating with Atta and Khalid Shaikh Mohammed back in Afghanistan at the local Kinko's, a few miles away, through simple Internet chat groups. None of the hijackers had their own computers. They also used the Internet on local computers to buy their seats on Flight 77, listing their real names, and then simply went to Baltimore-Washington International Airport to pick them up.

They used 133 different prepaid calling cards to call from various pay phones, cell phones, and landlines. For more than a year, the NSA had occasionally picked up Almihdhar's phone calls to the Al Qaeda safe house in Yemen, never knowing that his calls were coming from the United States—or possibly even the same town.

On the afternoon of September 10, they checked out of the Valencia and piled into their blue Toyota Corolla with California license plates, registered to Almihdhar. Merging into the south-bound traffic on Route 1, much of it homeward-bound NSA employees, they headed for the Marriott Residence Inn in Herndon, near Dulles International Airport. The next day, September 11, they had an early-morning plane to catch, American Airlines Flight 77, which would have as its final destination the south wall of the Pentagon.

Also on September 10, NSA's vacuum cleaner swept in two more messages culled from that day's electronic haystack. The first contained the phrase "The match begins tomorrow," and the second said "Tomorrow is zero hour." But even though they came from suspected Al Qaeda locations in Afghanistan, no one would translate them until September 12.

PART III

DECEPTION

In the onyx darkness, George W. Bush switched on the brass side-light next to his bed. The soft glow gave the President's bedroom the feel of an old but formal country inn, the kind that might be found in Williamsburg or Newport during the season. Pale-cream wallpaper overlaid with a diagonal pattern of blue and pink bunches of flowers; Early American wooden chairs decorated with whimsical, chip-carved lunettes; a scorched fireplace beneath a milky-white mantel; scrollwork made of Italian Carrera marble.

Behind heavy drapes, a pair of floor-to-ceiling windows looked through the towering southern magnolias, planted in 1830 by President Andrew Jackson in memory of his wife, Rachel, and across President's Park to the Washington Monument. Brightly lit against the early-morning light, the obelisk had the appearance of a spaceship about to rise. A spidery, antique chandelier of cut glass and gilded metal hung in the center of the room. On the floor near the bed, Barney, the family's Scottish terrier pup, lay like a small sack of coal. It was Tuesday, January 30, 2001, and George W. Bush had been president for ten days.

He strode quietly past the bedroom's walk-in closet and out to the West Sitting Hall where, four decades earlier, Jackie Kennedy answered correspondence with swirling penmanship on her father's French Empire desk. Passing through the eight-foot wooden doors into the cavernous Center Hall, he turned left into the small family elevator. Inside, columns carved in the old mahogany walls framed mirrors on three sides to reduce the feeling of claustrophobia. Hidden behind the elevator was a private circular stairway he sometimes used.

When the doors slid open at the basement level, the President crossed the Diplomatic Reception Room, encircled by Jean Zuber et Cie's pastoral scenes of North America. On the South Grounds, he stepped into the presidential limousine for the short ride to Fort Lesley J. McNair in southwest Washington for his morning jog.

Secluded away on the point of land where the Anacostia River merges into the Washington Channel, the old redbrick Army post offered privacy, security, and space—twenty-eight acres—for presidential runs. The old fort was originally constructed in 1791 to protect the nation's new capital city from invasion, but it failed when the British attacked in 1814. Washington was devastated; the White House was turned into cinders and Fort McNair was leveled. But thoughts of an attack on the nation and failed defenses were probably a long way from the mind of George W. Bush as he sprinted beside the neoclassic National War College in the cold morning air.

Back at the White House, a Secret Service agent nodded as the President, accompanied by Spot, stepped into the Oval Office. The small black and white English Springer spaniel was born in his father's White House a dozen years earlier. Just as Spot follows George W. Bush into the nation's most powerful office each morning, her mother, Millie, followed his father into the same place.

Bush crossed the Reagan-era ivory, beige, and terra-cotta rug. It had replaced Bill Clinton's royal blue oval carpet on the morning of the inauguration. From the beginning, Bush made it clear he wanted nothing left from the previous administration. Bold colors were out, peaches and cream were in. Workers lugged away the plush red and cream silk-covered sofas and replaced them with beige couches. The medallions and busts of Franklin D. Roosevelt and Harry S. Truman were returned to a dark basement storage room and the walls and tables were filled with family photos and rough-hewn artwork from Texas. On the north wall was one of the President's favorite paintings, Tom Lea's 1954 oil on canvas, "Rio Grande," borrowed from the El Paso Museum of Art. "Bush's taste in office decor is respectable Middle America," said one observer. The new style and decor "imply respectable, white, middle-aged, middle-class values. No perverts or radicals here."

Assassination, the fate of his alter ego William McKinley, was a topic that haunted George W. Bush since long before he became president. Not the possibility of his own violent death, but the assassination attempt against his father by Iraqi President Saddam Hussein shortly after the elder Bush lost the presidency.

In fact, if the intelligence George W. was given was correct, he might have lost nearly his entire immediate family, including his father, mother, wife, and two brothers. Just as he sought to avenge his father's political loss, he would one day go after the man accused of attempting to murder his father and the rest of his family. "After all," he would later comment, when speaking of the Iraqi leader at a Houston fundraiser, "this is the guy who tried to kill my dad."

The drama began in mid-April 1993 as much of the country was focused on the tense standoff in Waco, Texas, between Branch Davidian cult leader David Koresh and federal law-enforcement agents. About the same time that the FBI was flying two senior military officers to Waco to assess the situation, a few hundred miles to the south, in Houston, George H. W. Bush was quietly boarding a chartered Kuwaiti Airlines 747 for a trip to the Middle

East. A private citizen for the first time in more than a decade, the former president was being thanked and embraced by the Kuwaiti government, which hailed him as a liberating hero for forcing Iraq out of their country.

As the giant plane took off from Houston's Ellington Field on April 14, the only passengers were former President Bush, his wife Barbara, their two sons Marvin and Neil, his wife Sharon, and Laura Bush. Her husband, George W. Bush, who had always avoided foreign travel, stayed home to oversee his interest in the Texas Rangers baseball team and to make preparations for his run for the governorship. Several hours into the flight, the plane landed in Washington, D.C., to pick up former Secretary of State James Baker, former Treasury Secretary Nicholas Brady, and former White House Chief of Staff John Sununu. Once again airborne, the group toasted their reunion and looked forward to three days of victory celebrations.

But in Iraq, across the border from Kuwait, many were still bitter and hungry for revenge. According to a senior administration official during the Clinton administration, "During and immediately after the Persian Gulf war, Saddam, through his controlled media, indicated that President Bush would be held personally responsible for the war and would be hunted down and punished even after he left office." Prior to Bush's trip, the CIA began picking up some worrying indications that "the IIS [Iraqi Intelligence Service] was planning to assassinate Bush now that he had returned to private life and that the assassination attempt would occur only with authorization from Saddam Hussein." Other information the CIA received suggested "that Saddam Hussein had authorized the assassination attempt to obtain personal revenge and intimidate Kuwait and other Arab states."

On April 12, two days before the former president's departure from Texas, the Iraqi Intelligence Service (Mukhabarat) held a secret meeting in the southern Iraqi city of Basra, one hundred miles from Kuwait. Among those present was an Iraqi national named Wali al-Ghazali. According to Justice and FBI documents, the meeting was to carry out the final arrangements for the assassination of former President Bush and the Emir of Kuwait.

At the meeting, al-Ghazali was given a nondescript Toyota Land Cruiser, similar to thousands in Iraq and Kuwait—with one exception. Lining the skin of the vehicle was nearly two hundred pounds of plastic explosives connected to a detonator. It was enough to create a devastating blast with a kill radius of four football fields. Also hidden in the car were another ten bombs in the shape of cubes. They were to be planted elsewhere in commercial sections of Kuwait.

The powerful car bomb was specially constructed so that it could be detonated either manually by remote control, by an electronic timer, or by a push-pull suicide switch. Al-Ghazali was given a photograph of the building at Kuwait University where Bush was to receive an honorary degree. He was instructed to cross the border into Kuwait, then detonate the car bomb by remote control at the university close to the arriving motorcade. Finally, al-Ghazali was given a bomb-encased suicide belt and told that if all else failed he was to get as close to Bush as possible and then detonate it.

In the dark of the morning on April 13, the day before Bush was to leave Texas, al-Ghazali pressed down on the accelerator and turned his bomb-laden Land Cruiser toward Kuwait. A few hours later, he passed through the rough Kuwaiti border post of Salmi, a desert haven for smugglers and black marketers, where Iraq, Kuwait, and Saudi Arabia come together like wedges in a cake.

After he landed in Kuwait on April 15, the welcome must have seemed like salve on an open wound to George H. W. Bush, following his bitter election loss to Bill Clinton five months before.

Thousands of Kuwaitis, dressed in flowing white robes, greeted his plane like an Arctic whiteout. There were girls with baskets of flowers, whirling sword dancers, and a rose-red carpet. Dubbed "Operation Love Storm," the tribute included a perfume-scented motorcade route for the former commander-in-chief of Operation Desert Storm. As if still president, Bush and his family were feted and housed in the Emir's expansive Bayan Palace. "Literally everybody wanted to see the hero of Kuwait," said Taraq Al-Mezrem, the Kuwaiti official who handled press arrangements for the Bush trip. "We never had anything like it before."

Bush called the reception "terribly emotional and wonderfully fulfilling" and seemed to thoroughly enjoy himself as he toured oil fields once torched by Iraqi forces and greeted American troops. Then it was time for the major ceremony at Kuwait University. On the stage, Bush introduced his daughter-in-law. "Laura Bush's husband," he said, "is the owner of the Texas Rangers team. Now that I am just a citizen, I can root for any team I want."

No one on the stage or in the audience knew how close they might have come to death. Through a series of misadventures, the assassins had been caught shortly before Bush went to the university. Had the plan worked, there is little doubt that George W.'s father, mother, wife, two brothers, and one of their wives would have been killed.

According to a senior official from the Clinton administration, "From all the evidence available to it, the CIA [was] highly confident that the Iraq government at the highest levels directed its intelligence service to assassinate former President Bush." As a result, about two months later, President Bill Clinton ordered twenty-three Tomahawk guided missiles, each packed with a thousand pounds of high explosives, fired at the downtown Baghdad headquarters of Iraqi intelligence. Although most hit their target, three of the million-dollar missiles went off course and destroyed homes in the area, killing eight civilians, among them one of the country's most promising artists, Layla al-Attar.

President Bush was convinced (as was the Clinton administration) that Saddam Hussein had orchestrated the assassination attempts. But questions would quickly be raised about the quality of the intelligence and the evidence that led to the arrest and conviction of al-Ghazali and thirteen others suspected of involvement in the plot. "I tend to be extremely skeptical about this," a former CIA officer who worked in the region for years told the *Baltimore Sun*'s Scott Shane. "The Kuwaitis would not be reliable sources." And Seymour M. Hersh, in an article in *The New Yorker* magazine in November 1993, suggested that the Kuwaitis might have concocted the plot, or at least its connection to the Iraqi government. He also raised serious questions about the physical evidence that tied Iraq to the plot.

Even though al-Ghazali confessed and said his orders came from the Iraqi Intelligence Service, there was the possibility that torture or coercion was used. In a report on the trial, Amnesty International pointed out that "the defendants were not allowed access to lawyers before the trial. The right to be presumed innocent until proven guilty was seriously jeopardized by statements made by Kuwait's Public Prosecutor at a press conference on 16 May 1993. He stated that the defendants were criminals who allied with the devil and conspired with him to try to assault Kuwait's honoured guest . . . [and that] investigations proved without doubt that it was the Iraqi intelligence service which moved this rotten group of accused persons to execute the plans of the evil Iraqi regime."

That someone would order the killing of his wife, parents, and most of his immediate family—and almost succeed—would burn in George W. Bush, as it would in anyone. In private, his raw hatred for Hussein was evident. "The SOB tried to kill my dad," he snarled at one surprised visitor. "I was a warrior for George Bush," said George W. at another time. "I would run through a brick wall for my dad." Despite the magnitude of the crime, Hussein had never been brought to justice. Now, as president himself, George W. Bush would have a chance to bring justice to Hussein.

In a new administration that was determined to stay on message, the message for January 30 was support for "faith-based" education. Bush began the morning with an address to religious groups in the Indian Treaty Room of the Eisenhower Executive Office Building, and spent part of the afternoon at a nearby school addressing the virtues of his plan. Standing in front of a banner that showed black-and-white photos of caregivers and was emblazoned "Armies of Compassion," Bush said, "Real change happens street by street, heart by heart—one soul, one conscience at a time."

But soon after the "Armies of Compassion" sign was taken down, Bush turned his attention to armies of a different sort. Shortly after 3:30 P.M., the Bush national security team assembled around the polished wooden conference table of the Situation Room, down the stairs from the Oval Office. Along the walls, cherry paneling hides large television monitors and maps with small flashing lights. Just eighteen feet square, the tight conference room was once described by Nixon national security advisor Henry Kissinger as "uncomfortable, unaesthetic and essentially oppressive."

As the ten brown leather chairs around the table filled, place cards identified each of the players. On one side of Bush, who occupied the seat at the head of the table, was Vice President Dick Cheney, and on the other side sat Secretary of State Colin Powell. Opposite the President at the other end, National Security Advisor

Condoleezza Rice acted as stage manager. "Condi will run these meetings," said Bush. "I'll be seeing all of you regularly, but I want you to debate things out here and then Condi will report to me."

Then Bush addressed the sole items on the agenda for his first high-level national security meeting. The topics were not terrorism—a subject he barely mentioned during the campaign—or nervousness over China or Russia, but Israel and Iraq. From the very first moment, the Bush foreign policy would focus on three key objectives: Get rid of Saddam Hussein, end American involvement in the Israeli-Palestinian peace process, and rearrange the dominoes in the Middle East. A key to the policy shift would be the concept of "preemption."

The blueprint for the new Bush policy had actually been drawn up five years earlier by three of his top national security advisors. Soon to be appointed to senior administration positions, they were Richard Perle, Douglas Feith, and David Wurmser. Ironically, the plan was originally intended not for Bush but for another world leader, Israeli Prime Minister Benjamin Netanyahu.

At the time, the three officials were out of government and working for conservative pro-Israeli think tanks. Perle and Feith had previously served in high-level Pentagon positions during the presidency of Ronald Reagan. In a very unusual move, the former—and future—senior American officials were acting as a sort of American privy council to the new Israeli prime minister. The Perle task force to advise Netanyahu was set up by the Jerusalem-based Institute for Advanced Stategic and Political Studies, where Wurmser was working.

A key part of the plan was to get the United States to pull out of peace negotiations and simply let Israel take care of the Palestinians as it saw fit. "Israel," said the report, "can manage its own affairs. Such self-reliance will grant Israel greater freedom of action and remove a significant lever of pressure used against it in the past."

But the centerpiece of their recommendations was the removal of Saddam Hussein as the first step in remaking the Middle East into a region friendly, instead of hostile, to Israel. Their plan, "A Clean Break: A New Strategy for Securing the Realm," also signaled a radical departure from the peace-oriented policies of former Prime Minister Yitzhak Rabin, who was assassinated by a member of an extreme right-wing Israeli group.

As part of their "grand strategy," they recommended that once Iraq was conquered and Saddam Hussein overthrown, he should be replaced by a puppet leader friendly to Israel. "Whoever inherits Iraq," they wrote, "dominates the entire Levant strategically." Then they suggested that Syria would be the next country to be invaded. "Israel can shape its strategic environment," they said.

This would be done, they recommended to Netanyahu, "by reestablishing the principle of preemption" and by "rolling back" its Arab neighbors. From then on, the principle would be to strike first and expand, a dangerous and provocative change in philosophy. They recommended launching a major unprovoked regional war in the Middle East, attacking Lebanon and Syria and ousting Iraq's Saddam Hussein. Then, to gain the support of the American government and public, a phony pretext would be used as the reason for the original invasion.

The recommendation of Feith, Perle, and Wurmser was for Israel to once again invade Lebanon with air strikes. But this time, to counter potentially hostile reactions from the American government and public, they suggested using a pretext. They would claim that the purpose of the invasion was to halt "Syria's drug-money and counterfeiting infrastructure" located there. They were subjects in which Israel had virtually no interest, but they were ones, they said, "with which America can sympathize."

Another way to win American support for a preemptive war against Syria, they suggested, was by "drawing attention to its weapons of mass destruction program." The claim would be that Israel's war was really all about protecting Americans from drugs, counterfeit bills, and WMD—nuclear, chemical, and biological weapons.

It was rather extraordinary for a trio of former, and potentially future, high-ranking American government officials to become advisors to a foreign government. More unsettling still was the fact that they were recommending acts of war in which Americans could be killed, and also ways to masquerade the true purpose of the attacks from the American public.

Once inside Lebanon, Israel could let loose—to begin "engaging Hizballah, Syria, and Iran, as the principal agents of aggression in Lebanon." Then they would widen the war even further by using proxy forces—Lebanese militia fighters acting on Israel's behalf (as Ariel Sharon had done in the 1980s)—to invade Syria from Lebanon. Thus, they noted, they could invade Syria "by establishing the precedent that Syrian territory is not immune to attacks emanating from Lebanon by Israeli proxy forces."

As soon as that fighting started, they advised, Israel could begin "striking Syrian military targets in Lebanon, and should that prove insufficient, *striking at select targets in Syria proper* [emphasis in original]."

The Perle task force even supplied Netanyahu with some text for a television address, using the suggested pretext to justify the war. Years later, it would closely resemble speeches to justify their own Middle East war; Iraq would simply replace Syria and the United States would replace Israel:

Negotiations with repressive regimes like Syria's require cautious realism. One cannot sensibly assume the other side's good faith. It is dangerous for Israel to deal naively with a regime murderous of its own people, openly aggressive toward its neighbors, criminally involved with international drug traffickers and counterfeiters, and supportive of the most deadly terrorist organizations.

The task force then suggested that Israel open a second front in its expanding war, with a "focus on removing Saddam Hussein from power in Iraq—an important Israeli strategic objective in its own right—as a means of foiling Syria's regional ambitions."

For years the killing of Saddam Hussein had been among the highest, and most secret, priorities of the Israeli government. In one stroke it would pay Saddam Hussein back for launching Scud missiles against Israel, killing several people, during the Gulf War. Redrawing the map of the Middle East would also help isolate Syria, Iraq's ally and Israel's archenemy along its northern border. Thus, in the early 1990s, after the U.S.-led war in the Gulf, a small elite team of Israeli commandos was given the order to train in absolute secrecy for an assassination mission to bring down the Baghdad ruler.

The plan, code-named Bramble Bush, was to first kill a close friend of the Iraqi leader outside the country, someone from Hussein's hometown of Tikrit. Then, after learning the date and time of the funeral to be held in the town, a funeral Hussein was certain to attend, they would have time to covertly infiltrate a team of commandos into the country to carry out the assassination. The murder weapons were to be specially modified "smart" missiles that would be fired at Hussein as he stood in a crowd at the funeral.

But the plan was finally abandoned after five members of the team were accidentally killed during a dry run of the operation. Nevertheless, removing Saddam and converting Iraq from threat to ally had long been at the top of Israel's wish list.

Now Perle, Feith, and Wurmser were suggesting something far more daring—not just an assassination but a bloody war that would get rid of Saddam Hussein and also change the face of Syria and Lebanon. Perle felt their "Clean Break" recommendations were so important that he personally hand-carried the report to Netanyahu.

Wisely, Netanyahu rejected the task force's plan. But now, with the election of a receptive George W. Bush, they dusted off their preemptive war strategy and began getting ready to put it to use.

The new Bush policy was an aggressive agenda for any president, but especially for someone who had previously shown little interest in international affairs. "We're going to correct the imbalances of the previous administration on the Mideast conflict," Bush told his freshly assembled senior national security team in the Situation Room on January 30, 2001. "We're going to tilt it back toward Israel. . . . Anybody here ever met [Ariel] Sharon?" Only Colin Powell raised his hand.

Bush was going to reverse the Clinton policy, which was heavily weighted toward bringing the bloody conflict between Israel and the Palestinians to a peaceful conclusion. There would be no more U.S. interference; he would let Sharon resolve the dispute however he saw fit, with little or no regard for the situation of the Palestinians. The policy change was exactly as recommended by the Perle task force's "Clean Break" report.

"I'm not going to go by past reputations when it comes to Sharon," Bush told his newly gathered national security team. "I'm going to take him at face value. We'll work on a relationship based on how things go." Then he mentioned a trip he had taken with the Republican Jewish Coalition to Israel. "We flew over the Palestinian camps. Looked real bad down there," he said with a frown. Then he said it was time to end America's efforts in the region. "I don't see much we can do over there at this point," he said.

Colin Powell, Secretary of State for only a few days, was taken by surprise. The idea that such a complex problem, in which America had long been heavily involved, could simply be brushed away with the sweep of a hand made little sense. Fearing Israeli-led aggression, he quickly objected.

"He stressed that a pullback by the United States would unleash Sharon and the Israeli army," recalled Paul O'Neill, who had been sworn in as Secretary of the Treasury by Bush only hours before and was seated at the table. Powell told Bush, "The consequences of that could be dire, especially for the Palestinians." But Bush just shrugged. "Sometimes a show of strength by one side can really clarify things," he said. "Powell seemed startled," said O'Neill.

Over the following months, to the concern of Powell, the Bush-Sharon relationship became extremely tight. "This is the best administration for Israel since Harry Truman," said Thomas Neumann, executive director of the Jewish Institute for National Security Affairs, a pro-Israel advocacy group. In an article in *The Washington Post* titled "Bush and Sharon Nearly Identical on Mideast Policy," Robert G. Kaiser noted the dramatic shift in policy.

"For the first time," wrote Kaiser, "a U.S. administration and a Likud government in Israel are pursuing nearly identical policies. Earlier U.S. administrations, from Jimmy Carter's through Bill Clinton's, held Likud and Sharon at arm's length, distancing the United States from Likud's traditionally tough approach to the Palestinians." Using the Yiddish term for supporters of Sharon's political party and referring to the new warm relationship between Bush and Sharon, a senior U.S. government official told Kaiser, "The Likudniks are really in charge now."

With America's long struggle to bring peace to the region quickly terminated, George W. Bush could turn his attention to the prime focus of his first National Security Council meeting: ridding Iraq of Saddam Hussein. Condoleezza Rice led off the discussion. But rather than mention anything about threats to the United States or weapons of mass destruction, she noted only "that Iraq might be the key to reshaping the entire region." The words were practically lifted from the "Clean Break" report, which had the rather imperial-sounding subtitle: "A New Strategy for Securing the Realm."

Then Rice turned the meeting over to CIA Director George Tenet, who offered a grainy overhead picture of a factory that he said "might" be a plant "that produced either chemical or biological materials for weapons manufacture." There were no missiles or weapons of any kind, just some railroad tracks going to a building; truck activity; and a water tower—things that can be found in virtually any city in the United States. Nor were there any human intelligence or signals intelligence reports. "There was no confirming intelligence," Tenet said.

It was little more than a shell game. Other photos and charts showed U.S. air activity over the "no-fly zone," but Tenet offered no more intelligence. Nevertheless, in a matter of minutes the talk switched from a discussion about very speculative intelligence to which targets to begin bombing in Iraq.

By the time the meeting was over, Treasury Secretary O'Neill was convinced that "getting Hussein was now the administration's focus, that much was already clear." But, O'Neill believed, the real destabilizing factor in the Middle East was not Saddam Hussein but the Israeli-Palestinian conflict—the issue Bush had just turned his back on. Ten years after the Gulf War, said O'Neill, "Hussein seemed caged and defanged. Clearly, there were many forces destabilizing the region, most particularly the Arab-Israeli conflict itself, which we were now abandoning."

The war summit must also have seemed surreal to Colin Powell, who said little during the meeting and had long believed that Iraq no longer posed a threat to the United States. As he would tell German Foreign Minister Joschka Fischer just a few weeks later, "What we and other allies have been doing in the region, have succeeded in containing Saddam Hussein and his ambitions . . . They don't really possess the capability to attack their neighbors the way they did ten years ago . . . Containment has been a successful policy."

In addition to the "Clean Break" recommendations, David Wurmser only weeks before the NSC meeting had further elaborated on the way the United States might go about launching a preemptive war throughout the Middle East. "America's and Israel's responses must be regional, not local," he said. "Israel and the United States should adopt a coordinated strategy, to regain the initiative and reverse their region-wide strategic retreat. They should broaden the conflict to strike fatally, not merely disarm, the centers of radicalism in the region—the regimes of Damascus, Baghdad, Tripoli, Tehran, and Gaza. That would reestablish the recognition that fighting with either the United States or Israel is suicidal. Many in the Middle East will then understand the merits of being an American ally and of making peace with Israel."

In the weeks and months following the NSC meeting, Perle, Feith, and Wurmser began taking their places in the Bush administration. Perle became chairman of the reinvigorated and powerful Defense Policy Board, packing it with like-minded neoconservative super-hawks anxious for battle. Feith was appointed to the highest policy position in the Pentagon, Undersecretary of Defense for

Policy. And Wurmser moved into a top policy position in the State Department before later becoming Cheney's top Middle East expert.

With the Pentagon now under Secretary of Defense Donald Rumsfeld and his deputy, Paul Wolfowitz—both of whom had also long believed that Saddam Hussein should have been toppled during the first Gulf War—the war planners were given free rein. What was needed, however, was a pretext—perhaps a major crisis. "Crises can be opportunities," wrote Wurmser in his paper calling for an American-Israeli preemptive war throughout the Middle East.

Seeing little reason, or intelligence justification, for war at the close of the inaugural National Security Council meeting, Treasury Secretary Paul O'Neill was perplexed. "Who, exactly, was pushing this foreign policy?" he wondered to himself. And "why Saddam, why now, and why [was] this central to U.S. interests?"

CHAPTER 11

CAPITOL HILL

Israel had always been a central focus for Perle, Feith, and Wurmser. As a young staffer on Capitol Hill working for Democratic Senator Henry "Scoop" Jackson, Perle built his reputation as a pro-Israel activist. "Richard Perle and Morris Amitay [a staffer for Connecticut Democratic Senator Abraham Ribicoff] command a tiny army of Semitophiles on Capitol Hill and direct Jewish power in behalf of Jewish interests," wrote Stephen D. Isaacs, *The Washington Post*'s former New York bureau chief, in his 1975 book *Jews and American Politics.*

"The new Jewish activists," wrote Isaacs, "plunge forward on narrowly Jewish causes with scant regard for the 'old liberalism.' When once upon a time all Jews in positions of power would have concentrated their attentions on the naming of a new Supreme Court justice for the United States, one of the most important of the new Jewish activists was more concerned with arms for Israel."

Isaacs was referring to Perle, who told him, "I had all three of my telephone lines tied up, juggling calls, working on a Jackson amendment on aid to Israel. The telephone rang, and it was the Washington representative of one of the Jewish organizations. I figured he was calling in with a report on the response of some senator to our [aid to Israel] lobbying efforts. He wanted to talk about [William H.] Rehnquist [nominated to the Supreme Court]. I said, 'Jesus Christ, don't you know we're in the middle of a crisis?' And he said, 'Well, I also wanted to talk about that,' and I said, 'Well, what do you know?' And the other crisis he had in mind was Bangladesh."

Among Jackson's greatest supporters were members of the neoconservative movement. Predominantly Jewish, they were turned off by the counterculture movements of the 1960s, disillusioned with the Great Society, offended by the "anti-American" sentiments of the left, and fearful of the expansionist aims of the United Nations. At the core of the movement was a small but prolific band of sedentary intellectuals and think tank warriors, including Norman Podhoretz and Irving Kristol. In limited-circulation journals, they wrote longingly of a muscular expansion of American power and influence around the world, a rollback of communism and an end to détente with the Soviets, and the creation of a seamless bond between Israel's interests and America's military and foreign policy.

"I think the term [neoconservative] has something to do with the sense that those of us who are now called neoconservatives were at one time liberals," said Perle. "And I think that's a fair description, and I suppose all of us were liberal at one time. I was liberal in high school and a little bit into college. But reality and rigor are important tonics, and if you got into the world of international affairs and you looked with some rigor at what was going on in the world, it was really hard to be liberal and naive."

For Jackson, Perle was far more than a simple staffer, running around putting briefing books together or drafting constituent correspondence. One newspaper called him "the quintessential Washington operator," because of his ability to manipulate the news and conventional opinions. He was also known as "a great collector of sensitive information," something that occasionally raises security questions. Nevertheless, the two became a power team. "Jackson and Perle have established themselves as active players in the policy-making process, a status rarely achieved on Capitol Hill," said reporter Robert G. Kaiser in *The Washington Post* in 1977. Others found Perle arrogant, difficult to deal with, and single-minded.

Aided by Perle, Jackson quickly became Israel's number-one man in the Congress, constantly pushing for more and more money with fewer restrictions. In fiscal year 1970, Israel received military credits from the United States worth $30 million. But thanks to a Jackson amendment, the next year the amount sky-rocketed to $545 million. By 1974, it had reached an extraordinary $2.2 billion, more than seventy times what it had been just four years earlier. "We have a hero, and his name is Henry Jackson," gushed Mitchell Wohlberg, a Washington, D.C., rabbi. "More than any other leader on the American political scene, Senator Henry Jackson has been there in our times of trouble and pain."

Beyond Israel, the other major focus of Perle and Jackson was weapons of mass destruction—Soviet ballistic missiles. Jackson was the leading advocate of an antiballistic missile system that would be able to knock down incoming nuclear warheads. It was one of the most controversial and contentious issues of the day. Opponents argued that building such a system would be the opening shot in a new arms race. Not only would the United States have to compete with the Soviet Union on building more and bigger missiles, it would now have to also compete in building more and bigger anti-missile systems. But Jackson and his supporters argued that the Soviets had already deployed such a system around Moscow and America was falling behind.

One of his principal outside consultants helping to prepare legislation to push such a system through Congress was a University of Chicago mathematician who specialized in strategic warfare planning, Albert J. Wohlstetter. Among a small cadre of intellectual hawks, their weapons of choice were slide rules and slim pieces of squeaky chalk. Wars were fought not on battlefields but on blackboards covered with advanced mathematical formulas, like hieroglyphics on an ancient Egyptian tomb. Their language was Pentagonese, cluttered with acronyms and infused with the arcane euphemisms of mass death—kill ratios, throw weight, megatons. And they wore uniforms of tweed and corduroy as they shuttled from think tank to faculty lounge to corporate boardroom.

Born in New York in 1913, Wohlstetter went on to serve as a consultant for the War Production Board during World War II and later joined RAND. At RAND, Wohlstetter's work helped lead to the Cold War concept of "fail-safe." The idea was that bombers armed with nuclear weapons would be launched immediately toward Russia at the first indication of an attack, but forbidden from dropping their loads until they received an encrypted confirmation message from the President. He also helped develop the theory of "second-strike deterrence," where some missiles would be "hardened"—buried in the ground—to be able to survive a first strike in order to retaliate with a second strike. "To deter an attack means being able to strike back in spite of it," he wrote in his 1958 paper "The Delicate Balance of Terror."

By the 1960s, Wohlstetter was becoming known as the intellectual godfather of Cold War hawks. He strongly opposed any form of détente or disarmament, and instead developed strategies not for passive deterrence but for active fighting and winning both conventional and nuclear wars. These ideas included building smarter bombs and taking preemptive action—attacking first with surgical, pinpoint strikes against key military targets.

Wohlstetter also weighed in firmly in favor of American expansionism. "He was a firm believer in a global order," noted writer Khurram Husain, "underwritten by America's might and secured through the export of American secular and humanistic values to the rest of the world. In his view America could not be a great power without a worldwide web of interests."

In 1962, Wohlstetter left RAND but remained a part-time consultant and, after brief stints at Berkeley and UCLA, joined the University of Chicago's Political Science Department in 1964. There he continued his nuclear weapons research as well as his opposition to détente and disarmament. Slowly, he began developing a cultlike following among some of his students and others within the right-wing establishment. In Scoop Jackson, Wohlstetter found a soul mate. Throughout his career, Jackson considered initiatives to bring the arms race under control to be "appeasement," and constantly fought against them.

In 1969, he and Wohlstetter began fighting their biggest political battle as they tried to win passage of a bill that would fund development of an anti-ballistic missile system (ABM). The ABM debate was scheduled for the summer of 1969, with Jackson leading the battle on behalf of the Nixon administration and Wohlstetter acting as his principal theoretician. With enormous stakes riding on the outcome of the vote, Wohlstetter needed all the help he could get and decided to call two students he thought might be able to help out. Their names were Richard Perle and Paul Wolfowitz.

"I, at the time, was a graduate student of Albert Wohlstetter at the University of Chicago," recalled Wolfowitz, who was twenty-four at the time. "It was during the ABM debate in 1969 . . . And on the morning of the debate, lucky for me, Albert was in California, so I had the good fortune to be the one to take our charts to Senator Jackson all by myself and brief him. I had never personally met a senator in my life and I probably would've been awestruck at that time by even the most insignificant member of that great body. And there I was, face-to-face with one of the titans."

Richard Perle, then twenty-five years old, also recalled the first time all four—Perle, Wolfowitz, Jackson, and Wohlstetter—came together. "Albert Wohlstetter phoned me one day. I was still a graduate student at Princeton doing some research in Cambridge, Massachusetts, and he said, 'Could you come to Washington for a few days and interview some people and draft a report on the current debate shaping up in the Senate over ballistic missile defense,' which was a hot issue in the 1969 debate. This was in 1969. And he said, I've asked somebody else to do this too, and maybe the two of you could work together. The someone else was Paul Wolfowitz."

Perle had first met Wohlstetter while in high school in California. "Albert's daughter, Joan, was a classmate at Hollywood High School," he recalled. "We sat next to each other in Spanish class. She passed, I didn't, but she invited me over for a swim and her dad was there. We got into a conversation about strategy, a subject I really didn't know much about. Albert gave me an article to read—that was typical of Albert. Sitting there at the swimming pool, I read the article, which was a brilliant piece of exposition, and obviously so. We started talking about it . . . it was called the 'Delicate Balance of Terror.' It became quite a famous article in foreign affairs, and it was a way of looking at the strategic relationship between the United States and the Soviet Union and the product of the serious piece of research that he had done as the director of the Research Council at the RAND Corporation in Santa Monica."

Following Hollywood High, Perle went on to graduate from the University of Southern California and then Princeton with a master's degree in politics in 1967, before beginning studies for his Ph.D.

To Wolfowitz, Wohlstetter registered a blank: "One of my professors at Cornell said, 'And by the way there's this guy Albert Wohlstetter who's just moving to [University of] Chicago from

RAND, and you and he would probably get along very well.' I'd never heard of the man, if that tells you something about how unconnected I was to the field. This was 1965. I arrive in Chicago. The first student/faculty tea I'm introduced to Wohlstetter, and he said, 'Oh, are you related to Jack Wolfowitz?' I said, as a matter of fact that's my father. He said, I studied mathematics with him and Abraham Wald at Columbia."

The ensuing ABM debate become one of the most dramatic events in the history of the Senate. "I was told later that Scoop literally 'mopped the floor' with Senator Symington's chart," said Wolfowitz, who like Perle would become a protégé of both Wohlstetter and Jackson. The vote was 51 to 50 in favor of the missile system, with Vice President Spiro T. Agnew breaking the tie.

The Cold War between the United States and Russia would eventually end and Albert Wohlstetter and Scoop Jackson would quietly disappear from the scene. But their protégés, Paul Wolfowitz and Richard Perle, would become their intellectual disciples.

After his stint in Washington with Jackson and the ABM treaty, Wolfowitz returned to the University of Chicago to continue his doctoral studies and then accepted a teaching position at Yale. While there, he began hammering away on his dissertation. His topic was nuclear proliferation in the Middle East, and he argued that the United States must do whatever it can to prevent even the hint of weapons of mass destruction from being introduced into the area.

Wolfowitz also argued that American security was dependent not just on defending traditional allies from Communist incursion. Equally important, he said, was going on the offense when necessary to protect America's vital economic interests, such as oil. They were the thoughts and words of a geopolitical activist, eager to use force and preemption to advance American power, words that must have greatly pleased his dissertation advisor, Albert Wohlstetter.

In February 1980, Richard Perle quit Jackson's office and joined Abington Corporation, an international consulting firm, to earn substantially more than his Senate staffer pay. His chief client was an Israeli arms company called Soltam Ltd. For much of his Senate career, he and his wife, Leslie Barr, who worked at the Department of Energy and later at Commerce, lived in a town house on Capitol Hill. The extra income allowed Perle to buy an aging, shingle-style, Postmodern three-bedroom bungalow in the fashionable Washington, D.C., neighborhood of Chevy Chase.

But his days in the private sector ended with Reagan's election. Nicknamed "The Prince of Darkness," Perle became the Pentagon's new Assistant Secretary of Defense for International Security Policy, a job that dealt with nuclear weapons issues worldwide, among other things.

In turn, he nominated a young lawyer named Douglas Jay Feith as his Deputy Assistant Secretary. It was an extraordinary appointment for someone just six years out of law school with only two years of experience in defense issues. But he was seen by many as Perle's protégé.

After receiving his bachelor's degree from Harvard, Doug Feith had gone on to Georgetown Law. While there he joined up with Joseph Churba, a longtime friend and associate of Rabbi Meir Kahane, whose violent Jewish Defense League was declared a terrorist organization in both the United States and Israel. Feith and Churba coauthored an op-ed piece for *The Washington Post* that praised the tough, anti-Palestinian policies of newly elected Prime Minister Menachem Begin.

In 1981, he joined the Reagan administration's National Security Council as a Middle East expert, but he lasted only about a year. Nevertheless, Richard Perle took him under his wing as his special assistant in 1982, before skyrocketing him to the Deputy Assistant Secretary position in 1984.

At the close of the Reagan years, many of the neocons, including Perle and Feith, left government, having received a chilly reception from George Bush, Sr., when he became president. Soon after leaving the Pentagon and into the 1990s, Feith began turning more and more extreme in his pro-Israel and anti-Arab and -Palestinian views. He churned out constant diatribes in Israeli newspapers complaining about the Israeli government's policy on settlements (there should be more) or the Oslo peace process (it should end—he was even against the Camp David peace accords), or the Occupied Territories (they belong to Israel), or the Palestinians (they belong in Jordan), or Iraq (there should be regime change). Rashid Khalidi, director of Columbia University's Middle East Institute, called Feith's published opinions "quite extreme."

Beyond angry newspaper opinions, Feith denounced President George H. W. Bush for his "mistreatment of Israel" and even organized a committee to fight him—the Committee on U.S. Interests in the Middle East—complete with a full-page ad in *The New York Times*. He advised the Israeli government to pressure the White House to depose Saddam Hussein; led a Senate effort to pressure the Clinton administration to move the U.S. embassy from Tel Aviv to Jerusalem; became the head of a right-wing pro-Israel special-interest group, The Center for Security Policy; became a founding member of One Jerusalem, an Israeli organization determined to prevent any compromise with the Palestinians over the fate of any part of Jerusalem; and became the vice chairman of the advisory board of the Jewish Institute for National Security Affairs, a pro-Israel, defense-related special-interest group.

During these years, Feith was also putting together a legal practice. He teamed up with L. Marc Zell, a fellow associate from his days at the Washington law firm of Fried, Frank, Harris, Shriver and Kampelman. Like Feith, Zell had turned into a zealot on the issue of Jewish settlements in the Occupied Territories. In the late 1980s, he became an orthodox Jew and decided to join the right-wing Israeli settler movement. U.S. policy has always been, and continues to be, adamantly opposed to Israeli settlements.

"Feith is a partner of Zell, and Zell is a leading settler," said Rashid Khalidi, Columbia University's Middle East Institute director. "He lives in a settlement; he is an advocate of expansion of Israeli settlements in the Occupied Territories. He and Feith are ardent, committed, extremist Likud supporters—that is to say, they support a policy of Israel's expansion, they support a policy of crushing the Palestinians, they support the expansion of settlements."

"I can bear personal witness to Feith's adamancy on the issue [of settlements]," said Larry Cohler-Esses. "As a reporter during the late 1980s and early 1990s for *Washington Jewish Week*—whose attorney he was—I debated him several times over dinner on the very notion of Palestinian peoplehood."

A few months after the Palestinian uprising known as the Intifada began, in December 1987, Feith's partner, Zell, flew to Israel to lend his support to the settlers. He had received his welcoming indoctrination into the settler movement the year before in Israel by Gush Emunim ("bloc of the faithful"), the point on the spear for the extreme-right-wing Israeli settlement group.

Just a few years earlier, Gush Emunim devised a plot to blow up the Temple Mount—the Dome of the Rock—the third-holiest site in Islam. Their goal was to start a cataclysmic war between Jews and Muslims to hasten the coming of the Messiah and also to scuttle the Camp David accord, which called for the return of land under Israeli control to the Palestinians. The act was never carried out, only because in the end the plotters could not get rabbinical backing.

Soon after moving into the right-wing settlement of Alon Shvut, about twenty minutes south of Jerusalem, Zell and Feith opened their Jerusalem office and the two began soliciting Israeli-American business. While Marc Zell remained on the front lines of the settlement movement in Israel, Feith, the managing partner of the firm, was the settler's man in Washington. In July he joined with Perle, David Wurmser, and Wurmser's Israeli-born wife, Meryav, to develop the foreign-policy position paper "Clean Break" for Israeli Prime Minister Benjamin Netanyahu.

Soon after helping to write the report, David Wurmser became the director of the Middle East Studies Program at the American Enterprise Institute, where Perle also worked. His position was funded by Irving Moscowitz, a wealthy American who was a key financial backer of Jewish settlements in Israel's Occupied Territories. Meryav Wurmser founded an organization, Memri, that translates Arabic press reports that highlight negative views of the West.

A few months after they finished the "Clean Break" proposal, Feith's Center for Security Policy issued a paper titled "Israeli Settlements: Legitimate, Democratically Mandated, Vital to Israel's Security and, Therefore, in U.S. Interest." The document claimed, "Israel is fully entitled to expand existing settlements or build new ones in the disputed territories."

By 1997, Feith was going so far as to call for Israel to repudiate the Oslo peace accords and launch a full-scale war against the Palestinians in the Occupied Territories. "Repudiate Oslo," he wrote in a paper titled "A Strategy for Israel." Such a violent move, he acknowledged, would lead to a "massive upheaval in the territories, and the prospect of confrontation with 50,000 or so PA [Palestinian Authority] policemen with automatic weapons." Then he added coldly, "Any strategy for repudiating Oslo must therefore take into account the price in blood Israel would have to pay."

Following Feith's call for a war against the occupied Palestinians, Perle, Wolfowitz, Rumsfeld, and a small group of neocons signed a letter to President Clinton pleading with him to make the ouster of Saddam Hussein the "aim of American foreign policy" and to use military force. If he agreed, they wrote, they would "offer our full support in this difficult but necessary endeavor." Clinton, however, made only a token effort, lobbing cruise missiles into Iraq, and refused to involve United States forces in a ground war to oust Hussein.

But Perle and Wolfowitz soon found a sympathetic ear with George W. Bush, and at the start of his candidacy he named them as top advisors to his foreign policy team, then being coordinated by Condoleezza Rice.

Thus, it was little wonder that during his first National Security Council meeting, when the only topics on the agenda were Israel and Iraq, Treasury Secretary Paul O'Neill thought that all the issues had already been decided. "The meeting had seemed scripted," he thought. "Rumsfeld had said little, Cheney nothing at all, though both men had long entertained the idea of overthrowing Saddam. . . . Was a multipronged assault on Saddam Hussein really a priority in early 2001?" What most concerned him was that the entire thrust of the meeting had been only about the "hows" of the attack. But it was the "whys" that still confused him.

CHAPTER 12

It was predawn when Secretary of Defense Donald Rumsfeld emerged from his $3,350,000 three-story brick house in the Kalorama section of Washington and stepped into the back of his armored SUV. Named for the Greek word for "beautiful view," Kalorama is a small residential neighborhood that sits on a low hill near the edge of the city's gray-columned Federal heart. It is a land of faux-Tudor mansions and staid embassies with colorful flags and shiny gold plaques. Black Lincolns, many with red, white, and blue diplomatic tags, prowl the neighborhood like silent panthers, and residents such as California Senator Dianne Feinstein and former Treasury Secretary Lloyd Bentsen line the pages of the "green book," Washington's social register.

As his convoy snaked its way through downtown Washington on the morning of September 11, 2001, Rumsfeld, with slicked-down hair and wire-rimmed bifocals, and dressed in his trademark tab-collar shirt and gray suit, thumbed through a copy of the *Early Bird,* a compilation of that morning's most important national and international press clippings. He was checking for coverage of his talk to the Pentagon workforce the previous day. In that speech, Rumsfeld had declared war against the country's most serious enemy.

"The topic today," he said, "is an adversary that poses a threat, a serious threat, to the security of the United States of America. This adversary is one of the world's last bastions of central planning. It governs by dictating five-year plans. From a single capital, it attempts to impose its demands across time zones, continents, oceans and beyond. With brutal consistency, it stifles free thought and crushes new ideas. It disrupts the defense of the United States and places the lives of men and women in uniform at risk."

The enemy was not Saddam Hussein or Osama bin Laden. It was, said Rumsfeld, "the Pentagon bureaucracy. Not the people, but the processes. Not the civilians, but the systems. Not the men and women in uniform, but the uniformity of thought and action that we too often impose on them."

In the early morning of September 11, 2001, the greatest threat facing the nation, according to Rumsfeld, was Pentagon red tape. But within hours he would be gunning for a different enemy, a target of opportunity located in Baghdad.

Shortly after the devastating explosion caused when American Airlines Flight 77 slammed into the Pentagon, Rumsfeld and other officials evacuated to the bombproof War Room—the National Military Command Center—in the Pentagon's basement. Then, at five minutes past noon, CIA Director George Tenet passed him the information intercepted by NSA at 9:53 that morning, only minutes after the crash.

A bin Laden operative in Afghanistan, Tenet related, had telephoned a number in the former Soviet republic of Georgia and asked if he had "heard good news." At the same time, he had indicated that at least one more target was yet to be hit. Ten minutes later, United Flight 93 crashed in Pennsylvania en route to a fourth target in Washington.

Yet despite the implications that a member of bin Laden's team appeared to have foreknowledge of one of the attacks,

Rumsfeld dismissed the intelligence as "vague," that it "might not mean something," and there was "no good basis for hanging hat." The clear evidence aside, it was not the Afghan cave dweller that Rumsfeld was interested in.

At 2:40 that afternoon, an aide to the Defense Secretary jotted notes of Rumsfeld's conversations. Written deep in the War Room, the notes describe the Pentagon chief as wanting "best info fast; judge whether good enough hit S.H. [Saddam Hussein] at same time. Not only U.B.L. [Osama bin Laden]." "Go massive," he noted. "Sweep it all up. Things related, and not."

From the notes it was clear that the attacks would be used as a pretext for war against Saddam Hussein. Despite the fact that there was absolutely no evidence implicating the Iraqi leader, Rumsfeld wanted to "hit S.H. at same time." The idea was to "sweep" him up, whether "related" to 9/11 or "not." Wolfowitz had the same idea and quickly began talking up an Iraqi connection in conference calls with other officials, including Cheney.

Twelve hours later, around two o'clock on the morning of September 12, Counterterrorism Coordinator Richard Clarke headed back to the White House for a series of meetings. He had just left the building a little more than an hour before in order to take a shower and put on some clean clothes. "I expected to go back to a round of meetings examining what the next attacks should be," he recalled, "what our vulnerabilities were, what we could do about them in the short term." Clarke continued:

> Instead, I walked into a series of discussions about Iraq. At first I was incredulous that we were talking about something other than getting Al Qaeda. Then I realized with almost a sharp physical pain that Rumsfeld and Wolfowitz were going to try to take advantage of this national tragedy to promote their

agenda about Iraq. Since the beginning of the administration, indeed well before, they had been pressing for a
war with Iraq. My friends in the Pentagon had been
telling me that the word was we would be invading Iraq
sometime in 2002. On the morning of the 12th DOD's
focus was already beginning to shift from Al Qaeda.

By the afternoon on Wednesday, Secretary
Rumsfeld was talking about broadening the objectives
of our response and "getting Iraq" . . . I vented. "Having
been attacked by Al Qaeda, for us now to go bombing
Iraq in response would be like our invading Mexico after
the Japanese attacked us at Pearl Harbor." . . . Later in
the day, Secretary Rumsfeld complained that there were
no decent targets for bombing in Afghanistan and that
we should consider bombing Iraq, which, he said, had
better targets. At first I thought Rumsfeld was joking.
But he was serious and the President did not reject out
of hand the idea of attacking Iraq. Instead, he noted
that what we needed to do with Iraq was to change the
government, not just hit it with more cruise missiles, as
Rumsfeld had implied.

A few days later at Camp David, Wolfowitz would tell Bush that
the terrorist attacks created an opportunity to strike Iraq. Nearly four
years before, Wolfowitz had written an article for the conservative
Weekly Standard magazine in which he argued that the U.S. should
go after Saddam Hussein. "We will have to confront him sooner or
later—and sooner would be better," he wrote in the December 1994
issue of the magazine, which had the words "Saddam Must Go: A
How-to Guide" boldly stretched across its cover. Wolfowitz's coauthor on the article was Zalmay M. Khalilzad, whom George W.
Bush would name as his special envoy to Iraqi opposition groups.

A month after the article, both of them, together with Donald Rumsfeld, Richard Perle, James Woolsey, and several other neo-conservatives, would sign a letter urging President Bill Clinton to begin "implementing a strategy for removing Saddam's regime from power." Referring to the letter, *The Washington Post*'s Glenn Kessler wrote: "Many advocates of action were skeptical that Hussein could be contained indefinitely, even by repeated weapons inspections, and they viewed his control of Iraq—and his possible acquisition of weapons of mass destruction—as inherently destabi-lizing in the region. Many were also strong supporters of Israel, and they saw ousting Hussein as key to changing the political dynamic of the entire Middle East."

On September 17, shortly after the group returned from Camp David and just six days after the attacks, Bush signed a Top Secret two-and-a-half-page order that laid out his plan for going to war in Afghanistan. At the same time, the document directed the Pentagon to begin planning military options for an invasion of Iraq.

Two days later, Richard Perle convened a meeting of his Defense Policy Board and among those present was Defense chief Rumsfeld. Saddam Hussein was the central topic. Invited as a guest of Perle was Ahmed Chalabi, the head of the Iraqi National Congress, an anti–Saddam Hussein group. It was a significant move. For years, Chalabi had been the man Perle and Wolfowitz had wanted to run Iraq once they got rid of Saddam Hussein.

Within hours of the attacks, an effort was begun to quickly create a believable case showing Hussein's ties to the attacks, Al Qaeda and bin Laden. One of the first people Rumsfeld, Wolfowitz, Feith, and Perle turned to was David Wurmser. He was charged with putting together a very secret intelligence unit that would bypass the normal channels and report directly to Feith.

Like Feith, Wurmser was a Perle protégé and an original

member of Perle's task force that advised Israeli Prime Minister Netanyahu and recommended a war to oust Saddam Hussein. Just weeks before Bush took office, recall, Wurmser was pushing an expanded version of the plan, one calling for an all-out American-Israeli preemptive war in the Middle East. He recommended that the two countries join forces to "strike fatally, not merely disarm, the centers of radicalism in the region—the regimes of Damascus, Baghdad, Tripoli, Tehran, and Gaza."

In his paper, Wurmser also suggested that "crises can be opportunities," an idea that seemed to coincide with Rumsfeld's plan to use the day's attacks as an excuse to invade Iraq. Thus Feith quickly got in touch with his old friend and asked him to set up a small and very secret intelligence unit in his office. By then, as the Undersecretary of Defense for Policy, Feith was the third-ranking official in the Pentagon after Deputy Secretary Paul Wolfowitz.

Among those told of the plan was conservative journalist Arnaud de Borchgrave, the editor-at-large of the equally conservative *Washington Times*. "When this writer first heard from prominent neoconservatives in April 2002 that war was no longer a question of 'if' but 'when,' the *casus belli* had little to do with WMDs," he said. "The Bush administration, they explained, starkly and simply, had decided to redraw the geopolitical map of the Middle East. The Bush Doctrine of preemption had become the vehicle for driving axis-of-evil practitioners out of power."

While every effort was made to tie Saddam Hussein to 9/11, Perle and a number of leading neoconservatives sent a letter to Bush less than a week after the attacks arguing that he immediately focus on a war with Iraq regardless of whether he can show a connection. "Dear Mr. President," it said. "It may be that the Iraqi government provided assistance in some form to the recent attack on the United States. But even if evidence does not link Iraq directly to the attack, any strategy aiming at the eradication of terrorism and its sponsors must include a determined effort to remove Saddam Hussein from power in Iraq."

Also joining Wurmser's secret intelligence unit was another neocon and Perle protégé, F. Michael Maloof, a longtime Pentagon civilian who had worked for Perle during the Reagan years. But within months of his joining the unit, he would be stripped of his Top Secret security clearance after an FBI probe linked him to a Lebanese-American businessman, Imad El Haje, under federal investigation for arms trafficking. Maloof's clearance had originally been suspended during the Clinton years, but in an unusual move, Feith personally fought to get it restored soon after Bush took office.

Given the cover name Policy Counterterrorism Evaluation Group, Wurmser's unit was little more than a pro-war propaganda cell. It was designed to produce evidence to support the pretexts for attacking Iraq. This involved going through old and new intelligence collected by the various agencies and finding loose ties between Saddam Hussein and Al Qaeda. A similar project was a "sociometric diagram" of links between Al Qaeda and other fundamentalist Islamic terrorist organizations, such as Hezbollah and Islamic Jihad, and secular states such as Iraq.

But the primary purpose of the unit was to come up with some basis to counter the CIA, whose analysts had consistently found no credible links between Al Qaeda and Hussein. The CIA's analysis, said Perle with his trademark arrogance, "isn't worth the paper it's written on."

"Let me be blunt about this," he said. "The level of competence on past performance of the Central Intelligence Agency in this area is appalling. They are defensive—and I think quite destructive—in suggesting that anybody who didn't stand up and salute and accept that the CIA was the source of all wisdom on this is somehow engaged in nefarious activity. [That's] really outrageous." Speaking of Wurmser's intelligence unit, Perle said,

"Within a very short period of time, they began to find links that nobody else had previously understood or recorded in a useful way."

But instead of an honest, unbiased review of intelligence such as the CIA was charged with producing, the Wurmser intelligence unit would pluck selective bits and pieces of thread from a giant ball of yarn and weave them together into a frightening tapestry.

Until he retired in October 2002, Gregory Thielmann was in charge of military assessments within the State Department's Bureau of Intelligence and Research. He said the makeup of the intelligence unit was a giveaway, indicating that they had no interest in true analysis. Like Feith, Wurmser spent most of his career as a pro-Israeli activist and had no background at all in intelligence. "Are they missile experts?" Thielmann asked. "Nuclear engineers? There's no logical explanation for the office's creation except that they [the Bush administration] wanted people to find evidence to support their answers about war."

Retired Air Force Lt. Col. Karen Kwiatkowski agrees. "It wasn't intelligence, it was propaganda," she said. "They'd take a little bit of intelligence, cherry-pick it, make it sound much more exciting, usually by taking it out of context, often by juxtaposition of two pieces of information that don't belong together."

The forty-three-year-old former Pentagon official worked in the office that housed the intelligence unit at the time, Feith's Near East South Asia (NESA) division. By the spring of 2002, Kwiatkowski had been in the military for nearly twenty years, published two books, earned a master's degree from Harvard, and had recently passed her comprehensive doctoral exams at Catholic University. In May of that year, when she was transferred to NESA from the Sub-Saharan Africa desk, the lifelong conservative found the atmosphere almost surreal.

"I was chatting with my new office mate, a career civil servant working the Egypt desk," she recalled. "As the conversation moved into Middle East news and politics, she mentioned that if I wanted to be successful here, I shouldn't say anything positive about the Palestinians. In nineteen years of military service, I had never heard such a politically laden warning." Kwiatkowski also discovered that most of the longtime career Pentagon civilians in the office, and some of the military, were quickly being transferred out to make room for new appointments, mostly from neoconservative and pro-Israel think tanks.

"I came to share with many NESA colleagues a kind of unease, a sense that something was awry," she said. "What seemed out of place was the strong and open pro-Israel and anti-Arab orientation in an ostensibly apolitical policy-generation staff within the Pentagon. There was a sense that politics like these might play better at the State Department or the National Security Council, not the Pentagon, where we considered ourselves objective and hard-boiled."

Beyond the cherry-picked items from the various intelligence reports, a key source of intelligence for Perle, Feith, and Wolfowitz came from the Iraqi National Congress. Exiled in London with a guerrilla army based in northern Iraq, an area protected for many years by a U.S.-enforced no-fly zone, the group was led by Ahmed Chalabi.

A fellow neoconservative, Chalabi was born in Iraq, received his Ph.D. in math from the University of Chicago—Paul Wolfowitz's alma mater—and had even studied under Albert Wohlstetter. Raised in a Shiite Muslim family with close ties to the monarchy, he fled Iraq when he was fourteen. After receiving degrees from both Chicago and MIT, he went to Jordan and a career in banking, but ended up with an absentee conviction for embezzlement and a twenty-two-year sentence.

Balding and with a slight paunch, an aristocratic manner, and a passion for finely tailored conservative suits, Chalabi fit in well with the neocons. They were his main base of support in the United States, where he spent much of his time. His relationship with Wolfowitz and Perle went back more than a decade. In 1985, Wohlstetter introduced Chalabi to Perle, then at the Pentagon, and later to Wolfowitz. The three have been close ever since.

Throughout much of the 1990s, Perle and the CIA were at war with each other over Chalabi and the issue of how best to get rid of Saddam Hussein. Perle favored a popular insurrection that would eventually install his man as president of Iraq. But the CIA and others had little trust in Chalabi or the idea of an internal uprising, believing it would be quickly crushed and lead to a sort of desert version of Kennedy's Bay of Pigs fiasco. "The CIA doesn't like him," said Perle, "because they don't control him, and they only like people they control."

Among those opposed was retired Marine General Anthony Zinni, the former commander of the U.S. Central Command, responsible for U.S. forces in the Middle East. Calling Chalabi and his associates "silk-suited, Rolex-wearing guys in London," he said the price of American support for the INC would be high. "The Bay of Pigs could turn into the Bay of Goats," he said. And a 1999 article in *Foreign Affairs*, titled "The Rollback Fantasy," said the INC plan was "militarily ludicrous and would almost certainly end in either direct American intervention or a massive bloodbath."

Instead, the CIA was in favor of a palace coup, led by a group of Army generals and the Iraqi National Accord, a rival exile organization. Eventually, the coup plot was discovered and a number of generals were arrested and executed. Chalabi says he warned the CIA in advance. But the CIA never trusted the intelligence Chalabi was providing, believing it was largely self-serving and unverifiable, certainly not worth the $326,000 a month they were supplying to his INC. As a result, they dropped him in the mid-1990s and have never since regretted it.

For Perle and the neoconservatives, their dream has always been to install Chalabi as president of Iraq. He was especially appealing as a future leader of Iraq because of his friendly relationship with Israel, as someone who would eventually grant diplomatic recognition of the state. "A senior administration official, who requested anonymity," noted Knight-Ridder reporters Jonathan S. Landay and Warren P. Strobel, "said the Pentagon officials were enamored of Chalabi because he advocated normal diplomatic relations with Israel. They believed that would have 'taken off the board' one of the only remaining major Arab threats to Israeli security."

For that reason, Perle spent a considerable amount of energy attempting to get not only U.S. backing to overthrow Hussein and replace him with Chalabi, but also American Jewish and Israeli support.

"The arguments against Chalabi have been without substance," said Perle. "If he emerged in a leadership position, that would be highly desirable, from the point of view of the future of Iraq. . . . He worked tirelessly to achieve Saddam's removal, and is the kind of modern liberal leader that we would hope to see not only in Iraq but throughout the Arab world."

In 1998, Wurmser met with Israel's permanent representative to the United Nations, Dore Gold, in an effort to get Israel to put pressure on the American Congress to approve a $10 million grant to Chalabi's group to fund an invasion. "Israel has not devoted the political or rhetorical time or energy to Saddam that they have to the Iranians. The case for the Iraqi opposition in Congress would be a lot more favorable with Israeli support," said Perle.

With regard to the American Jewish community, Perle said: "One can only speculate what it might accomplish if it decided to focus its attention on Saddam Hussein." The neocon-dominated Jewish Institute for National Security Affairs—where Perle, Feith, and Cheney all served on the board of advisors—had also worked closely for years with Chalabi. Its executive director, Tom Neumann, said, "It is a good idea for the American Jewish community to do anything it can to change the government of Iraq."

Beginning in the mid-1990s, Chalabi and his crew of INC defectors were shunned by the CIA and the State Department. They considered him little more than a con man trying to wrangle large payments and to get them to start a war so he could be installed as president. In addition to his Jordanian bank-fraud conviction, he was unable to account for much of the money the CIA had given his group in the past.

The Pentagon, however, had a different agenda, and in the spring of 2002 both Wolfowitz and Rumsfeld began seeking Bush's intervention to grant Chalabi $90 million from the Treasury. Although Congress had authorized $97 million for Iraqi opposition groups under the 1998 Iraq Liberation Act, because of State Department objections most of that had not been expended. State had argued that it would be throwing good money after bad because Chalabi hadn't accounted for previous monies given to him.

"The [INC's] intelligence isn't reliable at all," said Vincent Cannistraro, the CIA's former chief of counterterrorism. "Much of it is propaganda. Much of it is telling the Defense Department what they want to hear. And much of it is used to support Chalabi's own presidential ambitions. They make no distinction between intelligence and propaganda, using alleged informants and defectors who say what Chalabi wants them to say, [creating] cooked information that goes right into presidential and vice-presidential speeches."

Nevertheless, to his fellow neocons now running the government, Chalabi had always been their Iraqi "president in waiting," and the waiting was now over. Thus, a major effort was made to use Chalabi's unreliable defectors and hyped anti-Saddam charges to channel disinformation to the media and help sell their war to the American public through the press.

One of their biggest coups came in 2001 when Chalabi offered *The New York Times*'s Judith Miller a worldwide print exclusive opportunity to interview a recent Iraqi defector then living in exile in Thailand. The man, an engineer named Adnan Ishan Saeed al-Haideri, claimed that he had personal knowledge of hundreds of bunkers for chemical, biological, and nuclear weapons research hidden throughout Iraq. Some of them, he said, he helped build himself. Among the locations was one located beneath Baghdad hospital and others in Saddam's presidential compounds.

At the same time, a similar exclusive TV deal was offered to the Australian Broadcasting Corporation through freelance tele-journalist Paul Moran. It was expected that hundreds of both print and television organizations around the world would quickly latch on to the story and start an avalanche of publicity, greatly influencing public opinion against Iraq.

But it was later discovered that Moran was anything but a dis-interested journalist. It turns out he had previously worked exten-sively for Chalabi and the INC, making anti-Saddam propaganda films. Worse, he also worked for a shadowy American company, The Rendon Group, that had been paid close to $200 million by the CIA and Pentagon to spread anti-Saddam propaganda worldwide.

The firm is headed by John W. Rendon, a dapper man often seen in dark suits and monogrammed shirts, who calls himself "an information warrior and a perception manager." Its specialty is manipulating thought and spreading propaganda. Working qui-etly for the American government, Rendon's company has played roles in the toppling of Panama's President Manuel Noriega, the first Gulf War, the Balkans, and Haiti. "They're very close-mouthed about what they do," said Kevin McCauley, one of the editors of *O'Dwyer's PR Daily*. "It's all cloak-and-dagger stuff."

Soon after the attacks of September 11, the company received a $100,000-a-month contract from the Pentagon to offer media strategy advice. Among the agencies to whom it provided recommendations was the Orwellian-sounding Office of Strategic Influence, another Feith creation that was apparently intended to be a massive disinformation factory. "When I get their briefings," said one senior official, "it's scary." As a storm of protests began to mount, Torie Clarke, the Pentagon's chief spokeswoman and Deputy Assistant Secretary for Public Affairs, warned Feith of "blowback." She argued that OSI would undermine "the trust, credibility, and transparency of our access to media."

The Rendon Group has taken in a great deal of cash vilifying Saddam Hussein. In 1991, following the Gulf War, President George H. W. Bush signed a presidential order directing the CIA to launch a covert operation to undermine the Iraqi leader. The CIA, in turn, passed along a sizable amount of money to The Rendon Group to turn world opinion against Hussein.

One of the company's first actions was to create the Iraqi National Congress, a name they came up with, as a Hussein opposition group; and in October 1992, Rendon protégé Ahmed Chalabi was placed in charge of the group. The covert operation was run out of an office in London, on Catherine Place near Buckingham Palace. "The INC was clueless. They needed a lot of help and didn't know where to start," said Thomas Twetten, the CIA's former deputy director of operations.

The man helping to arrange the al-Haideri interviews in Thailand for Moran and Miller was INC media spokesman Zaab Sethna. He had a similar background steeped in American-sponsored anti-Saddam propaganda. Sethna and Moran had met about a decade earlier in Kuwait. Following the Gulf War, they were asked by The Rendon Group to work as propagandists for the INC as contract employees. "He continued to work with The Rendon Group over the years," said Sethna about Moran, who died in March 2003 as result of a suicide bombing in Sulymania, Iraq, where he was on assignment for the Australian Broadcasting Corporation. Among those at the funeral was John Rendon, who had flown halfway around the word to pay his respects.

Unlike Moran, there is no indication that the Judith Miller of *The New York Times* was connected in any way to The Rendon Group. Nevertheless, her closeness to both Chalabi and the Pentagon has raised a number of eyebrows. While covering the search for weapons of mass destruction in Iraq, one military officer complained that Miller sometimes "intimidates Army soldiers by invoking Defense Secretary Donald Rumsfeld or Undersecretary Douglas Feith." And *The Washington Post*'s media critic, Howard Kurtz, asked, "Could Chalabi have been using the *Times* to build a drumbeat that Iraq was hiding weapons of mass destruction?"

In the end, nothing was found, not a single bunker. Al-Haideri claimed that the evidence had probably been moved. "Well, gosh, how do you move an underground facility?" laughed Scott Ritter, a former UN weapons inspector in Iraq. "It's the classic defense of the fabricator to say, 'Well, they're moving it, they're hiding it.'"

Ritter said he used to hear the same excuses from Chalabi when Ritter worked as a weapons inspector in Iraq. "That was what Ahmed Chalabi always told us every time we uncovered his data to be inaccurate," said Ritter. "He said, 'Well, they changed scenes, they're too clever for us, they're too fast, they respond too quickly.' No Ahmed, no Mr. al-Haideri, you're just liars. And it's time the world faced up to that—they're liars, they misled us, and they have the blood of hundreds of brave Americans and British service members on their hands and thousands of innocent Iraqis who perished in a war that didn't need to be fought."

The entire story may have been little more than a U.S.-sponsored psychological warfare effort—The Rendon Group's specialty—to gin up the American public's fear over Saddam Hussein. If so, it would have been illegal under U.S. law, which forbids the use of taxpayer money to propagandize the American public. "I think what you're seeing," said Ritter, "is the need for the United States government to turn to commercial enterprises like The Rendon Group to do the kind of lying and distortion of truth in terms of peddling disinformation to the media that the government normally can't do for itself."

Having largely shunned the CIA's analysis, the Pentagon's top leadership was instead dependent on selectively culled intelligence from Wurmser, a man who had long pushed his own radical agenda for the Middle East, and the bogus information from Chalabi and his defectors. It was a dangerous exercise in self-deception. Their task now was to frighten and deceive the rest of the country, and there was no better way than with the image of a madman a few screws away from a nuclear bomb. Like perfect timing, a man in Rome turned up with the proof.

In the fall of 2001, as George W. Bush and British Prime Minister Tony Blair began working together to build a coalition of support for a war in Iraq, a shadowy meeting took place amid the noisy espresso bars and busy trattorias in central Rome. A few days earlier, a mysterious call had been received at Italy's Military Intelligence and Security Service, the SISMI. Someone was offering to sell information on Iraq's efforts to regenerate its nuclear weapons program through the purchase of tons of uranium from Niger, a small West African country known for its poverty and expensive rocks.

Off and on for decades, the Niger embassy had been a key target of the SISMI's eavesdroppers. A cluttered apartment behind an armored door, it was located on the sixth floor of 10 Via Antonio Baimonte in the bustling Mazzini district of Rome. As the third-most-important country in the world for export of yellowcake—milled uranium oxide, a key ingredient for nuclear weapons—the apartment occasionally provided a keyhole for spies into the world of nuclear proliferation.

Nearly two decades earlier, in 1983, a telephone tap led to the SISMI discovering a failed Iraq bid to buy Niger uranium. Earlier, in 1981 or 1982, Iraq did legally acquire 2.8 kilograms of the ore. Following the Gulf War, United Nations weapons inspectors completely dismantled and demolished Iraq's nascent nuclear program. Now someone was offering evidence that Iraq was looking to rebuild its atomic infrastructure—there was no other use for yellowcake.

Months earlier, over the long New Year's holiday, the Niger embassy suffered a break-in. When the staff arrived at work on the morning of January 2, 2001, the office looked like an earthquake had struck. Papers covered the gloomy corridor between the ambassador's office and those of the political advisor. Drawers had been pulled out and dumped upside down. Closets had been broken into, file cabinets torn open, and folders tossed about. Arfou Mounkaila, the second secretary, reported the crime to the carabinieri. But the thieves seemed to have been more interested in paper than property, since the only objects that appeared stolen were a Breil steel watch and three small vials of perfume.

At the meeting that fall, the mysterious individual handed

the agents from the SISMI a thick packet of documents in exchange for cash. It was an odd collection: a codebook; a series of letters laying the groundwork for a 1999 visit to Niger by Wissam al-Zahawiah, Iraq's ambassador to the Holy See; and a few telexes. Among them was one with the heading "003/99/ABNI/Rome," addressed to Niger's foreign minister. "I beg to bring it to your attention," it said, "that the Iraqi Embassy to the Holy See has informed me that His Excellency Wissam al-Zahawiah, Iraqi ambassador to the Holy See, will make an official visit to our country in his capacity as representative of Saddam, president of the Iraqi Republic. His excellency Zahawiah will be arriving in Niamey," the capital of Niger.

Back at Forte Braschi, the SISMI headquarters in Rome, the telex matched one that the SISMI had secretly intercepted several years earlier. That, plus the codebook, was grounds to believe the material was authentic.

But the most troubling documents were more recent and dealt with a 2000 deal by Iraq to purchase tons of uranium. There was a July 30, 1999, message requesting an "answer on the uranium supply," and a confidential memo dated three days earlier referring to the deal—No. 381-NI 2000—for the "supply of 500 tonnes of uranium."

Finally, there was the three-page memorandum of understanding between the two countries on the uranium. Dated July 6, 2000, and signed by Niger President Tandja Mamadou and Allele Habibou, Minister of Foreign Affairs and Cooperation, it noted that the deal for the five hundred tons of uranium oxide was legal and authorized under the Niger constitution of 1965. An accompanying letter of October 10 said it was being sent for information to the ambassador in Rome from the foreign ministry.

According to the documents, the five hundred tons of uranium was to be shipped "secretly by sea" on a Gabon-flagged ship.

Then it was supposed to be "transshipped in international waters."
Apparently, this meant that somehow, while two ships were bobbing alongside each other more than a dozen miles out in the
ocean, five hundred tons of metal would be moved from one ship
to another—an amazing feat. The uranium was supposedly
shipped on August 28 and would have arrived around the time of
September 11.

"Very good work done together with the personal emissary of
the Iraqi president," said the document. "It's understood that this
information is top secret and personal. Be on guard as far as all
embassy personnel are concerned." Despite the Top Secret warning, however, the document was stamped only "Confidential."

With little analysis, the intelligence experts should surely
have seen the trapdoors hidden in the documents. A letter dated
July 30, 1999, actually refers in the past tense to supposed deals
agreed to in Niamey a year later, on June 29, 2000. And the
October 10 letter had the heading "Conseil Militaire Supreme,"
an organization that went out of existence in May 1989. The signature was that of Minister of Foreign Affairs Allele Habibou,
who held the post from 1988 to 1989 and had been out of office
for more than a decade. And finally, while the letter was dated
October 10, it was supposedly stamped as received in Rome on
September 28—thus, it was received about two weeks before it was
ever sent, another form of magic.

Also, the agreement signed by President Mamadou says the
transaction was approved under the May 12, 1965, constitution,
but a new constitution was promulgated on August 9, 1999, and
the presidential signature bore little resemblance to that of the
real Tandja Mamadou. At the same time, the forger used an inaccurate representation of the national emblem.

And a September 3, 2001, document attempting to show a
connection to the attacks appears identical to the document out-

lining the ambassador's previous 1999 trip—same flight and time. The only thing that was changed was the date at the top of the page. Also, by September 4, 2001, al-Zahawiah was no longer ambassador, a slight problem.

The letters were obviously a blend of several genuine older documents, possibly obtained during the earlier break-in, which were used to masquerade the counterfeit newer ones. The purpose of the phony documents was to create the impression that the true purpose of the Iraqi ambassador's trip to Niger in 1999 was to secretly arrange a large shipment of uranium to Iraq in 2000 and that he may have had something to do with the attacks of 9/11. Both were exactly what the Bush administration was trying to convey to the American public.

In fact, al-Zahawiah's trip had nothing to do with uranium. After the United Nations inspectors destroyed all remnants of the atomic development program in the early 1990s, Iraq never actively pursued nuclear weapons again. Instead, the Iraqi ambassador was hoping to persuade heads of state in a number of West African countries to travel to Baghdad and thereby break the air embargo that had long been strangling the country. Libya's ruler, Muammar Ghadafi, had earlier engaged in a similar tactic, and as a result a number of West African leaders flew to Tripoli and broke the embargo.

At 6:25 P.M. on the evening of February 5, 1999, Air France Flight 730 touched down at Niamey's airport. It was the first stop on al-Zahawiah's whirlwind trip that would also take him to Benin, Burkina-Faso, and Congo-Brazzaville. The next day, he spent an hour meeting with Niger's then president, Ibrahim Bare Mainassara, who agreed to pay a visit to Baghdad—the only leader on the trip to do so. But prior to his scheduled visit, he was cut down by an assassin in April 1999. The entire trip took only a few days, and he was soon back in Rome. "I took it to be a routine assignment," al-Zahawiah said in 2003. "I had done this sort of thing before, and I was senior in the Foreign Ministry." Having first entered the Foreign Service in 1955, when the monarchy was in power, he retired to Jordan in 2000.

Some Italian officials have suggested that the seller was an "African diplomat." But it was unlikely anyone from the Niger embassy, because of the numerous mistakes and the sloppy way the documents were put together. However, the person had to have had access to some actual documents. From those documents, they would know of the trip by al-Zahawiah to Niger. With just some creative energy, a complex conspiracy could be created.

It may be that the stolen documents had been floating around in the netherworld of thieves and con men for months before someone thought of a scheme to use them. Intelligence services are often the target of elaborate scams. For a number of years, con men around the world, including in the United States, tried to sell phony information to spy agencies about a supposedly plutonium-like substance called "red mercury." On the other hand, it is not out of the question that a more sinister motive may have been behind the deal. Groups like the INC were desperately trying to get the United States and Britain to go to war with Iraq so they could assume power, and deception was a frequently used tactic.

In any case, the SISMI passed on details of the supposed Iraq-Niger deal to the Executive Committee of the Intelligence and Security Services (CESIS), which in turn passed it on to the Farnesina, the Italian Foreign Ministry, and to Prime Minister Silvio Berlusconi at his office in Rome's Palazzo Chigi. Only the Farnesina raised "strong objections" and "reservations" about the report—primarily from the African Countries Directorate. They were greatly concerned about the reliability of the information.

Nevertheless, the SISMI quickly got in touch with their British MI-6 liaison and, following a number of meetings in Rome and London, passed on a summary of the information, indicating that the source was "reliable." "The British bought it without assessing it in any way," said one SISMI official. Both MI-6 and the SISMI then passed the same summary on to the CIA.

In the world of espionage, information is the coin of the realm, and the more you give the more you get. "Reciprocal exchange of information," it is called. In the early fall of 2001, the SISMI certainly knew how valuable confirmation of an Iraqi nuclear deal would be for two countries looking for a war. At the same time, it is also standard practice to seldom pass on either details of how the information was obtained or actual copies of the raw documents—only a summary of the information contained in them. The documents themselves, and how they were obtained, may reveal the source, something that most intelligence professionals are extremely careful about.

At CIA, the item from Italy was not given much prominence. It was thirdhand information without any corroboration, and on its face seemed improbable. It was certainly not solid enough to include in the President's Daily Brief. Nevertheless, what was fool's gold to the CIA was real gold to the Feith-Wurmser intelligence unit, which quickly and secretly passed the item on to Vice President Cheney.

The next morning, during his regular CIA intelligence briefing, the Niger item was not included. Nevertheless, Cheney himself brought up the topic and asked the briefer to get him more information. A day or so later, the briefer came back and said there was such a report but that there were few other details. As background he was told that Iraq had acquired a large supply of uranium ore from Niger in the early 1980s but that following the Gulf War, the material was seized and placed under the protection of the United Nations.

Spurred on by Cheney's interest, the CIA began giving the

highly questionable Niger item more prominence. On January 30, 2002, the agency issued an unclassified report to Congress containing the phrase "Baghdad may be attempting to acquire materials that could aid in reconstituting its nuclear-weapons program." Still, it was not highlighted and it was couched in very ambiguous-sounding language.

Yet only a week or so later, in early February, as the item moved from intelligence professionals to the Bush inner circle, it made a Herculean leap in credibility. Speaking before a House International Relations Committee, Secretary of State Colin Powell declared, "With respect to the nuclear program, there is no doubt that the Iraqis are pursuing it." In fact, there was every doubt.

It was a reckless charge. Even Powell's own intelligence agency at State, the Bureau of Intelligence and Research (INR), thought the Italian intelligence report was junk and sent him a memo saying so. At the time, Greg Thielmann was a senior official in INR. "A whole lot of things told us that the report was bogus," he later said. "This wasn't highly contested. There weren't strong advocates on the other side. It was done, shot down."

At the CIA, the item was still on the bottom rung of the credibility ladder. "The DO thought this smelled," said one official. Nevertheless, as a result of Cheney's unusual special interest, it was decided to give it the equivalent of a quick diagnostic check rather than expend the time and money on a full-scale clandestine operation. The idea was to get someone from the agency's retirement community with African experience to go to Niger and check it out.

Hearing about the suggestion was Valerie E. Wilson, a DO employee whose husband, Joseph Wilson, had been a former ambassador to nearby Gabon and served in Niger and in several other African countries. He had also served as an envoy to Iraq. For many years, Valerie Wilson worked for the agency in the non-official cover (NOC) program, often under her maiden name, Plame. According to a congressional intelligence source, hers was one of the names that former CIA employee, and longtime Russian mole, Aldrich Ames turned over to the KGB.

Later, Plame worked as a case officer in Europe, and more recently was assigned to the nonproliferation division. There she posed as an energy analyst for a nonexistent front company known as Brewster-Jennings & Associates, located in Boston. In reality, her job was as a weapons proliferation analyst. Wilson suggested that her husband might be a good candidate for the brief, nonpaying check-out mission to Niger, and he was given the assignment. "Rather than waste a lot of time on this caper, this was a way to find out quickly if it merited more effort," said one intelligence official.

"The agency officials asked if I would travel to Niger to check out the story so they could provide a response to the Vice President's office," said Joseph Wilson. "In late February 2002, I arrived in Niger's capital, Niamey. . . . The city was much as I remembered it. Seasonal winds had clogged the air with dust and sand. Through the haze, I could see camel caravans crossing the Niger River [over the John F. Kennedy Bridge], the setting sun behind them. Most people had wrapped scarves around their faces to protect against the grit, leaving only their eyes visible."

The next morning, Wilson met with U.S. Ambassador Owens-Kirkpatrick at the embassy. "For reasons that are understandable, the embassy staff has always kept a close eye on Niger's uranium business," he said. "I was not surprised, then, when the ambassador told me that she knew about the allegations of uranium sales to Iraq—and that she felt she had already debunked them in her reports to Washington. Nevertheless, she and I agreed that my time would be best spent interviewing people who had been in government when the deal supposedly took place, which was before her arrival."

Over the next eight days, Wilson sipped sweet mint tea and chatted with several dozen people, from current officials to businesspeople associated with the uranium mines. "It did not take long to conclude that it was highly doubtful that any such transaction had ever taken place," he said. "Given the structure of the consortiums that operated the mines, it would be exceedingly difficult for Niger to transfer uranium to Iraq."

The government of Niger is not in control of the uranium. Instead, the nation's two mines, Somair and Cominak, are run by a French, Spanish, Japanese, German, and Nigerian consortium. From the time the ore is extracted from the ground; packed in hermetically sealed, numbered, and dated drums; and transported to Benin, where it is loaded onto ships, it is heavily guarded by gendarmes and the International Atomic Energy Agency.

"If the government wanted to remove uranium from a mine," said Wilson, "it would have to notify the consortium, which in turn is strictly monitored by the International Atomic Energy Agency. Moreover, because the two mines are closely regulated, quasigovernmental entities, selling uranium would require the approval of the minister of mines, the prime minister, and probably the president. In short, there's simply too much oversight over too small an industry for a sale to have transpired."

Wilson returned to Washington in early March and verbally gave his negative assessment to CIA officials, and later met with the State Department's African Affairs Bureau. There was no substance to the Italian intelligence report. On March 9, the CIA cabled Wilson's doubts around the intelligence community and passed a memo with his comments to the White House.

As the move toward war began gaining momentum in late August 2002, Feith created another new organization, the Office of Special Plans. Its purpose was to conduct advance war planning for Iraq, and one of its most important responsibilities was "media strategy." Hidden away on the Pentagon's fifth floor, one floor above Feith's office, it was a crowded warren of blue cubicles and narrow hallways packed with unused equipment and rolled-up maps. The musty scent of old concrete never seemed to leave the air.

Above all, the office was Top Secret. "We were instructed at a staff meeting that this office was not to be discussed or explained," said Kwiatkowski, "and if people in the Joint Staff, among others, asked, we were to offer no comment."

Picked to head the OSP was still another longtime Perle protégé, Abram N. Shulsky. He had worked with Perle both in Senator "Scoop" Jackson's office and at the Pentagon when Perle was Assistant Secretary of Defense during the Reagan years. Although the office appeared small on paper, with about eighteen full-time Pentagon employees, its ranks were beefed up with outside contractors and consultants.

According to a report in London's *Guardian* newspaper, the OSP also forged close ties to a parallel, ad hoc intelligence unit within Ariel Sharon's office in Israel. It was designed to go around the country's own intelligence organization, Mossad. The purpose of the unit, said *The Guardian*, was to provide key people in the Bush administration "with more alarmist reports on Saddam's Iraq than Mossad was prepared to authorize." Thus, the OSP was getting cooked intelligence not only from its own intelligence unit but also from a similar Israeli cell.

"None of the Israelis who came were cleared into the Pentagon through normal channels," one source familiar with the visits told *The Guardian*. Instead, Feith would wave them through without their having to sign the normal papers. "The exchange of information continued a long-standing relationship Mr. Feith and other Washington neo-conservatives had with Israel's Likud party," said the paper.

Colonel Kwiatkowski noticed the same sort of activity when she was assigned to escort a number of Israeli generals who had come to the Pentagon to visit Feith. "Once in Feith's waiting room," she said, "the leader continued at speed to Feith's closed door. An alert secretary saw this coming and had leapt from her desk to block the door." Nevertheless, the curious general seemed annoyed. "The leader craned his neck to look around the secretary's head as he demanded, 'Who is in there with him?'" Kwiatkowski recalled. Then, when she asked them to sign in, it was made clear to her that she had made a mistake. "No, no, no," Feith's secretary said quickly, frantically waving her hands. "It is not necessary, not at all."

Although deliberately kept in the shadows, Israeli intelligence worked closely with Feith and other parts of the Pentagon. But a study produced by Tel Aviv University's Jaffee Center for Strategic Studies indicates that Israel's vaunted intelligence services could find no indication that Iraq possessed banned weapons, despite their location and access to Middle East sources. "On the eve of the war," said the report, "Israeli intelligence on Iraqi capabilities resembled its counterparts in the United States and other Western countries. It had not received any information regarding weapons of mass destruction and surface-to-surface missiles for nearly eight years."

The report was written by Shlomo Brom, a retired brigadier general who was the former head of the Israeli military's Strategic Planning Division on the General Staff. Brom also charged that despite the fact that Israeli intelligence, like that of the United States, had no evidence of Iraqi weapons of mass destruction, the Israeli government, along with the media, deliberately hyped the dangers of Iraq before the war. "A review of statements made by the establishment during the two months leading up to the war," the report said, "shows that as the war drew nearer, the Israeli establishment began to sense that it had exaggerated its presentation of the threat."

As an example, said the report, "when Israeli intelligence became aware that certain items had been transferred by heads of the regime from Iraq to Syria, Israeli intelligence immediately portrayed it—including in leaks to the media—as if Iraq was moving weapons of mass destruction out of Iraq in order to conceal them."

Finally, following the discovery that there were no weapons of mass destruction, officials began asking, with regard to Saddam Hussein, "Why did he not do everything possible to convince Western governments that he was 'clean,' retaining no weapons of mass destruction? The answer is that from Saddam Hussein's perspective, he did do everything to respond to every whim of UNMOVIC [the UN inspectors], but to no avail, since the real aim of the United States was regime change and not Iraq's disarmament of weapons of mass destruction."

The bad Israeli intelligence also led to the creation of a special panel of Israel's parliament, the Knesset, to investigate the actions of the Israeli intelligence services in the lead-up to war. Led by Yuval Steinitz (Likud Party), chairman of the Knesset's Foreign Affairs and Defence Committee, the panel held over fifty sessions and called more than seventy witnesses, including Prime Minister Ariel Sharon. In March 2004, the panel found that Israeli intelligence warnings about Iraq's unconventional weapons were based not on facts, but simply on assessments and speculation.

According to Yossi Sarid, a prominent member of the Foreign Affairs and Defence Committee, Israeli intelligence knew beforehand that Iraq had no weapons stockpiles and misled President George W Bush. Israeli intelligence, he said, knew the threat was "very, very, very limited. . . . [But] Israel didn't want to spoil President Bush's scenario, and it should have." He also dismissed Britain's claim that Iraq could launch deadly weapons on forty-five minutes' notice. "It was known in Israel that the story that weapons of mass destruction could be activated in forty-five minutes was an old wives' tale," he said.

Sarid's charges were confirmed by former American weapons inspector Scott Ritter. He spent seven years as a senior U.N. inspector in Iraq and also served as the group's liaison with the Israeli intelligence service. Israel, he said, had long known that Iraq had no weapons of mass destruction. "The Israeli intelligence reached this conclusion many years ago," he said in 2004. He added that when he met with Israeli intelligence officials in 1998, they told him that Iraq had been reduced to the number-six threat, down from number one four years earlier.

Like Chalabi, Israel had a history of providing questionable information when it came to Iraq. Within days of 9/11, Israel's military intelligence service, Aman, was claiming that Iraq was behind the attacks. "Aman," said a September 19, 2001, article in the respected Jane's *Foreign Report*, "suspects that Iraq is the state that sponsored the suicide attacks on the New York Trade Center and the Pentagon in Washington."

During a closed meeting in Brussels in June 2002, Efraim Halevy, chief of Mossad, offered to NATO chiefs just the kind of intelligence later studies said Israel did not possess. "We have clear indications," he said, "that the Iraqis renewed their efforts" to develop nuclear weapons. He added, "Together with these efforts, we have reason to believe that the Iraqis have succeeded in preserving parts of their capability in the fields of biological and chemical warfare. We have partial evidence that they have renewed production of VX and perhaps even anthrax germs. Regarding launching systems, we have sufficient evidence to determine that they are investing every possible effort to preserve the capability they still have, and to increase them through new means."

Israel began its anti-Saddam propaganda campaign in April 1994 when Aman's deputy director, Brig. Gen. Yakov Amidror, flew secretly to New York for a meeting with top UN weapons inspector Rolf Ekeus. One of Ekeus's senior inspectors, Scott Ritter, became the central conduit for the data. Despite its lack of good intelligence on Iraq, Israel had a great incentive to come up with threatening information on Saddam Hussein's supposed weapons programs. In return, Aman was secretly provided with tremendous access to classified high-resolution imagery shot by a U-2 spy plane, which was on loan to the UN inspectors from the United States.

Ritter would travel to Aman's headquarters in Tel Aviv's Kirya complex with canisters of the film, which Aman would then secretly copy. Such distribution was beyond the scope of the CIA's original agreement with the UN team. The imagery was stamped with the caveat "REL UNSCOM/IAEA ONLY," restricting the photography exclusively to the UN special commission and to the International Atomic Energy Agency. On occasion, Ritter and others within the inspection team would meet with Aman's chief, Maj. Gen. Uri Saguy.

The strange arrangement began raising alarms within the U.S. intelligence community. Because of the great volume of Iraqi imagery being passed to Tel Aviv, many began worrying that the United States would ultimately be held responsible if Israel decided to use it as part of a future attack on Baghdad. It wouldn't be the first time. In 1981, Israeli warplanes launched a preemptive strike against an Iraqi nuclear reactor under construction at Osirak.

Adding to the concerns was the fact that by July 1995, Israel had passed the United States and become the single most important intelligence source for the Iraqi weapons inspectors since its creation in April 1991.

While the imagery Israel received was real, much of the "intelligence" the UN was given in return was not. One of Israel's first major contributions to the UN took place in September 1994 when liaison officers in Aman's Foreign Relations Department passed on information that Iraq possessed mobile biological weapons labs. Baghdad, it said, was hiding poison factories in red-and-white painted "Tip Top Ice Cream" refrigerator trucks. At night, said Aman, the bio-weapons ingredients were transported in unmarked green Mercedes tractor-trailers belonging to Segada Transportation Co., named after Saddam Hussein's wife.

But because it was found that neither company, in fact, existed in Iraq, some inspectors were skeptical from the start that mobile biological labs even existed. "They just didn't make sense from a technical or a security viewpoint," Raymond A. Zilinskas, a UN inspector at the time, told reporters Bob Drogin and Greg Miller of *The Los Angeles Times*. Zilinskas helped inspect sixty-one biological facilities in Iraq in 1994.

Finding nothing in over three years, some inspectors were still not ready to give up on what Israel claimed was Hussein's deadly germ labs on wheels. Thus, in December 1997 Ritter and his deputy flew to London, where they met with Ahmed Chalabi and his intelligence chief, Ahmed Allawi. "They told us they had the run of Iraq," said Ritter. "We outlined the gaps in our under-standing of the Iraqi program, including the mobile bio-weapons labs." At the time, Chalabi was being vigorously promoted within the United States by Richard Perle, Paul Wolfowitz, and the neo-conservative crowd as the man the United States should pick to replace Saddam Hussein, once "regime change" had occurred.

Some time following the meeting, a chemical engineer claiming to be an Iraqi defector showed up in a German refugee camp where he was given the prescient code name "Curveball" by the BND, German intelligence. The defector told of graduating from Baghdad University at the top of his class and then being recruited by Iraqi weapons engineers to design and build biological-warfare trucks for the Iraqi Army.

What Curveball never told anyone at the time, however, was that he was also the brother of one of Chalabi's top aides. Intelligence officials now suspect that he had been coached by Chalabi's INC to provide the false information. "They began feeding us information," said Ritter. "But nothing panned out. Most of it just regurgitated what we'd given them. And the data that was new never checked out." Thus, the phony tip from Israel now gained significantly greater credibility with the phony confirmation from Chalabi's man.

Despite the importance of the information, U.S. intelligence officials were never allowed to interview Curveball or even learn his name. All details, possibly at the request of the defector himself, had to come from liaison officers with the BND, who provided the CIA with Curveball's lengthy statements. But there was no way to interrogate or cross-examine a file.

The only other confirmation of the bio-weapons lab allegation came from two Iraqi defectors who had no direct evidence; they had simply heard reports of the program. A fourth defector, who claimed to be a major in Iraq's intelligence service, said the bio-trucks had been built to test biological agents. But the Defense Intelligence Agency, to its credit, recognized that the Iraqi officer appeared to be lying and to have also been coached by Chalabi's group. Thus in May 2002, a year before the war with Iraq, the agency posted a "fabricator notice" on him throughout the intelligence community. The CIA, however, never caught it.

But there were other warning signs that were also ignored. Among the documents in the BND file was an interview with another Iraqi defector, an engineer who had worked with Curveball, who completely contradicted his former associate, saying they had never worked on such a program. At other times the BND also tried to warn the CIA about the credibility of the Iraqi sources.

Thus, despite the lack of verification, the information was given enormous credibility in the fall of 2002 as the Bush administration stepped up their relentless pursuit of war. As a result, when the UN inspectors returned to the country in November 2002, checking out the information and locations became one of their highest priorities. But in the end, after more than seventy raids and an intensive investigation involving taking samples at every location, they came up with nothing. "We didn't find anything," said one of the weapons hunters.

Undeterred, the Bush administration continued to make the bogus claims a central pillar of their go-to-war strategy. "This is the one that's damning," said the CIA's former chief weapons hunter, David Kay, who called Curveball an "out-and-out fabricator." He added, "This is the one that has the potential for causing the largest havoc in the sense that it really looks like a lack of due diligence and care in going forward."

Having absorbed Wurmser's intelligence unit, one of the Office of Special Plans' jobs was to use the selectively culled pieces of raw intelligence in a governmentwide PR campaign. "Talking points" containing the intelligence items and analysis were distributed to officials to ensure that they were all lined up behind the same "get-Saddam" message. Wurmser, in the meantime, transferred to a senior position at the State Department and then to Vice President Cheney's office as his Middle East advisor. Cheney, along with his chief of staff, archneoconservative I. Lewis (Scooter) Libby, had been one of the key people pushing the separate intelligence channel.

"They pushed an agenda on Iraq," said Kwiatkowski, "and they developed pretty sophisticated propaganda lines which were fed throughout government, to the Congress, and even internally to the Pentagon—to try and make this case of immediacy, this case of severe threat to the United States. . . . They were political, politically manipulated. They did have, obviously, bits of intelligence in them, but they were created to propagandize."

The group especially targeted the doubters and nonbelievers, from the CIA to the Secretary of State. "This was creatively produced propaganda spread not only through the Pentagon but across a network of policymakers," said Kwiatkowski. OSP "needed to convince the remaining holdovers. Colin Powell, for example. There was a lot of frustration with Powell; they said a lot of bad things about him in the office. . . . That is not normal, that is a bypassing of normal processes." She added that the OSP had a "very close relationship" with Vice President Cheney's office.

Another thing that troubled Kwiatkowski was the sort of enemies list maintained by her office. In addition to Powell, another person targeted was former Marine General Anthony Zinni, the former Commander of Middle East Forces as the head of Central Command. Bush later named him a special envoy to the area. "He spoke out publicly as President Bush's Middle East envoy about some of the things he saw," said Kwiatkowski. "Before he was removed by Bush, I heard Zinni called a traitor in a staff meeting. They were very anti anybody who might provide information that affected their paradigm. They were the spin enforcers."

In the end, said Kwiatkowski, the public heard what they were supposed to hear, what the OSP wanted them to hear. "They spent their energy gathering pieces of information and creating a propaganda story line," she said, "which is the same story line we heard the president and Vice President Cheney tell the American people in the fall of 2002.

"The very phrases they used are coming back to haunt them," she said, "because they are blatantly false and not based on any intelligence. The OSP and the Vice President's office were critical in this propaganda effort—to convince Americans that there was some just requirement for preemptive war. . . . The Congress was misled, it was lied to. At a very minimum, that is a subversion of the Constitution. A preemptive war based on what we knew was not a pressing need is not what this country stands for."

Once Feith's intelligence unit had cherry-picked the most damning items from the streams of U.S. and Israeli reports, they were then sent to the OSP to be turned into "analysis" and "talking points." Then the OSP would brief senior administration officials. These officials would then use the OSP's false and exaggerated intelligence as ammunition when attempting to hard-sell the need for war to their reluctant colleagues, such as Colin Powell, and even to allies like British Prime Minister Tony Blair.

According to one former senior Pentagon official who worked closely with Feith's offices, their goal was not just "how to fight Saddam Hussein but also how to fight the NSC, the State Department, and the intelligence community," which were not convinced of Hussein's involvement in terrorism.

For example, in late summer 2002 Feith's small intelligence unit completed its "study" on the links between Al Qaeda and Saddam Hussein. Feith then had the two analysts who worked on it—Christopher Carney, a naval reservist and associate professor of political science at the University of Pennsylvania; and Defense Intelligence Agency analyst Christina Shelton—brief Rumsfeld.

Then, on August 15, Feith took the pair to the CIA to see if he could change any minds there. Among the officials present was Tenet. But most of the participants quickly saw the "study" for what it was and, according to one report, were "nonplussed." "Much of it," one participant jotted in his notes, "we had discounted already." In the end, the briefing was largely ignored.

Nevertheless, without notifying the agency, Feith's road show turned around and gave the same briefing at the White House for senior officials in the National Security Council and the Vice President's office. Among those present were Deputy National

Security Advisor Stephen J. Hadley and Libby, Cheney's chief of staff. But this time they added a slide harshly critical of the CIA for disagreeing with them on the unproven links between Iraq, Al Qaeda, and the 9/11 attacks.

Despite the inaccuracy of the information contained in the high-level briefings, the top-down pressure worked and the CIA quickly reversed itself. On October 7, the agency's deputy director, John E. McLaughlin, noted in a letter to the Senate Intelligence Committee, "We have solid evidence of senior level contacts between Iraq and al-Qa'ida going back a decade." He added, "Growing indications of a relationship with al-Qa'ida, suggest that Baghdad's link to terrorists will increase, even absent U.S. military action." But despite the occasional contacts, there was no indication that the two groups had been involved in any operational activities.

Hadley and Libby were part of another secret office that had been set up within the White House. Known as the White House Iraq Group (WHIG), it was established in August 2002 by Chief of Staff Andrew H. Card, Jr., at the same time the OSP was established in Feith's office. Made up of high-level administration officials, its job was to sell the war to the general public, largely through televised addresses and by selectively leaking the intelligence to the media.

In June 2002, a leaked computer disk containing a presentation by chief Bush strategist Karl Rove revealed a White House political plan to use the war as a way to "maintain a positive issue environment." But the real pro-war media blitz was scheduled for the fall and the start of the election season "because from a marketing point of view, you don't introduce new products in August," said Card.

At least once a week they would gather around the blonde conference table downstairs in the Situation Room, the same place the war was born on January 30, 2001, ten days into the Bush presidency.

Although real intelligence had improved very little in the intervening nineteen months, the manufacturing of it had increased tremen-
dously. In addition to Hadley and Libby, those frequently attending
the WHIG meetings included Karl Rove; Condoleezza Rice; communications gurus Karen Hughes, Mary Matalin, and James R.
Wilkinson; and legislative liaison Nicholas E. Calio.

In addition to ties between Hussein and 9/11, among the most
important products the group was looking to sell as Labor Day 2002
approached were frightening images of mushroom clouds, mobile
biological weapons labs, and A-bomb plants, all in the hands of a
certified "madman." A key piece of evidence that Hussein was
building a nuclear weapon turned out to be the discredited Italian
documents purchased on a street corner from a con man.

The WHIG began priming its audience in August when Vice
President Cheney, on three occasions, sounded a shrill alarm over
Saddam Hussein's nuclear threat. There "is no doubt," he declared,
that Saddam Hussein "has weapons of mass destruction." Again
and again, he hit the same chord. "What we know now, from various sources, is that he . . . continues to pursue a nuclear weapon."
And again: "We do know, with absolute certainty, that he is using
his procurement system to acquire the equipment he needs in order
to enrich uranium to build a nuclear weapon."

Facing network television cameras, Cheney warned, "We now
know that Saddam has resumed his efforts to acquire nuclear
weapons. . . . Among other sources, we've gotten this from firsthand
testimony from defectors, including Saddam's own son-in-law."
The relative was Hussein Kamel, who defected to Jordan in 1995
with a great deal of inside information on Iraq's special weapons
programs, which he managed. He was later convinced by Saddam
to return to Iraq, but executed by the ruler soon after his arrival.

But what Kamel told his interrogators was the exact opposite of what Cheney was claiming he said. After numerous debriefings by officials from the United States, the UN, and Jordan, he said on August 22, 1995, that Saddam had ended all uranium-enrichment programs at the beginning of the Gulf War in 1991 and never restarted them. He also made it clear that "all weapons—biological, chemical, missile, nuclear—were destroyed." Investigators were convinced that Kamel was telling the truth, since he supplied them with a great deal of stolen raw data and was later murdered by his father-in-law as a result. But that was not the story Feith's OSP, Bush's WHIG, or Cheney wanted the American public to hear.

At the same time that Cheney began his media blitz, Ariel Sharon's office in Israel, as if perfectly coordinated, began issuing similar dire warnings concerning Hussein and pressing the Bush administration to go to war with Iraq. Like those from Cheney, pronouncements from Sharon's top aide, Ranaan Gissin, included frightening "evidence"—equally phony—of nuclear, as well as biological and chemical, threats.

"As evidence of Iraq's weapons building activities," said an Associated Press report on the briefing, "Israel points to an order Saddam gave to Iraq's Atomic Energy Commission last week to speed up its work, said Sharon aide Ranaan Gissin. 'Saddam's going to be able to reach a point where these weapons will be operational,' he said. . . . Israeli intelligence officials have gathered evidence that Iraq is speeding up efforts to produce biological and chemical weapons, Gissin said."

It was clear, based on the postwar reviews done in Israel, that Israeli intelligence had no such evidence. Instead, the "evidence" was likely cooked up in Sharon's own Office of Special Plans unit, which was coordinating its activities with the Feith/Wurmser/Shulsky Office of Special Plans. The joint get-Saddam media blitz would also explain the many highly secret visits by Israeli generals to Feith's office during the summer.

"Israel is urging U.S. officials not to delay a military strike against Iraq's Saddam Hussein, an aide to Prime Minister Ariel Sharon said Friday," the AP report continued. "'Any postponement of an attack on Iraq at this stage will serve no purpose,' Gissin told the Associated Press. 'It will only give him [Saddam] more of an opportunity to accelerate his program of weapons of mass destruction.'"

As expected, Sharon's call was widely publicized and increased pressure on Congress, which often bows to Israel's wishes, to vote in favor of the Bush war resolution. "Israel To U.S.: Don't Delay Iraq Attack," said a CBS News headline. "Israel is urging U.S. officials not to delay a military strike against Iraq's Saddam Hussein, an aide to Prime Minister Ariel Sharon said Friday," said the report.

The story also made news in London, where the *Guardian* newspaper ran the headline: "Israel Puts Pressure on US to Strike Iraq." It went on, "With foreign policy experts in Washington becoming increasingly critical of the wisdom of a military strike, and European governments showing no willingness to support an attack, the Israeli prime minister, Ariel Sharon, wants to make it clear that he is the US president's most reliable ally."

It was as if the Feith-Wurmser-Perle "Clean Break" plan had come full circle. Their plan for Israel to overthrow Saddam Hussein and put a pro-Israel regime in his place had been rejected by former Israeli Prime Minister Benjamin Netanyahu. Now Bush, with Sharon's support, was about to put it into effect.

Across the Atlantic, British Prime Minister Tony Blair also contributed to the war fever by releasing a much-hyped report that reinforced the White House theme that Iraq was an imminent threat not only to the United States but also to Britain. In addition to including a reference to the bogus Iraq-Niger uranium deal, the report—later dubbed the "doggie dossier"—made another frightening claim. It warned that Iraq could launch a deadly biological or chemical attack with long-range ballistic missiles on British tourists and servicemen in Cyprus with just forty-five minutes' notice.

Only after the war would it be publicly revealed that the reference was not to a strategic weapon that could reach Cyprus, but simply to a short-range battlefield weapon that could not come anywhere close to Cyprus. And because all the missiles were all disassembled, even to fire them on the battlefield would take not forty-five minutes but days of assembly and preparation. At least three times prior to the war, Blair was warned by intelligence officials that the report was inaccurate, but he made no public mention of it.

The disinformation blitz continued into early September, timed for the congressional elections and in order to prepare the country for Bush's preemption decision and possible United Nations fight. On September 7, Bush told reporters gathered at Camp David about alarming new evidence. "A report came out of the . . . IAEA [International Atomic Energy Agency]," he said, "that they [Iraqis] were six months away from developing a weapon. I don't know what more evidence we need."

A week later, on September 14, Bush repeated his nuclear charge during his weekly radio address. "Saddam Hussein has the scientists and infrastructure for a nuclear-weapons program, and has illicitly sought to purchase the equipment needed to enrich uranium for a nuclear weapon." But, again, there was no new report. The IAEA document he was referring to was from 1996, and it described a weapons program the inspectors had long ago destroyed.

Off on the sidelines, George Tenet was one of the few who knew the truth. But instead of speaking out, he was quietly attempting to stick his finger in the dike by trying to persuade first the British and then the White House to stay away from the Italian Niger report.

Defense Secretary Donald Rumsfeld warned that time was short and the threat imminent. "No terrorist state poses a greater or more immediate threat to the security of our people, and the stability of the world, than the regime of Saddam Hussein in Iraq," he told Congress that September.

With no reason to think they were being lied to, the public was left to believe that Saddam Hussein had restarted his nuclear weapons program and was just six months away from having a working atomic bomb. "Senior officials made statements which I can only describe as dishonest," said senior State Department intelligence official Gregory Thielmann, who saw much of the intelligence. "They were distorting some of the information that we provided to make it seem more alarmist and more dangerous. . . . I thought there were limits on how much one was willing to do in order to twist things."

The only thing left was for the national media to give the bogus information its imprimatur. Like clockwork, that happened the next morning, Sunday, September 8, when *The New York Times* published a major story under the stark headline "U.S. Says Hussein Intensifies Quest for A-Bomb Parts."

Written by veteran reporters Judith Miller and Michael Gordon, it stated that "more than a decade after Saddam Hussein agreed to give up weapons of mass destruction, Iraq has stepped up its quest for nuclear weapons and has embarked on a worldwide hunt for materials to make an atomic bomb, Bush administration officials said today." Emphasizing the need for speed to eliminate the Iraqi leader, they quoted an official as saying, "The closer Saddam Hussein gets to a nuclear weapon, the harder he will be to deal with."

The proof, according to the article, was the Iraqi leader's alleged attempted purchase of "specially designed aluminum tubes, which American officials believe were intended as components of centrifuges to enrich uranium." The article concluded, "Mr. Hussein's dogged insistence on pursuing his nuclear ambitions, along with what defectors described in interviews as Iraq's push to improve and expand Baghdad's chemical and biological arsenals, have brought Iraq and the United States to the brink of war."

As icing on the cake, the reporters quoted the vivid imagery of unnamed administration officials as worried that "the first sign of a 'smoking gun' . . . may be a mushroom cloud" and that, according to one defector, "all of Iraq is one large storage facility." Few words are as easy for the public to understand, or evoke more emotion, as "A-bomb" and "mushroom cloud."

As if the entire event had been scripted, administration officials had all agreed days earlier to appear on the Sunday talk shows that same morning. Once the cameras clicked on, they made generous use of the allegations contained in the article, now free from worries about releasing classified information. It was a perfect scheme—leak the secrets the night before so you can talk about them the next morning.

"It's now public," said Dick Cheney during his appearance on *Meet the Press*, that Saddam Hussein "has been seeking to acquire" the "kind of tubes" needed for the production of highly enriched uranium, "which is what you have to have in order to build a bomb." Condoleezza Rice, on CNN's *Late Edition* with Wolf Blitzer, regurgitated the "We don't want the smoking gun to be a mushroom cloud" phrase from the morning's article.

On Fox News, Colin Powell talked of the "specialized aluminum tubing" that "we saw in reporting just this morning." And on CBS's *Face the Nation*, Donald Rumsfeld tied it all in to September 11. "Imagine a September 11 with weapons of mass destruction," he said, which would kill "tens of thousands of innocent men, women, and children."

The series of events produced exactly the sort of propaganda coup that the White House Iraq Group had been set up to stage-manage. First OSP supplies false or exaggerated intelligence; then members of the WHIG leak it to friendly reporters, complete with prepackaged vivid imagery; finally, when the story breaks, senior officials point to it as proof and parrot the unnamed quotes they or their colleagues previously supplied.

Bush later evoked the mushroom-cloud scenario himself during his major address to the nation from Cincinnati in October 2002. "The Iraqi regime is seeking nuclear weapons," he said. "Does it make any sense for the world to wait . . . for the final proof, the smoking gun that could come in the form of a mushroom cloud?" And in November, General Tommy R. Franks, the chief of the U.S. Central Command, said inaction might provoke "the sight of the first mushroom cloud on one of the major population centers on this planet."

Times reporter Judith Miller was an obvious choice for the leaks. Several times before, she had turned information from Iraqi defectors into front-page stories. As she acknowledged in a May 2003 internal e-mail to *Times* Baghdad bureau chief John Burns, her dealings with Chalabi went back a long time. "I've been covering Chalabi for about 10 years," she said, "and have done most of the stories about him for our paper, including the long takeout we recently did on him. He has provided most of the front page exclusives on WMD to our paper."

But relying on Iraqi defectors—especially those supplied by Chalabi—was risky business. Many journalists who covered national security during the Cold War knew that the bulk of information provided by defectors—then from the Soviet Union—had to be taken with a grain of salt. The more exaggerated their charges, the better the chances of receiving political asylum or even large payments from intelligence agencies. It was a constant problem for CIA case officers and analysts.

Using the aluminum-tube story to kick off their "Get Saddam" media blitz, the White House claimed it backed up their charges that Iraq posed a dangerous, immediate threat to America. Ultimately, just four days after the story appeared, again as if the whole event had been planned, President Bush himself referred to the tubes in his dramatic speech before the United Nations General Assembly. "Iraq has made several attempts to buy high-strength aluminum tubes used to enrich uranium for a nuclear weapon," he said.

Yet by now a number of experts in the field, including many within the U.S. government working for nuclear research labs, were beginning to question the validity of the claims contained in the story. Among those was State Department intelligence and proliferation expert Gregory Thielmann.

"It was not a difficult assessment for us to arrive at, ultimately," Thielmann said, "that the Department of Energy experts were correct in seeing these tubes as being not well suited for uranium-enrichment centrifuge rotors, but were, in fact, for something else. As we explored the alternative possibilities, we really came up with a very good fit. It was for the casings of Iraqi artillery rockets—the kind that are used in multiple-launcher rocket systems." In fact, that is the purpose Iraq had previously claimed.

An expert called on by the U.S. nuclear laboratory at Oak Ridge also agreed that the tubes were unlikely for use in a centrifuge. "It would have been extremely difficult to make these tubes into centrifuges," said Houston G. Wood, founder of the Oak Ridge Centrifuge Physics Department. "It stretches the imagination to come up with a way. I do not know any real centrifuge experts that feel differently."

While Miller's article continued to serve the war policies of the Bush administration well, a team of reporters from Knight-

Ridder's Washington bureau decided to look into the story and found it contained far more smoke than fire. "We began hearing from sources in the military, the intelligence community, and the foreign service of doubts about the arguments the administration was making," bureau chief John Walcott told reporter Michael Massing in the *New York Review of Books*.

"These people," Walcott added, "were better informed about the details of the intelligence than the people higher up in the food chain, and they were deeply troubled by what they regarded as the administration's deliberate misrepresentation of intelligence, ranging from overstating the case to outright fabrication."

At the time, Knight-Ridder was virtually alone among national news organizations attempting to look behind the aluminum tubes story. "In the period before the war," wrote Michael Massing, "U.S. journalists were far too reliant on sources sympathetic to the administration. Those with dissenting views—and there were more than a few—were shut out. Reflecting this, the coverage was highly deferential to the White House. This was especially apparent on the issue of Iraq's weapons of mass destruction—the heart of the President's case for war. Despite abundant evidence of the administration's brazen misuse of intelligence in this matter, the press repeatedly let officials get away with it."

Knight-Ridder reporters Warren Strobel and Jonathan Landay found a number of senior U.S. officials with access to intelligence on Iraq who thought the administration claims were fraudulent. "While President Bush marshals congressional and international support for invading Iraq," Strobel, Landay, and Walcott wrote, "a growing number of military officers, intelligence professionals, and diplomats in his own government privately have deep misgivings about the administration's double-time march toward war."

These officials, they said in the fall of 2002, "charge that administration hawks have exaggerated evidence of the threat that Iraqi leader Saddam Hussein poses—including distorting his links to the al-Qaida terrorist network. . . . They charge that the administration squelches dissenting views and that intelligence analysts are under intense pressure to produce reports supporting the White House's argument that Saddam poses such an immediate threat to the United States that pre-emptive military action is necessary."

Meanwhile, three days after the Sunday media blitz, Senator Bob Graham (D–Fla.), chairman of the Senate Select Committee on Intelligence, sent a secret letter to George Tenet demanding that the agency weigh in on the controversy. He asked that the CIA issue its own analysis in the form of a National Intelligence Estimate (NIE) prepared by the National Intelligence Council (NIC), a sort of community-wide think tank.

From the start, the White House Iraq Group was hoping to avoid any interference as they continued to take the mushroom-cloud image to the public. They knew "there were disagreements over details in almost every aspect of the administration's case against Iraq," one official told Barton Gellman and Walter Pincus of *The Washington Post*. And they did not want "a lot of footnotes and disclaimers."

Senior State Department intelligence official Gregory Thielmann agreed. "Instead of our leadership forming conclusions based on a careful reading of the intelligence we provided them," he said, "they already had their conclusion to start out with, and they were cherry-picking the information that we provided to use whatever pieces of it that fit their overall interpretation. Worse than that, they were dropping qualifiers and distorting some of the information that we provided to make it seem more alarmist and more dangerous than the information that we were giving them. . . . There seemed to be an unseemly eagerness to believe any information which would portray the Iraqi threat as being extremely grave and imminent."

Thus, the NIE was rushed out in just two weeks—a process that usually takes months—and despite the lack of valid intelligence, it continued to boost the Iraq "nuclear threat" charge. A "key judgment," concluded the NIE, was that Hussein was intent on acquiring a nuclear weapon. It added, "Most agencies assess that Baghdad started reconstituting its nuclear program about the time that UNSCOM inspectors departed—December 1998." The NIE then included the phony Italian Niger claim. According to "a foreign government service," it said, Iraq had arranged to purchase "several tons of 'pure uranium' (probably yellowcake)" in Niger.

The NIE also contained a frightening section indicating that Iraq might launch drones—unmanned aerial vehicles (UAVs)—loaded with deadly germs against the United States. "Baghdad's UAV," it said, "could threaten Iraq's neighbors, U.S. forces in the Persian Gulf and if brought close to, or into, the United States, the U.S. homeland."

George Tenet and Dick Cheney later explained the drone threat in more detail to members of Congress. They were hoping to convince the legislators to vote in favor of giving Bush a blank check to launch his preemptive war against Iraq. In a bug-proof room, they laid out what they said was the "smoking gun," proving that Iraq was a grave threat to the United States. Later, other House and Senate members were given the same briefing.

The "smoking gun" turned out to be a fleet of UAVs with the potential for delivering deadly quantities of chemical and biological agents. In addition, they said, Iraq had also sought software used for producing sophisticated maps of cities along the East Coast of the United States.

Florida Democratic Senator Bill Nelson was one of those convinced by what he heard. "I was one of seventy-seven Senators who voted for the resolution in October of 2002 to authorize the expenditure of funds for the President to engage in an attack on Iraq. I voted for it," he later said. A key reason for his vote, he said, was information "very convincing to me that there was an imminent peril to the interests of the United States."

According to Nelson, "I was looked at straight in the face and told that Saddam Hussein had the means of delivering those biological and chemical weapons of mass destruction by unmanned drones, called UAVs, unmanned aerial vehicles. Further, I was looked at straight in the face and told that UAVs could be launched from ships off the Atlantic coast to attack eastern seaboard cities of the United States. . . . It was in a highly classified setting in a secure room."

Later, Secretary of State Colin Powell, in his presentation before the United Nations Security Council on February 5, 2003, used the UAV threat as a key justification for going to war: "Iraq could use these small UAVs, which have a wingspan of only a few meters, to deliver biological agents to its neighbors or, if transported, to other countries, including the United States."

But the intelligence, like virtually all the rest, was bogus. The drones, it was later determined, were made for observation, not delivery of chemical or biological agents. Instead of chambers for holding germs or powder, they had only glass viewing ports and brackets to hold cameras. There was no room for anything else.

The mapping software of the U.S. east coast was equally a fabrication. Iraq, like many countries, had simply been offered the program by an Australian company that produced maps similar to the kind anyone can obtain for free from MapQuest or any other mapware offered on the Internet. "The software," said one official, "apparently produced maps not much better than those sold at gasoline stations." But it was all moot anyway, since Iraq neither asked for the software nor ever purchased it. "The vendor," said an official, "in the interest of making further sales, suggested this to the Iraqis, and there was no confirmation that we could find that the Iraqis had actually purchased the software."

"We now know," said Senator Nelson in January 2004, "after the fact and on the basis of [CIA chief weapons inspector] Dr. [David] Kay's testimony today in the Senate Armed Services Committee, that the information was false; and not only that there were not weapons of mass destruction—chemical and biological—but there was no fleet of UAVs, unmanned aerial vehicles, nor was there any capability of putting UAVs on ships and transporting them to the Atlantic coast and launching them at U.S. cities on the eastern seaboard. . . . The degree of specificity I was given a year and a half ago, prior to my vote, was not only inaccurate; it was patently false."

What Nelson was not told was that even within the CIA there was disagreement over the information, just as there was concerning the uranium from Niger. "Not only was it in vigorous dispute," said Nelson, "there was an outright denial that the information was accurate. That was all within the intelligence community."

During his State of the Union address to Congress in January 2003, President Bush used both the phony UAV threat and the bogus Niger uranium allegations in his argument for war with Iraq. "The British government," he said, "has learned that Saddam Hussein recently sought significant quantities of uranium from Africa." Again, the American public was left with the image of nuclear annihilation.

CHAPTER 13

LANGLEY

In the days, weeks, and months following the September 11 attacks, the CIA was in chaos as it scrambled to quickly beef up its ranks with case officers, analysts, linguists, and paramilitary specialists. For many working at the agency, there was a renewed sense of mission as they drew together to fight a common enemy—terrorism in general and Al Qaeda in particular. But within a few months, for many the morale once again began to drop through the floor as they began getting pressure to come up with Saddam Hussein's fingerprints on 9/11 and Al Qaeda.

One of those who felt the pressure was a DO case officer who spent years running agents overseas, but who had been reassigned to the unit charged with finding weapons of mass destruction (WMD) in Iraq, a part of the Counter-Proliferation Division. According to the official, the group never found any indications of WMD in Iraq. "Where I was working, I never saw anything—no one else there did either," the person said.

Nevertheless, there was a great deal of pressure to find a reason to go to war with Iraq. And the pressure was not just subtle, it was blatant. At one point in January 2003, the person's boss called a meeting and gave them their marching orders. "And he said, 'You know what—if Bush wants to go to war, it's your job to give him a reason to do so,'" according to the official. It was the first time the official had ever heard anyone order employees to slant their analysis for political purposes.

"And I said 'All right, it's time, it's time to go,'" said the official. "I remember, when it happened I looked around and I said 'This is awful.' He said it at the weekly office meeting. And I just remember saying, 'This is something that the American public, if they ever heard, if they ever knew, they would be outraged.' The fact that we're sitting in the meeting and we're not outraged at this, and we can't do anything—it was just against every moral fiber of my being. He said, 'If President Bush wants to go to war, ladies and gentlemen, your job's to give him a reason to do so.' . . . He said it to about fifty people. And it's funny because everyone still talks about that—'Remember when [he] said that.'"

Though the case officer still holds a very high security clearance and works on similar activities within the intelligence community, the person left the WMD unit. It is the cult of secrecy within the CIA, the person said, that keeps people from speaking out. "No one is willing to say the emperor has no clothes—no one is willing to say that," said the official. "Your job is just to salute and say okay. . . . I said to another colleague how embarrassed I was, and he said you better be careful, someone's going to report you."

When the official arrived in the office, others there mentioned that Vice President Cheney had also made very unusual visits to the agency to pressure analysts to come up with something to justify the war. "Before I got there," said the official, "Cheney came and literally went around to people saying find something. I was in there at the time when everyone said, 'Remember when Cheney came in, said we needed to find something nuclear?' Everyone was talking about it still—I think it was like November or December."

Another former CIA official who heard agency employees complain of pressure from above to slant intelligence reports was Larry Johnson, who later served as deputy director of the State Department's Office of Counter Terrorism. A registered Republican, he voted for George W. Bush and contributed financially to his 2000 presidential campaign. In February 2004 he said:

> By April of last year, I was beginning to pick up grumblings from friends inside the intelligence community that there had been pressure applied to analysts to come up with certain conclusions. Specifically, I was told that analysts were pressured to find an operational link between Osama bin Laden and Saddam Hussein. One analyst, in particular, told me they were repeatedly pressured by the most senior officials in the Department of Defense.
>
> In an e-mail exchange with another friend, I raised the possibility that "the Bush administration had bought into a lie." My friend, who works within the intelligence community, challenged me on the use of the word, "bought," and suggested instead that the Bush administration had created the lie. . . . I have spoken to more than two analysts who have expressed fear of retaliation if they come forward and tell what they know. We know that most of the reasons we were given for going to war were wrong.

In congressional testimony, former CIA Counterterrorism chief Vince Cannistraro said that in the weeks and months leading up to the war in Iraq, the White House had exerted unprecedented pressure on the CIA and other intelligence agencies to come up with evidence linking Iraq to Osama bin Laden and Al Qaeda.

Pressure was also placed on analysts, he said, to show that Baghdad was trying to build a nuclear bomb. "They were looking for those selective pieces of intelligence that would support the policy," Cannistraro said.

In written testimony, Cannistraro said that Vice President Dick Cheney and his top aide, Lewis (Scooter) Libby, went to CIA headquarters to press mid-level analysts to provide support for the claims. Cheney, he said, "insisted that desk analysts were not looking hard enough for the evidence." Cannistraro indicated his information came from current agency analysts.

"Analysts feel more politicized and more pushed than many of them can ever remember," one intelligence official told Greg Miller and Bob Drogin of *The Los Angeles Times*, speaking on condition of anonymity. "The guys at the Pentagon shriek on issues such as the link between Iraq and Al Qaeda. There has been a lot of pressure to write on this constantly, and to not let it drop."

"After 9/11," said another DO case officer who also still works in the intelligence community, "I think a lot of people at the agency sought a renewed sense of mission—like 'Okay, now I'm really going to have something to go after, now we have something to focus on.'" But for many, that was lost when the administration began pushing for intelligence on behalf of their war in Iraq. Yet the agency simply went along instead of fighting back.

"I was working from the headquarters end in our Iraqi operations," said the official. "In talking to the specialists, people who had worked on Iraqi issues or Iraqi WMD for years, they said to me, 'I always knew we didn't have anything.' This was before the war. But I mean, it was sort of horrific to me. . . . I talked to analysts and I talked to WMD experts, and I said, 'Okay, is there a link between Al Qaeda and Iraq?' 'No, there's not a link.' 'Do we have evidence of all this WMD we're talking about?' 'No, we don't have it.' And then it was like a snowball, and all of a sudden we were at war.

"Everybody that I was talking to who did know about the issues were saying we didn't have anything, and of course nobody's speaking up. Who can they speak up to? There's no forum for someone who's involved in operations to talk to anyone and say, 'We don't have any Iraqi assets, we don't have information on WMD, we don't have anything there.' But yet we all kind of knew it."

The CIA, said the official, was deliberately misused by the Bush administration. "I understand that it [the CIA] serves the President and the administration, but my thought is that it should serve the President and the administration in providing intelligence. And what has happened is that it serves the agenda—or at least for the Bush administration it's serving the agenda of this administration, which is not what the CIA is supposed to do."

The official then brought up the order issued at the staff meeting that "if Bush wants to go to war, it's your job to give him a reason to do so. . . . The fact that someone could say that in the agency and get away with it is just disgusting," said the official. "He said that to his full staff. I can't believe that someone would say that openly and get away with it. But there was a lot of that. . . . My dissent was that the role of the agency had become: provide support for what the administration's viewpoint was. And for me that was the final straw. It was criminal the way we were implicitly deceiving people. . . . You know, what I heard from everyone was that this had been planned for a long time."

Still another longtime DO officer, who primarily worked in the Central Asia Division, heard directly from a colleague about the outside pressure on agency personnel. "He was saying to me," said the DO officer, "'Well, the administration pressured us to say things that probably weren't true.' And I said, 'Whether that's true or not, we're still responsible, because we walk around saying we're not a political animal, we have no political ties to anybody, we are our own organization, yet we caved.'

"If that's really what happened," added the DO officer, "this leadership needs to go, because we're not supposed to cave. Our leadership needs to go, they need to be run out on a rail, because that's not our charter and we walk around saying that we would never do that. It's so much of a cult, and we're so insulated. We have pretend oversight from Congress, but really we have no oversight."

Compounding the problem was the fact that the agency had virtually no reliable sources in Iraq. "What was happening from my view," said the DO officer assigned to the headquarters Iraq unit, "was that the agency was scrambling at the eleventh hour to get some kind of agents in Iraq and we didn't really have any, or if we did it was so compartmentalized that I, working in Iraqi operations, didn't know about it. And it was sort of disheartening to me, because I thought 'Okay, now here's really a critical moment and we're a critical agency,' and I can see what's going on behind the scenes with a bunch of bubblers sitting here at headquarters supporting this war that we don't really have any intelligence to at least provide the support that the administration was looking for."

Instead of ethnically compatible CIA case officers with native language skills, most of the DO employees assigned to Iraq were standard collegiate-looking officers with, at best, rudimentary language skills and Cold War tradecraft. As a result, the intelligence community continued to depend heavily on Chalabi and his INC, despite the group's severe credibility problems.

As part of the long-awaited plan to put their man in charge of Iraq, senior Pentagon officials had Chalabi and several dozen of

his men flown to Kuwait and then transported to Baghdad. There
they were driven through the city in a parade—widely ignored—
as if the conquest of Iraq had been their personal handiwork.
Chalabi was named to the unelected twenty-five-member Iraqi
Governing Council, but he and his followers were shunned by
many because he had last lived in the country when he was a
young boy.

The INC's primary intelligence organization is its
Information Collection Program (ICP). Because of the lack of
qualified CIA case officers, it is the ICP that conducts approximately 20 percent of all verbal debriefings of Iraqi prisoners,
insurgents, and defectors. Originally, Chalabi and his INC were
handled by the State Department, but officials there discovered
that the organization was improperly handling taxpayers' dollars.
Thus, in 1992 oversight of the INC was transferred to the
Pentagon's Defense Intelligence Agency, which pays the group
about $4 million a year. The question is, what does the United
States get for that large amount of money?

To answer the question, the DIA conducted an internal
assessment of the information on Iraq provided by Chalabi's defectors and concluded that most of it "was of little or no value." To
make matters worse, several of the defectors introduced to
American intelligence agencies "invented or exaggerated their
credentials as people with direct knowledge of the Iraqi government and its suspected unconventional weapons program." The
DIA review, said the report, "concluded that no more than one-
third of the information was potentially useful, and efforts to
explore those leads since have generally failed to pan out."

"A huge amount of what was collected hasn't panned out.
Some of it has turned out to have been either wrong or fabricated,"
said one senior administration official. "The evidence now sug-
gests that at some points along the way, we may have been duped

by people who wanted to encourage military action for their own reasons." But Chalabi has his country back and is unrepentant. "As far as we're concerned, we've been entirely successful," said Chalabi. "That tyrant Saddam is gone, and the Americans are in Baghdad. What was said before is not important."

For much of the 1990s, the CIA spent little time attempting to penetrate the upper reaches of the Iraqi government, because the country was crawling with United Nations weapons inspectors—in essence, free spies. But once the inspectors suddenly left in 1998, following a major flap over their connections to the CIA, the agency was left out in the cold. "Back then we did not have any high-level penetration of the Iraqi Ministry of Health or Defense—no high-level penetrations there at all," said a DO case officer who worked in the Iraq chemical-biological warfare area during that period.

With such a paucity of raw intelligence, analysts were reduced to little more than guesswork when it came to Iraq's capabilities. "We had bits and pieces of things, but nothing to indicate that there was this massive, active program," said the case officer. "They had experimented, they had produced some, but we had no evidence that at that time in 2000 there were large quantities. So when I went back, in 2003, I was briefly . . . back there so I talked to some of my friends still working at the [Iraq] counterproliferation desk, and they were just all surprised. The first question was: 'What weapons of mass destruction?'" This was before the start of the war, the officer said. "So they were just asking, 'What weapons of mass destruction?'"

By the time the war was approaching, the agency had only three sources, none of whom were apparently still in Iraq and none who had ever been close to Saddam Hussein's upper leadership. Desperate, the DO was simply reduced to spreading large amounts of cash around Baghdad in little more than a fishing expedition. Virtually all the sources turned out to be bad. One passed on Saddam Hussein's supposed hidden location, thus triggering the start of the war two days prematurely. But, like the rest, the information was wrong.

"We had some information from the Central Intelligence Agency, that they had an unimpeachable source that Saddam Hussein was going to be in a residence in a bunker at Dora Farm," said Marc Garlasco. Working in the bowels of the Pentagon on the opening days of the war in Iraq, Garlasco was chief of high-value targets on the Joint Staff. But there was no bunker and no Hussein. "We were zero for fifty in all the strikes against high-value targets," he said. "The problem was, while the weapons were extraordinarily accurate, and they hit the targets precisely, none of the fellows were actually there." Instead, Garlasco said, the missiles killed more than one hundred innocent civilians.

"We did not have enough of our own human intelligence," conceded George Tenet. "We did not ourselves penetrate the inner sanctum." It was the same story as in Afghanistan, as well as in Iran, North Korea, and most other trouble spots around the world. Instead of developing their own penetration agents, the agency instead depended on the questionable reliability of "émigrés and defectors," said Tenet.

Of the CIA's three sources, one came through Ahmed Chalabi and provided bad information on Iraq's supposed mobile germ-weapons labs. The agency received information from the other two via liaison relationships with friendly foreign intelligence agencies—poor substitutes for its own agents.

One of the two, according to Tenet, had "direct access to Saddam and his inner circle." With CIA case officers present in the room, the source told his handlers that Iraq had developed no nuclear capability and was simply "dabbling" in germ warfare to no effect. But he also said that Iraq maintained a stockpile of chemical weapons, along with mobile missiles tipped with chemical warheads aimed at Israel. The other source, whom Tenet described as having "access to senior Iraqi officials," stated flatly that chemical and biological weapons were being produced. In that case, however, the CIA case officers were not allowed to be in the room during the interrogation.

Lack of knowledge about the human sources providing the information they were supposed to evaluate was a critical problem for CIA analysts before and during the war. The analysts were told only about the "reliability" of the source, but they were given no other information regarding such critical factors as the amount of actual access to the information the person was providing—did the person have firsthand, secondhand, or thirdhand access to the data, for example. "This is something the analysts have sought for years and have never been able to get," said one former senior agency analyst.

Ostensibly, the purpose of restricting the information had to do with protecting the agent's identity, but it also had a great deal to do with turf battles between the case officers in the Directorate of Operations and the analysts in the Directorate of Intelligence. According to the agency's director of intelligence, Jamie Miscik, DO case officers working the Iraq issue would sometimes deliberately mislead analysts by trying to boost the credibility of reports coming from only a single source. To make it seem that multiple sources were involved—and enhance the credibility of their reports—they would occasionally describe a single source several different ways in the same report.

Still another problem analysts faced when reviewing the Iraq information was reliance on what was known as "inherited assumptions." This was when the analysts failed to recalibrate their viewpoints in examining reports despite the changing political or social environment in the area they were studying.

Following the war, Miscik saw this problem as "the single most important aspect of our tradecraft that needs to be examined." The issue was especially acute when experienced analysts passed on information to those fresh to the field. "How do we ensure that we are not passing along assumptions that haven't been sufficiently questioned or reexamined?" she asked.

In the end, the three Iraq sources—who often contradicted one another—were hardly the proper basis on which to make a decision to go to war. In fact, Tenet would later admit that his agency "never said there was an 'imminent' threat."

But if the intelligence didn't indicate that Iraq posed an imminent threat, then what was the reason for the constant "imminent threat" drumbeat coming out of the administration? Given the end result, it appears that the real purpose of the "imminent threat" fearmongering was to serve as a pretext for war. A war that had nothing to do with "imminent threat" but everything to do with rearranging the map of the Middle East.

In an incredible irony, it was the CIA—not Iraq—that was hiding suspected weapons locations from the inspectors. While Iraqi officials were allowing the inspectors to go anywhere they wished throughout the country in the months prior to the war, the CIA was secretly keeping from them the locations of many of the sites they needed to inspect.

In the months leading up to America's rush to war, many were arguing that the inspectors should be given more time, and questions were being raised as to whether the United States was deliberately holding back on information. But both Tenet and Condoleezza Rice claimed that the UN inspectors had been briefed on all of the sites identified as "high value and moderate value" in the weapons hunt. The White House also said constantly that all intelligence on weapons sites was being shared with the inspectors.

Finally, on March 6, 2003, Rice sent a letter to Senator Carl Levin of the Senate Intelligence Committee insisting that "United Nations inspectors have been briefed on every high or medium priority weapons of mass destruction, missile and U.A.V. [unmanned aerial vehicle]-related site the U.S. intelligence community has identified." Tenet testified before Congress on February 12, 2003, saying virtually the same thing.

But, in fact, the CIA had been deliberately withholding from the inspectors 20 percent of the known locations. Of the 105 sites the intelligence community had identified as most likely housing banned weapons, 21 of them were deliberately kept secret from the UN. Given the new information, Senator Levin now believes that Tenet misled Congress and has called his actions "totally unacceptable."

The CIA claimed that it believed that the inspectors already knew of the sites not provided, but Levin found that excuse lame at best. He said it was his belief that the Bush administration withheld the critical information because it wanted to convince the American people that the United Nations—led hunt for weapons in Iraq had run its full course before the United States began its invasion. In fact, there were still many sites the inspectors were planning to search.

In addition to a lack of intelligence on Iraq, another problem facing the DO in the run-up to the war in Iraq were numerous distractions caused by a series of serious internal scandals and the struggle to keep a lid on them. They ranged from the disappearance of an agent as a result of careless tradecraft by one of the agency's prize chiefs of station to high-level suspicions of espionage.

In a very serious breach, the CIA chief in one of the agency's largest and most-sensitive stations took a walk-in defector to his home and then drove him back into the city in broad daylight and dropped him off in a public area. As the CIA chief should have expected, he was under surveillance most of the time, and soon after he dropped off the defector, the man was arrested and later disappeared. Leaving no doubt as to what happened, liaison officers with the foreign intelligence service called the station chief in and warned him about conducting espionage in their country.

As if the scandal were not bad enough, CIA Headquarters had been warned repeatedly about the station chief, who had previously served as chief of another station. According to officials familiar with the case, case officers in the other station virtually mutinied against him because of his drinking problem. "His drinking was during the day, it was in the morning," said one knowledgeable official. "He would come in just reeking of beer."

The problem also affected his relationship with the local intelligence service. "They were taking us for a ride every which way but loose," said one official, who also said the station chief was "abusive and would scream at people." Once the station chief left and was headed for a promotion, a number of the CIA officials at the station sent a protest to headquarters. To prevent the matter from being "swept under the rug," the officers sent their complaint not to the DO but to the Office of Medical Services.

Eventually, the officers were assured that the matter would be taken care of and the station chief would be disciplined. Instead, he was named as chief of one of the agency's premier stations. But just eight months into his tour, he committed the grievous error in tradecraft that resulted in the disappearance of a potential key defector. Following the incident, the chief of station was recalled and demoted, and he left the agency.

Another major distraction in the DO were suspicions about one of its deep-background "non-traditional platform" (NTP) employees. The person was also an SIS-3, a member of the agency's Senior Intelligence Service, which is made up of the highest-ranking agency employees, equivalent to military generals or navy admirals. For several years, the person had been allowed to write his own performance evaluations. In them he would list the projects he had worked on and the organizations within the agency he had assisted. But when the agency suddenly audited his evaluation, they found it was mostly fraudulent.

A senior-level evaluator, said one knowledgeable NTP official, "went around to each of the divisions and said, 'Well, he's worked on this case for you and this case for you—can you give me some remarks on his performance?' And without exception all of them came back and said, 'He hasn't worked with us in years.'

"They started pulling back more and more layers of this," said the official, "and they brought him home and said, 'Who have you been working for? What have you been doing?' And he's traveling overseas all the time. 'Where are you going?' It's not only a management problem, it's also a CI [Counter-Intelligence] problem. 'You're going overseas all the time—what are you doing when you go if you're not working for anybody? Where are you getting the money?' And this guy is one of the two or three most senior guys. . . . Knowing him as I did, I could not discern who he worked for or what function he had and I was ten paces away when he was in country. And he was a role model for all of us, so to speak."

During an early-2004 interview the official said the case would likely be swept under the carpet. "This fellow would say, 'I'm off to Switzerland to support such and such a case,'" said the official. "If you go to Switzerland every quarter and you say it's for business and your money is from the government and you're not actually doing anything, there are lots of implications there. And for this to be one of the most senior guys, it's a terrible thing. It's unfolding even as we speak. He's still there. And he's on the carpet now, and they're going to give him a chance to reform."

Flush with millions of dollars in post-9/11 budget increases, the DO launched a mad hiring rush as the administration began gearing up for war with Iraq. But quantity did not translate into quality, and instead of producing usable intelligence, the scramble often produced only chaos and confusion. Lack of adequate linguists to handle the surge of increased raw intelligence was a critical problem.

In response, the agency began paying out millions of dollars to a score of established and start-up private companies. Nicknamed "beltway bandits" because many had offices around the Route 495 beltway circling Washington, these contractors would recruit current and former CIA employees at up to double their salaries.

Once on board, they were frequently assigned back to their same offices at CIA doing the same work, but now the taxpayers were paying them up to twice as much. Others were assigned even less sophisticated work than they were originally performing. Because of the slapdash nature of the rush to expand, the quality of intelligence produced by some of these contractors has become questionable.

"The money is incredible—I doubled my salary to go out and come back in and continue doing what I was doing," said one former DO official. "They're all former DO officers, and basically what these companies are doing, they have this net and all these people trickling out of the agency, they're just catching them. It's like fruit on the ground, because the agency doesn't have the people that they need to do these jobs. But the problem is these jobs are mindless—because once again there's no structure applied to the task at hand. So we're all just sitting there looking at each other, and we're making a ridiculous amount of money."

Many of the people were hired to analyze the hundreds of hard drives seized overseas in Afghanistan, Iraq, and other locations as part of the war on terrorism. But because much of the data is in Arabic or other languages which few analysts or agents read or speak, often the information simply collects dust.

"The first contract I was on I left, because I said this is fraud," said a DO officer turned contractor. "There was over a million dollars sitting in that [CIA] office—just the salary we collected, not to mention the extra money that goes to these companies. We sat there all day and same-timed each other, which is like instant messaging. We would just same-time each other all day. And after about three months of that, I went to my company and I said you need to get me off this contract or I'm going to another company or I'm leaving altogether.

"Basically what we were doing," said the person, "is we were looking for any ops leads in these hard drives—through e-mail— things that were found residually on hard drives. Anything you do in the computer is somewhere engraved in a hard drive, and so we could look for tools to mine. . . . Sometimes we got hard drives that were probably a couple of weeks old, because these are hard drives from where we went out and either rendered people or we raided places and we would just scoop up—not we, but the agents who were out there—the military would just scoop up hard drives in a big old Santa Claus bag and send them back."

The problem came when the information was not in English, which was most of the time. According to the contractor:

A lot of it was in Arabic, and none of us spoke Arabic— just a little problem. It would just sit there. It would just sit there. But none of us really knew what we were doing, and we had management who didn't know what they were doing either.

The problem is, and I just can't stress enough what the agency does to tackle their problems—they just throw people and money at the issue. It doesn't matter what the outcome is, it doesn't matter what the product of that is. It's just comforting to them to know that in this office next to me, he's got twenty people sitting there, doesn't matter what they're doing, but we've got them sitting there and that makes me feel like I'm getting something done, you know that we're tackling this problem.

After September 11 happened, I think working from a position of chaos is understandable, because we were all shell-shocked. Everybody was like sleeping at the agency, we'll read traffic, we'll put out cables, whatever you want, we'll man telephones. There was a lot of momentum for out-of-box kind of thinking and free-thinking and everything else. But it was a very chaotic time, and what we were able to accomplish was probably very good given what we were working under.

Two years after September 11, it's not acceptable to continue to be working from that same position of chaos, because we haven't stepped back—we let the momentum carry us along, but we fell back on the old ways of doing things, which is just shove people on the problem.

According to the former DO official turned contractor, the surge in staffing the agency's Counterterrorism Center [CTC] has left many of the agency's area divisions around the world depleted. Because of the "need to surge hundreds and hundreds at CTC," said the contractor, "there's nobody in these area divisions any-more, everybody's working the CT target. Africa Division is smaller now than the number of people we have in Baghdad. The entire division. And the people in Baghdad are just sitting."

Afghanistan has also proved difficult for the agency, said a number of current and former agency DO officials. According to one:

> We were talking to teams in the field who were in Afghanistan every night. I was working the night shift all the time, and I would talk to the guys because that's when they were awake and doing things. [They were] using a secure phone via Inmarsat, and then we have a STU [Secure Telephone Unit] on the other end—we had several teams.
>
> I would ask, What's going on? How are you all doing? They weren't doing anything. They weren't doing anything. And they were so frustrated. People were leaving. . . . There was one team that just left, they just up and left, because they were going to be extended and they had already stayed over their stay or whatever, and they had sent messages saying we're not doing any-thing here, and we've got family, and we have jobs, and we hear now that you're thinking of extending us—and this was probably a day before the helicopter was sup-posed to come and take them away. They got on that hel-icopter and they left.
>
> Their job was to collect intelligence. But this is what was happening—you'd go into this village and you'd have ten or fifteen people come up to you and go, "I know where bin Laden is." So you give them a hun-dred bucks and you never see them again. [The infor-

mants were also given a handheld GPS—global positioning system—to pinpoint exact locations.]

The GPS was to be taken to wherever bin Laden was, and they would write down the latitude and longitude. And so a lot of cable traffic has come and gone based on all of this information, from all of these people who come in and say they know where bin Laden is. And of course, they don't—they want the money. Or if someone does in all good faith, they only heard it through a cousin who heard it from their cousin who heard it from a cousin who heard it from a cousin. It's so ineffective. I'm not saying that that's not the right way to go about it, but what I am saying is it's not working. It's not been working now for two years. Let's think of another way to do that.

Because the war in Iraq, which the Pentagon had promised would be over quickly—followed by happy, cheering crowds—instead quickly dissolved into a quagmire, the CIA was caught short. Instead of the eighty-five Clandestine Service officers it had originally planned to send, it was forced to rush to the battlefield four times that number.

By the spring of 2004, more than three hundred full-time case officers were packing the Baghdad station and more than half a dozen outlying bases. Overall, CIA personnel in country by then had soared to more than five hundred—including contractors—eclipsing even Saigon station at the height of the Vietnam War more than three decades earlier.

Despite the surge, quantity did not translate into quality. Many of the new arrivals had little or no training in either the right languages, interrogation skills, or tradecraft. By 2004, the total number of CIA employees fluent in Arabic was still only eighty-three, and many of them spoke a dialect not used in Iraq. This has required the agency to become heavily dependent on translators, a problematic situation in terms of both security and effectiveness. Thus, there was little improvement in penetrating Iraqi resistance forces or learning who was behind the insurgency.

To make up for the green arrivals, the agency has been forced to turn to hundreds of volunteers from its reserve force of home-bound retirees, many of whom have long been away from the field and are of limited usefulness. Also, because they are rotated in and out so quickly—often for just ninety days at a time—there is little time to accomplish much. The confusion has also had a detrimental effect on the agency's relationship with a number of regional Iraqi leaders who have become frustrated over their inability to establish liaison relations with CIA officers. According to one former case officer who still maintains close ties to the agency, the CIA was stretched to the limit. "With Afghanistan, the war on terrorism, with Iraq, I think they're just sucking wind," he said.

Among the other handicaps faced by the station is the endless violence that has forced the agency to require that all employees leaving secure facilities be accompanied by an armed bodyguard. Under such conditions, developing sources and conducting clandestine meetings are all but impossible. "How do you do your job that way?" asked one former CIA official who had spent time in Iraq. "They don't know what's going on out there."

There has also been a tug-of-war between local military commanders who want more and better tactical intelligence to help prevent the daily attacks, and senior officials in Washington who are trying to discover long-term plans and establish a chain of command. This and other management problems led the agency to close a number of its Iraqi bases and pull the station chief out of Baghdad before the person's tour was up. The person, who had previously run a far less complex station in the Middle East, was replaced in December 2003 by a Clandestine Service officer who had previously run CIA operations in Bosnia and Kosovo. The new chief was the third since May of 2003.

At the same time that insurgents in Iraq are sniping away at the CIA on the battlefield, senior defense and military officials are taking aim at the agency in the windowless back rooms of the Pentagon. Few realize that while George Tenet may be the nominal head of America's vast intelligence empire, he really controls a mere 15 percent of it.

The rest is under the direct operational control of the Secretary of Defense, Donald Rumsfeld. This includes the National Security Agency, the largest of all the spy agencies; the National Reconnaissance Office, which builds, controls, and manages the spy satellite program; the National Geospatial-Intelligence Agency, which analyzes the imagery from the spy satellites; the Defense Intelligence Agency; and a number of others.

For years Rumsfeld, and other defense chiefs before him, had wanted to consolidate their control over America's spy world by creating their own intelligence czar—a sort of Pentagon equivalent to George Tenet. But also for years, the move had been fought by the various CIA directors, backed up by members of Congress, especially by many on the House and Senate Intelligence Committees. Nevertheless, in 2003, Rumsfeld was able to pull off a major coup when Congress finally gave him permission to establish such a post, known as the Undersecretary of Defense for Intelligence.

To the surprise—and disappointment—of many, Tenet barely lifted a finger in protest. A number of sources believe that Tenet's near obsession with running the day-to-day operations of the CIA left him with little time or interest for directing the activities of the rest of the intelligence community. Thus, within minutes of the attacks of September 11, with Rumsfeld suddenly becoming the administration's top warrior, his intelligence coup was almost inevitable.

The merging of the war on terrorism and the war in Iraq has also led to the blurring of the lines between CIA paramilitary operations and the Pentagon's special forces operations. This, together with the new concept of preemptive wars, has many worried. While there are strict laws governing the CIA's covert operations abroad, there are far fewer restrictions on the Pentagon's growing cadre of commandos, SEALs, special forces, Delta Team, and assorted other down-and-dirty fighters. Congressional oversight of the military's unconventional forces is considerably less than that of civilian intelligence operations.

Since the September 11 attacks, Rumsfeld has greatly boosted the budget of the U.S. Special Operations Command—SoCom— which is based at MacDill Air Force Base in Tampa, Florida. It has also granted expanded authority to the command, allowing its 50,000 fighters to play a far more significant role in the war on terrorism—previously the CIA's exclusive domain.

Technical intelligence wasn't much better than human intelligence on Iraq. The satellites could see only the exteriors of buildings, not what was going on inside. And because of the extensive use of difficult-to-tap buried and fiber-optic cables, as well as sophisticated encryption and communications security, NSA was not able to listen to Saddam Hussein or his inner circle. As a result, the agency mostly focused its attention on intercepting wireless Iraqi military communications and eavesdropping on commercial traffic.

"Sigint [signals intelligence] was monitoring the movement of cargo whenever they had a tip-off about certain cargo, especially cargo from China to Iraq, or Russia to Iraq," said one intelligence official involved with Iraq. "That's what they monitored. Sometimes they would get the bill of lading, and then on there it would list equipment. But it was usually a lot of dual-use items. Things that could be used in a vaccine program—very legitimate use—equipment as well." Sigint, said the official, "is given a higher degree of credibility than humint [human intelligence]. There's more respect. I think hands down their [NSA's] linguistic capabilities are probably more respected [than that of the CIA]."

In a sense, it is a sort of vicious circle. NSA needs human intelligence sources to help tell it where, and to whom, to listen. So poor humint ultimately results in poor Sigint. "The more humint you get, the better Sigint you get," said a senior intelligence official. "Because the more humint you get, the more your Sigint is able to cope with the volume that is inherent in just throwing a blanket over a communications network, then trying to sort out what it is you have underneath the blanket. The more humint you have the more precise you can be, and therefore the more effective you can be with Sigint."

Following the attacks of September 11, NSA had a major decision to make. It had to decide whether to continue to go forward with its massive, long-term reorganization plan, designed to revitalize the agency workforce and modernize its worldwide eavesdropping network, or quickly change gears to focus on the immediate terrorist threat. On September 13, the agency's director, Lt. Gen. Michael Hayden, called a meeting in his office to make the decision.

"We had all the senior leadership of the agency in this room," said Hayden. "About thirty-five people . . . all the key leaders. We had them all in the room. I said, 'Okay, we had a plan and we had a transformational road map and we made some decisions, now this [9/11] has happened. Do we need to revisit any of the trajectories that we put the agency on?' And this was one of those frank and wide-ranging discussions. Every man and woman in the

room said, 'Go faster. No change in direction. If anything, accelerate all the changes under way.'"

Ironically, at a time when most of the intelligence agencies
were recalling previously retired workers, NSA went ahead with
their plan to offer incentives for employees to take early outs.
"This was within thirty days of the attack," said Hayden, "with
the whole system stretched by the challenges of the new war. We
had a lot of people leave and actually paid some people to leave."
The problem was that many of the people at NSA had the right
skills for the wrong targets. The agency had to move out many of
the longtime Soviet linguists and high-frequency specialists to
make room for Urdu and Dari speakers, and experts at dissecting
and reverse-engineering the Internet.

"We cannot squeeze any more juice out of retraining," said
Hayden. "We had spent a decade trying to retrain people for the
new kinds of missions, and now it was time to get new people in
here. And the only way you can get new people in here is to let
other people go. And we were criticized for that. Someone who's as
good at her job as [Congresswoman] Jane Harmon, the senior
member on the [House Intelligence Committee], and pays a lot of
attention to us and is very conscientious and comes out to visit us
and is very supportive, even she kind of said, 'What is this all
about?' And said so in a public way, and I quietly pointed out to her,
'It was a tough decision, but it was a right decision.'"

NSA's personnel problems began in the early 1990s with the
end of the Cold War. "We were a third smaller at the end of the
1990s than we were at the beginning," said Hayden. "We downsized in the worst possible way—we shut the front door. For most
of the decade of the 1990s, we hired fewer than 200 people a
year—civilians—in an agency that had over 20,000 civilians in
1990; 15,000 by 2000." By 2004, according to Hayden, the new
recruits had jumped to 1,500 a year.

But of those numbers, the largest group hired were not code breakers but security guards. "Number one, security—we've got to defend ourself," said Hayden. "Garrison no longer equates to sanctuary. So we're hiring guards. We're renting some, too. Number two, we've increased our polygraphers. Number three, linguists. Number four, analysts. And there almost ain't a number five. . . . We focused on what I call wartime languages—Arabic, all the languages of Afghanistan, and then selected languages in other parts of the world, Horn of Africa."

According to Hayden, as the rush to war began gathering steam, most of the intelligence NSA was able to pick up was ambiguous and far from solid with regard to weapons of mass destruction. "When I asked our best analysts to characterize our Sigint now, in comparison to the humint, as an overall assessment, they characterized the Sigint as either ambiguous or confirmatory of the humint," said Hayden. At the time, however, there was very little humint.

Adding to the ambiguity problem was the fact that much of what Hussein was receiving was dual-use—items that could be used for either innocent or nefarious purposes. Hayden's Sigint analysts, he said, "brought up an additional fact that made this hard. Saddam was living under a sanction regime. Most commercial transactions which in other parts of the world would have been legitimate transactions were in many cases in Iraq violations of the sanctions. So an awful lot of commercial transactions were of an ambiguous nature that involved dual-use materials or dual-use equipment."

These transactions, said Hayden, "were conducted in an almost clandestine sort of way. Now, how do you distinguish that clandestinity as evidence of pursuing WMD, as opposed to simply a reflection of living under a regime in which commercial transactions that otherwise would be viewed as normal, here have to be conducted in a secretive sort of way? . . . When you're looking at the evidence here, say you're a Siginter [a signals intelligence analyst] and you're looking at an intercept. It's admittedly ambiguous—you may give country x the benefit of the doubt, but if country x is Iraq, this is a guy who you know has lied about his weapons of mass destruction program, so there's a tendency here to be suspicious about even ambiguous activity."

In addition to looking for WMD, NSA also played a large role in the Bush administration's efforts to spy on the United Nations weapons inspectors and pressure undecided members of the UN Security Council to vote in favor of its go-to-war resolution.

The agency's highly secret eavesdropping operations targeting the United Nations dates back to its very first organizing conference in 1945. In April of that year, representatives of more than fifty countries crowded into a San Francisco opera house to negotiate a framework for a new world order. But the American delegates also had a secret weapon.

As coded messages between the foreign delegations and their distant capitals passed through U.S. telegraph lines in San Francisco, copies were covertly turned over to Army code breakers. Other messages were intercepted at a secret listening post known as Two Rock Ranch north of San Francisco. The intercepts were then forwarded to Arlington Hall, the Army's code-breaking headquarters, over forty-six special secure teletype lines.

The decrypts revealed how desperate France had become to maintain their image as a major world power after the war. Messages from Colombia provided details on quiet disagreements between Russia and its satellite nations as well as "Russia's prejudice toward the Latin American countries." Spanish decrypts indicated that their diplomats in San Francisco were warned to oppose a number of Russian moves. "Red maneuver . . . must be stopped at once," said one intercepted message. Another, from Czechoslovakia, indicated their opposition to the admission of Argentina.

The United States pushed hard to locate the organization on American soil, largely to accommodate the eavesdroppers and code breakers of NSA and its predecessors. The Russians, on the other hand, were also happy to have it on American soil—it gave them a reason to ship dozens of new spies across U.S. borders.

Nearly sixty years later, the United Nations was still a key target for American eavedroppers and code breakers. Among those high on NSA's list was Hans Blix, the chief of the Iraq weapons inspectors. He had previously served at the International Atomic Energy Agency from 1981 to 1997. Discovering the bugging operation during the run-up to war, he labeled it "disgusting." Blix said: "You are cooperating with the people who sit across the desk one day and if the next they are listening to you, it is an unpleasant feeling." Asked if it was morally questionable, he replied: "Well, I don't know what morals they have. Questionable, yes."

Blix became convinced that the United States was spying on him when, two weeks before the start of the war, John Wolf, the Assistant Secretary of State for Nonproliferation, showed him two photographs of Iraqi weapons that could only have come from the UN weapons office. "He should not have had them," said Blix. "I asked him how he got them and he would not tell me, and I said I resented that." Blix suspected that the NSA was monitoring his secure fax and had deciphered his encryption algorithm.

Blix's mobile phone was also monitored, as was the headquarters for his UN inspection team in Baghdad's Canal Hotel. Transcripts of his conversations were shared with senior British officials. "The only saving grace is that neither Dr. Blix or anyone else among us would speak about sensitive matters on mobile telephones," said one UN official. "So they would not have heard anything earth-shattering just by that. But I suspect there were other, more widespread interceptions. There were plenty of attempts to undermine us."

At the time, the United States was angry with Blix because he and Dr. Mohamed El Baradei, head of the International Atomic Energy Agency, had asked for more time to finish their weapons inspection in Iraq. The Bush administration, hell-bent to launch its war, opposed any extension and would do almost anything to frustrate Blix.

"I think they had a set mind," said Blix. "They wanted to come to the conclusion that there were weapons. Like the former days of the witch hunt, they are convinced that they exist, and if you see a black cat, well, that's evidence of the witch. . . . You could say that Iraq was perhaps as much punitive as it was preemptive. It was a reaction to 9/11 that we have to strike some theoretical, hypothetical links between Saddam Hussein and the terrorists. That was wrong. There wasn't anything. The Americans and British created facts where there were no facts at all. The Americans needed [Iraq to have] WMD to justify the Iraq war."

A clear indication that WMD was simply a pretext for the Bush administration's long-planned war was the fact that no revised National Intelligence Estimate was produced prior to the push for the war resolution. By then, in February 2003, the newly returned inspectors had spent three nonstop months checking out virtually all of the questionable locations listed in the CIA's NIE. And despite taking thousands of samples, they found no indications of hidden quantities of chemical, biological, or nuclear weapons—anywhere.

While the U.S. intelligence community was studying pictures of suspect buildings from space, the UN inspectors were swabbing the insides of those same locations with cotton balls. They would later be put through sophisticated tests designed to detect even the most minute trace of germs or banned chemicals. On November 28 they inspected al-Dawrah, on December 9 they tested the suspected buildings in Fallujah, two days later they went to Ibn Sina and Tarmiyya, and on and on. They were all locations identified in the highly secret NIE.

"By the time the inspectors left the plant today, after four hours," wrote one reporter who accompanied inspectors through the suspected location at al-Dawrah, "they had concluded that the plant was no longer operational—not for the production of toxins, and not for animal vaccines either. Reporters who were allowed to wander through the plant after the inspectors left found the place largely in ruins. Apparently, it had been abandoned by the Iraqis after 1996, when the weapons inspectors took heavy cutting equipment to the fermenters, containers and pressurized tubing and valves used in the toxin production."

As more inspectors poured in, permission was granted for U-2s to begin crisscrossing the country. Never before had there been such an opportunity to collect so much close-up humint, Sigint, and photint on a target country. But the Bush administration simply ignored it all, demanded the inspectors leave and make way for the bombs and the tanks.

Richard Butler, Blix's predecessor, was also angry over the UN bugging operation during the run-up to war. "What if Kofi Annan had been bringing people together last February in a genuine attempt to prevent the invasion of Iraq, and the people bugging him did not want that to happen, what do you think they would do with that information?"

Butler also had a great deal of personal experience as a frequent bugging target. "I was utterly confident that in my attempts to have private conversations, trying to solve the problem of disarmament of Iraq, I was being listened to by the Americans, British, the French, and the Russians," he said. "They also had people on my staff reporting what I was trying to do privately. Do you think that was paranoia? Absolutely not. There was abundant evidence that we were being constantly monitored."

A key target of the NSA was Secretary General Kofi Annan. According to his predecessor, Boutros Boutros-Ghali, "From the first day I entered my office they said, 'Beware, your office is bugged, your residence is bugged, and it is a tradition that the member states who have the technical capacity to bug will do it without any hesitation.' That would involve members of the Security Council. The perception is that you must know in advance that your office, your residence, your car, your phone is bugged."

In February 2004 British Member of Parliament Clare Short, a former member of Prime Minister Tony Blair's cabinet, set off a storm when she admitted that in the weeks prior to the launch of the Iraq war she had read secret transcripts of UN Secretary General Kofi Annan confidential conversations. The transcripts were likely made by NSA and shared with its sister British eavesdropping agency, the Government Communications Headquarters (GCHQ), which passed them on to the prime minister's office.

"The U.K. in this time was also getting, spying on Kofi Annan's office and getting reports from him about what was going on," said Short. She added, "These things are done. And in the case of Kofi's office, it's been done for some time. . . . I have seen transcripts of Kofi Annan's conversations. In fact, I have had conversations with Kofi in the run-up to war, thinking, 'Oh dear, there will be a transcript of this and people will see what he and I are saying.'"

By January 2003, NSA was turning its giant ears toward the undecided members of the UN Security Council. Three months earlier, largely as a result of its avalanche of phony intelligence, the Bush administration won the support of both houses of Congress for a war with Iraq. With the country largely convinced, Bush reluctantly went along with Colin Powell's recommendation to convince the rest of the world through a United Nations resolution authorizing the use of force against Iraq.

On November 8, the Security Council passed Resolution 1441, warning of "serious consequences" if Iraq did not take a "final opportunity to comply with its disarmament obligations." To Washington, that translated into an authorization to launch its war against Iraq if they failed to comply fully, but London disagreed. With a population far less supportive of military action against Iraq, Prime Minister Tony Blair's government suggested that a second resolution, specifically authorizing war, would be required before the launch of an all-out UN-backed invasion. Reluctantly, primarily as a favor to his friend Blair, Bush agreed to the recommendation.

By late January the Bush and Blair administrations had determined that Iraq had failed to fully disarm and as a result they were putting tremendous pressure on the uncommitted members of the Security Council to vote in favor of its tough go-to-war resolution. On the other side, arguing against the war, were France, Germany and Russia. Thus the "Middle Six," as they became known—Angola, Cameroon, Chile, Mexico, Guinea, and Pakistan—suddenly became top candidates for America's friendship, and key targets for NSA's eavesdropping.

They were like cheats at a poker game; knowing what cards were in other players' hands would give the United States a critical advantage. By listening in as the delegates communicated back to their home countries, the NSA would be able to discover which way they might vote, which positions they favored or opposed, and what their negotiating positions would be.

They also could pick up indications of what they needed, such as a highway, a dam, or a favorable trade deal, and, in a subtle form of bribery, provide the country with a generous "aid package" to help pay for the construction.

Among the things NSA tapped into was a secret meeting of the Middle Six, who were seeking, in a last-ditch effort, to come up with a compromise resolution to avert the war in Iraq by giving the weapons inspectors more time to finish their work. According to former Mexican ambassador to the UN Adolfo Aguilar Zinser, the Americans somehow learned of the meeting and intervened. They could only have learned of the plan, said Zinser, as a result of electronic surveillance. As soon as the Americans found out about the meeting, Zinser claimed, "They said, 'You should know that we don't like the idea and we don't like you to promote it.'"

Having already won over the U.S. Congress and the American public, the Bush administration was not about to let a half-dozen Third World countries get between them and their war. Thus, on January 31, the NSA ratcheted up its targeting on the Middle Six. Frank Koza, the Sigint Department's deputy chief of staff for Regional Targets, sent a Top Secret/Codeword memo to the NSA's partners in Britain, Canada, Australia, and New Zealand asking for help:

"As you've likely heard by now, the Agency is mounting a surge particularly directed at the UN Security Council (UNSC) members (minus US and GBR [Great Britain] of course) for insights as to how membership is reacting to the on-going debate RE: Iraq, plans to vote on any related resolutions, what related policies/negotiating positions they may be considering, alliances/dependencies, etc.——the whole gamut of information that could give US policymakers an edge in obtaining results favorable to US goals or to head off surprises."

Koza added, "I suspect that you'll be hearing more along these lines in formal channels—especially as this effort will probably peak (at least for this specific focus) in the middle of next week, following the SecState's [Secretary of State Colin Powell's] presentation to the UNSC."

It was during that address by Powell that the Bush administration would make their last major argument before launching the war—and their most persuasive because of the respect accorded Powell.

CHAPTER 14

SECURITY COUNCIL

Like Hollywood producers, the White House Iraq Group was looking for a media spectacular to sell not just the American public but
the rest of the skeptical world on the need to go to war with Iraq.
The answer was to replay the scene from the 1962 Cuban missile
crisis when Kennedy administration UN Ambassador Adlai
Stevenson confronted his Soviet counterpart in the Security
Council over ballistic missiles in Cuba. While the whole world
watched, Stevenson proved the Russians were hiding weapons of
mass destruction on Castro's island.

Four decades later, the role of Stevenson would be played by
Secretary of State Colin Powell, backed up by a twenty-first-century sound and light show. As probably the most trusted member
of the Bush administration, Powell would be the perfect choice
and the Security Council the ideal venue to sell the WHIG's spu-
rious claims against Iraq.

Powell compared the assignment to when he received his
marching orders a decade earlier during the Gulf War. Then, as
Chairman of the Joint Chiefs of Staff, he was watching CNN
when President George H. W. Bush addressed the nation from the
Oval Office. The Iraqi invasion of Kuwait "will not stand," said

the President. "I think I just got my orders," Powell told those around him, according to a knowledgeable source.

Now, as President George W. Bush, during his State of the Union address, told the nation that he would send his Secretary of State to the United Nations to make his case for war, Powell had the same reaction. "I just got my orders," he later told his associates.

With little time to prepare for the February 5, 2003, Security Council address, Powell assembled a small task force of trusted aides to go over the intelligence and put together his presentation. And right from the start, the WHIG handed Powell the "script" he was supposed to follow. "Here's the document prepared over at the White House for my script," he told an associate.

Early the next morning, the small group of aides arrived at CIA Headquarters, where they planned to assemble Powell's presentation with the help of an assortment of intelligence professionals. They were given space in the seventh-floor corner offices of the National Intelligence Council (NIC), just down the hall from George Tenet's suite. It was the NIC that had produced the National Intelligence Estimate on Iraqi weapons of mass destruction three months earlier, so many of the experts were close at hand.

But according to a 2004 interview with a senior official closely associated with the event, the Powell aides saw problems the minute they began reading the fifty-page White House "script." "We went through that for about six hours—item by item, page by page," said the official, "and about halfway through the day I realized this is idiocy, we cannot possibly do this, because it was all bullshit—it was unsourced, a lot of it was just out of newspapers, it was—and I look back in retrospect—it was a [Undersecretary of Defense for Policy Douglas] Feith product, it was a Scooter Libby [Vice President Cheney's chief of staff] product, it was a Vice President's office product. It was a product of collusion between that group. And it had no way of standing up, any-where. I mean it was nuts."

The "script" had been prepared by top Libby and Cheney aide John Hannah, according to the official. Hannah was assigned to Powell's team to help prepare the presentation. Hannah was also one of the key officials receiving the largely bogus raw intel-ligence from Chalabi's INC, according to a memorandum obtained by *Newsweek*. "The memo not only describes Cheney aide Hannah as a 'principal point of contact' for the program," wrote Mark Hosenball and Michael Isikoff, "it even provides his direct White House telephone number." The other official named on the memo was William Luti, head of Feith's Office of Special Plans at the Pentagon.

The script "was a prepared document supposedly written by Scooter Libby," said the official. He said he later "found out that . . . John Hannah, in the Vice President's office, who works for Scooter Libby, actually wrote it. Scooter actually may have done some things, but John wrote it, I think. . . . And John came amply papered in order to support that document, but what he was amply papered with was not a professional intelligence trail, it was a trail to a newspaper article, it was a trail to an INC defector, it was a trail to someone else's speech that was as unsupportable as that. So we tossed it out."

Instead of the Cheney office "script," the team decided to use the NIC's National Intelligence Estimate (NIE) on Iraq. While not as bad as the "script," the NIE was also a thrown-together collec-tion of half-baked intelligence, including such things as the Italian Niger yellowcake claim.

Concerned with the rejection of their "script," members of the WHIG came over to CIA to watch Powell rehearse his presen-tation in George Tenet's conference room and assure themselves that he was still following the party line. There were "three major rehearsals, with everybody coming over from the White House," said the official, "with the exception of the President. Condi Rice came over, Scooter Libby came over, Steve Hadley—Condi's deputy—came over." George Tenet was also present.

"On a number of occasions," said the official, Powell "simply said, 'I'm not using that, I'm not using that, that is not good enough. That's not something that I can support.' And on each occasion he was fought by the Vice President's office in the person of Scooter Libby, by the National Security Advisor [Condoleezza Rice] herself, by her deputy [Steve Hadley], and sometimes by the intelligence people—George [Tenet] and [Deputy CIA Director] John [McLaughlin]."

Much of the fighting between Powell and the WHIG officials was over what the official said was "the garbage on terrorism." This included such things as the discredited connections between Saddam Hussein and the 9/11 attacks, and meetings between hijacker Mohamed Atta and an Iraqi intelligence official in Prague, Czech Republic. "Cutting some of that stuff out was fought hard by the National Security Advisor [Rice], the Deputy National Security Advisor [Hadley], Scooter Libby from the Vice President's office. They wanted that stuff back in there. And on one occasion the Secretary actually threw the paper down on the table and said, 'I'm not saying that.' And that was the tenor throughout, even when we did two more rehearsals in New York City."

Even after Powell threw material out, it would occasionally be quietly put back in. "One of the most outrageous ones was the Mohamed Atta meeting in Prague," said the official. "Steve Hadley on one occasion [put] it back in. We cut it and somehow it got back in. And the Secretary said, 'I thought I cut this?' And Hadley looked around and said, 'My fault, Mr. Secretary, I put it back in.' 'Well, cut it, permanently!'" yelled Powell.

"It was all cartoon," said the official, "the specious connections between Al Qaeda and Saddam Hussein, much of which I subsequently found came probably from the INC and from their sources, defectors and so forth, [regarding the] training in Iraq for terrorists. It was like a chronology of contacts between terrorists, and in particular Al Qaeda or Al Qaeda associates, with the Mukhabaret, the Iraqi intelligence service, Saddam Hussein, whatever, and it just didn't hold together."

With regard to the origin of some of the material, the official said, "No question in my mind that some of the sources that we were using were probably Israeli intelligence. That was one thing that was rarely revealed to us—if it was a foreign source."

With regard to the terrorist connections, said the official, the truth was opposite from what they were projecting. At every opportunity, Saddam Hussein spurned any relationship with Al Qaeda and terrorist organizations. "You would almost always find that Saddam Hussein or someone in his government had rebuffed the attempt by the terrorist organization, whoever it might have been, to get training from, funds from, or establish some kind of operational relationship between Iraqi intelligence and themselves. It had almost always been rebuffed.

"And so it didn't make sense to be talking about contacts which clearly had happened but didn't turn into anything. That didn't become a relationship. It didn't become a sponsorship, or a host-sponsor type of thing." But the truth was not what the WHIG was hoping to pass on to the American public.

Powell was so concerned about the quality of intelligence he was getting that he told Tenet, "George, you're going to be there with me at the UN, you're going to be sitting behind me. You have got to put your imprimatur on it—this is your presentation as much as it is mine." Tenet agreed. "Mr. Secretary," he said, "I've got to go defend it on the Hill after you say it. And that's going to be a much tougher audience. So I'm standing behind it one hundred percent."

On February 5, 2003, Powell took his seat at the round Security Council table and made his case to the world. It was a powerful and convincing performance, particularly because of his assertive language and lack of qualifiers. "My colleagues," he said, "every statement I make today is backed up by sources, solid sources. These are not assertions. What we're giving you are facts and conclusions based on solid intelligence."

But Powell knew that the case was anything but solid and was based almost entirely on poor guesswork. He began with what he likely thought would be the most dramatic and convincing evidence—by playing actual NSA intercepts of Iraq military personnel. "What you're about to hear is a conversation that my government monitored. It takes place on November 26 of last year, on the day before United Nations teams resumed inspections in Iraq. The conversation involves two senior officers, a colonel and a brigadier general, from Iraq's elite military unit, the Republican Guard."

The colonel says, "We have this modified vehicle . . . What do we say if one of them sees it?" He notes that it is from the al-Kindi company. "Yeah, yeah. I'll come to you in the morning. I have some comments. I'm worried you all have something left."

A second intercept, recorded on January 30, 2003, involves a conversation between Republican Guard headquarters and an officer in the field. "There is a directive of the [Republican] Guard chief of staff at the conference today," says headquarters. "They are inspecting the ammunition you have . . . for the possibility there are forbidden ammo . . . We sent you a message yesterday to clean out all of the areas, the scrap areas, the abandoned areas. Make sure there is nothing there. . . . After you have carried out what is contained in the message, destroy the message." The officer agrees.

And a third intercept, said Powell, "shows a captain in the Second Corps of the Republican Guard being ordered by a colonel to 'remove the expression "nerve agents" from wireless instructions.'"

In years of monitoring Iraqi communications, that was the best NSA had—comments about a "modified vehicle," an order to get rid of some "forbidden ammo," and an order to "remove the expression 'nerve agents' from wireless communications." Even NSA Director Hayden agreed that they were little more than ambiguous.

"We were asked, what do you have," said Hayden in a late-January 2004 interview. "And we surfaced several, including these three. . . . If you take a textural analysis of that, they are ambiguous. That said, you don't have to be a dishonest or intellectually handicapped person to be very suspicious about when the guy's saying remove all references to this from your codebooks, or the other guy saying 'I've got one of the modified vehicles here.'"

Asked, "Modified in what way?" Hayden said, "Well, we don't know. That's the ambiguity. So we went ahead and played them. . . . In my heart, each one of them individually could be explained away as this, that, or the other. Collectively they made a reasonably good package. . . . Now you say they're ambiguous. And I admit that, yeah, I can intellectualize and you can explain away some of these things. . . . For example, let's just take the one about 'remove all references to "nerve agents" in your codebooks.' If I'm innocent and I'm on the other side of the fence—[I might say] 'Oh, give me a break, for God's sake, we all have codebooks, we all need references in it, you tell me you don't have codewords for nerve agents on the battlefield. All modern armies have those codewords, you idiots.'"

Given the obvious ambiguity of the intercepts, Hayden was surprised that the Iraqis did not argue that case more strongly.

"They didn't do that. What they said was, these are third-class forgeries that any high school student can fabricate. That was very interesting to me, because rather than taking the textual criticism and attacking them on their merits, or lack of merit, they dismissed them as forgeries. I just looked at it and said, 'Well, why are you going down that track?' It lessened the sense of ambiguity. Whatever lingering sense of ambiguity about these intercepts was in my mind got lessened by the Iraqi government's response to it."

Even within Powell's small task force, the NSA intercepts—the most dramatic evidence they had—was looked upon as ambiguous. "If Captain Hindi with a Republican Guard unit was saying, 'Take nerve agents out of his CEOI—out of his communicating instructions,'" said the senior official, "that could have a double meaning. I mean, we took it as having a meaning that they didn't want the inspectors to know they had nerve agents. But it could be the other side of the coin, too—they got rid of them, so they're taking it out of the CEOI because they don't need it anymore."

But the public was never told how weak and ambiguous the best evidence was. They would be told the opposite.

In addition to hearing the intercepts, Powell brought up the frightening topic of biological weapons. "Saddam Hussein has investigated dozens of biological agents, causing diseases such as gas gangrene, plague, typhus, tetanus, cholera, camel pox, and hemorrhagic fever. And he also has the wherewithal to develop smallpox." Then he warned, "One of the most worrisome things that emerges from the thick intelligence file we have on Iraq's biological weapons is the existence of mobile production facilities used to make biological agents.

"Let me take you inside that intelligence file and share with you what we know from eyewitness accounts," said Powell. "We have firsthand descriptions of biological-weapons factories on wheels and on rails. The trucks and train cars are easily moved and are designed to evade detection by inspectors. In a matter of months, they can produce a quantity of biological poison equal to the entire amount that Iraq claimed to have produced in the years prior to the Gulf War. . . . We know that Iraq has at least seven of these mobile biological-agent factories." Powell then unveiled dramatic drawings of these germ factories on wheels. For proof, Powell pointed to multiple human sources:

> The source was an eyewitness, an Iraqi chemical engineer who supervised one of these facilities. He actually was present during biological-agent production runs. . . . This defector is currently hiding in another country, with the certain knowledge that Saddam Hussein will kill him if he finds him. . . . His eyewitness account of these mobile production facilities has been corroborated by other sources.
>
> A second source, an Iraqi civil engineer in a position to know the details of the program, confirmed the existence of transportable facilities moving on trailers. A third source, also in a position to know, reported in summer 2002 that Iraq had manufactured mobile production systems mounted on road trailer units and on rail cars. Finally, a fourth source, an Iraqi major, who defected, confirmed that Iraq has mobile biological research laboratories, in addition to the production facilities I mentioned earlier.

But despite Powell's hard sell and dramatic flourishes, the evidence was all bad, largely supplied by Chalabi's team of con men. According to a March 2004 interview with a senior official involved in the presentation:

We had four sources for the biological labs, four sources. About a month ago we found out that one of them had fallen away, and then about two weeks ago I found out that two more had fallen away. And yesterday I learned that the fourth source had probably fallen away.

George [Tenet] is saying all around town that three of the four are absolutely bogus. I make this point, only because that is one of the things that the Secretary of State of the United States looked at the DCI [Director of Central Intelligence] of the United States and said, "George, are you sure about these mobile labs, because we were putting a lot of stuff up on the screen." And George said, "Mr. Secretary, that's a slam dunk." And that's the way he talks—I mean, when he says something like that, basketball, when he says something like that, you go with it. Because George was standing by it.

There were three sources for the labs as production facilities, and there was a fourth for the labs as a research facility in addition to production. To George's credit, he admitted it. That source had been declared a fabricator a year or two before we put the presentation together but the CIA had lost computer contact for that information. And so when it was run through the computers, it didn't show up. But in their subsequent scrub, that he ordered to find how they so screwed up, they found it. And so he had to come forward and say, "Well, that fourth source, it wasn't worth anything, and we even declared it not being worth anything two years or so before you did the presentation."

I don't think he's [Powell] happy—how could he be?

In October 2002, the Pew Research Center for People and the Press took a survey and found that 66 percent of Americans said they believed Saddam Hussein was involved in the 9/11 attacks, despite the lack of proof. With regard to weapons of mass destruction, 79 percent believed that Iraq currently possessed—or was close to possessing—nuclear weapons. Three months later, a Knight-Ridder poll found that "half of those surveyed said one or more of the September 11 terrorist hijackers were Iraqi citizens. In fact, none was."

Thus, the Bush administration's massive disinformation campaign, abetted by a lazy and timid press, succeeded spectacularly in driving the public to support its long-planned war. In the end, it was the power of lies, not logic, that was the deciding factor. At the same time, the fact that several of the key players most aggressively pushing the war had originally outlined it for the benefit of another country years earlier raises the most troubling conflict-of-interest questions.

Never before has the United States launched a preemptive war. And only once before, in Vietnam, have so few manipulated so many at such a great price. "We were wrong, terribly wrong," said former Defense Secretary Robert S. McNamara about the Vietnam War. "We were all wrong," said former CIA weapons hunter David Kay about the war in Iraq. "We were all wrong."

BAGHDAD

PREWAR INTELLIGENCE

At 3:15 A.M. on March 20, 2003, an iron rain began to fall over Baghdad as the first of 29,199 bombs plunged toward earth.

Only six weeks earlier, Colin Powell had delivered his now infamous address before the UN Security Council. Made up almost entirely of false charges, it was intended to sell a skeptical world on a preemptive American war with Iraq. To sell the American public, a constant stream of Bush administration officials and neoconservatives began appearing daily on cable talk shows, right-wing radio programs, and mainstream networks.

Many claimed that the war would be a quick and easy "cake-walk." On ABC's *Nightline*, Kenneth Adelman, a member of Richard Perle's Defense Policy Board and, like Perle, a leading neoconservative, engaged in blatant fearmongering. "I would ask everybody," he said, "do we really want to go into Iraq once Saddam gets a nuclear weapon? And that will happen before the next presidential election. Before 2004 he will have nuclear weapons capability." He added, "The fact is that once we go into Iraq, and liberate Iraq, two things will happen immediately: the Iraqi people will start dancing in the street, and week after week, month after month, inspectors from around the world will find vats of biological weapons, vats of chemical weapons, tremendous progress on nuclear weapons. And every week, if not more, people will say, 'God, that was a close call. Thank God we stopped that production.'"

The concept that the American invaders would be greeted by enthusiastic, flower-throwing Iraqis, the way Allied troops were greeted while marching to victory in Paris during World War II, was constantly driven home by administration officials. It had long been one of the leading fantasies of neoconservatism, based on a naive lack of understanding of the Arab world. "Like the people of France in the 1940s, they view us as their hoped-for liberator," said Deputy Defense Secretary Paul Wolfowitz a little more than a week before the invasion. "They know that America will not come as a conqueror." Four days later, Vice President Dick Cheney echoed the faulty belief on *Meet the Press*. "We will, in fact, be greeted as liberators," he said.

Like the neocons, George Tenet and many in his CIA were also caught by surprise when American troops discovered their paths were strewn with roadside bombs instead of garlands of flowers. Shortly before the invasion, CIA officials were so convinced that American soldiers would be welcomed warmly that they suggested sneaking hundreds of small American flags into Iraq so that the Iraqis could demonstrate their gratitude. The event would then be videotaped and beamed throughout the Arab world as part of a secret CIA propaganda operation. The military, however, wisely rejected the plan.

Indeed, that the invasion would quickly devolve into a protracted, bloody guerrilla war was hardly even considered by the CIA. In a National Intelligence Estimate prepared in January 2003, two months before the war began, the possibility of a postwar insurgency was relegated to the final paragraph of the document's thirty-eight pages. "There was never a buildup of intelligence that says: 'It's coming. It's coming. It's coming. This is the end you should prepare for,'" complained General Tommy R. Franks, the former head of the United States Central Command, speaking of the insurgency. "It did not happen. Never saw it. It was never offered."

The depth of the CIA's troubles became clear during the summer of 2004. After a yearlong investigation, the Senate Select Committee on Intelligence released its report on the agency's judgments concerning Iraq in the lead-up to war. The unanimous 511-page report was scathing in its language and angry in its tone. The panel concluded that the intelligence put forth by the agency to justify going to war was both unfounded and unreasonable. It painted a picture of a dysfunctional organization that continually rejected evidence that did not fit into its preconceived biases and that sometimes passed on flawed analysis based on dubious or discredited sources. It even found instances in which analysts may have misrepresented information by submitting reports that distorted the facts in order to strengthen their case that Iraq possessed weapons of mass destruction, including nuclear programs.

With regard to the most important intelligence assessments, such as the question of whether Saddam Hussein actually possessed mobile biological-weapons laboratories, sought aluminum tubes for nuclear weapons, or was working on a program to attack the United States with chemical or biological weapons on drone aircraft, the committee was unanimous: none of those things was true and the CIA's analysis was completely wrong. Also unsubstantiated by intelligence reporting was the claim that Iraq likely possessed chemical and biological weapons. "Most of the major key judgments" in the controversial October 2002 National Intelligence Estimate "either overstated, or were not supported by, the underlying intelligence reporting," the committee report declared. "A series of failures, particularly in analytic tradecraft, led to the mischaracterization of intelligence."

Far from being an imminent threat, Iraq had become little more than a hollow shell. By 1999, the intelligence community viewed Saddam Hussein as a washed-up dictator with a military decaying under the weight of economic sanctions and American military pressure. "The body of assessments showed that Iraqi military capabilities had steadily degraded following defeat in the first Gulf War in 1991," the report noted. "Analysts also believed those capabilities would continue to erode as long as economic sanctions remained in place." The report blamed the agencies for failing "to clearly characterize changes in Iraq's threat to regional stability and security, taking account of the fact that its conventional military forces steadily degraded after 1990."

Despite the intelligence community's dim view of Hussein as a serious and immediate threat to the U.S., a small group of hardcore neoconservatives in 1998 lobbied the Clinton administration to support regime change in Iraq—by force if necessary. The group, made up of Paul Wolfowitz, Donald Rumsfeld, Richard Perle, and about a dozen others, sent Clinton a letter urging his administration to implement "a strategy for removing Saddam's regime from power." But Clinton viewed the longstanding policy of containing Saddam Hussein "in a box" a success. Thus, while voicing support for the general principle of regime change in Iraq, he preferred letting the Iraqi people take the initiative and never considered war with Iraq an option.

By January 2003, when the Bush administration was ratcheting up its claims of Iraq's imminent threat, the intelligence reports were continuing to say the exact opposite—that Saddam Hussein had no intention of attacking the United States, unless he was about to be attacked first. The intelligence assessment found that "Saddam probably will not initiate hostilities for fear of providing Washington with justification to invade Iraq. Nevertheless, he might deal the first blow, especially if he perceives that an attack intended to end his regime is imminent." But intelligence estimates are only predictions, and when they don't agree with a president's preconceived views, they are often ignored.

The committee put the greatest portion of the blame for the intelligence disaster on the doorstep of CIA Director George J. Tenet, who decided, after having viewed drafts of the Senate report the month before, to announce his resignation. Throughout his seven years as Director of Central Intelligence, Tenet had always wanted to be seen as the agency's strong protector, its bodyguard and cheerleader. He would walk the halls, an unlit cigar protruding from the corner of his mouth, and bask in the glow of friendly nods and warm greetings from agency employees. But eventually Tenet changed course. Instead of championing the views of his analysts to officials inside the White House, he ended up championing the President's war inside the CIA. The Senate committee harshly criticized Tenet for his failure to halt the stream of bogus sources, exaggerated reports, and misjudgments that eventually led to his confirming the administration's charge that Iraq possessed weapons of mass destruction and posed a near-term danger to the United States.

Tenet was also criticized for his failure to manage the intelligence community in his role as Director of Central Intelligence (DCI). "While the DCI was supposed to function as both the head of the CIA and the head of the Intelligence Community," the committee report charged, "in many instances he acted only as head of the CIA." Thus, because the CIA makes up only about 15 percent of the entire American spy world, the other 85 percent—including the National Security Agency, the National Reconnaissance Office, and the National Geospacial-Intelligence Agency—were often ignored by Tenet. Had he focused more on managing the country's vast spy world effectively rather than simply telling the White House what it wanted to hear, such as the "slam dunk" comment, it's possible that some of the intelligence estimates might have been more accurate.

The committee even blasted Tenet for failing in the area in which he took the most pride: rebuilding the agency's highly secret human spy organization, the Clandestine Service. According to the report, after the UN weapons inspectors departed Iraq in 1998, the CIA was left spyless in the country. The committee placed the blame on "a broken corporate culture and poor management." Specifically, it pointed to a lack of risk-taking in both developing of secret foreign sources and infiltrating operations officers into critical foreign countries. "Such operations are difficult and dangerous," the committee said, "but they should be the norm of the CIA's activities."

Another serious problem was the pressuring of intelligence professionals, especially in the lower and middle ranks, to conform to the White House message that Iraq possessed weapons of mass destruction and had links with Al Qaeda. In an evaluation requested by Tenet of the Iraq weapons intelligence failure, former CIA deputy director Richard Kerr wrote, "Requests for reporting and analysis of [Iraq's links to Al Qaeda] were steady and heavy in the period leading up to the war, creating significant pressure on the intelligence community to find evidence that supported a connection." The CIA's own ombudsman also complained to the Senate committee that he "felt the 'hammering' by the Bush administration on Iraq intelligence was harder than he had previously witnessed in his 32-year career with the agency."

Normally the CIA Director would protect his people from that kind of pressure. But according to a written statement issued by Senator Rockefeller and other Democrats on the committee,

Tenet decided against intervening directly whenever employees told him that they felt pressure while writing analytical papers on Iraq. "In his interview with the committee, Director Tenet confirmed that some agency officials raised with him personally the matter of the repetitive tasking and the pressure it created during this time period," read the Democratic statement. But rather than asking administration officials to halt efforts designed to influence his employees, Tenet simply asked his people to ignore the repeated questions. Ultimately Tenet lost sight of his role. Instead of the country's apolitical eyes and ears around the world, a spymaster charged with telling the President the bad as well as the good, he simply became the President's cheerleader, shouting slam dunk when he should have been asking for a time-out.

"In the end, what the President and the Congress used to send the country to war was information provided by the intelligence community, and that information was flawed," said Senator Pat Roberts, a Republican from Kansas and the chairman of the panel. Long a vocal supporter of the war, after the report was finished even Roberts said he was not sure that Congress would have authorized the invasion if it had known of the contrary intelligence—and lack of intelligence—prior to the vote.

To many within the intelligence community, it was clear that the Bush administration was determined to go to war regardless of what the intelligence indicated. On the day before Secretary of State Colin Powell's address before the UN Security Council, for example, a military intelligence officer became alarmed that Powell was relying on a number of informants the officer knew to be dubious. One in particular was a source code-named Curveball. As an expert in biological warfare and the only American intelligence official to have actually spent time with Curveball, he decided to issue an urgent warning to the deputy chief of the CIA's Iraqi task force. The CIA official, however, knew that objecting to the war, even with grave concerns about the veracity of the intelligence going to the Secretary of State and the White House, was useless. He therefore rejected the suggested warning. "Let's keep in mind the fact that this war's going to happen regardless of what Curveball said or didn't say," the senior CIA official wrote to the military intelligence officer in an e-mail obtained by the committee, "and that the Powers That Be probably aren't terribly interested in whether Curveball knows what he's talking about."

WARTIME INTELLIGENCE

In the opening days of the war, as the bombs began to pour, the American spy world was desperately attempting to locate key Iraqi command centers and top military and civilian officials so they could be attacked prior to the arrival of U.S. ground troops. But because of the CIA's absolute lack of reliable human intelligence in Iraq, the job of pinpointing the regime's top leaders fell largely to NSA and its ultrasecret signals intelligence effort. It would be an extremely difficult task because of Iraq's extensive use of buried fiber-optic cables, its complex encryption system, and the lack of prewar intelligence.

For a number of years during the 1990s, NSA was able to secretly monitor a number of key Iraqi government communications links as a result of a covert operation run jointly with the CIA. The targets were Iraqi walkie-talkie and mobile radio transmissions used by the Iraqi government to coordinate its weapons concealment efforts. But because these low-powered VHF signals were frequently too weak to be picked up by aircraft or spy satellites, a more low-tech system was needed. The answer was Operation Shake the Tree, which involved manning a series of commercially bought scanners which they tuned to the Iraqi military frequencies.

By 1996, however, the NSA and CIA had come up with a far

more ambitious signals intelligence plan, this one directed at higher-level military communications carried over evasive microwave channels. These signals, used for high-volume telephone traffic, travel from transmission tower to transmission tower in a pencil-straight line. Thus, in order to monitor them, an antenna must be placed in, or very near, the invisible channel. To do this, the spy agencies decided to secretly bug an existing system of remote television cameras installed by the UN to keep a continuous watch on critical facilities, such as weapons bunkers. By the mid-1990s, there were more than three hundred of these cameras throughout Iraq. Periodically, inspectors would travel to the remote locations, change the magnetic tapes, and then review the exposed film back at their headquarters. But in 1996, with the permission of the Iraqi government, the system was changed to allow the monitoring equipment to automatically transmit the video images back to UN offices in Baghdad. This enabled the inspectors to watch the distant sites in near real time and eliminated the need to retrieve videotapes manually.

It also gave signals engineers in the American intelligence community a unique opportunity. Soon, U.S. spies disguised as television technicians began arriving in Iraq to "assist" the inspectors and help install the new video equipment. The technicians covertly installed antennas in a number of the cameras that were located near key Iraqi microwave channels. Telephone communications picked up by the antennas were either retransmitted up to spy satellites or stored in mini-recorders and sent as superfast "burst" signals to U-2 spy planes. Unlike the previous scanner operation, this one was kept completely secret from both the weapons inspectors in Baghdad and their superiors back at United Nations headquarters in New York. The decision to keep it secret was made because the information the spy agencies were after was primarily routine military intelligence, important to Pentagon war planners but not to the UN team. Another key factor was the extreme sensitivity of the eavesdropping technologies being used. Even Britain's GCHQ—their NSA—was kept in the dark, a rare exception.

Ultimately this deception played a major role in the demise of the inspection team in Iraq. When word of the operation leaked, it confirmed to many the frequent charge made by Saddam Hussein that the UN mission was riddled with American spies and was little more than a front for the CIA. The revelation greatly distressed the leader of the inspection force, Richard Butler, an Australian diplomat. "If all this stuff turns out to be true, then Rolf Ekeus [Butler's predecessor] and I have been played for suckers, haven't we?" Butler commented to one close associate. "I've spent a lifetime of helping build and defend the nonproliferation regimes. Piggybacking in this manner [by U.S. intelligence] can only serve the interests of those who reject meaningful efforts at arms control."

The NSA thus lost its ability to eavesdrop on domestic Iraqi communications. In the 1990s it had also listened in on international communications in and out of the country. This was done from thousands of miles away at remote listening posts and from satellites in space. The key targets were Iraq's two Intelsat earth stations (one for satellites over the Atlantic Ocean and the other for satellites over the Indian Ocean); an Intersputnik earth station for Russian satellites; and an Arabsat earth station (though its use was primarily television).

But in the lead-up to war, hearing what was being said domestically was far more important than what was being discussed internationally. With the inspectors gone and the cameras turned off, NSA had become hard of hearing in Iraq. The agency did, however, still have one card up its sleeve: tapping into the growing network of handheld mobile satellite telephones in use throughout the country. For a number of years the major company providing satellite phone service was Inmarsat. But in 2001, a new satellite telephone service opened in the Middle East. The company, Thuraya Satellite Telecommunications Co., offered satellite phone service throughout Iraq and the rest of the region using two spacecraft in geostationary orbit (22,300 miles) and an earth station in the United Arab Emirate city of Sharjah. Through aggressive marketing, by mid-2002 there were more than 65,000 of the company's phones in use, and the minutes used per day was double the company's expectations.

With little wonder, in 2001 Thuraya's satellites quickly became key targets of NSA listening posts from Menwith Hill in England to Diego Garcia in the middle of the Indian Ocean. The uplinks were intercepted by the agency's supersecret Orion communications intelligence satellite network, a constellation of spacecraft in geostationary orbit with massive 150-foot dish-shaped antennas.

Soon after the September 11 attacks, in a major change, NSA director Michael Hayden ordered that determining the location of callers and receivers suspected of involvement in terrorism be placed on a higher priority status than deciphering and translating the actual conversations. This was a result of the continuing difficulty in acquiring adequate numbers of competent translators, an inability to decipher many of their target's homemade verbal codes, and the need to capture—or kill—suspected terrorists quickly. Another factor was the growing use of encryption and NSA's inability, without spending excessive amounts of computer time and human energy, to solve commercial systems more complex than 256 bits.

Fortunately for NSA, many of Iraq's senior officials communicated with the small blue Thuraya handheld satellite phones, which could also be used for terrestrial mobile calls. A key advantage for the spy agency was the fact that the phones contained global positioning system (GPS) chips that revealed their coordinates to NSA. At Ft. Meade, as the Bush administration began moving closer to its invasion of Baghdad, analysts studying intercepted Iraqi conversations were making progress. They successfully matched some of the phones to a number of senior officials and, at various times, were able to determine their locations within a broad geographic area. It was part of a plan to decapitate the Iraqi leadership at the start of the war.

Several months earlier the NSA had successfully used this same method to track down a key Al Qaeda suspect in a remote part of Yemen. On November 4, 2002, an analyst at NSA headquarters at Ft. Meade received an alert when computers picked up a call from an important, but long-dormant, telephone number. The number belonged to a satellite phone used by a senior Al Qaeda operative, who was a possible suspect in the bombing of the USS *Cole*. His name was Salim Sinan al-Harethi, also known as Abu Ali. At the time of the alert, al-Harethi was riding in a car with five other individuals, including an American, in the remote eastern Marib province of Yemen. Half the earth away, in a windowless room at NSA headquarters, the analyst was listening in on the satellite phone. An Arabic linguist, for years he had been eavesdropping on members of Al Qaeda and knew the identities of many members simply by the sounds of their voices. But this time he couldn't make out who was speaking. Moments later, however, for a brief six seconds, he did overhear the voice of al-Harethi in the background. "He's in the backseat and he's giving the driver directions," said the analyst excitedly, according to an intelligence official familiar with the operation. "That's him," shouted the analyst as a colleague was quickly called over to confirm his opinion. After the tape was played back, the second analyst agreed.

At the same time, and in the same general vicinity as the car carrying al-Harethi, a CIA-controlled Predator aircraft was quietly flying overhead, too high to be seen from the ground. Unmanned, remotely controlled, and armed with a deadly Hellfire missile, the drone was part of a CIA operation designed to target and kill suspected senior Al Qaeda members. Quickly alerted by NSA, the CIA operations officers directed the aircraft to target the car and then pressed the fire button. Seconds later the missile struck and the crowded vehicle exploded in a ball of flames, killing all of the occupants. It was the first successful assassination-style murder in the CIA's history.

The Bush administration had approved a highly secret assassination program following the September 11 attacks. A formal document, known as a presidential finding, set out the legal and executive branch authority for the CIA to carry out the "targeted killings." Those high on the CIA's secret hit list include not only Osama bin Laden and his deputy Ayman al-Zawahiri, but also many lesser officials, some of whom the United States knows little about. Although assassination was outlawed by the Ford administration in the mid-1970s, the Bush White House avoids the prohibition by labeling the targets "enemy combatants."

When it came to Iraq, however, the Bush administration was far more interested in war than assassination. But without any intelligence agents on the ground at the start of the conflict, the military was forced to rely on NSA to locate members of Saddam Hussein's regime. The eavesdroppers quickly found that targeting an isolated car in an unpopulated desert was far different than pinpointing an individual in a densely populated city. Complicating the matter was the fact that Thuraya's GPS chips were only accurate within a 100-meter radius—more than three football fields. Thus the location of the caller could be anywhere within a vast 31,400-square-meter area, much of it densely packed urban neighborhoods.

This meant that killing Iraqi officials with Tomahawk cruise missiles and 2,000-pound penetrator bombs was less a matter of precision targeting and more like firing blindly into very large crowds. While the weapons landed exactly where they were supposed to, not a single senior Iraqi official was hit—a 100 percent failure rate. Instead, it was innocent Iraqi civilians who were killed, a fact that would make it difficult for the Bush administration to convince many Iraqis that the United States was genuinely interested in helping them.

CIVILIAN DEATHS

Many of the weapons used in the air attacks were deadly cluster bombs that opened up like clamshells to spew hundreds of mini-bombs over densely populated areas, causing hundreds of civilian casualties. According to a U.S. Central Command report, over the first three weeks of the war more than ten thousand cluster munitions were dropped, dispersing nearly two million bomblets—about one a second for three straight weeks. Thousands more cluster bombs fell from British planes and ground launchers. According to a Human Rights Watch report, "Although cluster munitions strikes are particularly dangerous in populated areas, U.S. and U.K. ground forces repeatedly used these weapons in attacks on Iraqi positions in residential neighborhoods." It concluded, "U.S. and U.K. ground forces were found to have caused significant numbers of civilian casualties with the widespread use of cluster munitions, particularly in populated areas."

Adding to the civilians' terror was the fact that cluster bomblets often fail to explode when they hit soft ground or sand, turning them into instant land mines. With an average failure rate of 5 percent, as many as 90,000 live bombs were left in backyards and playgrounds throughout the country. As a tragic result, for weeks, months, and even years after the attack, thousands of Iraqi civilians, many of them children, were killed or maimed when they accidentally stepped on one of the lethal munitions or picked them up as toys or scrap metal. "Bomblets are what kids pick up. There is a nice ribbon on the end. It's nice for carrying," said an officer at the Baghdad Civil-Military Operations Center. Dr. al-Ubaidi, an Iraqi physician at al-Najaf Teaching Hospital, saw the problem close-up while treating dozens of child victims. "Cluster bombs sometimes look like beautiful things," he said. "Children like to play with them. [The bomblets] are here and there, every-where on farmland. They look shiny."

With little resistance from the Iraqi Army, U.S. and coalition troops quickly swept into Baghdad. On live television, American soldiers pulled down the statue of Saddam Hussein, wrapped its head in an American flag, and then turned his palace into an iso-lated, impenetrable fortress to house their army of occupation. In Washington, the Bush administration cheered the images from Iraq on their television screens, claiming they validated their the-ory that the occupation would be welcomed. But despite years of harsh treatment under Hussein, in the eyes of many in Iraq, one bloody dictator had simply been replaced by another.

Throughout the Arab world also, many were happy to see the end of Saddam Hussein but at the same time were distrustful of an American occupation. "Please, America must hear our voices," pleaded Diaa Rashwan, a political scientist at Cairo's Ahram Center for Political and Strategic Studies. "The American media and people are in a state of euphoria right now, but they are not seeing it the way we are seeing it at all. The Arab street is very frustrated, and to America, I repeat, I repeat, I repeat, the real war hasn't started yet. We have to be careful with such euphoria. It will only increase the feelings of anger in the Arab world. No Arabs want to welcome an occupying power." The managing editor of

Cairo's *Al-Ahram Weekly*, Hani Shukrallah, offered a similar warning. "They may want Saddam out. But in a few weeks they will be doing the same thing to a picture of George Bush."

Among those sampling the reaction throughout the Middle East was *The Washington Post*'s Emily Wax and Alia Ibrahim. They wrote, "Repeatedly analysts said U.S. trust could be rebuilt only when the Palestinian-Israeli conflict was resolved." It was a view reflected by Saudi political scientist Turki Hamad. "For all people in the Arab world, the Palestinian problem is the only problem they have with the United States," he said. "If the U.S. succeeds in solving it, then people will change their minds about America." For some within the Middle East, especially those with memories of Jordan's brutal treatment of Palestinian refugees following the Israeli occupation of the West Bank, there was a certain amount of hypocrisy in the charge.

As many in the Arab world had predicted, the short war quickly became a long and bloody occupation. Innocent Iraqi civilians continued to suffer the brunt of the casualties. But contrary to the images coming across American television screens, the deaths and injuries were primarily caused not by the insurgents and their high-profile car bombs but by American forces with their little-publicized massive air strikes in heavily populated areas. That was the conclusion of a study published in the prestigious British medical journal *The Lancet*. The publication said that about 100,000 Iraqi civilians—more than half of them women and children—have died in Iraq since the invasion, mostly as a result of air strikes by coalition forces. That the U.S. military was killing and maiming, by the tens of thousands, the very people it had come to liberate was a fact the Bush administration hoped would remain hidden. To that end, the Pentagon has stuck to its official policy of refusing to acknowledge Iraqi civilian deaths and injuries.

Without official involvement, any accurate accounting of

civilian deaths is almost impossible. Human Rights Watch attempted to determine the statistics by visiting a large number of
hospitals, but they found that many of the records were little more
than bloodstained notebooks with handwritten notes. Another
problem was that in a Muslim nation the dead were buried almost
immediately. Nevertheless, the Associated Press canvassed 60 of
Iraq's 124 hospitals immediately after major combat operations
came to an end and concluded that at least 3,420 civilians died in
the initial fighting. *The Los Angeles Times* conducted a smaller
survey, visiting 27 hospitals in Baghdad and its suburbs, and estimated that at least 1,700 civilians died and more than 8,000 were
wounded in the capital alone. Human Rights Watch found that
civilian casualties were also high outside Baghdad and that many
of the dead were women and children. In al-Nasiriyya, for example, 169 children were killed. One resident, Ali Kadhim Hashim,
lost 14 members of his family, including his wife, children, and
parents.

According to *The Lancet* study, most of the deaths—nearly
80 percent—were the result of American bombing runs. "Most
individuals reportedly killed by coalition forces," noted the report,
"were women and children." Clare Short, who earlier had
resigned from Prime Minister Tony Blair's cabinet to protest the
war, exclaimed, "It is really horrifying. When will Tony Blair stop
saying it is all beneficial for the Iraqi people since Saddam Hussein
has gone? How many more lives are to be taken? It is no wonder,
given this tragic death toll, that the resistance to the occupation is
growing."

The survey was conducted by a distinguished group of scientists at Johns Hopkins University and led by Dr. Les Roberts of the
Bloomberg School of Public Health; contributors included medical and social scientists from Columbia University and the College
of Medicine at Al-Mustansiriya University in Baghdad. The report

criticized the United States for ignoring Iraqi civilian deaths. "U.S. General Tommy Franks is widely quoted as saying 'We don't do body counts,'" the authors noted, pointing out that occupying armies have responsibilities for protecting civilians under the Geneva conventions. "We were shocked at the magnitude but we're quite sure that the estimate of 100,000 is a conservative estimate," concluded Dr. Gilbert Burnham, a coauthor of the study. For example, the directors deliberately did not include in their calculations deaths from the American attacks on Fallujah.

While the survey was criticized by some because of the way it was conducted, without official assistance the only alternative was simply to ignore the problem. Others noted the great difference in numbers between *The Lancet* report and an estimate by a group called www.iraqbodycount.net that put the number of civilian deaths at just under seventeen thousand. But one of the researchers who works for the website, Scott Lipscomb, an associate professor at Northwestern University, was not surprised. "We've always maintained that the actual count must be much higher," he cautioned.

Despite the lack of help from the American occupation forces, the Iraqi Ministry of Health conducted a survey to determine how Iraqis were being killed, and their conclusions were very similar to those of the Johns Hopkins study. Two-thirds of the Iraqi deaths were the result of operations by U.S. and coalition forces and Iraqi police, and only one-third was caused by insurgent attacks. "Anyone who hates America has come here to fight: Saddam's supporters, people who don't have jobs, other Arab fighters," said Dr. Walid Hamed, an employee of the Ministry of Health who worked on the study. "All these people are on our streets. But everyone is afraid of the Americans, not the fighters. And they should be." As more and more civilians, broken and bloody, were pulled from the rubble of their houses following U.S.

bombing runs, the anger, fear, and resentment toward the United States spread.

QUAGMIRE?

Scattered across those same killing fields, the number of Americans dying was also growing significantly and increasing almost every week. In early September 2004, a soldier with the 1st Cavalry Division from Fort Hood, Texas, died fighting in the streets of Baghdad. By then, such a death would have barely received notice, except for the fact that he or she became the one thousandth American to die in the conflict. The Pentagon refused to release the name of the victim. By the same day more than 7,000 Americans had been wounded.

Around the United States, small gatherings of antiwar protesters and relatives of service members killed in the conflict marked the milestone with sadness and dignity. At Lake Merritt, in Oakland, California, nearly 250 people from surrounding neighborhoods gathered at the colonnade on the lake's edge, where they held candles in silence. Placards read, "1,000 DEAD," "QUAGMIRE," "NO END IN SIGHT," and passing drivers leaned on their horns in support. *The Houston Chronicle* called the number "a bloody threshold." Vigils in 900 other cities around the country drew upward of 40,000 people.

As usual, but especially with an all-voluntary military, it was the young and the poor, those with the least education and those from small and rural towns, that paid the highest price. They were also the ones who tended to vote for the Bush administration. More than half of those killed came from the lowest-paid enlisted ranks, with only about 12 percent from the officer corps. When a young Marine named Kyle Codner was killed, he was a nineteen-year-old corporal with a high school education who left his job at J.R.'s Mini Mart in Shelton, Nebraska, to join the Marines. In his yearbook, Codner was named as the student "Most Likely to Kick Some Terrorist Butt."

Many who joined the military out of high school believed the false claims of the Bush administration that Saddam Hussein was somehow connected to the terrorist attacks of September 11 or to Al Qaeda. Ever hungry for more raw recruits to send to the front lines in Iraq, especially as the battle disintegrated into a deadly and protracted guerrilla war, military recruiters began combining high-pressure tactics with jingoistic calls for patriotism. Their key targets were schools in working-class neighborhoods and students who had little prospect for further education.

For example, at McDonough High, a public school in a working-class neighborhood in Pomfret, Maryland, recruiters chaperone dances; pass out coffee mugs, key chains, and flashy brochures in the cafeteria; and blitz prospects with home visits and at least half a dozen calls each. Among the tactics advocated in recruiting manuals is the use of tricks such as looking up details of prospects in yearbooks and then pretending to "mysteriously" have great insight into the student when they meet. Thirty-seven miles away, at McLean High in the more affluent community of McLean, Virginia, recruiters face limits on the number of visits and then must line up behind dozens of college recruiters. There are no military chaperones at the prom, and talk in the cafeteria is of college campuses, not of battle zones.

According to a survey of the Pentagon's recruitment system, students from schools like McDonough are six times as likely to wind up in boot camp as students from schools like McLean. As Kurt Gilroy, who directs recruiting policy in Secretary Rumsfeld's office says, the idea is "to go where the low-hanging fruit is. In other words, we fish where the fish are." But as the pool of possible recruits continued to shrink as the war expanded, the army was forced to change its rules in 2004 so that it could accept more high school dropouts—up to one out of four recruits.

Once in Iraq, three out of four soldiers who were killed died as a result of homemade-bomb explosions, small-arms fire, or rocket attacks. The powerful roadside bombs, known as improvised explosive devises (IEDs), turned trucks and armored personnel carriers into molten heaps of scrap metal, and American soldiers—those who lived—into amputees and paraplegics. Convinced the country would instantly turn friendly and cooperative once Baghdad was captured, little attention was paid to securing the massive quantities of Iraq's explosive ordnance stored in nearly every part of the country. It was a deadly mistake; much of the arsenal fell under the control of the insurgents who used it to wreak havoc throughout the country, killing thousands of American troops and Iraqi civilians. According to the director general of the National Mine Action Authority in Iraq, there may have been more than 600,000 tons of abandoned munitions throughout the country—enough to blow up every U.S. soldier in Iraq with about four and a half tons of explosives each. "I've never seen so much ordnance, and I've been in the Balkans, northern Iraq, and Afghanistan," exclaimed coalition official John Thompson.

Indeed, among the most monumental mistakes of the war was the military's failure to secure many key Iraqi ammunition storage facilities as they rushed toward Baghdad, expecting to be greeted by cheering crowds followed by a quick trip home. At the time, counterintelligence agent David DeBatto was posted with the Army National Guard's 223rd Military Intelligence Battalion at Camp Anaconda, a former Iraqi air force base about 50 miles north of Baghdad. In early May 2003 he was informed by a local Iraqi about a large abandoned weapons storage facility a few kilometers to the south of Anaconda. He and some members of his team went there to check it out and found a huge base about five square miles or more with dozens of both above- and below-ground storage buildings. "I was stunned to see vast amounts of weapons simply lying around on the ground littering the base," he recalled. "Some of these weapons included surface-to-air and air-to-air missiles, land mines, rocket-propelled grenades, small-arms ammunition, hand grenades, detonator caps, plastic explosives, and other assorted ammunition and weaponry. It was quite a frightening sight." DeBatto repeatedly reported the discovery up the chain of command but nothing was ever done.

"For the next several weeks I continued to receive reports from my sources in the community that the weapons were still at the storage facility," DeBatto said. "There were still no guards, and the looting was continuing. I made three or four more trips to the site between May and August and confirmed that the facility was in fact unsecured and that weapons and ammunition were still exposed. On one such visit I actually saw some Iraqis in the distance driving a pickup truck and stopping at bunkers inside the storage facility, no doubt helping themselves."

It wasn't just the small dumps that got overlooked; the United States also failed to secure Iraq's single largest ammo dump, known as Al Qaqaa. The massive facility was about 30 miles south of Baghdad and filled with tan humplike ammo bunkers in neat rows as far as the eye could see. Containing more than 380 tons of extremely potent conventional explosives, material that could be used for everything from making missile warheads to detonating nuclear weapons, the giant storage facility had been carefully monitored by United Nations inspectors for years. Much of the explosives consisted of superpowerful HMX (high melting-point explosive), RDX (rapid detonation explosive), and PETN (pentaerythritol tetranitrate). Some of those same ingredients were used in the bomb that brought down Pan Am Flight 103 over

Lockerbie, Scotland, in 1988. For that explosion, less than a pound was used. Larger amounts of the same material were used in the terrorist bombing of a Moscow apartment complex in September 1999 that left nearly 300 people dead.

HMX and RDX have long been the explosives of choice for terrorists. While packing an enormous blast, they are also easy to move because they are insensitive to shock and physical abuse during transportation and handling. Even hitting the material with a hammer will not set it off. Instead, it takes a detonator, such as a blasting cap, to make it blow. It is also easy to disguise during shipment across borders. "The immediate danger" of the stolen explosives, according to an expert with experience in Iraq, "is its potential use with insurgents in very small and powerful explosive devices. The other danger is that it can easily move into the terrorist web across the Middle East."

According to experts with the International Atomic Energy Agency (IAEA), as well as officials in Washington, HMX and RDX can be used to implode a nuclear weapon, which is why the UN inspectors carefully monitored it. The enormous blast caused by the materials could be directed inward toward a hollow sphere containing uranium or plutonium, crushing it into a critical mass and thus causing a nuclear explosion.

Shortly before the war started, the IAEA had placed seals on the bunkers and issued a number of public warnings outlining the extreme danger of the explosives. The IAEA specifically informed American officials of the need to keep the facility under tight security. But following the U.S. invasion, military forces simply made a few brief visits to the weapons base without installing any kind of security.

Units of the 101st Airborne Division spent about two or three weeks near Al Qaqaa beginning on April 10. At the time, the facility was still crawling with weapons, as was confirmed by a camera crew from KSTP-TV, an ABC affiliate in Minneapolis-St. Paul. On April 18 they shot videotape of the troops breaking into a number of the bunkers. At the time, the doors to the facilities were secured with chains and locks that had to be severed with bolt cutters. Also still intact and uncut were the IAEA seals, lead disks attached to very thin wires that were wrapped around the doors of the bunkers. The troops snapped off the seals and entered the gloomy bunkers to find neatly stacked boxes, crates, and barrels of three kinds of HMX containers. Inside the boxes they observed the highly explosive white powder.

After examining the bunkers, the troops simply left the doors open. "It would have been easy for anybody to get in," said Joe Caffrey, the television crew's photographer. Another member of the team, reporter Dean Staley, noted that a red Toyota pickup truck with Iraqis inside arrived as they were leaving. "Our impression was they were looters," he said. "This was a no-man's-land. It was a huge facility, and we worried that they were bad guys who might come up on us." Thus when the 101st departed for Baghdad a week or so later, they left the weapons dump as unguarded as it had been when they arrived. The looters and future insurgents wasted little time stripping the base. After learning of the problem in May 2003, an internal IAEA memorandum was written alerting Washington that terrorists might be in the process of helping "themselves to the greatest explosives bonanza in history." The White House, however, ignored the warning. Thus, intent on finding the nuclear weapons that didn't exist, Washington ignored the real weapons that did exist.

Through such actions and inactions, the Bush administration turned Iraq into a grizzly death factory for Americans and innocent Iraqi men, women, and children. Its invasion created the insurgency, its brutal occupation kept it growing, and its utter lack of planning and foresight armed it with a virtually unlimited supply of powerful weapons. This makes for bitter irony. The Bush administration invaded Iraq in large part to keep weapons of mass destruction out of the hands of terrorists. Now because of its invasion and lack of planning, the Bush administration is responsible for weapons of mass destruction going into the hands of terrorists.

Among those who may have been victims of the explosives stolen from the Al Qaqaa weapons storage base was UN Special Representative to Iraq Sergio Vieira de Mello. He and many of his staff were killed on August 19, 2003, when a truck bomb exploded at the Canal Hotel, which served as the UN's headquarters in Baghdad. Less than two weeks later, another truck loaded with explosives killed ninety-one people at the Imam 'Ali Shrine in al-Najaf. Since then, hardly a day has gone by without American troops and Iraqi civilians falling victim to the abandoned weapons. Given that international law requires an occupying force to protect the civilian population, something that the U.S. has clearly failed to do, it is understandable that growing segments of Iraqi society have come to hate America. This hatred, emphasizes Egyptian President Hosni Mubarak, is the best recruiting tool for the insurgent forces and for creating more Osama bin Ladens.

The result is a seemingly endless downward spiral. The more the occupation creates hatred, the more recruits are drawn to the insurgency, and the more the insurgency grows, the more the United States increases its bombing and bloodshed, which ends up killing mostly civilians and driving more and more angry Iraqis and other Muslims into the insurgency.

THE ISRAEL FACTOR

During the summer of 2002, as Israeli generals were quietly slipping in and out of the Pentagon for their meetings with Feith, the FBI began a highly classified espionage investigation that would eventually focus on top-secret documents flowing out of his office and into the hands of Israeli intelligence agents. Feith had long had extremely close ties to Israel and its far-right political parties over the years. In fact, according to former CIA counterterrorism chief Vince Cannistraro, Feith was fired from a job in the National Security Council early in the Reagan years for leaking classified information to Israel. The FBI's principal target was Israel's powerful Washington-based lobby, the American Israel Public Affairs Committee (AIPAC), which the FBI suspected of acting as a conduit for Israeli espionage. At the same time, the agency was also concerned that Israel might be engaged in illegal influence-peddling in the hopes of manipulating American policy toward Iraq and Iran, two of Israel's most hated Arab neighbors.

The question of Israeli espionage has long dogged Richard Perle and a number of his close associates. According to Seymour Hersh's book on Henry Kissinger, *The Price of Power*, in the fall of 1970, the FBI allegedly overheard Perle passing classified information he had obtained from the National Security Council to the Israeli embassy. At the time, Perle was a staff member working for Washington Senator Henry "Scoop" Jackson, and the FBI was conducting an extensive wiretapping operation on the Israeli embassy in Washington, D.C. A summary of the tape was sent to FBI Director J. Edgar Hoover, who in turn sent a copy to H. R. "Bob" Haldeman, President Nixon's chief of staff.

Despite the incident, during the Reagan administration Perle became the Pentagon's Assistant Secretary of Defense for International Security Policy, a post where he earned the nickname "The Prince of Darkness." Shortly after taking office, Perle named Stephen D. Bryen to fill the post of deputy undersecretary of defense for Trade Security Policy, a key job involving the transfer of highly sensitive technology. At the time Bryen was the executive director of the Jewish Institute for National Security Affairs (JINSA), a pro-Israel special-interest group specializing in attracting defense equipment and dollars to Israel, but only two years earlier he had been under Justice Department investigation for espionage on behalf of Israel.

At the time of the Bryen investigation, the CIA had also become very concerned about Israeli penetration of the U.S. government. A report issued by the agency warned, "The Israelis devote a considerable portion of their covert operations to obtaining scientific and technical intelligence. This has included attempts to penetrate certain classified defense projects in the United States and other Western nations." It added, "The Israeli intelligence service depends heavily on the various Jewish communities and organizations abroad for recruiting agents and eliciting general information. . . . Israeli agents usually operate discreetly within Jewish communities and are under instructions to handle their missions with utmost tact to avoid embarrassment to Israel."

It was a precipitous warning. On September 19, 1979, around the same time that the CIA report went out, Jonathan Jay Pollard was hired by U.S. Naval Intelligence as an intelligence research specialist. He would eventually become a major spy for Israel's highly secret Office of Scientific Liaison of the Ministry of Defense, passing to Israeli intelligence more than 800,000 pages of highly classified documents.

During and after the arrest and conviction of Pollard on espionage charges, Justice Department investigators remained convinced that there was at least one other American citizen working inside the U.S. government who was spying for Israel, sometimes referred to as Mr. X. "Their fears were based on more than just a hunch," wrote Wolf Blitzer in his book on the Pollard case, *Territory of Lies.* "During their many hours of interrogating Pollard, they discovered to their absolute horror that the Israelis had been rather specific in 'tasking' him to obtain certain top-secret documents. Indeed, Pollard was often asked to obtain classified documents by their code numbers and titles. U.S. counter-intelligence agents quickly concluded that Israel must have had at least one other agent on the inside providing the names of the documents. Perhaps that agent did not have a 'courier card,' like Pollard." The FBI was never able to discover the identity of the mystery coconspirator, a fact that in 2004 greatly worried the agents looking into the connections between the Pentagon, AIPAC, and Israel.

With Pollard, the drive to sell out his country to benefit Israel came from within. It was a point he made in a series of letters he wrote to friends and family from his prison cell: "I utterly reject the notion that Israelis can pay in blood for our homeland's defense while complacent American Jews, safe behind their credit cards and miles of intervening ocean, can indulge in what I call 'pocketbook' Zionism. It doesn't work that way.... When we accepted the covenantal yoke we pledged our bodies and souls, not a yearly tax-deductible contribution to a country of stand-ins.... Eilat, and Kiryat Arba, and Jerusalem are first and foremost Jewish cities which are part of our people's sacred territorial inheritance from God. As such, the Land demands the unequivocal loyalty of every diaspora Jew—even if that entails placing one's life in harm's way."

For some other officials in the government, especially those who are Jewish, the pressure to help Israel at the expense of their own country sometimes came from without. One former senior official who knows just how much pressure Israel and its supporters can exert is Dr. Dov S. Zakheim, until 2004 the Pentagon's undersecretary of defense (comptroller) and chief financial officer for the Department of Defense.

Appointed by Secretary of Defense Donald Rumsfeld in 2001, for three years Zakheim held the purse strings for the Department of Defense as the Pentagon's top financial officer. But during the Reagan administration, when he was deputy undersecretary of defense for Planning and Resources, a senior position in what is now Douglas Feith's office, the pressure to help Israel secretly was at times enormous. What made the problem especially acute was that he decided that a joint U.S.-Israeli project, an aircraft known as the Lavi, was a total waste of taxpayers' money and needed to be killed. But given his Jewish Orthodox background, Zakheim's decision to cancel the program was viewed by many Israelis as nothing less than treachery.

"I had heard of the virtual brutality with which the Israelis dealt with those who opposed them," he noted, "especially if they were Jewish." What angered Zakheim was "the Israeli refusal to understand that I viewed matters from an American perspective," he said. "The prevailing Israeli view—and that of some Americans, I might add—seems to have been that I was guilty of dual loyalties by putting *America* first. My first loyalty should have been to Israel. I should have viewed disputes between our two countries from an *Israeli* perspective. What was bad for Israel must be *ipso facto* bad for America. Even if it was not, it should be. Dual loyalty is an Israeli obsession." [Zakheim's emphasis]

But it was the reaction from hard-liners within the American Jewish community that surprised Zakheim the most, "especially when my family was dragged into the fray, which seemed to be happening with ever-increasing frequency," he said. "I started to receive hate mail and nasty phone calls, but got used to them, as I did to being called a 'traitor.' But it is those incidents that in some way involved my parents, children, wife, and other members of my family that stand out most sharply in my memory. . . . Chaim, my eldest son, was told by his camp counselor that his father was a traitor. . . . I found equally upsetting my abandonment by the Orthodox community of which I had been a part since birth. Time and again I found Orthodox leaders, rabbis, and institutions unwilling to acknowledge that I had any connection with their denomination."

Two decades after Pollard's arrest, it is clear that Israeli spying in the United States, and its interest in Pentagon officials, continues. In 2004 government officials told Bob Drogin and Greg Miller of *The Los Angeles Times* that "Israel secretly maintains a large and active intelligence-gathering operation in the United States that has long attempted to recruit U.S. officials as spies and to procure classified documents." A former intelligence official familiar with the FBI probe told the reporters, "There is a huge, aggressive, ongoing set of Israeli activities directed against the United States. Anybody who worked in counterintelligence in a professional capacity will tell you the Israelis are among the most aggressive and active countries targeting the United States. They undertake a wide range of technical operations and human operations. People here as liaisons . . . aggressively pursue classified intelligence from people. The denials are laughable."

Among those long troubled by the fact that Pollard's Mr. X had never been identified was David Szady, the FBI's top spy catcher as assistant director for Counterintelligence. At sixty years old, the thirty-two-year veteran of the FBI is lean and tall at 6' 4". He became the FBI's chief counterspy in March 2001, only weeks after the arrest of fellow agent Robert Hanssen, who became among the most damaging Russian moles in American history. Szady's assignment was to completely revamp the way counterintelligence is conducted in the post–Cold War years, a plan known as CI-21: Counterintelligence for the 21st Century. That means focusing on allies, such as Israel, as well as adversaries. "It's no longer just our traditional adversaries who want to steal our secrets," said Szady shortly before the AIPAC case became public, "but sometimes even our allies. And how they go about it has changed." Szady listed Israel among the leading countries involved in economic spying in the United States, spying that has increased in recent years and is costing U.S. firms billions of dollars. "The threat is huge," he said.

Now Szady was searching for another spy. "He has never stopped looking for Mr. X," said one observer. The problem, however, was that even if he found him, there was a good chance the case would be quickly and quietly dealt with so as not to embarrass Israel. According to *The American Prospect*, since the Pollard case at least six sealed indictments have been issued against individuals for espionage on Israel's behalf. "It's a testament to the unique relationship between the United States and Israel that those cases were never prosecuted," noted the article. "According to the same sources, both governments ultimately addressed them through diplomatic and intelligence channels rather than air the dirty laundry." A number of career Justice Department and intelligence officials who have worked on Israeli counterespionage told the *Prospect* of "longstanding frustration among investigators and prosecutors who feel that cases that could have been made successfully against Israeli spies were never brought to trial, or that the investigations were shut down prematurely." Szady was hoping the suspects in his AIPAC investigation would not end up with similar get-out-of-jail-free cards.

Tipped off by a series of e-mails that were brought to an investigator's attention, Szady began placing AIPAC under a microscope in the summer of 2002. Nearly every investigative tool was used, from national security wiretaps on office and home phones authorized by the highly secret Foreign Intelligence Surveillance Court, to hidden photography and even undercover surveillance.

The reason for such concern was that among the material the FBI feared AIPAC officials might have transferred to Israel was extremely sensitive cryptologic—code-making, code-breaking, and communications interception—information from the ultrasecret

National Security Agency. In a highly unusual move, the FBI began investigating meetings between AIPAC personnel and White House officials and other senior national-security officials in Washington. One administration source who spoke to *Newsweek* described the case as "the most significant Israeli espionage investigation in Washington since Jonathan Pollard." Yossi Alpher, a former official with the Israeli intelligence service Mossad, said it could even be worse because of AIPAC's alleged involvement. "The insinuation that AIPAC, an American Jewish lobby, is engaged in espionage is in some ways worse than Pollard, who as a single individual could be described as off-balance," he said.

AIPAC today is one of the most powerful and influential lobbies in Washington. The group's muscle began to bulge beginning in 1980 when Thomas Dine, a veteran Capitol Hill staffer, took over as executive director from Morris Amitay, a onetime partner of Feith and Perle. A whistle-thin Midwesterner with a boyish face, Dine inherited a sizable organization. In six years, Amitay had fattened AIPAC's bank account from $400,000 to $1.2 million and boosted its membership to 8,000. During Dine's dozen years at the helm, the lobby's budget exploded by a factor of ten, to $15 million, with a membership of 50,000 and a staff up from two dozen employees to 158. "AIPAC became an all-purpose pressure machine," said writer J. J. Goldberg, editor of the *Forward*, the long-established Jewish newspaper. "Dine openly trumpeted AIPAC's clout, boasting about 'Jewish political power' to mass audiences, in the obvious belief that an outsized reputation would intimidate the opposition. AIPAC," said Goldberg, "had only one issue: Israel. A friend of Israel was a friend of AIPAC, period."

In the late 1980s David K. Shipler of *The New York Times* reported that AIPAC had become "a major factor in shaping United States policy in the Middle East. . . . The organization has gained power to influence a presidential candidate's choice of staff, to block practically any arms sales to an Arab country and to serve as a catalyst for intimate military relations between the Pentagon and the Israeli army. Its leading officials are consulted by State Department and White House policy makers, by senators and generals."

Soon after the FBI launched its secret investigation of AIPAC in 2002, National Security Adviser Condoleezza Rice and her deputy Stephen Hadley became two of the very few Bush administration officials who were informed. Thus, at the same time bureau agents were aiming their long-range cameras at the lobby, top Bush administration officials and members of Congress continued to work closely with the organization. In 2002, AIPAC's annual conference included fifty senators and ninety representatives from both parties, as well as more than a dozen senior administration officials. In May of 2004, in the middle of the investigation, President George W. Bush made an appearance at AIPAC's annual conference in Washington and offered his thanks to the organization for "serving the cause of America" by alerting the public about the threat posed by Iran's nuclear weapons development.

That same month the FBI's espionage investigation was focusing on a number of the Bush administration's most senior officials, people with a long past of close ties to Israel who were now heavily involved with the war in Iraq. One of the people bureau agents contacted was Stephen Green, a former United Nations worker and the author of two books on U.S.-Israeli relations. They asked him to come to Washington for a meeting with the agents, a meeting that took place on June 22 in an office in northern Virginia.

"They were extraordinarily well-informed," said Green. "It was apparent they've been at this for a while." According to Green, the questions went back decades. Seated across an oval table, the agents focused on a small group of neoconservatives. The names that came up included those of Feith, Wolfowitz, Richard Perle, Feith consultant Michael Ledeen, Feith employee Harold Rhode, and Stephen Bryen, the Reagan Pentagon official who was the subject of an earlier Israeli espionage investigation. Green asked why the agents were looking into the past links between the Bush officials and Israel. "It's a present issue," they told him.

Another major focus of the FBI's wide-ranging investigation was meetings between Americans working for AIPAC and diplomats from the Israeli embassy. It was during one of those stakeouts, in early 2003, that the FBI discovered a key connection. At the time, the bureau's secret cameras and tape recorders were focused on a luncheon meeting involving two lobbyists for AIPAC, Steve Rosen, the director of foreign policy issues, and Keith Weissman, a senior Middle East analyst. Also present was Naor Gilon, the chief of political affairs at the Israeli embassy and a specialist on Iran's nuclear weapons program. Then, suddenly, a senior Pentagon intelligence official walked into the picture and took a seat at the table. Although agents were initially unaware of the man's identity, they were shocked when they put a name to the face a short time later.

His name was Lawrence A. Franklin, a Brooklyn-born career Defense Intelligence Agency analyst and colonel in the Air Force reserve in his late fifties. Originally a Soviet specialist, with the end of the Cold War in the early 1990s, Franklin earned a doctorate in East Asian studies from St. John's University in New York and transferred to the agency's Middle Eastern division as an Iranian specialist. During the late 1990s, while stationed at the Pentagon with the Air Force reserve, he traveled to Israel on eight occasions and also spent time working in the U.S. embassy in Tel Aviv with the military attaché's office.

In the summer of 2001, Franklin, whose support for Israel was ardent, public, and unequivocal according to colleagues, moved

into Feith's office as one of two senior intelligence analysts specializing in Iran. The Israeli newspaper *Haaretz* interviewed a number of people who described him as an "ideologue who believes
wholeheartedly in the neoconservative approach." "Everything by
him is black and white," one colleague said, adding, "One of the
reasons he was brought into the Near East and South Asia desk was
his political beliefs." In addition to working on Iran issues,
Franklin, according to his résumé, also worked on Iraq within
Feith's highly secret Office of Special Plans. His immediate boss
was William J. Luti, deputy undersecretary of defense for Near
Eastern and South Asian Affairs, the key division responsible for
developing defense policy for both Iraq and Iran.

Like regime change in Iraq, regime change in Iran had
always been a top priority for both Israel and many neoconservatives in the Bush administration, who hoped that after a quick war
with Iraq, Iran would be next. Eventually the debate over Iran
within the Bush administration came down to a quiet battle
between two powerful groups. The hard-core neocons in Feith's
and the vice president's office were exploring ways to overthrow
the Iranian government. They were also pushing for aggressive
action, including the possibility of military strikes on Tehran's
nuclear program if it came close to producing a nuclear weapon.
Others, however, at the State Department and CIA were advocat-
ing a more cautious approach.

At one point a top-secret policy document known as a
National Security Presidential Directive was drafted for President
Bush, setting out a number of arguments and options concerning
Iran. One person who read the document said it had the ring of a
"glorified op-ed looking at how engagement [with Iran] doesn't
work and how the U.S. needs a more robust strategy." Many of the
neocons felt its tone was far too moderate. It was details from that
highly secret presidential discussion paper, as well as other equally

sensitive information, that the FBI believes Franklin allegedly passed through AIPAC to Israeli intelligence. A U.S. intelligence official told *Newsweek* that at first Franklin allegedly attempted to pass the document to one of the people at the table. "But his alleged confederate was 'too smart,' the official said, and refused to take it. . . . Instead, he asked Franklin to brief him on its contents—and Franklin allegedly obliged. Franklin also passed information gleaned from more highly classified documents, the official said." *Newsweek* added, "If the government is correct, Franklin's motive appears to have been ideological rather than financial."

Some investigators believe that other documents and more than one individual may have been involved in the espionage. They also believe that a key reason for the spying was anger over the fact that the proposed policy was not sufficiently tough toward Iran. Passing it to AIPAC, therefore, would give Israel an opportunity to influence U.S. policy while it was still being made. Hardline Israelis and many neoconservatives had always viewed Iran as the bomb on Israel's doorstep. In the years following the 9/11 attacks, Israel's concern over Iran's nuclear development escalated sharply. By the summer of 2004, Israeli officials were warning that they might even attack Tehran unilaterally, launching strikes against the country's nuclear facilities—facilities Iran has always claimed were solely for peaceful nuclear power. In response, the Iranian military warned, "If Israel should dare attack our nuclear installations, we will come down on its head like a heavy hammer crushing its skull."

As the investigation into AIPAC and Franklin progressed, agents began uncovering other suspicious activities involving Iraq and Iran, and all roads seemed to lead to the plush Pentagon office of Douglas Feith. One involved a close friend and associate of Franklin and Feith by the name of Michael Ledeen, whom the *Jerusalem Post* has called "Washington's neocon guru." In the late

1970s Ledeen served as the first executive director of the Jewish Institute for National Security Affairs, a group that specializes in pressuring the Pentagon and Congress to supply money and weapons to Israel. (Until his appointment to the Pentagon, Feith also held a senior position with the organization.) Then in the early 1980s, after losing his job as a consultant with the State Department, Ledeen approached the Pentagon's Noel Koch, the principal assistant secretary of defense for International Security Affairs, and asked to be placed on his rolls as a terrorism consultant—to be paid only when used. Koch agreed, but later greatly regretted his decision.

In 1988, in an extraordinary yet almost unknown letter to the House Judiciary Committee, which oversees the Justice Department and FBI, Koch virtually accused Ledeen of being a spy and said the CIA listed him as an "agent of influence of a foreign government," that government reportedly being Israel. Asking the committee to investigate Ledeen, Koch said his former consultant "lied about efforts to acquire by ruse classified information for which he had no legitimate claim, and, while he lived in Italy [as a correspondent for *The New Republic* magazine], was carried by the CIA chief of station in Rome as an agent of influence of a foreign government [Israel], according to a current ranking official of the CIA who was associated with the activities of the Rome station in that period."

One incident was particularly suspicious to Koch. Ledeen wanted his help in acquiring several highly secret CIA debriefings of a defector from a Middle Eastern country. The former senior Pentagon official speculated that someone had given Ledeen the titles and asked him to try to get copies of them. In his letter to the committee, Koch then made reference to an unnamed spy, most likely Israeli spy Jonathan Pollard who, in a similar way, had been tasked with certain specific requests by the mysterious American official, Mr. X. "Someone had to tell him what to steal," said Koch, who also had repeatedly attempted to get the FBI to investigate Ledeen. But senior FBI official Oliver "Buck" Revell, a friend of Ledeen, constantly rebuffed him.

In the mid-1980s Ledeen played a major role in the Iran-contra arms scandal as a go-between with Israeli officials. Also among his principal contacts was Iranian arms dealer Manucher Ghorbanifar who, like Ahmed Chalabi, was dismissed as little more than a con man by the CIA. According the Final Report of the Independent Counsel for Iran-Contra, Ghorbanifar was "well known to the American intelligence community as a prevaricator. The CIA had concluded, after past interaction with Ghorbanifar, that he could not be trusted to act in anyone's interest but his own. So strong were the CIA's views on Ghorbanifar that the agency issued a 'burn notice' in July 1984, effectively recommending that no U.S. agency have any dealings with him."

Despite Ledeen's suspicious background and Koch's charge that he was an agent of influence for Israel, Feith hired him shortly after the 9/11 attacks as a consultant in his Office of Special Plans. Soon after his arrival, Ledeen in turn set up a meeting in Rome with Ghorbanifar, along with several Iranian dissidents. Joining Ledeen were two of Feith's employees. One was Larry Franklin, who would soon come under investigation as an alleged Israeli spy. The other was Harold Rhode, another arch neoconservative and one of the key architects of the Iraq war and occupation.

"Rhode practically lived out of [Ahmed] Chalabi's office," said a former senior U.S. intelligence official close to members of the Coalition Provisional Authority in Baghdad. The official told Richard Sale, United Press International's intelligence correspondent, "Rhode was observed by CIA operatives as being constantly on his cell phone to Israel." The information that the intelligence officials overheard Rhode passing to Israel was "mind-boggling" and "dealt with U.S. plans, military deployments, political projects, discussion of Iraq assets, and a host of other sensitive topics," the official added.

According to *Jerusalem Post* correspondent Matthew Gutman, the meeting between Ghorbanifar and the small group of Pentagon neoconservatives was an attempt to secretly redirect White House policy toward their private goals. "The purpose of the meeting with Ghorbanifar," he wrote, "was to undermine a pending deal that the White House had been negotiating with the Iranian government. At the time, Iran had considered turning over five Al Qaeda operatives in exchange for Washington dropping its support for Mujahideen El Khalq (MEK), an Iraq-based rebel Iranian group listed as a terrorist organization by the State Department."

For years the neocons had promoted support for the MEK as a possible opposition force against the Iranian government, just as they promoted Ahmed Chalabi and his INC as an opposition force against the Iraqi regime of Saddam Hussein. But with the MEK it was always a devil's bargain. The group had to make peace with Hussein in order to establish bases in Iraq from which to launch attacks against Iran. Therefore when the United States recently branded the MEK a terrorist organization, many frustrated neoconservatives expressed great anger. Despite the opposition group's record of terrorism against the Iranian government, the neocons wanted to continue developing the MEK into a weapon aimed at Tehran. Thus the interest on the part of the Iranians to trade five captured Al Qaeda soldiers for the Bush administration's agreement to abandon its support for the MEK.

But as the *Jerusalem Post* noted, a key objective of the meeting with Ghorbanifar was to secretly find a way to undermine the possible White House-Iranian deal. To the neocons, the value of their future anti-Iran army greatly outweighed the benefit that might come to the U.S. as a result of its interrogation of the Al Qaeda operatives, despite the fact that among the information that might flow from the terrorists were details on future operations or even clues to the location of Osama bin Laden. The "meetings suggest the possibility that a rogue faction at the Pentagon was trying to work outside normal U.S. foreign policy channels," said *The Washington Monthly*, which investigated the meeting. Its purpose, cautioned the magazine, was "to advance a 'regime change' agenda not approved by the president's foreign policy principals or even the president himself."

At the time of the meeting, the FBI's investigation of AIPAC as a conduit for Israeli spying was fully under way, as was the war in Iraq. With the discovery of the alleged involvement of Larry Franklin, investigators quickly turned their attention to Doug Feith's Pentagon office and the possible involvement of other senior Pentagon officials.

In addition to looking closely at the suspicious activity involving Feith's office, Ghorbanifar, and Iran, FBI agents began looking closely at the suspicious activity involving Feith's office, Chalabi, and Iraq. Most explosively, they began investigating another potential espionage case. This one focused on whether Chalabi, or someone from his group, had received and then passed on to the Iranians in early 2004 extremely sensitive details of American code-breaking successes against the Iranian government. It was information that could have come only from highly cleared U.S. officials. Clues to the espionage may have been discovered when Iraqi officials raided Chalabi's Baghdad compound in May 2004. The security breach resulted in a massive loss of intelligence on Iran and a major effort by NSA to try to repair the damage.

Two years after the AIPAC probe got under way, in the summer of 2004, the FBI decided it was time to begin showing its hand.

Franklin was quietly approached, shown evidence that he had given classified information to AIPAC, and asked to secretly cooperate with the investigation. Hoping for leniency when the case was over, he agreed to help the agents. One case involved top-secret White House and NSA documents going to Israel and the other case concerned top-secret NSA information going to Iran. Both were extremely serious and both had links to Feith's Pentagon office.

FBI agents first aimed Franklin at AIPAC and told him to arrange another luncheon meeting with his two AIPAC contacts, Rosen and Weissman. Then they told him to pass on some very "secret" and urgent information—that a group of Iranians was closely watching a number of Israelis operating in the Kurdish region of northern Iraq and that they intended to kill them. He was also told to stress that because his access to the White House was limited, he was concerned that the Bush administration was unaware of the large number of Iranian agents operating in Iraq. Franklin was to ask his AIPAC contacts to stress this point in meetings with U.S. officials.

The idea was to have Franklin offer the information as bait and then, as the FBI's cameras and wiretaps were rolling, see if the AIPAC officials in turn passed the "secret" information on to Israeli embassy officials—a violation of the U.S. espionage laws. According to a report in the *Jerusalem Post*, that is exactly what they did. It is possible that agents from the FBI and NSA were also monitoring Israeli embassy communications as the "secret" information from AIPAC was transmitted to Tel Aviv.

Next, the agents pointed Franklin toward Ahmed Chalabi. On a hot, late August afternoon, with FBI agents nearby listening in and an FBI script in front of him, Franklin made a "pretext call" to one of his Iraqi exile acquaintances, someone who had spent the past decade working with Chalabi's INC. Could he recall,

Franklin asked the Iraqi in his heavy Brooklyn accent, whether he had heard anyone discussing America's ability to intercept and decode the Iranian government's secret communications? The questions, which concerned specific Pentagon officials and went on for close to half an hour, startled the Iraqi. But he could offer no confirmation.

A few weeks later the decision was made to start shaking the tree. On Friday, August 27, 2004, FBI agents went to AIPAC offices, flashed their credentials, and asked to speak with Steven Rosen, the group's director of foreign policy issues, and Keith Weissman, one of its experts on Iran. After answering a few brief questions, the two shocked officials refused to say any more and instead asked to speak to an attorney. Nevertheless, the agents seized a number of computer hard drives, including that of Rosen. In an unusual move, two days later on a Sunday, agents showed up at the front door of Feith's house. Others paid visits to Luti, Paul Wolfowitz, Peter Rodman, the assistant secretary of defense for International Security Affairs, and others.

Over the next week, FBI agents began questioning dozens of government officials specifically about the Bush administration's neocon cabal—Feith, Wolfowitz, Richard Perle, Harold Rhode, David Wurmser, and others. "The initial interest was: Do you believe certain people would spy for Israel and pass secret information?" said one source interviewed by the FBI about the Pentagon employees. The officials whose names came up during questioning all had strong ties to Israel.

It took little time for news of the investigation to leak, and on August 27, CBS was the first to break the story. The speed of the disclosures caught some investigators off guard. At the time, the Justice Department had been preparing a request to the State Department to have an Israeli diplomat declared persona non grata for allegedly having received classified U.S. intelligence from

AIPAC sources. This was apparently Israeli embassy official Naor Gilon, who'd had frequent meetings with Franklin.

Despite their vocal protests over the investigation, knowing that the FBI had conducted both video and audio surveillance AIPAC carefully responded by not denying that its staffers held numerous meetings with Franklin or even passed information from him to Israeli officials. Instead, what they said was that AIPAC did not *knowingly* receive or pass along any *classified* information, which would likely be an argument the organization would use if they were to eventually get charged with espionage.

In October, about six weeks after the investigation became public, Franklin decided to drop his publicly paid, court-appointed attorney. Instead, he hired well-known Washington lawyer Plato Cacheris, who had represented Aldrich Ames, Robert Hanssen, and other spies. Soon after, he rejected a plea bargain in which he would have had to agree to plead guilty to one or more charges. Although the charges were less than the government could have brought, Franklin still felt them too severe. "Any charge of espionage will be met with fierce resistance," warned Cacheris. Franklin also terminated all cooperation with the bureau in its effort to trap AIPAC officials. "Who pushed Franklin—who for months seemed vulnerable—to stop cooperating?" asked *The American Prospect.* "And who is paying for his expensive new lawyer?"

Nevertheless, on December 1, after a brief lull during the presidential election and after a grand jury had been assembled to listen to the evidence, the FBI, for the second time in three months, conducted another surprise raid on AIPAC's Capitol Hill offices. This time they seized stacks of computer files connected to Rosen and Weissman and handed out subpoenas to four more senior officials. The officials were ordered to appear before a grand jury under the jurisdiction of U.S. Attorney Paul McNulty, a Bush-

Ashcroft appointee for the Eastern District of Virginia in Alexandria. The four were AIPAC executive director Howard Kohr, managing director Richard Fishman, communications director Renee Rothstein, and research director Rafi Danziger.

For many ardent supporters of Israel, unaccustomed to being on the defensive, the first reaction was simply to try to bully the government, through both slander and raw political power, into closing down the investigation. Democratic Congressman Robert Wexler, whose district along the east coast of Florida contains a large Jewish community, made one attempt by throwing down the old anti-Semitism card. In a letter he sent to President Bush, he suggested that the "driving force" behind the investigation was anti-Semitism. He then urged an investigation of FBI counterintelligence chief David Szady for having a "purported anti-Semitic record at the CIA and FBI," and asked the administration to consider removing "Mr. Szady from the AIPAC case and dismiss him from his post." Szady had no such record and Franklin, the only person targeted, was in fact a practicing Roman Catholic.

On the other hand, Democratic Congressman John Conyers of Michigan saw in the investigation a much more frightening picture, one in which a "rogue element in the American government may have been working with a foreign government," that rogue element being a small group of neoconservatives connected to the office of Doug Feith.

How much of a factor, if any, support for Israel played in the ultimate decision to launch the preemptive war against Iraq, a war that has proved disastrous, is still shrouded in secrecy and fog. But the fact that the question is even being raised is more than troubling and needs to be answered. The Franklin investigation, writes correspondent Nathan Guttman in Israel's *Haaretz*, "breathes new life into the assertion that Israeli, and not American, interests led to the war in Iraq."

What is now clear is that the original justification for the invasion—that the United States was in imminent danger from the threat of Iraqi weapons of mass destruction—was fraudulent, as many in the CIA and other intelligence agencies were quietly warning. Instead, it was simply a pretext for a war long advocated by a small group of hard-line neoconservatives with their own agenda. The man who might have made a difference was George Tenet, but rather than fight or resign in protest, he chose instead simply to go along. It was a "slam dunk" decision.

On December 14, 2004, in a glittery ceremony in the East Room of the White House, President George W. Bush hung around the neck of George Tenet a heavy gold medal on royal blue velvet ribbons. It was the Presidential Medal of Freedom, the nation's highest civilian honor, whose previous recipients have included Mother Teresa and Pope John Paul II. Among those in the audience applauding were Secretary of Defense Donald Rumsfeld and Vice President Dick Cheney. "Tenet grinned broadly," said news accounts about the former CIA director, who had also recently received a $5 million book contract.

That same day two more Marines were killed in Iraq, bringing the total number of servicemen killed in the conflict to more than 1,100. In Baghdad, a suicide bomber blew up seven people and wounded at least thirteen at a Green Zone checkpoint. Farther to the north, in Mosul, gunmen killed a provincial council member and soldiers discovered eight more bodies of Iraqis, bringing the number of Iraqi police killed by insurgents over the past six weeks to more than 150. And in Washington, the Pentagon announced that the U.S. military would have a record high of 150,000 troops on the ground in Iraq through the January 30 election. According to the announcement, these troops might also stay "a little bit after"; how long is still unclear.

NOTES

4   "Watch supervisor, I have a possible": William B. Scott, "Exercise Jump-Starts Response to Attacks," *Aviation Week & Space Technology* (June 3, 2002).

4   "Part of the exercise": Hart Seely, "Amid Crisis Simulation, 'We Were Suddenly No-Kidding Under Attack,'" *Newhouse News Service* (January 25, 2002).

5   "American eleven heavy with you passing through"; "Traffic ten o'clock": "Transcript of Flight 11," *The New York Times* (October 16, 2001).

5   3.1 million parts: Boeing 767 Fact sheet, The Boeing Company.

5   "When his hands were dirty"; Ogonowski's background: Dave Weber and Ed Hayward, "Pilot's Greatest Love Was His Family," *The Boston Herald* (September 12, 2001).

6   the move was on; details of what went on during the assault: Michael Woodward, an American Airlines ground manager at Boston's Logan Airport who was in contact with one of the flight attendants on the plane at the time. See "Calm Before the Crash," *Primetime*, ABC News (July 18, 2002).

6   "Don't do anything foolish": Mark Clayton, "Controller's Tale of Flight 11," *The Christian Science Monitor* (September 13, 2001).

7   "We have more planes": Peter Grier, "A Changed World," *The Christian Science Monitor* (September 17, 2001).

8   "We have a hijacked aircraft and I need to get you some sort of fighters": Transcript, "9/11," ABC News (September 11, 2002).

8   "some F-16s or something": Hart Seely, "Amid Crisis Simulation, 'We Were Suddenly No-Kidding Under Attack,'" *Newhouse News Service* (January 25, 2002).

8   "American 11 heavy": William B. Scott, "Exercise Jump-Starts Response to Attacks," *Aviation Week & Space Technology* (June 3, 2002).

8   "We were going by the old-fashioned method": Transcript, "9/11," ABC News (September 11, 2002).

9   "I have FAA on the phone": Transcript, "9/11," ABC News (September 11, 2002).

9   "He says it's going to New York": Hart Seely, "Amid Crisis Simulation, 'We Were Suddenly No-Kidding Under Attack,'" *Newhouse News Service* (January 25, 2002).

9   "Listen, and listen to me very carefully": Transcript, "Calm Before the Crash," *Primetime*, ABC News (July 18, 2002).

9   "Pray for us": Transcript, "Calm Before the Crash," *Primetime*, ABC News (July 18, 2002).

10   "Boss, I need to scramble"; "Go ahead and scramble them": Transcript, "9/11," ABC News (September 11, 2002).

11   "I see the water": Transcript, "Calm Before the Crash," *Primetime*, ABC News (July 18, 2002).

12   *"Oh my God, all my people"*; Details on Steve McIntyre and the employees of the American Bureau of Shipping are derived from: John McLaughlin and Alison Bate, "Cheating Death," *Lloyds List* (September 17, 2001).

12   "Oh, my God!": Transcript, "Calm Before the Crash," *Primetime*, ABC News (July 18, 2002).

13   "I just picked up an ELT on 121.5": "Transcript of United Airlines Flight 175," *The New York Times* (October 16, 2001).

13   "Anybody know what": "Transcript of United Airlines Flight 175," *The New York Times* (October 16, 2001).

14   "Oh, God. My brother works": Hart Seely, "Amid Crisis Simulation, 'We Were Suddenly No-Kidding Under Attack,'" *Newhouse News Service* (January 25, 2002).

14   "He says, 'You're not gonna believe'": Transcript, "9/11," ABC News (September 11, 2002).

14   "Looks like he's heading southbound": "Transcript of United Airlines Flight 175," *The New York Times* (October 16, 2001).

15   "We heard a suspicious transmission": "Transcript of United Airlines Flight 175," *The New York Times* (October 16, 2001).

15   "Duff, you're super": Transcript, "9/11," ABC News (September 11, 2002).

16   "We have more planes": Peter Grier, "A Changed World," *The Christian Science Monitor* (September 17, 2001).

16   "This just in": Transcript, "CNN Breaking News," Cable News Network (September 11, 2001).

17 "Oh, my God, I don't believe it": Joline Gutierrez Krueger, "The Eye of the Storm," *The Albuquerque Tribune* (September 10, 2002).

17 "The President was surprised": Transcript, "Terror Hits the Towers," *World News Tonight*, ABC News (September 14, 2003).

18 "Mr. Director, there's a serious problem": Dan Balz and Bob Woodward, "America's Chaotic Road to War," *The Washington Post* (January 27, 2002).

18 "The immediate image I had": Interview with Lt. Gen. Michael V. Hayden, January 20, 2004.

20 "I thought that was a big fire for a small plane": Interview with Lt. Gen. Michael V. Hayden, January 20, 2004.

21 "Where the hell is the third fire-stair?": John McLaughlin and Alison Bate, "Cheating Death," *Lloyds List* (September 17, 2001).

21 "We're having a smoke condition": Transcript, Port Authority of New York and New Jersey for September 11, 2001 (August 29, 2003).

22 "The situation on 106": Transcript, Port Authority of New York and New Jersey for September 11, 2001 (August 29, 2003).

22 "Listen, this is Tony Savas": Transcript, Port Authority of New York and New Jersey for September 11, 2001 (August 29, 2003).

22 "I'm at work": Transcript, Port Authority of New York and New Jersey for September 11, 2001 (August 29, 2003).

23 "It's the other building"; this and subsequent quotes from Beverly Eckert and Sean Rooney are derived from: Michael Howerton, "Bittersweet Goodbye: Stamford Widow Finds Solace in Final Phone Call," *Stamford Advocate* (date not available).

23 "The first two flights were dark": John McLaughlin and Alison Bate, "Cheating Death," *Lloyds List* (September 17, 2001).

24 "UAL175," he said, "do you read New York?": "Transcript of United Airlines Flight 175," *The New York Times* (October 16, 2001).

24 "We may have a hijack": "Transcript of United Airlines Flight 175," *The New York Times* (October 16, 2001).

24 "Hey, John, are you watching this on TV?": "Get These Planes on the Ground," *20/20*, ABC News (October 24, 2001).

26 "Runway three zero, taxi into position": "Transcript of American Airlines Flight 77."

27 "Good Luck . . . I usually say": "Get These Planes on the Ground," *20/20*, ABC News (October 24, 2001).

27 "American 77, Indy": "Get These Planes on the Ground," *20/20*, ABC News (October 24, 2001).

27 "Wow! Look at that"; "We've lost an aircraft over Manhattan"; "Can you see him out the window?": Alan Levin, Marilyn Adams, and Blake

Morrison, "Amid Terror, a Drastic Decision: Clear the Skies" *USA Today* (August 12, 2002).

28   "It appears that there is more": *Good Morning America*, ABC News (September 11, 2001).

29   "Jesus Christ": "Rooftop Rescues: Why Weren't There Any on September 11?" *World News Tonight*, ABC News (November 8, 2001).

30   "Oh my God!": H. Darr Beiser, "Amid Terror, a Drastic Decision"; Alan Levin, Marilyn Adams and Blake Morrison, "Clear the Skies," *USA Today* (August 12, 2002).

30   "Boom, boom": "America Remembers," *Dateline*, NBC News (September 10, 2002).

31   "Just letting you know": John McLaughlin and Alison Bate, "Cheating Death," *Lloyds List* (September 17, 2001).

32   "Come on, everyone"; "You can't go down": Dennis Cauchon, "Four Survived by Ignoring Words of Advice," *USA Today* (December 19, 2001).

34   "You didn't want NORAD": Interview with Lt. Gen. Daniel O. Graham (December 1984).

34   "It has all the inputs from all the assets": Harvard University, Center for Information Policy Research, Program on Information Resources Policy, Seminar on Command, Control, Communications and Intelligence (Cambridge: Harvard University, 1980), Raymond T. Tate lecture, p. 30.

35   "My intention . . . was to plumb": Interview with Lt. Gen. Michael V. Hayden, January 20, 2004.

36   "I was sitting outside the classroom": Transcript, Bush Town Hall Meeting, Florida, December 4, 2001, CNN.

36   "When we walked into the classroom": Transcript, Bush Town Hall Meeting, California, January 5, 2002, White House website: http://www.whitehouse.gov/news/releases/2002/01/20020105-3.html.

37   He reportedly did not enter the class until 9:04: Dana Milbank and Mike Allen, "Bush Vows Retaliation for 'Mass Murder,'" *The Washington Post* (September 12, 2001).

37   "A second plane hit the second tower"; "America is under attack": Transcript, "The President's Story," *60 Minutes II*, CBS News (September 10, 2003).

37   "They had declared war on us": Dan Balz and Bob Woodward, "America's Chaotic Road to War," *The Washington Post* (January 27, 2002).

39   Myers's actions on 9/11; "It was initially pretty confusing": Sgt. 1st Class Kathleen T. Rhem, USA, "Myers and Sept. 11: 'We Hadn't Thought About This,'" American Forces Press Service (October 23, 2001).

39   "Captain, this is impossible": Transcript, "Rooftop Rescues: Why Weren't

There Any on September 11?" *World News Tonight*, ABC News (November 8, 2001).

40   "People falling out of building": "Second-by-Second Terror Revealed in Calls to 911," *New York Daily News* (September 30, 2001).

40   "There's body parts all over the place": Transcript, Port Authority of New York and New Jersey for September 11, 2001 (August 29, 2003).

41   "A hundred and twenty people trapped on the 106th floor": "Second-by-Second Terror Revealed in Calls to 911," *New York Daily News* (September 30, 2001).

41   "The roof of the South Tower": "Rooftop Rescues: Why Weren't There Any on September 11?" *World News Tonight*, ABC News (November 8, 2001).

41   "You guys never": "Transcript of Flight 77," *The New York Times* (October 16, 2001).

43   "I don't think any fighter pilot": Jack Sullivan, "Fargo Pilots Remember Sept. 11 Duty," Associated Press (August 19, 2002).

43   "Fast-moving primary target": "Get These Planes on the Ground," *20/20*, ABC News (October 24, 2001).

43   "Oh my God!": "Get These Planes on the Ground," *20/20*, ABC News (October 24, 2001).

44   "Barbara is on the phone"; this and other details concerning Ted and Barbara Olson are derived from: Ted Olson interview, *Larry King Live*, CNN (September 14, 2001).

46   "He's twelve miles west": "Get These Planes on the Ground," *20/20*, ABC News (October 24, 2001).

46   "We're moving now, sir; we're moving": Nancy Gibbs, "Special Report: Day of the Attack," *Time* (September 12, 2001).

46   "Women, drop your heels": Transcript, "The President's Story," *60 Minutes II*, CBS News (September 10, 2002).

46   "Six miles"; "And we waited": "Get These Planes on the Ground," *20/20*, ABC News (October 24, 2001).

47   "It's an American Airlines plane": Transcript, Arlington, Virginia, Police Department, September 11, 2001, Associated Press (September 18, 2001).

47   "It looked like a plane coming in for a landing": Paul Haring, "Pentagon Crash Eyewitness Comforted Victims," Military District of Washington News Service (September 28, 2001).

48   "I saw it crash into the building": Paul Haring, "Pentagon Crash Eyewitness Comforted Victims," Military District of Washington News Service (September 28, 2001).

48   "Did you see that?": "USA Under Terrorist Attack," Associated Press (September 12, 2001).

48   "Dulles, hold all of our inbound": "Get These Planes on the Ground," *20/20*, ABC News (October 24, 2001).

48   "I did and I didn't want to": Ted Olson interview, *Larry King Live*, CNN (September 14, 2001).

49   "It was the first time": Transcript, "9/11," ABC News (September 11, 2002).

50   ". . . as part of its dual mission": http://www.dcandr.ang.af.mil/113wing/pa/html/wg_units.html (January 21, 2001).

50   "I have no idea what's going on"; details of Lt. Col. Marc H. Sasseville's mission: William B. Scott, "F-16 Pilots Considered Ramming Flight 93," *Aviation Week & Space Technology* (September 9, 2002).

51   "Order everyone to land!": H. Darr Beiser, "Amid Terror, a Drastic Decision"; Alan Levin, Marilyn Adams and Blake Morrison, "Clear the Skies," *USA Today* (August 12, 2002).

52   "As they were walking through the door": Interview with Lt. Gen. Michael V. Hayden, January 20, 2004.

53   "All non-essential personnel": Interview with Lt. Gen. Michael V. Hayden, January 20, 2004.

55   "Beware, cockpit intrusion": "'Nobody move, please': Transcripts from Sept. 11 Reveal Voice from Cockpit," Associated Press (October 16, 2001).

55   "Good Morning, Cleveland": Karen Breslau, Eleanor Clift, and Evan Thomas, "The Real Story of Flight 93," *Newsweek* (December 3, 2001).

55   "Somebody call Cleveland?": Karen Breslau, Eleanor Clift, and Evan Thomas, "The Real Story of Flight 93," *Newsweek* (December 3, 2001).

56   "Ladies and gentlemen": Karen Breslau, Eleanor Clift, and·Evan Thomas, "The Real Story of Flight 93," *Newsweek* (December 3, 2001).

56   "There's smoke!"; "With that we all rushed to the window": Senator Tom Daschle with Michael D'Orso, *Like No Other Time: The 107th Congress and the Two Years That Changed America Forever* (New York: Crown, 2004), p. 107.

57   "A plane is heading for the Capitol!": Transcript, "Sept. 11 Scramble," ABC News (September 14, 2003).

57   "The scene was total chaos": Senator Tom Daschle with Michael D'Orso, *Like No Other Time: The 107th Congress and the Two Years That Changed America Forever* (New York: Crown, 2004), p. 110.

57   "There was starting to be": John F. Harris, "Congress Reassesses Its Security Plans," *The Washington Post* (September 14, 2001).

57   "People were just as fearful": Transcript, "Sept. 11 Scramble," ABC News (September 14, 2003).

57   "They are dying": "Second-by-Second Terror Revealed in Calls to 911," New York *Daily News* (September 30, 2001).

57 Eighty-three elevator mechanics from ACE Elevator had left the two buildings: Dennis Cauchon, "For Many on Sept. 11, Survival Was No Accident," *USA Today* (December 19, 2001).

58 Eckert asked him how bad the smoke was now; details concerning Beverly Eckert and Sean Rooney are derived from: Michael Howerton, "Bittersweet Goodbye: Stamford Widow Finds Solace in Final Phone Call," *Stamford Advocate* (date not available).

59 "It's down!": Transcript, "Clear the Skies," BBC Television (September 1, 2002).

60 "If we had intercepted": Kevin Dennehy, "I Thought It Was the Start of World War III," *The Cape Cod Times* (August 21, 2002).

61 "I have determined, of course": Transcript, "Clear the Skies," BBC Television (September 1, 2002).

61 "I was thinking"; details concerning employees of American Bureau of Shipping and Steve McIntyre are derived from: John McLaughlin and Alison Bate, "Cheating Death," *Lloyds List* (September 17, 2001).

61 "Get out!": Dennis Cauchon, "For Many on Sept. 11, Survival Was No Accident," *USA Today* (December 19, 2001).

63 "As the President sat down": Transcript, "9/11," ABC News (September 11, 2002).

64 Details on Outpost Mission were derived from: Ted Gup, "The Doomsday Blueprints," *Time* (August 10, 1992).

65 "The significance of saying to a pilot"; "The President had given us permission"; "United Airlines Flight 93 will not"; "Sir, what are they gonna do?" "As military men": Transcript, "9/11," ABC News (September 11, 2002).

65 "The significance of saying to a pilot;" "The President had given us permission;" "United Airlines Flight 93 will not;" "Sir, what are they gonna do?"; "As, as military men": Transcript, "9/11," ABC News (September 11, 2002).

65 "DOD, DOD": Richard A. Clarke, *Against All Enemies: Inside America's War on Terrorism* (New York: Simon & Schuster: 2004), p. 8.

66 "The New York controller": Transcript, "Clear the Skies," BBC Television (September 1, 2002).

69 "It seemed we were 'wheels up'": Transcript, "Sept. 11 Scramble," ABC News (September 14, 2003).

70 "They've been unsuccessful"; "simply never happened"; "White House Drops Claim of Threat to Bush": Mike Allen, *The Washington Post* (September 27, 2001).

70 "We would have to run this country": Ted Gup, "The Doomsday Blueprints," *Time* (August 10, 1992).

75   Details on Mount Weather: See Ted Gup, "The Doomsday Blueprints," *Time* (August 10, 1992).

76   Details on Mount Weather and Mount Pony were derived from: *Atomic Audit: The Costs and Consequences of U.S. Nuclear Weapons Since 1940* (Washington, DC: The Brookings Institution, 1998).

77   Details on Site R: See Ted Gup, "Civil Defense Doomsday Hideaway," *Time* (December 9, 1991).

78   "We don't even have to turn on the news": Howard Altman, "Chasing Shadows," *Philadelphia CityPaper.Net* (March 14–21, 2002).

80   Details on the congressional bunker were derived from: *Atomic Audit: The Costs and Consequences of U.S. Nuclear Weapons Since 1940* (Washington, DC: The Brookings Institution, 1998); Ted Gup, "The Ultimate Congressional Hideaway," *The Washington Post Magazine* (May 31, 1992).

80   "Two of my security people": Transcript, "Clear the Skies," BBC Television (September 1, 2002).

81   "I'm thinking to myself": Transcript, "Sept. 11 Scramble," ABC News (September 14, 2003).

81   "Immediately upon landing": Tom Daschle with Michael D'Orso, *Like No Other Time: The 107th Congress and the Two Years That Changed America Forever* (New York: Crown, 2003), p. 115.

81   "I expect each station"; U.S. Army Logistics Command: Ronald Kessler, *The CIA at War: Inside the Secret Campaign Against Terror* (New York: St. Martin's Press, 2003), p. 204.

83   "Everyone is watching": Joline Gutierrez Krueger, "9.11.01 Our Day of Infamy," *The Albuquerque Tribune* (September 10, 2002).

83   "We seemed to be flying forever": Transcript, "9/11," ABC News (September 11, 2002).

83   "The military operator came back": Transcript, "The President's Story," *60 Minutes II,* CBS News (September 10, 2002).

85   "Secure calls just take": Kenneth T. Walsh, *Air Force One: A History of the Presidents and Their Planes* (New York: Hyperion, 2003), p. 33.

86   "The strange part about it was": Joline Gutierrez Krueger, "9.11.01 Our Day of Infamy," *The Albuquerque Tribune* (September 10, 2002).

86   "He looked nervous;" "It was not our best moment": David E. Sanger and Don Van Natta Jr., "In Four Days, a National Crisis Changes Bush's Presidency," *The New York Times* (September 16, 2001).

86   "When Bush finally appeared": Dan Balz and Bob Woodward, "America's Chaotic Road to War," *The Washington Post* (January 27, 2002).

87   "looked grim": Judy Keen, "Danger Grounds President's Priorities for the Day," *USA Today* (September 12, 2001).

87   "Where's the President?"; NBC's Tim Russert: Jake Tapper, "Bush Challenged," *Salon* (September 11, 2001).

87   "If he stayed away . . . he could": William Langley, "Revealed: what really went on during Bush's 'missing hours,'" *Daily Telegraph* (December 16, 2001).

87   "Air Force One, got two F-16s": Transcript, "The President's Story," *60 Minutes II*, CBS News (September 10, 2002).

87   "We were not told": "Conversation with Major General Larry Arnold," *Code One* (January 2002).

90   "nerve-racking": Transcript, "American Morning with Paula Zahn," CNN (October 17, 2002).

91   "Who do you think did this to us?": Transcript, "The President's Story," *60 Minutes II*, CBS News (September 10, 2002).

91   "Get your ears up": Dan Balz and Bob Woodward, "America's Chaotic Road to War," *The Washington Post* (January 27, 2002).

91   "I am stunned that he has not come home": David E. Sanger and Don Van Natta Jr., "In Four Days, a National Crisis Changes Bush's Presidency," *The New York Times* (September 16, 2001).

91   "This is not 1812": Elisabeth Bumiller, David E. Sanger, "A Somber Bush Says Terrorism Cannot Prevail," *The New York Times* (September 12, 2001).

91   "Do we have permission": Dan Balz and Bob Woodward, "America's Chaotic Road to War," *The Washington Post* (January 27, 2002).

91   "We were able to determine": "Clear the Skies," BBC Television (September 1, 2002).

92   "Republican advisers to the administration": David E. Sanger and Don Van Natta Jr., "In Four Days, a National Crisis Changes Bush's Presidency," *The New York Times* (September 16, 2001).

95   Details on ADX Florence were derived from: Michael Taylor, "The Last Worse Place," *San Francisco Chronicle* (December 28, 1998).

96   "Khaled, he was so, so smart": Farhan Bokhari, Victoria Burnett, Charles Clover, Mark Huband, and Roel Landingin, "The CEO of al-Qaeda," *The Financial Times* (February 15, 2003).

99   whose mother was Palestinian; "Palestinian by choice": James Bone and Alan Road, "Terror by Degree," *The Times* (London) (October 18, 1997).

99   "Since the U.S. government": James Bone and Alan Road, "Terror by Degree," *The Times* (London) (October 18, 1997).

101 "This is the Liberation Army"; "OUR DEMANDS ARE"; calculations were not very accurate this time: U.S. Senate, Committee on Judiciary,

Subcommittee on Technology, Terrorism, and Government Information, Statement by J. Gilmore Childers, Esq., and Henry J. DePippo, Esq., "Foreign Terrorists in America: Five Years After the World Trade Center" (February 24, 1998).

102 "I drive myself," Details concerning Hayden's office: Interview with Lieutenant General Michael V. Hayden (February 2, 2000), personal observation.

105 "As an agency . . . we now face our greatest": NSA, DIRNSA's Desk, NSA Newsletter (February 2000), p. 3.

106 "The target changed overnight": Background briefing by a senior NSA official.

107 "The powers that be are trying to kill it": Interview with a senior NSA official, August 2001.

107 "There are still things that you can pick up": Interview with a senior NSA official, August 2001.

108 "Today you have no idea where that information": Interview with a senior intelligence official.

108 "There was nothing more important": Interview with a former senior NSA official, September 2001.

109 "The career path from college": Interview with Maureen Baginski, April 2001.

111 "There's so much out there": Neil King Jr., "In Digital Age, U.S. Spy Agency Fights to Keep From Going Deaf," *The Wall Street Journal* (May 23, 2001).

111 "U.S. intelligence operates what is probably": Admiral William O. Studeman, Remarks at the Symposium on "National Security and National Competitiveness: Open Source Solutions" (December 1, 1992).

111 "We are digging out": Joint Inquiry, testimony of NSA Director Michael V. Hayden (October 17, 2002).

111 Hayden chose Beverly Wright: NSA, "Director of National Security Agency Welcomes Ms. Beverly Wright, Chief Financial Manager," National Security Agency Newsletter (February 2000), p. 2.

112 "This is simply insufficient": Commission on the Roles and Capabilities of the United States Intelligence Community, Preparing for the 21st Century: An Appraisal of U.S. Intelligence (Washington, DC: GPO, 1996), p. 96.

112 "NSA downsized about one-third": Joint Inquiry, testimony of NSA Director Michael V. Hayden (October 17, 2002).

112 "Forty years ago": Lt. Gen. Michael V. Hayden, USAF, Director, National

Security Agency, Address to Kennedy Political Union of American University, 17 February 2000.

113 "an act of God": Neil King, Jr., "Big Technology Players Vie to Upgrade NSA Computers," *The Wall Street Journal* (March 13, 2001).

113 "What we said basically": NSA, videotape, "Address by Timothy Sample at the Cryptologic History Symposium" (October 27, 1999).

114 "Our agency must undergo change": NSA, DIRNSA's Desk, NSAN (January 2000), p. 3.

114 "responsible anarchists"; details on inside panel's report: Bob Brewin, Daniel Verton, William Matthews, "NSA Playing IT Catch-Up," *Federal Computer Week* (December 6, 1999), p. 1.

115 "In a broad sense": Interview with Lt. Gen. Michael V. Hayden (February 2, 2000).

115 "Even the best game plan": NSA, DIRNSA's Desk, NSAN (January 2000), p. 3.

116 "Cultural pride has reemerged": Renee Meyer's remarks were derived from a lecture she gave at NSA on June 11, 2001, at which the author was present.

116 "NSA is . . . not well-positioned": U.S. Library of Congress, Congressional Research Service, Richard A. Best, Jr., "The National Security Agency: Issues for Congress," Report RL 30740 (Updated January 16, 2001). (unpaginated).

117 "We truly are speaking truth": John J. Lumpkin, "CIA's Top Analyst Informs President," Associated Press (November 3, 2002).

118 "multimodality learner": Walter Pincus, "Under Bush, the Briefing Gets Briefer; Key Intelligence Report by CIA and FBI Is Shorter, 'More Targeted,' Limited to Smaller Circle of Top Officials and Advisers," *The Washington Post* (May 24, 2002), p. A33.

119 "The Presidential Daily Brief was the first": George H. W. Bush, remarks at the conference "U.S. Intelligence and the End of the Cold War," Texas A&M University (November 19, 1999).

118 Charles A. Peters; "He did not want us talking": Vernon Loeb, "The Spy Chief Who Came In From Cold War; CIA Honoring Ex-President Bush," *The Washington Post* (April 23, 1999), p. A35.

119 "The relationship between the President": Walter Pincus and Vernon Loeb, "CIA Resurfaces, In the Oval Office; Tenet, Bush Develop Close Relationship," *The Washington Post* (July 29, 2001), p. A05.

119 "The former president reinforced": Elisabeth Bumiller, "C.I.A. Chief Prospers From Bond With Bush," *The New York Times* (December 17, 2002).

120 "really hit it off": Walter Pincus and Vernon Loeb, "CIA Resurfaces in the Oval Office; Tenet, Bush Develop Close Relationship," *The Washington Post* (July 29, 2001), p. A05.

120 "They're pragmatists": Elisabeth Bumiller, "C.I.A. Chief Prospers From Bond With Bush," *The New York Times* (December 17, 2002).

121 Once described by a family friend: All Politics, CNN (March 28, 1997).

121 "Nobody who knew me": George Tenet, Address at the 1999 Alumni of the Year Awards, Benjamin N. Cardozo High School (June 11, 1999).

121 "Starting out with nothing": George Tenet, Address at the 1999 Alumni of the Year Awards, Benjamin N. Cardozo High School (June 11, 1999).

121 "When I went to high school": George Tenet, Address at the 1999 Alumni of the Year Awards, Benjamin N. Cardozo High School (June 11, 1999).

122 "I didn't go to law school": George Tenet, Address at the 1999 Alumni of the Year Awards, Benjamin N. Cardozo High School (June 11, 1999).

122 "Read 'lobbying,'": Rick Horowitz, "By George, He Knows the Guy," at Everybody Comes to Rick's website (March 27, 1997): http://yesrick.com/rh32097.htm.

123 Room SH-219: Paul De La Garza, "Sen. Graham Oversees World of Intrigue," *St. Petersburg Times* (July 22, 2001).

125 "A pretty appropriate description": Milt Bearden and James Risen, *The Main Enemy: Inside the CIA's Final Showdown with the KGB* (New York: Random House), p. 377.

125 "When David Rolph walked into the embassy": Milt Bearden and James Risen, *The Main Enemy: Inside the CIA's Final Showdown with the KGB* (New York: Random House), p. 490.

126 "The CIA did not have any high-level agents": Milt Bearden and James Risen, *The Main Enemy: Inside the CIA's Final Showdown with the KGB* (New York: Random House), p. 397.

126 "The CIA had no agents inside": Milt Bearden and James Risen, *The Main Enemy: Inside the CIA's Final Showdown with the KGB* (New York: Random House), p. 386.

126 "The CIA had no human intelligence": Milt Bearden and James Risen, *The Main Enemy: Inside the CIA's Final Showdown with the KGB* (New York: Random House), p. 399.

126 "In truth": Milt Bearden and James Risen, *The Main Enemy: Inside the CIA's Final Showdown with the KGB* (New York: Random House), pp. 397–398.

127 "Washington is full of people": Eric Pooley, "CIA Nominee: Take Two," *Time* (3/24/97).

127 "I'm registered in one party": Barbara Slavin, "Tenet on a Mission to 'Serve Everyone,'" *USA Today* (3/24/97).

128 "My high school soccer coach": George Tenet, Address at the 1999 Alumni of the Year Awards, Benjamin N. Cardozo High School (June 11, 1999).

128 "Puff Daddy": Barbara Slavin, "Tenet on a Mission to 'Serve Everyone,'" *USA Today* (October 11, 2000).

129 "I'll come in and his door"; Nurith C. Aizenman, "Can George Tenet Save the CIA?" *The New Republic* (March 22, 1999).

129 "I know most of you": George Tenet, Address at the 1999 Alumni of the Year Awards, Benjamin N. Cardozo High School (June 11, 1999).

129 "Laugh as much as you can": George Tenet, Address at the University of Oklahoma Graduation Ceremony (May 10, 2003).

129 "I called Tenet": Richard W. Stevenson, "President Asserts He Still Has Faith in Tenet and CIA," *The New York Times* (July 12, 2003).

130 "The CIA is good at stealing": Jeff Stein, "Spy Business Leaves Little Room for Intelligence," *Newsday* (December 7, 1995), p. 48.

130 "We never recruited a spy": Robert M. Gates, *From The Shadows: The Ultimate Insider's Story of Five Presidents and How They Won the Cold War* (New York: Simon and Schuster, 1997), p. 560.

130 "Perhaps the most compelling": CIA, Gates quoted in John H. Hedley, "The Intelligence Community: Is it Broken? How to Fix It?" *Studies in Intelligence* (1996), p. 18.

130 "U.S. intelligence assets on the ground": James A. Baker III with Thomas M. DeFrank, *The Politics of Diplomacy, 1989–1992* (New York: G.P. Putnam's Sons, 1995), p. 7. This view was also shared by General Norman Schwarzkopf, who said, after the war, "Our human intelligence was poor." (H. Norman Schwarzkopf and Peter Petre, *It Doesn't Take a Hero* [New York: Bantam Books, 1992], p. 319.)

130 "The greatest weakness of CIA's performance": Richard L. Russell, "CIA's Strategic Intelligence in Iraq," *Political Science Quarterly* (Summer 2002), p. 205.

131 "The CIA had no spies worthy of the name in India": Tim Weiner, "Report Finds Basic Flaws in U.S. Intelligence Operations," *The New York Times* (June 3, 1998).

132 "We made a school bus disappear": Robert Baer, *See No Evil: The True Story of a Ground Soldier in the CIA's War on Terrorism* (Three Rivers Press, 2003).

132 Description of Harvey Point Defense Testing Activity: Jon Elliston, "Bomb School," *Durham Independent* (June 5, 2002).

133 "The incendiary projectile would": Victor Marchetti and John E. Marks, *The CIA and the Cult of Intelligence* (New York: Alfred A. Knopf, 1974), pp. 111–112.

134 "Hardly an Islamic fundamentalist": Ben Anderson, "Terror in the Philippines," Correspondent, BBC (June 15, 2003).

135 "Put 0.5g of sodium hydroxide": Matthew Brzezinski, "Boom and Bust," *The Washington Post Magazine* (December 30, 2001).

138 "Murad's idea is that": Jim Gomez and John Solomon, "Authorities Warned of Hijack Risks," Associated Press (March 5, 2002).

138 "What do you mean by Liberation Army?": Transcript, Abdul Hakim Murad interrogation, Philippines Police, January 7, 1995.

138 If the U.S. government keeps supporting Israel: Matthew Brzezinski, "Boom and Bust," *The Washington Post Magazine* (December 30, 2001).

139 "When the invasion of Afghanistan started": Robert Fisk, "Anti-Soviet Warrior," *Independent* (London) (December 6, 1993).

139 "We transported heavy equipment": Transcript of Osama bin Laden interview by Peter Arnett, CNN (March 1997).

142 "It is quite obvious": Israel Shahak, "Strategic Aims of the 1996 Israeli Invasion of Lebanon," Columbia University, Middle East and Jewish Studies Department.

142 "My God, my God": Matthew Rothschild, "Interview with Robert Fisk," *The Progressive* (July 1998).

143 "It was a massacre": Robert Fisk, "Massacre in a Sanctuary; Eyewitness," *Independent* (London) (April 19, 1996).

143 "It is unlikely": United Nations, "Report of the Secretary-General's Military Adviser Concerning the Shelling of the United Nations Compound at Qana on 18 April 1996," May 1, 1996.

144 "How easily we killed them": James Walsh, "Anatomy of a Tragedy," *Time* (international edition) (May 20, 1996).

144 "Around the Middle East": James Walsh, "Anatomy of a Tragedy," *Time* (international edition) (May 20, 1996).

145 "we will no longer be relevant": Vernon Loeb, "Inside Information," *The Washington Post* (January 10, 2001).

145 "a world-renowned operator": Vernon Loeb, "At Hush-Hush CIA Unit, Talk of a Turnaround; Reforms Recharge Espionage Service," *The Washington Post* (September 7, 1999).

145 "There was a reluctance to take risks": Walter Pincus, "Top Spy Retiring from CIA; Downing Led Revamp of Clandestine Service," *The Washington Post* (July 29, 1999).

146 "Ordinary people are not inclined": Vernon Loeb, "At Hush-Hush CIA Unit, Talk of a Turnaround; Reforms Recharge Espionage Service," *The Washington Post* (September 7, 1999).

146 "At the end of the day": George Tenet, Address at Georgetown University's Oscar Iden Lecture (October 18, 1999).

147 "Yesterday's code clerk": Interview with a very senior intelligence official.

147 "the Live Room": Tom Bowman, Scott Shane, "Espionage From the Front Lines," *The [Baltimore] Sun* (special series December 3–5, 1995).

148 "My spies save the world"; "I'll probably get indicted for this"; Pavitt background: James Pavitt address to the University of Missouri Alumni Association, summer 2000.

152 "Our resources were perilously depleted": Interview with James Pavitt, April 2001.

153 They have the three sets: Interview conducted in late 2003.

156 "You've got the close family": Interview conducted in late 2003.

157 seventy-nine since the agency was formed: Vernon Loeb, "CIA Reports Officer Killed in Prison Uprising," *The Washington Post* (November 29, 2001).

157 forty-one New Jersey law-enforcement officers died: National Law Enforcement Officers Memorial Fund website at: http://www.nleomf.com/FactsFigures/Statestats01.doc.

157 "You're asking them to leave the mother ship": Interview conducted in late 2003.

158 "I think the biggest issue is control": Interview conducted in late 2003.

158 "One case I ran for a long time": Interview conducted in late 2003.

159 "I saw a lot of backbiting and backstabbing": Interview conducted in late 2003.

160 "It's absolutely appalling": Interview conducted in late 2003.

162 Details on Ziyad Khalil are derived from Mark Morris, "Jihad phone' linked to former Missouri student," *The Kansas City Star* (September 19, 2001)

164 "We look upon those heroes": Transcript of Osama bin Laden interview by Peter Arnett, CNN (March 1997).

165 "My Muslim Brothers of the World": Osama bin Laden, "Declaration of War Against America," August 23, 1996.

165 "It should not be hidden from you": Osama bin Laden, "Declaration of War Against America," August 23, 1996.

166 "hold you responsible for all of the killings": Osama bin Laden, "Declaration of War Against America," August 23, 1996.

167 "Regarding the American people": Transcript of Osama bin Laden interview by Peter Arnett, CNN (March 1997).

167 "The war has just begun": Transcript of interview with Osama bin Laden by ABC News producer Rahimullah Yousafasi (January 1999).

167 "The Nairobi embassy": Salah Najm, film transcript, "Usamah Bin-Laden, The Destruction of The Base" (June 10, 1999). Bin Laden interviewed by Jamal Isma'il.

168 Details concerning the calls between London and Afghanistan are derived from Vernon Loeb, "NSA Intercepts Are Foundation of Bombing Case," *The Washington Post* (January 8, 2001).

168 Details concerning the legal status of the embassy bombing suspects are derived from United States Attorney, Southern District of New York, Press Release, May 29, 2001.

170 "The Jews and crusaders": Peter Finn, "Hamburg's Cauldron of Terror," *The Washington Post* (September 11, 2002).

171 "He maintained a simple life": Dafna Linzer, "Binalshibh, From Secular Student to Islamic Extremist," Associated Press (September 14, 2002).

172 "The group's discussions became": Peter Finn, "Hamburg's Cauldron of Terror," *The Washington Post* (September 11, 2002).

172 "By October 1999 at the latest": Douglas Frantz with Desmond Butler, "Sept. 11 Attack Planned in '99, Germans Learn," *The Los Angeles Times* (August 30, 2002).

172 "The goal of every Muslim": Georg Mascolo, Holger Stark, "Operation Holy Tuesday," *Der Spiegel* (October 27, 2003).

173 "Why do you use an ax": Georg Mascolo, Holger Stark, "Operation Holy Tuesday," *Der Spiegel* (October 27, 2003).

174 "They wanted to go off": Interview with senior intelligence official, December 2003.

177 Directorate of Operations named Gary Schroen: Steve Coll, *Ghost Wars: The Secret History of the CIA, Afghanistan, and Bin Laden, from the Soviet Invasion to September 10, 2001* (New York: The Penguin Press, 2004).

179 "If fundamentalism comes to Afghanistan": Michael Griffin, *Reaping the Whirlwind* (London: Pluto Press, 2001), p. 5.

179 2,300 missiles delivered; Afghanistan by then contained more personal weapons: Steve Coll, *Ghost Wars: The Secret History of the CIA, Afghanistan, and Bin Laden, from the Soviet Invasion to September 10, 2001* (New York: The Penguin Press, 2004), p. 249.

182 "Oh my God"; "I hope he runs out of bullets": Patricia Davis and Maria Glod, "CIA Shooter Kasi, Harbinger of Terror, Set to Die Tonight; U.S. Supreme Court, Virginina Governor Warner Deny Late Appeals," *The Washington Post* (November 14, 2002); Frank Green and Rex Springston, "Kasi Dies for CIA Killings," *Richmond Times Dispatch* (November 15, 2002).

183 "I shot approximately ten rounds": *Mir Aimal Kasi v. Ronald J. Angelone,* U.S. Court of Appeals, Fourth Circuit, August 15, 2002.

183 "Like a suicide bomber": Patricia Davis and Maria Glod, "A Muslim 'Gets Even' with the CIA," *The Washington Post* (November 15, 2000).

184 Details on the FD/Trodpint team were derived from: Steve Coll, *Ghost Wars: The Secret History of the CIA, Afghanistan, and Bin Laden, from the Soviet Invasion to September 10, 2001* (New York: The Penguin Press, 2004), p. 249.

186 "It was surreal"; details of Kasi's capture: Patricia Davis and Maria Glod, "A Muslim 'Gets Even' with the CIA," *The Washington Post* (November 15, 2000).

187 "We issue the following fatwa": Osama bin Laden, "Jihad Against Jews and Crusaders" (February 23, 1998).

187 "We predict a black day": Transcript, "Interview with Osama bin Laden," ABC News (May 28, 1998).

189 "As of late 1999 no program"; "NOCs haven't really changed": Reuel Marc Gerecht, "The Counterterrorist Myth," *The Atlantic Monthly* (July/ August 2001).

189 "We would almost never in any operation": Interview with a senior intelligence official, December 2003.

191 "We were always told": Interview with a former NOC, January 2003.

205 "U.S. Policy on Counterterrorism": U.S. Policy on Counterterrorism, The White House, June 21, 1995.

207 Details on Lacrosse satellites were derived from: Craig Covault, "Secret NRO Recons Eye Iraqi Threats," *Aviation Week & Space Technology* (September 16, 2002).

209 "the intelligence wasn't that solid": Bob Woodward and Thomas E. Ricks, "CIA Trained Pakistanis to Nab Terrorist," *The Washington Post* (October 3, 2001).

210 "As an American citizen": Tim Weiner and James Risen, "Decision to Strike Factory in Sudan Based Partly on Surmise," *The New York Times* (September 21, 1998).

210 "the distant enemy": Ayman al-Zawahiri, Knights of the Distant Prophets.

211 "I think that raid really helped": Bob Woodward and Thomas E. Ricks, "CIA Trained Pakistanis to Nab Terrorist," *The Washington Post* (October 3, 2001).

211 "A few months ago, and again this week": "There are No Expendable American Targets," *The Washington Post* (August 21, 1998).

211 "We must now enter a new phase in our effort": James Risen, "U.S. Failed

to Act on Warnings in '98 of a Plane Attack," *The New York Times* (September 19, 2002).

211 "UBL is actively planning against U.S. targets"; "The intelligence community has strong": Joint Inquiry, testimony of Staff Director Eleanor Hill (September 18, 2002).

212 "We never had enough officers": Joint Inquiry, Findings and Conclusions, Part One.

212 "In hindsight . . . I wish I had said": George Tenet testimony, Joint Inquiry, October 17, 2002.

213 "As I declared war against Al Qaeda": George Tenet testimony, Joint Inquiry, October 17, 2002.

213 "Senator Kyl once asked me": Joint Inquiry, Findings and Conclusions, Part One.

216 "Let's just blow the thing up": Steve Coll, *Ghost Wars: The Secret History of the CIA, Afghanistan, and Bin Laden, from the Soviet Invasion to September 10, 2001* (New York: The Penguin Press, 2004), p. 465.

216 "The rest of the CIA and the intelligence community": Joint Inquiry, testimony of Staff Director Eleanor Hill (September 10, 2002).

217 "take direction from the ladies": Joint Inquiry, Part 1, "Findings and Conclusions," p. 64.

218 "They despised the FBI": Interview with an FBI official, early 2004.

218 "If you get a guy that becomes a little bit too flashy": Transcript, interview with Barry Mawn, head of the FBI's New York office 2000–2002, "The Man Who Knew," *Frontline*, PBS (October 2002).

218 "The working relationships were difficult at times": Interview with a senior intelligence official, December 2002.

219 "Rich was seen by some": Steve Coll, *Ghost Wars: The Secret History of the CIA, Afghanistan, and Bin Laden, from the Soviet Invasion to September 10, 2001* (New York: The Penguin Press, 2004), pp. 557–558.

219 "Unfair trials, torture and ill-treatment were routinely associated": Report, "Uzbekistan," Amnesty International (December 2002).

220 boiled to death: Nick Paton Walsh, "US Looks Away as New Ally Tortures Islamists," *The Guardian* (May 26, 2003).

220 to smuggle large amounts of opium; "not a very good group of people to begin with": Steve Coll, *Ghost Wars: The Secret History of the CIA, Afghanistan, and Bin Laden, from the Soviet Invasion to September 10, 2001* (New York: The Penguin Press, 2004), pp. 540, 538.

221 "At this time": Joint Inquiry, Findings and Conclusions, Part One, pp. 91–92.

222 "We knew that some guys that looked": Interview with a senior intelligence official, December 2003.

223 "we need to continue the effort to identify these travelers": National Commission on Terrorist Attacks Upon the United States, staff statement two.

224 "They refused to tell us": Interview with FBI official, December 2003.

225 Details concerning Yazid Sufaat were derived from: Mark Fineman and Bob Drogin, "Terror: In Malaysia, a Jailed Cal State Graduate Helps Unravel Al Qaeda's Southeast Asia Network," *The Los Angeles Times* (February 2, 2002).

228 Details on TIPOFF: Joint Inquiry, testimony of Staff Director Eleanor Hill (September 18, 2002).

229 sitting on at least fifty-eight other suspected terrorists: Joint Inquiry, testimony of Staff Director Eleanor Hill (September 18, 2002).

232 "I remember playing football": "John Walker Lindh," *People in the News*, CNN (2002).

233 "We train volunteers in the most basic skills": Mark Kukis, "My Heart Became Attached," *Salon* (August 25, 2003).

235 "bin Laden had sent forth some fifty people": Indictment, *United States of America v. John Walker Lindh.*

235 "there should have been five planes": Oliver Burkeman, "Al-Qaida Captive May Have Been Planning Fifth Hijack," *The Guardian* (October 12, 2002).

235 "fifteen more operations were pending": David Johnston and Don Van Natta Jr., "9/11 Inquiry Eyes Possible 5th Pilot," *The New York Times* (October 10, 2002).

236 "We don't even think about it": Matthew Purdy and Lowell Bergman, "Where the Trail Led," *The New York Times* (October 12, 2003).

236 "The coming weeks will hold important surprises": "Taliban Leaders Dismiss U.S. Reports of a Terrorist Plot," Associated Press (June 21, 2001).

236 "To all the mujahideen, your brothers": "Video Shows bin Laden Urging Muslims to Prepare for Fighting," CNN (June 20, 2001).

237 "He was eager to know Islam": T. R. Reid and Keith B. Richburg, "Shoe Bomb Suspect's Journey Into Al Qaeda," *The Washington Post* (March 31, 2002).

237 "The U.S. and Israel are the enemy": T. R. Reid and Keith B. Richburg, "Shoe Bomb Suspect's Journey Into Al Qaeda," *The Washington Post* (March 31, 2002).

238 "His trip to Jerusalem further emboldened"; "It angered him to see 'Jews with guns'": "Accused Shoe Bomber Says He Acted Alone," CNN (September 12, 2002).

238 "reported to an associate in Afghanistan": Government's Sentencing Memorandum, *United States of America vs. Richard Covin Reid* (January 17, 2003).

239 "Without America, there would be no Israel": Government's Sentencing Memorandum, *United States of America vs. Richard Covin Reid* (January 17, 2003).

241 Richard Clarke met in the Situation Room with top domestic law enforcement officials: David Johnston And Eric Schmitt, "Uneven response on Terror Seen in Summer of 2001," *The New York Times* (April 3, 2001).

241 "Based on a review of all-source reporting": Joint Inquiry, Staff Statement, Part One, September 18, 2002.

241 "We are going to be struck soon": Transcript, Cofer Black testimony before the Joint Inquiry, September 26, 2002.

245 hijackers entered the U.S. a total of thirty-three times: National Commission on Terrorist Attacks Upon the United States, Hearings, Staff Statement No. 1, January 26, 2004.

245 "The innovation al Qaeda introduced": Transcript, Doris Meissner testimony before the National Commission on Terrorist Attacks Upon the United States, January 26, 2004.

247 "Throughout the summer of 2001": Transcript, Lt. Gen. Michael V. Hayden testimony before the Joint Inquiry, October 17, 2002.

247 "unprecedented": Transcript, Staff Director Eleanor Hill testimony before the Joint Inquiry, September 18, 2002.

248 "It's central": Interview of a senior intelligence official, December 2003.

249 "The match begins tomorrow"; "Tomorrow is zero hour": David Ensor, "More Clues Before September 11 Surface," *Newsnight with Aaron Brown*, CNN (June 19, 2002).

255 "Bush's taste in office decor": Glancey, "A Wolf in Sheep's Fittings," *The Guardian* (January 24, 2001).

255 "this is the guy": Thomas M. DeFrank, "Bush Calm, Cool Over War," *New York Daily News* (March 9, 2003).

256 "During and immediately after the Persian Gulf war"; "the IIS [Iraqi Intelligence Service] was planning": Report, U.S. Department of Justice, "The Bush Assassination Attempt."

256 "Operation Love Storm"; "Literally everybody wanted to see": Scott Shane, "When the Threat of Hussein Hit Home for Bush," *Baltimore Sun* (February 23, 2003).

258 "terribly emotional"; "Laura Bush's husband": Scott Shane, "When the Threat of Hussein Hit Home for Bush," *Baltimore Sun* (February 23, 2003).

258 "From all the evidence available": The White House, Background Briefing by Senior Administration Officials (June 26, 1993).

259 "I tend to be extremely skeptical": Scott Shane, "When the Threat of Hussein Hit Home for Bush," *Baltimore Sun* (February 23, 2003).

259 Seymour M. Hersh: Seymour M. Hersh, "A Case Not Closed," *The New Yorker* (November 1, 1993).

259 "the defendants were not allowed": Kuwait, Five Years of Impunity: Human Rights Concerns Since the Withdrawal of Iraqi Forces, *Amnesty International* (February 1996).

260 "The SOB tried to kill": Thomas M. DeFrank, "Bush Calm, Cool Over War," *New York Daily News* (March 9, 2003).

260 "I was a warrior for George Bush": *A Charge To Keep: My Journey to the White House* (New York: Perennial, 1999), p. 182.

260 "Real change happens": Transcript, address by George W. Bush at the Fishing School, January 30, 2001.

261 "Condi will run these meetings": Ron Suskind, *The Price of Loyalty: George W. Bush, the White House and the Education of Paul O'Neill* (New York: Simon & Schuster, 2004), p. 70.

261 "Israel . . . can manage its own affairs"; "Whoever inherits Iraq": Study Group on a New Israeli Strategy Toward 2000, "A Clean Break: A New Strategy for Securing the Realm," The Institute for Advanced Strategic and Political Studies (Israel) (1996).

264 Bramble Bush: Amos Harel, "Ya'alon: Reporting plan to kill Saddam was 'irresponsible,'" *Ha'aretz* (December 17, 2003).

265 "We're going to tilt it back toward Israel": Ron Suskind, *The Price of Loyalty: George W. Bush, the White House and the Education of Paul O'Neill* (New York: Simon & Schuster, 2004), p. 71.

265 "I'm not going to go by past reputations": Ron Suskind, *The Price of Loyalty: George W. Bush, the White House and the Education of Paul O'Neill* (New York: Simon & Schuster, 2004), p. 71.

266 "He stressed that a pullback by the United States": Ron Suskind, *The Price of Loyalty: George W. Bush, the White House and the Education of Paul O'Neill* (New York: Simon & Schuster, 2004), p. 71.

266 "This is the best administration for Israel": Robert G. Kaiser, "Bush and Sharon Nearly Identical On Mideast Policy," *The Washington Post* (February 9, 2003).

266 "For the first time": Robert G. Kaiser, "Bush and Sharon Nearly Identical On Mideast Policy," *The Washington Post* (February 9, 2003).

267 "that Iraq might be the key to reshaping"; "that produced either chemical or biological"; details on the NSC meeting are derived from: Ron

Suskind, *The Price of Loyalty: George W. Bush, the White House and the Education of Paul O'Neill* (New York: Simon & Schuster, 2004), pp. 72–73.

268 "What we and other allies": Transcript, Secretary of State Colin Powell and German Foreign Minister On Iraq, February 22, 2001, American Embassy, Tel Aviv.

268 "America's and Israel's responses"; "Crises can be opportunities": David Wurmser, "Middle East 'War,'" American Enterprise Institute (January 1, 2001).

269 "Who, exactly, was pushing this": Ron Suskind, *The Price of Loyalty: George W. Bush, the White House and the Education of Paul O'Neill* (New York: Simon & Schuster, 2004), pp. 75–76.

271 "The new Jewish activists"; the Jewish organizations: Stephen D. Isaacs, *Jews and American Politics* (New York: Doubleday, 1974), pp. 248–249.

272 "I think the term has something": "The Making of a Neoconservative," *Think Tank with Ben Wattenberg*, PBS (November 14, 2002).

272 "the quintessential Washington operator"; "a great collector of sensitive information"; "Jackson and Perle have established": Robert G. Kaiser, "Behind-Scenes Power Over Arms Policy," *The Washington Post* (June 26, 1977).

273 "We have a hero": Peter J. Ognibene, *Scoop: The Life and Politics of Henry M. Jackson* (New York: Stein and Day, 1975), p. 182.

274 Wohlstetter's early background: Neil Swidley, "The Analyst," *Boston Globe* (May 18, 2003).

274 "To deter an attack": Albert Wohlstetter, "A Delicate Balance of Terror," RAND paper P-1472 (November 6, 1958).

274 "He was a firm believer": Khurram Husain, "American Dreams: Intellectual Roots of Neo-conservative Thinking," [Pakistan] *Herald* (March 2003).

275 "I, at the time, was a graduate student": Remarks by Deputy Secretary of Defense Paul Wolfowitz at the Henry M. "Scoop" Jackson Distinguished Service Award, Jewish Institute for National Security Affairs, November 18, 2002.

276 "Albert Wohlstetter phoned me one day": "The Making of a Neoconservative," *Think Tank with Ben Wattenberg*, PBS (November 14, 2002).

279 effort to pressure the Clinton administration: Hillel Kuttler, "Senators push Clinton to move US Embassy to Jerusalem," *The Jerusalem Post* (May 28, 1999).

280 "Feith is a partner of Zell": Dan Feidt, "Interview with Roundtable participant Rashid Khalidi," *The Mac Weekly* (October 17, 2003).

280 "I can bear personal witness": Larry Cohler-Esses, "One Track Minds on Two-Track Mideast Solutions, *The Forward* (January 24, 2003).

281 His position was funded: See David Wurmster, *Tyranny's Ally: America's Failure to Defeat Saddam Hussein* (Washington: AIE Press, 1999), p. xxiii.

281 "Repudiate Oslo"; "Any strategy for repudiating": Douglas J. Feith, "A Strategy for Israel," *Commentary* (September 1997).

282 "The meeting had seemed scripted": Ron Suskind, *The Price of Loyalty: George W. Bush, the White House and the Education of Paul O'Neill* (New York: Simon & Schuster, 2004), p. 76.

284 "The topic today": Transcript, Rumsfeld address at Pentagon, September 10, 2001.

284 "heard good news"; "best info fast"; "judge whether good enough hit S.H. [Saddam Hussein] at same time": "Plans For Iraq Attack Began," On 9/11," CBS News (September 4, 2002).

285 "I expected to go back to a round of meetings": Richard A. Clarke, *Against All Enemies: Inside America's War on Terror* (New York: Simon & Schuster, 2004), pp. 30–31.

286 "We will have to confront him sooner or later": Paul D. Wolfowitz and Zalmay M. Khalilzad, "Saddam Must Go," *Weekly Standard* (December 1997).

287 "implementing a strategy": January 26, 1998 letter to President Bill Clinton, located on the website for the Project for the New American Century: http://www.newamericancentury.org/iraqclintonletter.htm.

287 "Many advocates of action were skeptical": Glenn Kessler, "U.S. Decision On Iraq Has Puzzling Past," *The Washington Post* (January 12, 2003).

287 "strike fatally, not merely disarm": David Wurmser, "Middle East 'War,'" American Enterprise Institute (January 1, 2001).

288 "When this writer first heard": Arnaud de Borchgrave, "Iraq and the Gulf of Tonkin," United Press International (February 2, 2004).

288 "Dear Mr. President": *National Review* website at: http://www.national-review.com/document/document092101b.shtml.

289 "isn't worth the paper it's written on": Warren P. Strobel, Jonathan S. Landay and John Walcott, "Some in Bush Administration Have Misgivings About Iraq Policy," Knight-Ridder Newspapers (October 27, 2002).

289 "Let me be blunt about this": Transcript, Richard Perle interview on "Truth, War, and Consequences," *Frontline,* PBS (October 2003).

290 "Are they missile experts?": Eric Boehler, "Rumsfeld's Personal Spy Ring," *Salon* (July 16, 2003).

290 "They'd take a little bit of intelligence, cherry-pick it": Robert Dreyfuss and Jason Vest, "The Lie Factory," *Mother Jones* (January 26, 2004).

290 "I was chatting"; "I came to share": Karen Kwiatkowski, "In Rumsfeld's Shop," *The American Conservative* (December 1, 2003).

292 "The CIA doesn't like him": Transcript, Richard Perle interview on "Truth, War, and Consequences," *Frontline*, PBS (October 2003).

292 "silk-suited, Rolex-wearing guys in London": Robert Dreyfuss, "Tinker, Banker, NeoCon, Spy," *The American Prospect* (November 18, 2002).

292 "militarily ludicrous": Daniel Byman, Kenneth Pollack and Gideon Rose, "The Rollback Fantasy," *Foreign Affairs* (January/February 1999).

293 "A senior administration official, who requested anonymity": Jonathan S. Landay and Warren P. Strobel, "Pentagon civilians' lack of planning contributed to chaos in Iraq," Knight-Ridder (July 11, 2003).

293 "The arguments against Chalabi": Transcript, Perle interview, "Truth, War & Consequences," *Frontline*, PBS (October 9, 2003).

293 "Israel has not devoted": Seth Gitell, "Allies of Chalabi Meet Ambassador Gold, Warn of White House Folly," *Forward* (July 31, 1998).

294 "The [INC's] intelligence isn't reliable at all": Andrew Buncombe, "US paid $1m for 'useless intelligence' from Chalabi," *The Independent* (London), (September 30, 2003).

295 "an information warrior and a perception manager"; "They're very close-mouthed": Stephen J. Hedges, "When U.S. troops go into a war zone, John Rendon is rarely far behind," *Chicago Tribune* (May 12, 2002).

296 "When I get their briefings"; "blowback": Franklin Foer, "Flacks Americana," *The New Republic* (May 20, 2002).

296 "The INC was clueless": Franklin Foer, "Flacks Americana," *The New Republic* (May 20, 2002).

296 "He continued to work with the Rendon Group": "Paul Moran Story," *Dateline,* SBS Network Television (Australia) (July 23, 2003).

297 "intimidates Army soldiers"; "Could Chalabi have been using the *Times*": Howard Kurtz, "Embedded Reporter's Role in Army Unit's Actions Questioned by Military," *The Washington Post* (June 25, 2003).

297 "I think what you're seeing"; comments by Scott Ritter: "Paul Moran Story," *Dateline,* SBS Network Television (Australia) (July 23, 2003).

298 a shadowy meeting took place: The following account of the Niger document trail was pieced together through interviews with intelligence officials in American and several foreign intelligence agencies as well as a number of news accounts, including most importantly: Carlo Bonini and Giuseppe D'Avanzo, "Ecco il Falso Dossier Sull'uranio di Saddam," *La Repubblica* (July 16, 2003).

A few of the documents have surfaced or been mentioned. Among the likely genuine ones:

1. February 1, 1999, letter from Wissam al-Zahawiah, Iraqi ambassador to the Holy See, to the Niger Embassy in Rome. In Italian, it confirms al-Zahawiah's upcoming visit to Niger.

2. February 1, 1999, letter from Niger Embassy in Rome to the Minister of Foreign Affairs in Niger announcing Ambassador al-Zahawiah's proposed visit to Niger.

3. February 1, 1999, telex containing text identical to the preceding letter. Likely false documents:

1. July 27, 2000, letter from the president of Niger to Saddam Hussein confirming the agreement to furnish 500 tons of uranium. The document contains a comment by the Niger president that the agreement is in accord with Niger's constitution but it is a constitution long out of date.

2. June 28, 2000 (also possibly dated July 6—see below) "accord" between Niger and Iraq to furnish uranium to Iraq.

3. June 30, 2000, letter from the Niger Ministry of Foreign Affairs to Niger ambassador in Rome requesting him to contact Iraq's Rome ambassador, al-Zahawiah—who had by then retired—regarding the June 28 agreement. Date and contents appear altered.

4. July 6, 2000, three-page "accord" between Niger and Iraq for 500 tons of uranium oxide. It is supposedly signed by Niger President Tandja Mamadou and "minister of Foreign Affairs and Cooperation Ailele Elhadj Habibou" who actually left that job in 1989.

5. October 10, 2000, letter from Niger Minister of Foreign Affairs to Niger Embassy in Rome referring to an attached agreement to supply Iraq with uranium. The letter is stamped received on September 28, 2000, two weeks before it was supposedly created and signed by "Minister of Foreign Affairs" Ailele Elhadj Habibou who left that job in 1989.

6. February 7, 2001, letter in code from the Minister of Foreign Affairs.

7. June 14, 2002, meeting, referred to in an undated report, between the ambassadors of Sudan, Niger, Pakistan, Iraq, Libya, and Iran to establish a highly secret military force to assist nations facing western diplomatic aggression, such as sanctions, embargo, or accusations.

8. July 2001 Confidential deciphered letter from the Secretary of State of Niger to the Ambassador in Rome outlining shipping details for the uranium bound for Iraq.

9. August 28, 2001, letter from the Niger Minister of Foreign Affairs to the Ambassador in Rome confirming a shipment of uranium but no destination is listed.

10. September 3, 2001, letter from "Ambassador al-Zahawiah" (he had actually retired to Lebanon a year earlier) to Niger Embassy confirming a

September 2001 visit to Niger. Except for the date—likely altered—it is identical to the genuine February 1, 1999 letter listed above.

302 "I took it to be a routine assignment": Hassan Fattah, "Saddam's Niger Point-man Speaks," *Time* (October 1, 2003).

305 "A whole lot of things told us": "Follow the Yellowcake Road," *Time* (July 13, 2003).

306 "Rather than waste a lot of time": James Risen, "All Roads Lead to Iraq," *The New York Times* (October 3, 2003).

306 "The agency officials asked if I would": Joseph C. Wilson 4th, "What I Didn't Find in Africa," *The New York Times* (July 6, 2003).

308 "We were instructed at a staff meeting": Karen Kwiatkowski, "In Rumsfeld's Shop," *The American Conservative* (December 1, 2003).

308 "with more alarmist"; "None of the Israelis": Julian Borger, "The Spies Who Pushed For War," *The Guardian* (July 17, 2003).

309 "Once in Feith's waiting room": Karen Kwiatkowski, "Open Door Policy," *The American Conservative* (January 19, 2004).

309 "On the eve of the war": Shlomo Brom, "The War in Iraq: An Intelligence Failure?" Jaffee Center for Strategic Studies, Tel Aviv University (November 2003).

310 The bad Israeli intelligence also led: "The Iraq Blame Game: Israel," *Jane's Intelligence Report* (February 19, 2004).

310 In March 2004, the panel found: "Israeli Parliamentary Intelligence Probe Misses Focus," *Debka File* (March 28, 2004).

310 "Israel didn't want to spoil"; "The Israeli intelligence reached this conclusion": Associated Press, "Israel knew Iraq had no WMD says MP," *The Guardian* (February 4, 2004).

311 Israel's military intelligence service, Aman: Israel's American spy Jonathan Pollard has claimed in legal papers that most of his U.S. intelligence assignments came from Aman. See Jonathan Pollard v. Ehud Barak, Petition No. 6029/99, "Request to Produce Documents," October 21, 1999.

311 "We have clear indications": Transcript, Efraim Halevy address, "On September 11, World War III Started," before the NATO Council in Brussels, published in *Yediot Aharonot* (June 28, 2002).

312 The strange arrangement began raising alarms; the single most important intelligence source: Barton Gellman, "Israel Gave Key Help To U.N. Team in Iraq," *The Washington Post* (September 29, 1998).

313 hiding poison factories in refrigerator trucks painted in red-and-white "Tip Top Ice Cream": Bob Drogin and Greg Miller, "Iraqi Defector's Tales Bolstered U.S. Case for War," *Los Angeles Times* (March 28, 2004). See also

Barton Gellman, "Arms Inspectors 'Shake the Tree,'" *The Washington Post* (October 12, 1998).

313 "They just didn't make sense from a technical": Bob Drogin and Greg Miller, "Iraqi Defector's Tales Bolstered U.S. Case for War," *Los Angeles Times* (March 28, 2004).

313 "They told us they had the run of Iraq": Bob Drogin and Greg Miller, "Iraqi Defector's Tales Bolstered U.S. Case for War," *Los Angeles Times* (March 28, 2004).

313 Curveball: Details come from senior U.S. intelligence officials not assigned to the CIA as well as a *Los Angeles Times* report by Bob Drogin and Greg Miller: "Iraqi Defector's Tales Bolstered U.S. Case for War," *Los Angeles Times* (March 28, 2004).

314 "They began feeding us information": Bob Drogin and Greg Miller, "Iraqi Defector's Tales Bolstered U.S. Case for War," *Los Angeles Times* (March 28, 2004).

315 "We didn't find anything"; "This is the one that's damning": Bob Drogin and Greg Miller, "Iraqi Defector's Tales Bolstered U.S. Case for War," *Los Angeles Times* (March 28, 2004).

315 "They pushed an agenda"; "This was creatively produced"; "He spoke out publicly"; "They spent their energy": Marc Cooper, "Soldier for the Truth Exposing Bush's Talking-Points War," *LA Weekly* (February 20–26).

317 "how to fight Saddam": Dana Priest, "Pentagon Shadow Loses Some Mystique," *The Washington Post* (March 13, 2004).

317 "nonplussed"; "Much of it": Dana Priest, "Pentagon Shadow Loses Some Mystique," *The Washington Post* (March 13, 2004).

317 without notifying the agency: It would be more than a year before Tenet would even learn of the high-level briefings. But in November 2003, the CIA discovered that Feith's office had sent a memo to a congressional intelligence committee that contained much of that same inaccurate information. As a result, the agency forced Feith's office to retract it "because of our concerns with what the document said." But by then the war was long over. See Tenet testimony, United States Senate, Armed Services Committee (March 9, 2004).

317 gave the same briefing at the White House: Greg Miller, "Pentagon group's role in shaping White House views about ties between Hussein and Al Qaeda was greater than known, Senate panel hears," *The Los Angeles Times* (March 10, 2004).

318 "We have solid evidence": Dana Priest, "Pentagon Shadow Loses Some Mystique," *The Washington Post* (March 13, 2004).

318 "maintain a positive issue environment"; "because from a marketing point of view": Richard Gephardt, "Defend the Country, Not the Party," *The New York Times* (September 27, 2002).

320 "As evidence of Iraq's weapons building activities": Jason Keyser, "Israel Urges U.S. to Attack Iraq," Associated Press (August 16, 2002).

321 "Israel To U.S.: Don't Delay Iraq Attack": CBS News (August 16, 2002).

321 "Israel Puts Pressure on US to Strike Iraq": Jonathan Steele, "Israel Puts Pressure on US to Strike Iraq," *The Guardian* (August 17, 2002).

322 "No terrorist state poses a greater": Transcript, Secretary of Defense Donald Rumsfeld testimony before the House Armed Services Committee, September 18, 2002.

323 "Senior officials made statements": Transcript, Thielmann interview, "Truth, War & Consequences," *Frontline*, PBS (October 9, 2003).

323 "U.S. Says Hussein Intensifies Quest for A-Bomb Parts": Michael R. Gordon and Judith Miller, "U.S. Says Hussein Intensifies Quest for A-Bomb Parts," *The New York Times* (September 8, 2002).

324 "It's now public": Transcript, *Meet the Press*, NBC News (September 8, 2002).

324 "We don't want the smoking gun": Transcript, *Late Edition with Wolf Blitzer*, CNN (September 8, 2002).

324 "specialized aluminum tubing": Transcript, Fox News (September 8, 2002).

325 mushroom-cloud: Tenet would later claim that he would occasionally correct administration officials when they publicly misstated intelligence, but there is no evidence that this was done. Alternatively, if he had issued such warnings he was apparently too timid to follow them up since they not only continued, they grew both in frequency and degree of deception. See Tenet testimony, United States Senate, Armed Services Committee (March 9, 2004).

325 "I've been covering Chalabi": Howard Kurtz, "Intra-Times Battle Over Iraqi Weapons," *The Washington Post* (May 26, 2003).

326 "It was not a difficult assessment": Transcript, Thielmann interview, "Truth, War & Consequences," *Frontline*, PBS (October 9, 2003).

326 "It would have been extremely difficult to make": Barton Gellman and Walter Pincus, "Depiction of Threat Outgrew Supporting Evidence," *The Washington Post* (August 10, 2003).

326 "We began hearing from sources": Michael Massing, "Now They Tell Us," *The New York Review of Books* (February 26, 2004).

327 "While President Bush marshals congressional": Warren P. Strobel and Jonathan S. Landay, "Some administration officials expressing misgivings on Iraq," Knight-Ridder Newspapers (October 8, 2002).

328 "there were disagreements over details": Barton Gellman and Walter Pincus, "Depiction of Threat Outgrew Supporting Evidence," *The Washington Post* (August 10, 2003).

328 "Instead of our leadership": Transcript, Thielmann interview, "Truth, War & Consequences," *Frontline*, PBS (October 9, 2003).

329 "Baghdad's UAV": CIA, National Intelligence Estimate on Weapons of Mass Destruction in Iraq (Declassified version), October 2002.

329 "I was one of seventy-seven Senators who voted for the resolution": *Congressional Record*, January 28, 2004 (Senate), pp. S311–S312.

330 "Iraq could use these small UAVs": Transcript, Department of State, Secretary of State Colin Powell's Address Before the United Nations Security Council, February 5, 2003.

330 "The software": Glenn Kessler and Walter Pincus, "A Flawed Argument In the Case for War," *The Washington Post* (February 1, 2004).

331 "We now know": *Congressional Record*, January 28, 2004 (Senate), pp. S311–S312.

331 "The British government . . . has learned": Transcript, The White House, State of the Union address by President George W. Bush, January 2003.

333 "And he said, 'You know what'": Interview conducted in late 2003.

336 "They were looking for those selective pieces of intelligence": Edward Alden, "Naming of Agent Was Aimed at Discrediting CIA," *The Financial Times* (October 28, 2003).

336 "Analysts feel more politicized": Greg Miller and Bob Drogin, "CIA Feels Heat On Iraq Data," *Los Angeles Times* (October 11, 2002).

336 "After 9/11": Interview conducted in late 2003.

337 "He was saying to me": Interview conducted in late 2003.

339 "was of little or no value": Douglas Jehl, "Pentagon Agency Belittles Information Given by Iraqi Defectors," *The New York Times* (September 29, 2003).

339 "A huge amount of what was collected": Jonathan S. Landay, Warren P. Strobel and John Walcott, "Officials: U.S. still paying millions to group that provided false Iraqi intelligence," Knight-Ridder Newspapers (February 21, 2004).

340 "Back then we did not have": Interview conducted in late 2003.

341 "We had some information": Martha Raddatz, "U.S. Missile Strikes in Iraq Hit and Miss," ABC News (March 19, 2004).

341 "We did not have enough"; "direct access to Saddam"; "access to senior

Iraqi": Transcript, Tenet's prepared remarks for an address at Georgetown University (February 5, 2004).

342 "This is something the analysts": Walter Pincus, "CIA Alters Policy After Iraq Lapses," *The Washington Post* (February 12, 2004).

343 "the single most important aspect"; "How do we ensure": Walter Pincus, "CIA Alters Policy After Iraq Lapses," *The Washington Post* (February 12, 2004).

343 "never said there was an 'imminent' threat": Transcript, Tenet's prepared remarks for an address at Georgetown University (February 5, 2004).

344 "United Nations inspectors have been briefed"; "totally unacceptable": Douglas Jehl and David E Sanger, "CIA Admits It Didnt Give Weapon Data to the UN," *The New York Times* (February 21, 2004).

345 "His drinking was during the day": Interview conducted in late 2003.

346 "went around to each of the divisions": Interview conducted in early 2004.

347 "The money is incredible": Interview conducted in late 2003.

348 "The first contract I was on I left": Interview conducted in late 2003.

350 "We were talking to teams": Interview conducted in late 2003.

352 "With Afghanistan, the war on terrorism": Greg Miller, Bob Drogin, "CIA Struggles in Iraq, Afghanistan," *The Los Angeles Times* (February 21, 2004).

352 "How do you do your job": Dana Priest, "CIA faces unexpected hurdles in Iraq," *The Washington Post* (March 4, 2004).

354 "Sigint [signals intelligence] was monitoring": Interview conducted in late 2003.

355 "We had all the senior leadership of the agency": Interview with Lt. Gen. Michael V. Hayden, January 20, 2004.

359 "You are cooperating with the people": Ewen MacAskill, Blix: "I Was A Target Too," *The Guardian* (February 28, 2004).

359 "He should not have had them": Kim Sengupta and Kathy Marks, "Britain and US shared transcripts after bugging Blix's mobile phone," *The Independent* (February 28, 2004).

360 "I think they had a set mind": Warren Hoge, "Ex-UN Inspector has harsh words for Bush," *The New York Times* (March 16, 2004).

360 "The Americans and British created facts . . . to justify the Iraq war": Blix, *People's Daily* (February 24, 2004).

361 "By the time the inspectors left"; "Inspectors Find Only Ruins at an Old Iraqi Weapons Site," *The New York Times* (November 29, 2002).

362 "The U.K. in this time was also getting": Ed Johnson, "Britain Spied on UN's Annan," Associated Press (February 26, 2004).

364 "They said, 'You should know that we don't like the idea'": Martin Bright,

Peter Beaumont and Jo Tuckman, "A joint British and American spy op wrecked peace move," *The Observer* (February 15, 2004).

364 "As you've likely heard by now": Martin Bright, Ed Vulliamy, "Revealed: US dirty tricks to win vote on Iraq war," *The Observer* (March 2, 2003).

368 "I think I just got my orders": Interview conducted in March 2004.

379 "I would ask everybody": ABC *Nightline* (August 13, 2002).

380 "Like the people of France in the 1940s": Nicholas D. Kristof, "Iraq's not Vietnam," *The Washington Post* (April 4, 2003).

380 "We will, in fact, be greeted as liberators": Nicholas D. Kristof, "Iraq's not Vietnam," *The Washington Post* (April 4, 2003).

381 "There was never a buildup of intelligence": Michael R. Gordon, "U.S. Intelligence: Getting the Signals Wrong," *The New York Times* (October 20, 2004).

381 "Most of the major key judgments": U.S. Senate, Select Committee on Intelligence, Report on the U.S. Intelligence Community's Prewar Intelligence Assessments on Iraq, Additional Views of Senator Richard Durbin.

382 "The body of assessments showed": U.S. Senate, Select Committee on Intelligence, Report on the U.S. Intelligence Community's Prewar Intelligence Assessments on Iraq.

382 "a strategy for removing Saddam's regime from power": Letter, Project for a New American Century to President Clinton (January 26, 1998).

383 "Saddam probably will not initiate": U.S. Senate, Select Committee on Intelligence, Report on the U.S. Intelligence Community's Prewar Intelligence Assessments on Iraq.

383 "While the DCI was supposed to function": U.S. Senate, Select Committee on Intelligence, Report on the U.S. Intelligence Community's Prewar Intelligence Assessments on Iraq.

384 "a broken corporate culture and poor management": U.S. Senate, Select Committee on Intelligence, Report on the U.S. Intelligence Community's Prewar Intelligence Assessments on Iraq.

384 "Requests for reporting and analysis": Central Intelligence Agency, Report of Richard Kerr (July 2003).

385 "In his interview with the committee": U.S. Senate, Select Committee on Intelligence, Report on the U.S. Intelligence Community's Prewar Intelligence Assessments on Iraq, Additional Views of Vice Chairman John D. Rockefeller IV, Senator Carl Levin, and Senator Richard Durbin.

385 "In the end, what the President and the Congress used": *Meet the Press*, NBC News (July 11, 2004).

386 "Let's keep in mind the fact that this war's": Michael Isikoff, "The Dots Never Existed," *Newsweek* (July 19, 2004).

388 "If all this stuff turns out to be true, then Rolf Ekeus": Barton Gellman, "U.S. Spied on Iraqi Military via U.N.," *The Washington Post* (March 2, 1999).

390 "He's in the backseat and he's giving the driver directions": Interview with a senior intelligence official.

392 U.S. Central Command report: U.S. CENTCOM, executive summary of report on cluster munitions, 2003.

392 Although cluster munitions strikes are particularly dangerous": Human Rights Watch, *Off Target: The Conduct of the War and Civilian Casualties in Iraq,* 2003

393 "Bomblets are what kids pick up"; "Cluster bombs sometimes look like beautiful things": Human Rights Watch, *Off Target: The Conduct of the War and Civilian Casualties in Iraq,* 2003

393 "Please, America must hear our voices"; "They may want Saddam out"; "Repeatedly, analysts said U.S. trust"; "For all people in the Arab world": Emily Wax and Alia Ibrahim, "TV Images Stir Anger, Shock and Warnings of Backlash," *The Washington Post* (April 10, 2003).

395 Human Rights Watch attempted to determine: Human Rights Watch, *Off Target: The Conduct of the War and Civilian Casualties in Iraq,* 2003

395 the Associated Press canvassed 60: Niko Price "3,240 Civilian Deaths in Iraq," Associated Press (June 10, 2003).

395 *The Los Angeles Times* conducted a smaller survey: Laura King, "Baghdad's Death Toll Assessed," *Los Angeles Times* (May 18, 2003).

395 169 children were killed: Human Rights Watch, *Off Target: The Conduct of the War and Civilian Casualties in Iraq,* 2003

395 "Most individuals reportedly killed by coalition forces": Les Roberts, Riyadh Lafta, Richard Garfield, Jamal Khudhairi, Gilbert Burnham, "Mortality Before and After the 2003 Invasion of Iraq: Cluster Sample Survey," *The Lancet* (October 29, 2004).

395 "It is really horrifying": Jeremy Laurance and Colin Brown, "Revealed: War has cost 100,000 Iraqi lives," *The Independent* (October 29, 2004).

396 "U.S. General Tommy Franks is widely quoted as saying"; Les Roberts, Riyadh Lafta, Richard Garfield, Jamal Khudhairi, Gilbert Burnham, "Mortality Before and After the 2003 Invasion of Iraq: Cluster Sample Survey," *The Lancet* (October 29, 2004).

396 "We were shocked at the magnitude": Les Roberts, Riyadh Lafta, Richard Garfield, Jamal Khudhairi, Gilbert Burnham, "Mortality Before and After

the 2003 Invasion of Iraq: Cluster Sample Survey," *The Lancet* (October 29, 2004).

396 "We've always maintained": Elisabeth Rosenthal, "Study Puts Death Toll in Iraq at Over 100,000," *International Herald Tribune* (October 30, 2004).

396 "Anyone who hates America": Nancy A. Youssef, "More Iraqi civilians killed by U.S. forces than by insurgents data shows," Knight-Ridder Newspapers (September 24, 2004).

397 Placards read, "1,000 DEAD": Tai Moses, "The Meaning of One Thousand," http://www.alternet.org/story/19844/ (September 10, 2004).

398 "Most Likely to Kick Some Terrorist Butt": Monica Davey, "For 1000 Troops There Is No Going Home," *The New York Times* (September 9, 2004).

398 "mysteriously"; "to go where the low-hanging fruit is"; details on recruiting: Charlie Savage, "Military Recruiters Pursue Target Schools Carefully," *The Boston Globe* (November 29, 2004).

399 According to the director general of the National Mine Action Authority: Letter from Siraj Barzani, Director General, National Mine Action Authority in Iraq (October 9, 2003), reproduced in *Mine Action Support Group Newsletter* (October, 2003).

399 "I've never seen so much ordnance": Human Rights Watch, *Off Target: The Conduct of the War and Civilian Casualties in Iraq,* 2003

400 "I was stunned to see vast amounts of weapons": David DeBatto, "The looting of Iraq's Arsenal," *Salon* (October 29, 2004).

400 "For the next several weeks I continued": David DeBatto, "The looting of Iraq's Arsenal," *Salon* (October 29, 2004).

401 "The immediate danger": James Glanz, William J. Broad, and David E. Sanger, "Huge Cache of Explosives Vanished from Site in Iraq," *The New York Times* (October 25, 2004).

401 According to experts with the International Atomic Energy Agency: James Glanz, William J. Broad, and David E. Sanger, "Huge Cache of Explosives Vanished from Site in Iraq," *The New York Times* (October 25, 2004).

402 "It would have been easy for anybody"; "Our impression was they were looters": William J. Broad and David E. Sanger, "Video Shows GIs at Weapon Cache," *The New York Times* (October 29, 2004).

402 "themselves to the greatest explosives bonanza in history": James Glanz, William J. Broad, and David E. Sanger, "Huge Cache of Explosives Vanished from Site in Iraq," *The New York Times* (October 25, 2004).

403 emphasizes Egyptian President Hosni Mubarak: Elizabeth Becker, "The American Portrayal of a War of Liberation Is Faltering Across the Arab World," *The New York Times* (April 5, 2003).

404 Feith was fired from a job in the National Security Council: Richard Sale, "FBI Probes DOD Office," United Press International (August 28, 2004).

404 the FBI allegedly overheard Perle; wiretapping operation on the Israeli embassy: Seymour M. Hersh, *The Price of Power: Kissinger in the Nixon White House* (New York: Summit Books, 1983), pp. 321–322.

405 Jonathan Jay Pollard: Wolf Blitzer, *Territory of Lies: The Exclusive Story of Jonathan Jay Pollard* (New York: Harper & Row, 1989), pp. 8, 51.

405 "Their fears were based": Wolf Blitzer, *Territory of Lies: The Exclusive Story of Jonathan Jay Pollard* (New York: Harper & Row, 1989), p. 296.

406 "I utterly reject the notion": Robert I. Friedman, "Pollard's Prison Letters: A Portrait of a Fanatic," *The Washington Post* (June 19, 1988).

407 "I had heard of the virtual brutality": Dov S. Zakheim, *Flight of the Lavi: Inside a U.S.-Israeli Crisis* (Washington, D.C.: Brassey's, 1986), p. 21.

407 "the Israeli refusal to understand": Dov S. Zakheim, *Flight of the Lavi: Inside a U.S.-Israeli Crisis* (Washington, D.C.: Brassey's, 1986), p. 114.

407 "especially when my family": Dov S. Zakheim, *Flight of the Lavi: Inside a U.S.-Israeli Crisis* (Washington, D.C.: Brassey's, 1986), p. 115.

408 In 2004 government officials: Thomas E. Ricks and Robin Wright, "Analyst Who Is Target of Probe Went to Israel," *The Washington Post* (August 29, 2004).

408 "Israel secretly maintains a large and active intelligence-gathering operation": Bob Drogin and Greg Miller, "Israel Has Long Spied on U.S., Say Officials," *Los Angeles Times* (September 3, 2004).

408 "It's no longer just our traditional adversaries": FBI, "Interview with FBI Assistant Director Dave Szady" http://www.fbi.gov/page2/july04/szady 072004.htm (July 20, 2004).

408 Szady listed Israel among the leading countries; "The threat is huge": Edward Iwata, "Spy catcher focuses on economic espionage," *USA Today* (May 10, 2004).

409 "He has never stopped looking for Mr. X": Edwin Black, "FBI Official involved in controversial CIA discrimination case," *The Jewish Week, NYC* (September 24, 2004).

409 "It's a testament to the unique relationship": Laura Rozen and Jason Vest, "Cloak and Swagger," *The American Prospect* online (November 1, 2004).

409 "longstanding frustration among investigators": Laura Rozen and Jason Vest, "Cloak and Swagger," *The American Prospect* online (November 1, 2004).

409 Tipped off by a series of e-mails: Thomas E. Ricks and Robin Wright, "Analyst Who Is Target of Probe Went to Israel," *The Washington Post* (August 29, 2004).

409 might have transferred to Israel was extremely sensitive cryptologic: Susan Schmidt and Robin Wright, "Leak Probe More Than 2 Years Old; Pro-Israel Group's Possible Role at Issue," *The Washington Post* (September 2, 2004).

410 "the most significant": Michael Isikoff and Mark Hosenball, "And Now a Mole?" *Newsweek* (September 6, 2004).

410 "The insinuation that AIPAC, an American Jewish lobby": Molly Moore and John Ward Anderson, "Israel, Iran Trade Threats as FBI Investigates Spying," *The Washington Post* (August 30, 2004).

410 $400,000 to $1.2 million: J. J. Goldberg, *Jewish Power: Inside the American Jewish Establishment* (New York: Perseus Publishing, 1997), pp. 167, 202.

410 "AIPAC became an all-purpose pressure machine"; "AIPAC . . . had only one issue": J. J. Goldberg, *Jewish Power: Inside the American Jewish Establishment* (New York: Perseus Publishing, 1997), pp. 201, 215.

410 had become "a major factor": David K. Shipler, *The New York Times* (July 6, 1987).

411 "They were extraordinarily well-informed": Jason Vest and Laura Rozen, "Mole Hunt," *The American Prospect* online (September 3, 2004).

412 meeting involving two lobbyists for AIPAC: Bob Drogin and Greg Miller, "Israel Has Long Spied on U.S., Say Officials," *Los Angeles Times* (September 3, 2004).

412 Steve Rosen, the director of foreign policy issues, and Keith Weissman: Janine Zacharia, "How the FBI set up AIPAC," *Jerusalem Post* (December 5, 2004).

412 traveled to Israel on eight occasions: Nathan Guttman, "Analyst at Center of Spy Flap Called Naïve Ardently Pro-Israel," *Haaretz* (August 30, 2004).

412 ardent, public, and unequivocal; "ideologue who believes wholeheartedly": Nathan Guttman, "Analyst at Center of Spy Flap Called Naïve Ardently Pro-Israel," *Haaretz* (August 30, 2004).

413 Franklin, according to his résumé, also worked on Iraq within Feith's highly secret Office of Special Plans: Nathan Guttman, "Analyst at Center of Spy Flap Called Naïve Ardently Pro-Israel," *Haaretz* (August 30, 2004).

413 pushing for aggressive action, including the possibility of military strikes: Warren P. Strobel, "Alleged Pentagon leaks may be connected to Iran policy," Knight-Ridder Newspapers (September 2, 2004).

413 "glorified op-ed": Brian Bennett, Elaine Shannon, and Adam Zagorin, "Web of Intrigue," *Time* (September 5, 2004).

414 "But his alleged confederate was 'too smart'": Michael Isikoff and Mark Hosenball, "And Now a Mole?" *Newsweek* (September 6, 2004).

414 "Washington's neocon guru": Matthew Gutman, "Who is Larry Franklin?" *Jerusalem Post* (August 28, 2004).

415 "agent of influence" ... "lied about efforts": Letter, Noel Koch to the Honorable Hamilton Fish, Jr., Ranking Minority Member of the House Judiciary Committee (August 8, 1988).

416 "well known to the American intelligence community as a prevaricator": Lawrence E. Walsh, Independent Counsel, *Final Report of the Independent Counsel for Iran-Contra Matters*, Volume I: Investigations and Prosecutions (August 4, 1993).

416 "Rhode practically lived out": Richard Sale, "FBI Probes DOD Office," United Press International (August 29, 2004).

417 "The purpose of the meeting": Matthew Gutman, "Who is Larry Franklin?" *Jerusalem Post* (August 28, 2004).

418 "meetings suggest the possibility": Joshua Micah Marshall, Laura Rozen, and Paul Glastris, "Iran-Contra II Fresh Scrutiny on a Rogue Pentagon Operation," *The Washington Monthly* (September 2004).

418 turned their attention to Doug Feith's Pentagon office and the possible involvement of other senior Pentagon officials: Warren P. Strobel, "FBI espionage probe goes beyond Israeli allegations, sources say," Knight-Ridder Newspapers (August 29, 2004).

419 According to a report in the *Jerusalem Post:* Janine Zacharia, "How the FBI set up AIPAC," *Jerusalem Post* (December 1, 2004).

420 Feith, Wolfowitz, Richard Perle, Harold Rhode, David Wurmser; The officials whose names came up: Robin Wright and Dan Eggen, "Leak Inquiry Includes Iran Experts in Administration," *The Washington Post* (September 4, 2004).

420 the Justice Department had been preparing a request: Bradley Graham and Dan Eggen, "FBI Interviews Senior Defense Officials in Probe of Analyst; Investigators Looking at Contacts with Israelis," *The Washington Post* (August 31, 2004).

421 what they said was that AIPAC: Ori Nir, "ADL's Foxman Calls for Federal Investigation into Media Leaks," *Forward* (September 3, 2004).

421 "Any charge of espionage": Richard B. Schmitt, "Policy Analyst Is Said to Have Rejected Plea Deal," *Los Angeles Times* (October 6, 2004).

421 "Who pushed Franklin": Laura Rozen and Jason Vest, "Cloak and Swagger," *The American Prospect* online (November 1, 2004).

422 The four were AIPAC executive director: Janine Zacharia, "How the FBI set up AIPAC," *Jerusalem Post* (December 1, 2004).

422 "driving force": Letter, Wexler to Bush (September 29, 2004).

422 "rogue element in the American government": Eli Lake, "Conyers Calls for Hearings on 'Spy' Case," *New York Sun* (September 2, 2004).

422 "breathes new life into the assertion": Nathan Guttman, "Analysis/'Dual Loyalty' Slur Returns to Haunt American Jews," www.Haaretz.com (August 29, 2004).

423 "Tenet grinned broadly;" two more Marines were killed; "a little bit after": Ann Gerhart, "Bush Gives Medal of Freedom to 'Pivotal' Iraq Figures," *The Washington Post* (December 15, 2004).

ACKNOWLEDGMENTS

With deepest thanks to the many people who gave generously of their time and their courage, to help me tell this important story. Although they must remain unnamed, they will not go unheard.

I am also very grateful to Doubleday's editor-in-chief, Bill Thomas, for all his help, encouragement, and friendship. A warm thanks to my editor, Katie Hall, who deciphered my manuscript with the skill of a first-class code breaker. And my appreciation to Kris Dahl, my agent at International Creative Management, for always pointing me in the right direction. Many thanks also to Doubleday's Christine Pride and Michael Windsor and to Chris Fortunato and Tina Thompson for their hard work on *A Pretext for War*.

INDEX